GUIDE TO THE SMALL AND HISTORIC LODGINGS OF FLORIDA

THIRD EDITION

by Herbert L. Hiller
Illustrated by Charles Greacen

PINEAPPLE PRESS, INC.

Sarasota, Florida

Copyright © 1991 by Herbert L. Hiller

Library of Congress Cataloging-in-Publication Data
Hiller, Herbert L., 1931-
    Guide to the small and historic lodgings of Florida / by Herbert L. Hiller : illustrated by Charles Greacen. — 3rd ed.
      p. cm.
    ISBN 0-910923-78-7 : $14.95
    1. Hotels, taverns, etc.–Florida–Guide-books. I. Title.
TX907.H483 1990   89-70992
647.9475901–dc20   CIP

Third Edition

Printed in the United States by Arcata Graphics, Kingsport, Tennessee
Composition by Sherri Hill, in the typeface Goudy

DEDICATION

To Stephanie and Morris who led me to travel.
To Ted and Knut who led me to think about it.

ACKNOWLEDGMENTS

My view of the importance of a guidebook to small hotels as a way to satisfy the needs of preservation and of local economies, as well as the needs of vacationers looking for more satisfying local connections, was first presented to the Inter-American Foundation. The foundation chose not to fund that project for the Caribbean but did underwrite a year's study which helped lead me to the current project. I trust the guidebook will be instructive for tourism policymakers in the Caribbean.

As I began to research each section of Florida for the kinds of lodgings I was interested in, I was everywhere helped by local chambers of commerce, tourism development councils, and historical societies. Peggy Bulger Leatherbury, then of the Florida Folklife Center, put me in touch with folklorists around the state who helped me find out about worthwhile properties. So did Tavia McCuean, then of the Florida Trust for Historic Preservation. Linda and Dale Crider of Gainesville opened their rich resource of contacts among Florida's bicyclists, and State Bicycle Coordinator Dan Burden among state agencies. Myrtice Craig of Jacksonville helped scout out places, as did Marcella Schaible of Bed-and-Breakfast Tropical Florida in Coral Gables, and Danie Bernard of B&B Suncoast Accommodations in St. Petersburg Beach. I made good use of the archives at the Historical Museum of Southern Florida.

Thanks to the innkeepers of the state who responded when in 1988 I invited them to meet each other. They rewarded my intuition that they could strengthen Florida's innkeeping sector by working together. From that first meeting hosted by Ellison Ketchum, then at the Lakeside Inn in Mount Dora, came Inn Route, Inc. The Appendix contains information about how to be in touch with this nonprofit organization.

Thanks also to Cass Lewis for her keyboarding skills and Judy Johnson for her copyediting.

Special thanks to David Z. Orlow of Brooklyn, NY, who finally got me on track about publishers, to Sandy Pukel of Coconut Grove's Oak Feed Store who more than once when funds were low saw that I was well nourished while on the road, and to Erica Rand for her quiet space on Poinciana Avenue, and to Dick and Doris Nellius for theirs in the Roads.

I will remain forever indebted to Gloria Anderson, formerly at *Miami Today*, for having helped me discipline myself to the task by agreeing to publish my research as "Florida Wayfarer" in her newspaper.

Table of Contents

❖ Lodgings that provide meals in addition to breakfast.
✚ Lodgings that provide meals in addition to breakfast in season only.

INTRODUCTION

This book is the result of almost 30 years' work with tourism in Florida and the Caribbean. There and here I have observed that as tourists, we are steadily bombarded by advertising to reward humdrum lives with quick weekends of escape to help make the year of weeks bearable—not lead to change—and to consume in exotic surroundings a portion o f what we labor the year to produce. This may satisfy some, otherwise happy with the state of the world. But I am restless for change. No abrupt change. I like self discovery. I like how all of us have become more aware that we and the natural environment depend on each other, and how values besides making money are becoming important again. This prepares us for personal change. I believe the kind of vacation that leads to self discovery can pivot us from lives of bought pleasures to lives of self realization.

Small hotels and other intimate lodgings, by how they put us in touch with authentic hospitality elsewhere, can help us find authenticity in ourselves.

Massive corporate ad budgets blind us to this, so that most vacationers rarely find out about the inns, guest houses, and small hotels in most parts of the world. Instead, we get formula resorts. Everything from the number of rooms along corridors to the size of the grapefruits comes calculated by accountants. Though we ache to escape it, the corporate world shapes our getaway.

Intimate lodgings, on the other hand, even apart from the long-term change they avail, can supply short-term value for money because hospitality is genuine. Food is fresher. Information is easily forthcoming about hinterland features inaccessible by tour buses at the end of unpaved roads. Lodgings are often in buildings of native materials rich in architectural character and local memory. Rooms and suites are textured with crafts and antiques of their district. Guests feel themselves part of a real world that is not an ordinary world. Caring feels indispensable. Defenses trained for a hostile world relax.

More and more of us, rule-bound in the corporate world, look for the personal touch when we vacation. We are a big market that includes veteran travelers attuned to "high touch," and others who, after a few package tours, begin discovering what we have been missing.

Such notions were with me in the late Seventies when I was invited to White Springs to advise on how tourism might improve the quality of life in that turn-of-the-century resort town on the banks of the Suwannee River. Where once there had been dozens of hotels, only the Telford House remained. That was now a nursing home. There was the Stephen Foster Center in a beautiful park where Memorial Day Weekend each year the Florida Folk Festival brings together displays of Florida crafts accompanied by long days of traditional music and varieties of regional cooking. Nearby was home of the Suwannee River Crafts

Guild. Many old houses awaited restoration. Quiet hung over the town like moss draping the oaks.

I wanted to see the Telford house restored. The Telford and the Stephen Foster Center would be the active attractions. Fill the hotel with touring bicyclists, I counseled. Cycling had a future. The oil embargo had spurred bike sales to record numbers. You could see physical fitness was coming on. Touring cyclists would like the old town the way it was. No Hyatts, no Holiday Inns, no Hiltons would have to be built. With cyclists, tourism wouldn't become the tail wagging the dog.

Trouble was, there wasn't anybody who wanted to restore the old hotel, least of all its owners. Where else nearby could cyclists overnight? I had come too late by a few years for hotels in neighboring Lake City, Madison, Mayo, Monticello, and Suwannee Springs.

Chambers of commerce mostly could tell me only about motels. Sympathetic old-timers knew about old hotels, but mostly those that had become homes for the elderly, shelters for down-and-outers or migrant workers. Still others awaited the wrecker. From librarians, historians, folklorists, and other cyclists I learned that once small and grand hotels had welcomed visitors at almost every rail stop, river, and lake landing in this state opened up by railroaders and boatmen. But all over Florida the legacy was vanishing. For every livery stable, telephone exchange, and warehouse converted to lodgings, I heard about three or four others just gone :the Plantation Inn in Lake Wales, the Suwannee in Live Oak, the Colonial in White Springs, landmarks having outlived their progenitor railroads, finally themselves succumbing to knock-'em-down ways of business.

A few lodgings near White Springs fit their locales. One was the Jasper Hotel run by ancient Ann Greer in the next town north. Another was the Island Hotel in Cedar Key. There was the Izaak Walton Lodge in Yankeetown. These were enough for the bike tours to begin. They continued, and they prosper—albeit without the Telford House.

Other people took over the tours. I turned to researching old hotels. A sensitive writer, Gloria Jahoda, a decade before had published an introduction to the region she called *The Other Florida* (Charles Scribner's Sons, 1967) and it served as my inspiration.

Some railroad era architectural fantasies I found redeemed as university center, like Henry Flagler's Ponce de Leon, now Flagler College in St. Augustine, and Henry Plant's Tampa Bay, now the University of Tampa. Others, like Gainesville's Thomas Hotel, Ocala's Marion, Orlando's Angebilt, and the Longwood in its namesake town, I found modernized as offices, while Winter Haven's old Haven Hotel has escaped with its facade, but with its insides removed and implanted with condos. Flagler's Alcazar in St. Augustine has become a shopping arcade.

Hundreds more I found to exist only in memory or in Lucy Frisbie's photographic memoir, *Florida's Fabled Inns* (Imperial Publishing Company, 1980).

I learned that many old hotels have disappeared because newer highways have bypassed the old links between towns that grew up or grew and faded. They have disappeared from the sight of those who don't travel the byways. Otherwise, as relics, some remain. Among these, the Cassadaga Hotel stands by a loop road, its rooms no longer used by even the Southern Cassadaga Spiritualist Camp Meeting Association since its conversion to an old-age home. In New Port Richey, the same use has taken the Hacienda off the market. The Hotel James in Palatka is a rare Addison Mizner lodging that instead of sophisticates now houses laborers in that river town. The Fenway in Dunedin and the Fort Harrison and Gray Moss Inn in Clearwater have been taken over by religious groups. The Redland in Homestead and the Brahman in Kissimmee have lapsed forlorn. Rooms in the Largo Hotel go by the week, month, or season to Largo workers.

Others I discovered have lost the struggle of a half century and more. Trash and breakage mar their entries. Their signs advertise beds for the night. Some although standing, are lifeless, like El Vernona, John Ringling's "aristocrat of beauty" in Sarasota, or, still by the tracks, Haines City's Palm Crest, where seasonal guests once stepped from their Pullmans into its now boarded-up lobby at the onset of winter.

Some borderline ones, like the old Riverside Lodge in Moore Haven, that in isolation withstood the 1928 hurricane around Lake Okeechobee, go downhill, its restaurant and friendly piano bar replaced by a computer center for the owners' construction business. Others, like Deland's Putnam, hover between demise and revival, its restaurant service a slipping grasp, or await judgment 'midst hopes and disappointments, finally like Key West's La Concha, restored, or like the San Carlos, "gray lady of Pensacola," which may or may not be.

Those housing the elderly often are close for walking to stores, libraries, museums, parks, and waterfronts. On the up-scale side of such enterprise a group called Florida Senior Residences has restored three properties: the Regency Tower in Lakeland, the Sunset Bay in St. Petersburg, and the Manatee River Hotel in Bradenton. When rooms are available, the Manatee River takes overnight guests. Too bad that among others, Fort Myers' Edison Hotel was recently leveled.

None among these hotels for oldsters is more interesting than the arthritic Manhattan Hotel in St. Petersburg. Once the residence of city founder John Constantine Williams, it was long ago turned into a hotel. Since 1975 it has been in the National Register of Historic Places. It is an exemplar of turn-of-the-century gingerbread with multitudinous gables and a wraparound wood porch, the last example of Queen Anne architecture in its vicinity. The Manhattan is worth at least a look from the outside, and if you gain entry, don't hurry yourself. I found it a trove of memorabilia worthy of the Smithsonian, occupants and all.

Many Florida cities have tried to shake their dependency on tourism—Orlando excepted, of course. They have given up trying to make tourism a consistent 12-month business for supporting year-round populations. Downtown business leaders instead have charted municipal futures in banking, light and high-tech

13

industry, international trade and medicine, all pre-empting sites once occupied by hotels.

Before their economies were revitalized, Daytona Beach, Fort Lauderdale, Miami, and St. Petersburg all provided a warehouse service for their beachfront resort strips. When the tourists returned North after winter, commerce slowed. Vacation time for the locals. Indeed, many weren't local at all, but themselves had come only for winter, returning now to jobs serving tourists in New England or Great Lakes resorts. The Manasota Beach Club near Englewood and the Colony in Delray continue that pattern. New owners of Island City House and the Palms hope to revive it, twining these island properties with the once grand Bedford Springs Hotel in south-center Pennsylvania, perhaps to be restored by the same owners. Otherwise, along with the pattern, most old beachfront hotels have gone, too.

Some grand hotels have adapted. Those like the Belleview Mido in Clearwater, the Boca Raton Hotel, the Breakers in Palm Beach, the Casa Marina in Key West, and the Ponte Vedra Inn in its gracious north Florida community of the same name, began staying open year-round and taking conventions and incentive groups to keep busy. The Don CeSar in St. Pete Beach has succeeded in summers by attracting inland yuppies to the coast.

A few resist extending their season, enclaves of tradition—the Colony and Manasota Beach Club already noted—while Hillcrest Lodge in Babson Park and the Gasparilla Inn in Boca Grande provide only summer cottages without food.

As though old vacation habits weren't already slipping away, Disney attractions capitalize on modernity's extravagant rejection of the past by recasting tradition as nostalgia and completing the illusion that Old Florida and its legendary hospitality no longer exist.

But despite the changed habits of vacationing Northerners, Old Florida persists in a steady stream of restorations. Whole towns like Key West at times have lain dormant, and when revived, are prized for their look of the past which becomes treasured by those renewing in the present. In Apalachicola, Avon Park, Cassadaga, Coral Gables, Crescent City, Inverness, Mount Dora, New Smyrna Beach, St. Petersburg, and Winter Park, once fine hotels, many in historic districts, until recently stood sadly neglected. Now the Gibson, the Jacaranda, the Cassadaga, the Bilmore, Sprague House Inn, the Crown, the Lakeside Inn, the Heritage (formerly the Martha Washington), the Riverview, and the Park Plaza have all been handsomely restored. Around the state are many more architecturally intriguing old buildings, still sound, still unused, capable of reintegration into their neighborhoods as lodgings for visitors.

The investors are out there to restore them, usually ordinary people with a dream. An old building sparks intuition. The mind races down empty corridors of possibility, grabbing leftover impressions—from a college course or a magazine article—that fill in a picture of restored lobbies and canopied lawns. In the sprint of imagination there is a flash of tax credits. For a moment the thinly channeled dream expands into glowing panorama.

By now Florida is caught up in the revival spirit that has made historic preservation an important focus in contemporary America. Many recent migrants are establishing careers as innkeepers because they know the market exists for such lodgings everywhere. From Bailey House in Fernandina Beach to Inn by the Sea in Naples, Bayboro House in St. Petersburg, and Allison House Inn in Quincy, old family houses are being restyled for hospitality extended by new families to travelers.

These historic lodgings, large and small, offer the best way for travelers to get to know the places they visit. Only the Breakers maintains a full-time historian. But the others are run by people who care how their lodgings fit into their vicinities. Their pleasure is to tell about down-home restaurants, the pick of local performers, and myriad details that distinguish their localities from all others.

Despite this long history of specialized lodgings and their recent revival, hardly anyone yet thinks of Florida when extolling such hospitality. People who visit the state don't expect such lodgings to be found here. Florida is thought of for its manmade attractions, its glitter, and its places to stay that lavish fantasy lifestyles upon royalty-for-a-day throngs. That, or strips of undistinguished motels or lookalike high-rises.

All too abundant, these latter, but still only part of the story. Many small towns and historic districts in cities are choosing to safeguard their special character. In a state as significantly dependent on tourism as Florida, many more preservationists and environmentalists need to know that an alternate form of tourism can comport with their interests, that small and historic lodgings can bring the benefits of tourism and so strengthen local heritage without undue stress.

This guidebook seeks to provide a service to travelers who already know the special pleasures of small and historic lodgings elsewhere and would like to find their equivalents in Florida. Equally, the book should help guide all who are newly interested in such places and who for the first time can sample hospitality from a wide range of such properties here. I also have in mind the operators of these lodgings themselves, many of whom have needed this kind of exposure to the public, and who now, perhaps for the first time, stand to profit from their commitment to the ancient dedication of looking after the traveling public. May many more join them!

Coconut Grove
Fall, 1986, updated Spring, 1988, and Spring 1991

HOW TO USE THIS BOOK

Since most of the lodgings described in this book operate according to the personal tastes of their owners, rather than by standard formats of the hotel industry, I should explain some matters to help readers make best use of the guidebook. Let me start by explaining why there are 140 entries rather than 190 or 80. (There were 92 in the first edition, 108 in the second.)

Why Small and Historic?

The entries describe small as well as historic lodgings. Although a few of the small properties are not historic, no large ones are included that aren't. So there are places told about with as few as one room, and others with as many as 500. What they have in common is an approach to hospitality that starts with "sense of place." Operators of these lodgings themselves know about local life and hire or train others who work there, so that their lodgings are effective interpreters of their places. In every case, the lodgings described in the guidebook should help you as a traveler answer the question about the town or city you find yourself in: When I'm here, where am I?

Why Not Most Bed-and-Breakfasts?

Some of the entries are bed-and-breakfasts, though dozens more Florida B&Bs are not included. The distinction I generally rely on is that if the place has a sign out front with its trade name, puts out a brochure and rate card, and is mostly used for guests, then it qualifies. On the other hand, if the facility feels more like a private home and accommodates guests mainly in a spare bedroom or two, I have left it out. I've made one or two exceptions.

What About Other Places to Stay?

It goes without saying that even apart from bed-and-breakfasts, there are hundreds of other places not described in the book where visitors can expect close encounters with proprietors and maybe good insight into their surrounding areas. These might include many motels and small apartment houses stretched along both Florida coasts. Undoubtedly there are a few that might fit the criteria of this book. As I learn about them, they will be included in subsequent editions. But most motels and apartment houses are unexceptional, even if small, and since almost everywhere in the state I have been able to find places worth your attention in terms of their architecture or history or other special features, I feel I am not costing the reader any significantly worthwhile experience. Indeed, if just the

16

properties detailed in the book are helped to prosper because of it, we will all together have done something wonderful for encouraging others to get into the business of offering hospitable lodgings, and will have offered Florida travelers worthwhile experiences they might have otherwise missed.

Personal Commitment

I have personally inspected every place described in the book. I have overnighted in almost all. In no case has anyone been charged anything to be included in the book.

The only chain hotels described are the Casa Marina, a Marriott resort, and La Concha, a Holiday Inn, both in Key West. The only motel is Di Vito By The Sea in Hollywood. In each case, these are exceptional, though not likely to be everybody's favorites.

Only two places have any kind of restrictive policies. These are the Grove Isle Hotel in Coconut Grove, and the Useppa Island Club on Useppa Island. Both are membership facilities, but in each case guests are welcomed when recommended by members, and overnight use is available to those genuinely interested in membership. In the case of Useppa Island, day trips by boat are available, and in the case of Grove Isle, group visits can be arranged for touring the sculpture gardens.

Importance of Context

Just as the lodgings in this book help interpret their places, in telling about them I have developed their geographic and historical contexts. In some cases, this illuminates aspects of Florida that may be somewhat familiar to Florida watchers. For example, the Clewiston Inn is told about in terms of the environmental issues that affect sugar cane cultivation, without which there would be no inn in Clewiston. For the Art Deco District hotels, the context is the fitful history of Miami Beach tourism in which these properties are seen as contemporary resolutions.

I also talk about the people who own and operate these lodgings because seasoned travelers know how much these off-beat places to stay are ultimately reflections of their proprietors, and if the proprietors sound right, the places are likely to satisfy as adventures of the most agreeable sort.

Since there are so many approaches to operating intimate lodgings, readers with the time will find it worthwhile to read through the entries whether or not they plan to be in any given part of the state. Especially by reviewing the kinds of properties they are interested in in different parts of the state, readers will get a feeling for the range of possibilities such places offer. You can get an idea of why places excel and what may be lacking elsewhere. The guidebook does not rate these Florida lodgings according to objective standards. Instead, I tell about

17

each according to its essential appeal and note glaring deficiencies.

Readers who just want an overview about any particular property will find a summary phrase under each heading, and a data section following each narrative that details facilities and rate.

Matters Peculiar To Florida

You should know some things about the Florida calendar. From June through October is hurricane season. Most tropical storms collect in August and September. If you are in the state when one is coming, pay close attention to weather reports and make your moves on the side of caution.

Less threatening are certain intense weekends celebrated here and there around the state. Such events as Race Week in Daytona Beach (February), the Orange Bowl Festival in Miami (turn of the year), the legislative session in Tallahassee (late winter, spring), big football weekends in many cities, and local celebrations like Epiphany Celebration in Tarpon Springs (always Jan. 6th), Bamboleo in Tampa (late January), Isle of Eight Flags Shrimp Festival in Fernandina Beach (always first full weekend in May), and the Rattlesnake Festival and International Gopher Race in San Antonio (always the third Saturday in October), for example, all affect normal hotel policies. You can expect two- or three-night minimums, for high-season rates to apply even if it is otherwise off-season, and special deposit and probably restricted refund policies in case of cancellations. Keep in mind that the high season (with higher rates) for most of Florida is winter, although in the Panhandle it is summer, in the northeast it is spring, summer, and fall, and in the Daytona area, spring and fall—though obviously one or another property has its own way of rating its most attractive times of year.

While most properties differentiate their rates by time of year, many have year-round rates. Winder rate generally means December 15th through Easter; off-season generally means the rest of the year, though there may be other peaks. The data sections following each narrative in almost all cases give you a high-season and an off-season range of rates. But in some cases operators, when asked, had not yet set rates for their coming year. And it goes without saying that rates are subject to change without notice. This is also true of meal prices, and I daresay it is true of almost everything stated in the book. So how can you avoid surprises?

Avoiding Unpleasant Surprises

Obviously you want to be in touch with operators of the lodgings before you show up, or if you just show up unannounced, be prepared for variations from what you have read. Change isn't inevitable. Just be prepared for it.

Small and historic places don't change owners or managers more frequently than do conventional lodgings. Maybe less frequently. But the changes are likely to be more noticeable where ambiance and policies are the reflections of a person or couple than where they reflect corporation standards applicable through a national chain. Hence, the more reason for being in touch before you show up.

My recommendation is that you give yourself plenty of time to write for a brochure and rate card (always ask for both). Also write to the Florida Division of Tourism and ask for information about the vicinities of the lodgings you are interested in. The Division of Tourism address is included in the appendix, where you will also find other helpful references. When you have this information together with what the lodging operator has sent, you are better prepared to ask operators how well they can help you take advantage of what is in their vicinities. You can also ask if they pack picnic lunches. Do they offer excursions to particular places of interest? If not, who in their vicinity does? If there has been a change of ownership or management, ask if matters of particular interest to you that are described in the guidebook are change or unchanged.

There is much more you can ask about. The following list is only a guide. You can undoubtedly add your own considerations to it. But think about the following:

— A particularly good reading lamp by the bed.
— A particularly firm mattress.
— That the room has been treated for pests immediately before you arrive, but so there is no lingering odor.
— If a meal is included, for any special requests.
— If a kitchen is available, that all the burners and oven have been tested just before you arrive, and that all are in working order. Ask to have whatever you need for food preparation included in the inventory of supplies. If you are given a printed inventory on arrival, check it against what you actually take possession of.
— Ask that all windows be checked before you arrive, and the air-conditioning and heat. Insist that the air-conditioning not be noisy, and that any overhead fans be in good working order and not squeaky.
— You can ask that toilets be checked so that the water cycle completes in due time and the water doesn't continue to flow noisily after use.
— If you want use of a laundry or ironing board or hair dryer, ask for it in advance.
— Double-check telephone policies: Are local calls free? Is there a surcharge for long-distance calls? If a TV is available first-come, first-serve, ask if you can reserve it (assuming you want it).
— If it's important to you, ask for a room reserved for nonsmokers. You can ask owners who smoke to refrain while you're around.
— Especially at the smaller properties, are there curfew hours? Do you need a special key? What are the check-in and check-out times?
— Ask if the place is going to be sold or if new managers are planned for

around the time you plan to arrive. Ask what changes in policy this portends.

— Especially in the smaller places, you can negotiate for exceptional circumstances. Ask for a quiet room or one with sunshine in the morning or sunset in the evening. Ask for a room with a balcony or private entrance —whatever you'd like, ask for it.

— You may be able to deposit your booking by personal check but not pay by check for the balance due.

— Ask if a multi-night discount is available, or especially in larger properties, if a discount is offered to members of AAA or AARP.

— If you like to sleep in, make sure your room is away from the kitchen or from others likely to be out early.

It is always best to have everything of concern to you verified in writing.

Notes On Abbreviations, Additional Information, and Making Reservations

About abbreviations used in the data sections, AP stands for American Plan (three meals included), MAP stands for Modified American Plan (breakfast and dinner included), EP stands for European Plan (no meals included). Continental breakfast usually means a sweet roll, juice, and coffee. Expanded continental breakfast means more, but less than a full breakfast. AC stands for air-conditioning. AmEx is American Express, CB is Carte Blanche, DC is Diners Club, and MC is Mastercard.

Check the appendix for information about parks and camping in state facilities, about affiliates of American Youth Hostels in Florida, about bed-and-breakfast referral agencies in the state. Also listed are sources for county road maps and bike maps. There is a listing of lodgings that serve meals other than breakfast.

You can book any of the properties described here by yourself, but you may wish to use a travel agent. Agents are always helpful for arranging air tickets and many other services. However, many agents prefer not to book small properties because some properties do not pay commissions, and others may not pay promptly. If you have a travel agent who specializes in small properties, so much the better. Or if you have one interested in specializing in such properties, encourage him/her by asking that he or she handle the booking for you. Still, no harm making your own inquiries, and if you plan to book through an agent, inquire whether this is going to cost you an additional fee.

Finally, when you make reservations, or when your agent does, by all means let the proprietors know that you have read about their place in this book. This will make the guidebook more valuable to them. I welcome your comments about your experiences with the places I have described. I also welcome knowing about additional places in Florida you think fit the book's criteria but which I obviously don't know about. I also welcome word about your own favorite small and historic lodgings elsewhere in America or abroad. You can write to me care of Pineapple Press and insofar as possible, I will answer questions.

Enjoy the kind of vacation you've always wanted in Florida!

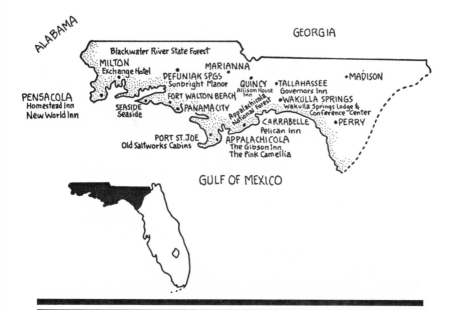

Map labels:
ALABAMA GEORGIA

Blackwater River State Forest
MILTON
Exchange Hotel MARIANNA
DEFUNIAK SPGS
Sunbright Manor QUINCY •TALLAHASSEE •MADISON
FORT WALTON BEACH Allison House Governors Inn
Inn
PENSACOLA •WAKULLA SPRINGS
Homestead Inn SEASIDE PANAMA CITY Wakulla Springs Lodge &
New World Inn Seaside Conference Center
CARRABELLE •PERRY
Pelican Inn
PORT ST.JOE APPALACHICOLA
Old Saltworks Cabins The Gibson Inn
The Pink Camellia

GULF OF MEXICO

THE PANHANDLE

Hospitality is impressive, though the news is mixed. Since the second edition of this book, **Magnolia's** has closed in Apalachicola, and the **Jasper Hotel** in Jasper. Thanks, Ann Greer, for a lifetime of hospitality. **New World Inn** in Pensacola has been taken over by the bank. Arden and Kay Anderson's superb hotel in a set of old warehouses couldn't make it through the downturn in business. Plans for a sizeable expansion, which would have spread operating costs over more rooms, never got underway. The Andersons will be missed in the trade.

On the good side.

The **Pink Camellia** gives Apalachicola rooms lost with Magnolia's, and very stylishly, full of art and color. **Sunbright Manor** in DeFuniak Springs could signal a rush of quality lodgings in the myriad Queen Anne houses of this beautiful old railroad town.

High praise for the **Old Salt Works Cabins** across San Blas Bay from Port St. Joe. These are park-quality lodgings of screen and ponderosa pine and cedar, forest hideaways Florida can use many more of. High praise, too, for **Allison House Inn** in Quincy. At last, quality lodgings in this vintage town. Also to be thankful for, the neat mix of overnight rooms, suites, and apartments at **Seaside**, the stylish resort enclave where developer Bob Davis dreamed childhood memories right onto the beach.

The **Governors Inn** in Tallahassee has given up its award-winning restaurant. **Wakulla Springs Lodge** has reopened as a state park and conference

23

center, still with the tacky fence around, but attractively managed by veteran hotelier John Puskar. Despite rumors, the lodge is definitely open to overnight guests and its lobby and dining room (and ice cream parlor) open to all.

Also worth knowing about in the Panhandle: Shirley and Bruce Gaver's one-room bed-and-breakfast and antique shop in a 1907 house in Havana (pronounced Háy-vana) [301 East 6th Avenue, Havana, FL 32333, (904) 539-5611], **Cobb's Gulfview Inn Bed & Breakfast**, open seasonally from April 1st through Labor Day [21722 West Highway 98A, Box 199, Sunnyside, FL 32461, (904) 234-6051].

The **Pensacola Hilton** remains notable because it incorporates into its lower levels the Louisville & Nashville Railroad station built in 1912-13 [200 East Gregory Street, Pensacola, FL, (904) 433-3336, (800) 348-3336]. And keep in mind the **Hopkins Boarding House** at 900 North Spring Street, Pensacola, FL (904) 438-3979, not because they take overnight guests but because in their beautifully maintained, broad-porched old white clapboard house the Hopkins family continues to provide Pensacola's finest home-cooked meals as they have since 1948, lunch and dinner daily except Mondays.

Though not in the Panhandle—and not even open—the **Telford House** in White Springs, which briefly in 1988 reopened as a country hotel, soon shut again under mismanagement. It remains for sale and in the right hands couldn't help but succeed in that Suwannee River town of historic hospitality.

Apalachicola — THE GIBSON INN
Victorian restoration in a Panhandle fishing port.

Maybe the best argument against the rehabilitation tax credit for historic preservation is that grown people like Neil Koun often react to it like they would to an illegal substance. They awaken stifled ambitions. They get wild-eyed and childlike. They throw money around and frenzy others into giving up perfectly normal lives.

Nobody had wanted the old Gibson Hotel. In any other place its location on the circle across from City Hall on the only road through town would have been prime for redevelopment. But until recently Apalachicola was just plain neglectful of its history, and the grand hotel had become a broken-down refuge for tramps.

Like most of what the locals call Apalach, the old Gibson—which used to be the old Franklin—had been well placed in its time. That was during the town's second heyday as a lumber port. The hotel's black cypress beams and polished hardwood floors, its double-decked all-around porch, made it a showplace of the river economy that for a time kept Apalachicola a busy world port.

Timber had been a canny adjustment. The river was as good for floating logs as it had been for cotton after Florida was transferred to the United States by Spain in 1821. When after the Civil War the railroads re-routed cotton to Eastern ports (closer to European markets), timbering kept the town going.

Later, when the cypress gave out, the same river system made oystering lucrative in the saline bay gently replenished by upland nutrients and the wash of the Gulf of Mexico, gentled by a string of barrier islands.

In 1983, Neil Koun was led to the place by a woman he had met on an airplane. Now he and his brother Michael were about to join the ranks of bored insurance agents, dentists with a little spare cash, geologists who fly their own planes—the normally cautious investors who, rather than corporate hoteliers coolly regarding Interstate sites and emotion-free 800 numbers, wind up saving old hotels.

Neil, an investment banker, had already talked Michael into giving up a secure executive post to run a small restaurant investment in an old inn in Fort Walton Beach, nearby in the Panhandle. Now Michael had the perfect outlet for his imagination and ambition and made up his mind to transform the rundown old Gibson into the glory of Apalachicola.

Fortunately, the deterioration was mostly superficial. Cedar shake shingles had protected the structure. You could see that the good cypress and heart pine were still there. Under the filth, the tongue-in-groove wainscoting, window casings, and trimwork were exquisite.

Double-hung windows now surround the downstairs. Two sets of double entry doors open behind a porch of rockers into a Victorian lobby sectioned off by wood posts and beams. A flaired staircase with richly turned balusters topped by museum-quality globe lamps bespeaks an era of plaid-weskited gents with pocket watches dealing in cotton futures from the saloon while waiting for the Lake Wimico & St. Joseph Railroad—Florida's first in 1839.

On three floors there are guest rooms, no two alike, full of antique white iron and four-poster beds with small-patterned headboards and Victorian motifs on muted fields of carpet. The owners' quarters are eaved into a fourth floor that leads to a widow's walk with cupola and a sweeping view of the small town as an architectural treasure in this remote bayou.

Upstairs around back, the banister porch goes every which way, opening down to a soaring first-floor dining room, which opens to the sky beyond canopied walks, a concourse of sloping roofs, balustrades, and rails in a great wandering. The eye leads, the legs follow. The place insists on exploration and discovery.

Since its reopening, the inn has been placed in the National Register of Historic Places.

Jo Ann Deering, who first managed the Gibson, is amazed that Neil and Michael could have walked into the mess and visualized what it could be.

"But people are looking to get into heritage," she says. "A lot of young people are going back. Maybe we get too modern too soon."

Gibson Inn, 100 Market St., Apalachicola, FL 32320. (904) 653-2191. Michael Koun, owner. 31 rooms with color cable TV, AC, heat, ceiling fan, direct-dial phone, bathroom (some with original clawfoot tubs). Restaurant, bar, big-screen TV for sporting events. Children of any age accepted, free in parents' room if no extra bed required. Designated smoking area in restaurant. AmEx, MC, Visa. Year-round rates: single or double $60 to $105. $5 for extra persons or pets. Restaurant meals: breakfast, $2.50 to $5; lunch, $3.75 to $8.50; dinner, $7.50 to $16.

Apalachicola — THE PINK CAMELLIA
Art-filled and quilt-comfy.

There are small towns where you can relocate and live for 40 years and still be an outsider. Then there's Apalachicola. Two years after showing up, Bill Barnes was vice president of the Downtown Merchants Association, director of the Chamber, and on the Economic Development Council. Needless to say, he and Carole Jayne took to Apalach right away.

They came with one business and started another, both adding what the town can use. Bill and Carole are artists. Between them they're jewelers, potters, enamelists, woodworkers, ceramists, leatherworkers, and printers. For years they've traveled America on the outdoor circuit. Now they're also bed-and-breakfast keepers. Their studio downtown and their Pink Camellia B&B a few blocks west both add attractions that can help develop low-profile tourism in this town where oystering in recent years has become chancy.

Bill and Carole came from Missouri to settle early in 1988. They turned the old Floyd House, which dates from 1897, into the Pink Camellia.

"We just jumped into this house," says Carole. "Four months later we were sobbing. We knew we'd bitten off more than we could chew."

The porches needed new support posts and spindle railings. The house, which had been closed for three years, needed new plumbing and wiring. A funeral director who owned it in the 1960s had torn out the fireplaces in the west rooms and enclosed the wraparound porch. He'd built a hideous ramp, dropped ceilings, and boarded up windows. He refused to put in a new septic system, so that after all the abominations, he never even opened. Subsequent owners left it the way they'd found it.

It took Carole and Bill nine months to restore the house. They also opened their gallery in the house, but later moved it to a space on Market Street. They kept their studio in the utility house back of their B&B.

Public rooms of the house are strikingly colorful, banded with dark red yielding to an orange-peach above. Rooms are filled with art, mainly Carole's and what she and Bill have collected. In the comfortable living room, Carole's work shows in framed paper and fabric pieces. There are Panamanian molas, cloisonne of Carole's, and antique vases from her great-grandmother. Furniture is mainly antique, set on Oriental rugs, though a new couch is large and cushiony. Where the gallery used to be, guests now have an antique pool table, library, TV, and comfortable sofa and chairs.

Morning coffee and newspapers are placed upstairs at 8:00. Full breakfast is served family style in the dining room at 9:00 on a Midwestern farm table with hideaway leaves beneath a wall of Haitian watercolors. Afternoons there are often hors d'oeuvres. Desserts and wine are usually set out for guests when they return from evening meals in town.

Downstairs has an antique wagon-wheel quilt in the hall and an upright piano. The carpeted staircase has a pine banister with white-painted spindles. The upstairs hall has a collection of Guatemalan and Nigerian masks, as well as two quilts. The signature feature of each guest room is the handbag displayed as art.

The Peach Room is soft and glowing with light beige carpet and a diamond patch quilt on an English slat bed. Accessories include a flotilla of ship models.

The Raspberry is outrageous in mismatched patchwork quilts and coral walls. The Green has an Eastlake dresser with hardware incised with cranes, palms, and flamingos.

The satiny suite is for honeymooners, with an Eastlake bed, yellow board walls, and lots of wicker. Bill's paternal grandmother cross-stitched the quilt. There's a huge oak marble-topped dresser with beveled mirror. Three lovely fans are displayed. A pair of folding doors leads to the large bathroom with a massive six-foot clawfoot tub.

The house is as colorful outside as inside. It's pink with gray trim under large canopied trees. The upstairs portico has diamond-shaped wood shingles. Bill says that sitting on the porch is all the outsider he feels like anymore. Guests feel they belong, too.

The Pink Camellia Inn, 145 Ave. E. (corner 12th St. and Hwy. 98), Apalachicola, FL 32320. (904) 653-2107. Carole Jayne and Bill Barnes, innkeepers. 3 rooms and 1 suite with full baths (1, tub only), AC, heat. Phone in library or remote phone available, free local and credit-card LD calls. TV in library. Children of any age accepted. Extra person $15. AmEx, MC, Visa, personal checks. Year-round rates: $60-$70 single, $65-$75 double, includes full breakfast, evening dessert generally provided, coffee and tea 1 hour before breakfast, wine in the afternoon. No smoking in rooms; only on porches. Recreation room with pool table. Off-street parking.

Carrabelle — PELICAN INN
Fully equipped apartments, little else but nature on remote barrier island.

A second shot at paradise sure beats a second shoot-out in Miami, so after two heart attacks, Cliff Shaw and his wife Gwen have settled in as born-again primitives on out-of-the-way Dog Island, a seven-mile island off the Big Bend of Florida.

There are only two jobs on Dog Island. Cliff's got both. He looks after the Pelican Inn for its Alabama owner, and tends the island for a private conservation trust.

"An excellent lifestyle with low pay," Cliff calls it, on an island one writer describes as "unspoiled by human ambition."

Maybe that's because Dog Island is in Franklin County, Florida's poorest per capita, a place where tourism hasn't outpaced conservation. It helps that plans for a bridge have never been pursued, and that even the ferry was abandoned first chance the county got. Now the only arrivals from time to time on privately run transportation are some of the hundred or so houseowners and the few who can be lodged in the seven units of the Pelican Inn, Dog Island's only quarters for visitors.

They find an island with pine stands, marsh, and beaches, and a ridge of dunes to 50 feet called "the mountains." Water birds flock, dive, and feast on abundant sea life that daily replenishes the shore with great stocks of shells. Walking, watching, and collecting alternate with fishing, boating, swimming, and sunning as outdoor things to do. You can walk for miles or hours and not see another person. The only litter may be a piece of glass, maybe a cup.

"You need to come for a week," says Cliff. "First day everybody's got things to do. Second day, maybe not. Third day they come to a dead stop. After that they sleep and do nothing that's not relaxing. The place is like a narcotic. Guests I take back to Carrabelle sure aren't the same people I carried over."

Nor is Cliff the same man who first came out in 1951. There weren't any buildings then. But he was too fired up on getting ahead in life. He worked for Orkin in Orlando, then Miami.

He had arrived for work one day in Miami when a policeman shouted: "Get down!" and threw him to the ground. Machine guns blazed. The cops were shooting it out with drug guys. Cliff decided to exit Orkin. Besides, a heart attack had started him thinking about retiring. A second heart attack convinced him. The Pelican Inn was looking for a manger. Cliff, with Gwen, came back.

The inn is clean and completely equipped for guests, who have to bring their own food and look after themselves. Each of the seven apartments on two floors includes a kitchen, modern bath with tub, and an arrangement of partitioned sleeping and sitting rooms. Sliding glass and screen doors lead to wood porches. A large common deck downstairs is set with tables, chairs, and chaise-lounges. It's a place for going barefoot all the time and leaving things unlocked.

Early in the morning everything is bathed in glow and shadow. The sea is yellow lit. Wind blows grasses expelled by a recent storm. Houses with cupolas built on spindly legs resemble old light stations.

Everything here yields to the sea. All is ordered by its setting. There is little to spare. There are no stores, no phones. Natural order prevails. You find yourself complying with given rhythm, some supreme mantra that brooks no forgetting.

Right as it is for many people, it isn't for all, so Cliff and Gwen try to paint the true picture. "On the mainland if someone's not happy they can pretty much check out. Here you have to wait till I've finished the chores—which may be next day—before I can carry anyone back," says Cliff.

He likes to spend time with everyone.

"If they want to do something I'm doing, they're welcome. I'll take people out shrimping sometimes. Or we'll drive them down the beach one way and let them walk back. If they don't want to be bothered, I don't bother them.

"If they forget to get something at the grocery store before coming over, we usually try to fill in."

The grocery store is in Carrabelle, three and a half miles directly, but about seven through the channels by boat with Cliff. In the summer, the ferry *Ruby B* ties up downtown where you can leave your car.

Things were getting built up awhile back. Then the Nature Conservancy bought out the largest property owner, and with deed restrictions sold in turn to the Cuyahoga Trust of Ohio. Today three-quarters of the island is maintained as a nature preserve, and apart from the Pelican Inn, the chief activity is development of an education and research program that Cliff also looks after.

Quiet, and you might say life-saving for those who show up, as well as for Cliff.

Pelican Inn, Box 5030 Dog Island, Carrabelle, FL 32322. (800) 451-5294. (No local phone.) Cliff Shaw, manager. 7 apartments with AC, heat, ceiling fan, bathrooms with tubs, full kitchens, all rooms now have microwaves, beaches, hiking trails, 15-foot puffer and 15-1/2-foot alluminum skiff, hot tub. Children of any age accepted, free in parents' room to any age (maximum of 4 persons per unit). No pets. AmEx, MC, Visa. Rates for March-October: $565 week, $250 weekend, $265 weekend plus Thursday or Sunday, $288 Monday-Thursday; Nov.-Feb., $475, $200, $220, $248. $125 nightly year-round. Transportation to island and back not included. Charge: $8.75 per person each way. Note: No restaurant or store on the island. Street parking for cars in Carrabelle.

DeFuniak Springs — SUNBRIGHT MANOR

Welcomed innkeeping in a town ripe for revival.

That DeFuniak Springs has a bed-and-breakfast in a grand mansion elates everyone who works for the revival of Florida's historic towns. Colorful personalities layer rich history here.

The house is Sunbright Manor. John Mitchell, who owns it with his wife, Byrdie, works 28 days at a time on an oil rig 80 miles into the North Sea from Aberdeen, Scotland.

Sunbright Manor was the retirement home of Gov. Sidney J. Catts. DeFuniak Springs was a grand winter resort, and famous on the Chautauqua circuit. With its remaining turn-of-the-century mansions, it is still one of Florida's loveliest towns almost a century after it was also one of the state's most cultured. Colonel deFuniak was born in Rome. He helped build the first railroad in Africa, fought alongside Garibaldi for Italian independence, then fled to America and enlisted in the Confederate Army. After the war, he entered the railroad business and became general manager and chief engineer of the Louisville & Nashville Railroad. He founded the little town that bears his name.

By 1885, a winter version of the Chautauqua, an educational and recreational assembly with a program of lectures and concerts, was coming to DeFuniak Springs each year for six weeks from February to April. College presidents and congressmen came from all over America.

The town prospered as a cultural center and as a health resort. The spring waters were said to equal in purity and restorative powers those at Poland and Waukesha. In a calculated dig at resorts that were opening in Tampa and along the east coast, the Hotel Chautauqua boasted of DeFuniak Springs that "The air is bracing and invigorating, free from the slightest taint of malaria."

Though the grand white-framed hotel is gone, a remnant of the Chautauqua Amphitheatre remains in a handsome white clapboard structure on Circle Drive that today houses chamber of commerce offices. Just beyond is the little white-frame library, opened in 1887, expanded several times since, and still in service.

The old town is centered a few blocks along the tracks. Just west where U.S. 331 zips traffic south to Panama City is John and Byrdie's bed-and-breakfast.

Though the house was built around 1886 for a Wisconsin family, its fame dates from the 1920s and 1930s when Governor Catts and his family lived here. Catts was famous in Florida's backwoods for campaigning in his Model T Ford, and for his slogan that "The only three friends a Florida cracker can trust are Sears Roebuck, the Lord Jesus, and Sidney J. Catts."

John and Byrdie bought Sunbright Manor in 1989 and restored it.

Sunbright Manor is irrepressibly Victorian, with brooding dark three-sided porches behind gay gingerbread trim—1,600 spindles and 33 columns worth. Clad in white clapboard with black trim and gray-lattice steprails, the house rises three stories in two grandly symmetrical sections crowned by an octagonal turret. Stained glass panes, tall casement windows, and a pair of oculus windows mark the house worthy of a governor.

Entry is through double doors with star-crinkly upper glass panels and a brass pull lock. To the right is the formal Victorian parlor with heavy blue, elaborately swagged curtains, ring-pull shades, and old-fashioned wallpaper. Furniture is heavy mahogany, with seating pieces in dowager blue velvet on a mustard yellow and pastel Oriental rug.

Guest rooms are full of antiques, with carved, scrolled beds and Eastlake dressers. There's a cushiony couch and TV on the second story of the turret.

Guest rooms have lacked lounge chairs and reading lamps, and the arrangement of parlor furniture has been awkward for conversation. These matters have been pointed out and have likely been corrected. You might ask.

Byrdie serves a full breakfast on Jewel Tea china in the formal dining room.

Your presence at Sunbright Manor will add to the promise of the town's renewal.

Sunbright Manor, 606 Live Oak, DeFuniak Springs, FL 32433. (904) 892-0656. John and Byrdie Mitchell, proprietors. 3 bedrooms, 2 with private bath (1 shares with the Mitchells) (all with showers and tubs, 1 with hot tub), AC, heat, ceiling fan. Color cable TV in lounge. House phone for free local or credit-card LD calls. Children of any age accepted, but require additional room. No pets. MC, Visa, personal checks. Year-round rates: single $40, double $50-$75, includes full breakfast, ice service, wake-up coffee and juice to rooms, sparkling fruit juice, cookies, mints with turndown service. No smoking. Off-street parking.

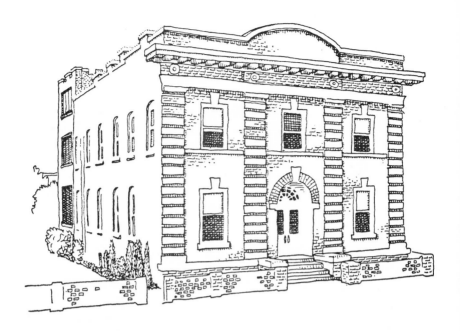

Milton – EXCHANGE HOTEL
Elegant inn in a small restored Panhandle office building.

Sleep comes sweetly now in a luxurious north Florida bed-and-breakfast where telephones once jangled. The Exchange Hotel is an excellent example of how neglected buildings can be recycled into contemporary lodging that makes the case for historic preservation.

Here, 20 miles northeast of Pensacola, Panhandle scion William S. Rosasco III has restored the original two-story telephone exchange that took guests once before in its 76-year history. Today it serves uniquely as an inn in an office building.

Five suites individually furnished with antiques and reproductions are on the second floor, a penthouse is upstairs, and below are offices that house Rosasco enterprises. Manager Tiffany Woodbury, answering the bell, can't be sure if she is letting in a honeymooning couple or an investor for land in northern Santa Rosa County.

You have to think long ago and far from hype for Milton. Geographically, New Orleans, Little Rock, and Nashville are closer than Miami. Culturally, the *Montgomery Advertiser* is sold in news racks. Recreationally, 17 percent of the county is set aside for public outdoor use. One of the cleanest American rivers, the Blackwater, flows from Alabama two blocks from the Exchange Hotel on its way to the Gulf of Mexico.

The historic district reminds that at the turn of the century, Santa Rosa County was still virtually a frontier in west Florida's great yellow pine forests, and Milton was a village of less than 2,000 inhabitants. Its populace consisted of a rough mixture of lumbermen, turpentine workers, boatmen, and farmers.

Just which "Milton" the town was named for is hard to say. Some say secessionist governor John Milton; others say it was named for the town's early days as a pine milling center. But in pioneer times the common names for the town were Scratch Ankle and Hard Scrabble, both derived from trade organized to avoid taxes which caused smugglers to get themselves cut up while landing in briar patches, and trying to scramble up the steep shoreside embankments to avoid notice.

Four-lane action just west of town centers around the shopping mall, Six Flags Plaza, developed by Bill Rosasco, along with the First National Bank of Santa Rosa County, which he serves as chairman.

But even life in the fast lane moves slowly through Milton—despite Eglin Air Force and many Navy bases nearby—because the county is dry. So apart from two plain motels, choice lodgings are in the old part of town where State Road 10 narrows to two lanes, and the Exchange Hotel occupies a prominent corner.

You might do a double-take on an evening stroll up from the river, where in one block you pass the Imogene Theater and in the next block the hotel. The Imogene (that's pronounced "Ima-Jean"), long a relic, has been restored. Once it was the model for Charles Sudmall, a turn-of-the-century Latvian immigrant, who hired the theater contractor to duplicate the brick-stack Federal-style look of the Imogene as a telephone exchange.

The duplicate barely served its original purpose before the exchange was moved to a more modest frame building next door. Curiously vaultlike and bureaucratic-looking for a place of hospitality, the Exchange had only brief success as a hotel before it lapsed into becoming a rooming house, then for a short while, a private dwelling, finally abandoned, condemned, and vandalized.

Bill Rosasco felt he owed himself one because he had tarried about resurrecting the 19th-century Rosasco family mansion until it burned down.

Restored and primped, the Exchange looks decorous as a painted wood soldier, a chorister with a yawning entry arch for a mouth, two half-drawn shaded windows upstairs for theatrical eyes, two windows below like two spots of rouge, and a flat cap of a parapet, in patriotic recital to the American flag out front.

Except for an unobstrusive rear addition, the building's exterior is largely unchanged from when it was new in 1914. The building is rectangular, built almost entirely of common red brick.

The concrete steps to the front door are a variety of sizes, indicating they were handcrafted and not mass produced. The entrance displays the original doors, hardware, and plaster over a beveled glass fanlight window. The lobby is basically restored as it was, including brick interior walls, posts, tongue-in-groove ceiling and stairwell. Steps creak under rich carpeting.

Antique furniture, reproductions, and decor used throughout the building are from the Rosasco family collection and are not part of the original hotel. The look reflects the Victorian and pre-World War I eras.

One of Florida's exceptional values at $48 double is the hotel's penthouse suite. It has two entries, one up a 31-step, two-story circular staircase direct from the parking lot. The suite is fully carpeted and furnished in the tawny colors of fall that match interior brick walls that once were exterior and show the marks of wear. The large space is country-comfy with no hotel aspects.

Since the hotel reopened early in 1983, people have come to deposit memorabilia of its earlier days. A painting of the original hotel, and old guest registers, have been returned. Tiffany recalls an overnight visit by an elderly woman who found the hole in a brick wall where she used to store her jacks as a child.

Guests are accepted with advance reservations only.

Exchange Hotel, 302 Elmira St., Milton, FL 32572. (904) 626-1500. Tiffany Woodbury, manager. 5 suites with AC, heat, bathrooms with tub, color cable TV, direct-dial phone, digital clock radio, VCR lounge. Penthouse also with jacuzzi. Children of any age accepted, free in parents' room under 12. No pets. All major credit cards. Year-round rates: $35 single plus $3 extra person. Penthouse $45 single, $48 double. Danish or English muffin, juice, and coffee $1.50. Smoking in guest rooms only. Private hotel parking. No handicap access.

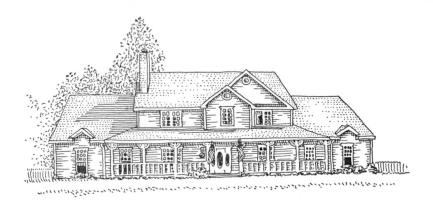

Pensacola — HOMESTEAD INN
Total roadside innkeeping in a replica
Williamsburg governor's house.

Neil Liechty prepares food the old-fashioned way. His cinnamon rolls rise three times. His ice cream is made with pure whipping cream. His berries are fresh as a wisecracking meter maid. Nothing's preserved—not even the old-fashioned west-of-Pensacola inn where he serves it all. Despite its Jamestown blue, Caswell rose, Secretary House red, and Eagle Tavern gold—"official" Williamsburg colors—the Homestead Inn is new as the four-lane highway it sits on. Meant to look old. Replica of a Williamsburg governor's house.

But as it says on the shingle, "Established in 1986."

No pretense here. Just Neil's genuine belief he's better off and so are his guests if he builds like he bakes—from scratch, instead of rehabbing an old place.

"Look," he shrugs. "When you take an historic house and put in new bathrooms and closets, it's remodeled. It's not old anymore. You try to rezone an old place. Zoning people aren't sympathetic to bed-and-breakfasts. There's never any end to the problems. My idea is let's make it look historical. Build a place to look like one you really like. Then put the warmth and the love in.

"People want the modern conveniences. I'm not going to tell them, 'Hey, we don't have TV or telephones in my place because they weren't in the original house.' There are certain things you have to have. If you want the business you have to go after it and provide for it. I can turn around financially a lot faster starting with a building that's new. I turn it around because of the food. Fresh home food makes people feel good together. Back to basics is what a lot of people are looking for."

At the Homestead Inn they find it. Made-to-order breakfast includes fruits and juices, grits and eggs, choice of quiches, sausage or ham, blueberry pancakes

36

with maple syrup, coffee cake or cinnamon roll, and freshly ground coffee. Come evening, included in the room rate there's homemade ice cream and desserts like pecan or chess pie, buttermilk pound cake, or something you might have asked for special that morning.

Most guests' favorite dining room is the one that joins the early-American kitchen where Neil's wife, Jeanne, and her helpers are cooking and baking all day.

Neil comes to how he does things from a Mennonite boyhood.

"I was raised to work," he says, "from day one. When I was five I started getting up at 5:15. I started washing down udders, sweeping the barn. My mom and dad, three brothers and two sisters—we lived off the land. If crops weren't good we didn't take vacations. I like working. Mennonites are farmers and builders. That's how our country started. I believe in this country. I have a relationship with my Creator."

Neil followed a brother to northwest Florida from Grabill, Indiana, and went into the motel business, then retirement centers.

"But I kept looking to give more personal service," he says. "I have this memory of Mennonite food and hospitality. If 40 or 50 folks didn't come by for dinner Sunday after church my people were disappointed."

Neil figured half a mile off the Interstate on a new four-lane highway was the place for his Williamsburg replica. "Right from the start I wanted the place busy like Sunday after church. I'm impatient."

Success was no surprise with year-round $59 to $79 rates—and that's with all the food for two. Neil also puts on food shows at the state fairgrounds, passes out recipes, gives away baked goods to the Chamber and Welcome Center, and caters occasions like downtown bank openings where he shows up with 100 pies baked the same morning and gallons of fresh ice cream. Fast-moving, fast-talking, he's still easy to like.

Guests especially take to the idea of a washer, dryer, and iron they can use. Also available are weights and rollers, since Neil was told by his doctor he needed more fitness in his life to balance out the stressful pace. There's a pool table and a 50-inch TV in addition to those in guest rooms.

The inn is looking more on the outside like it does on the inside as hundreds of blueberry bushes start bushing up, as the red maples, silver oaks, and magnolias fill in the piney spaces and overhang the shingled roof. It leaves the place looking more like a ranch house than a Tidewater mansion. Jeanne's tomato, corn, and pepper plants and her herb garden add charm.

Inside is better with its crocks and crafts that quickly soften the highway harshness. Old-fashioned floral wallpapers complement wood and cane chairs, down-home print upholstery, hand-embroidered pillows, hurricane lamps. Shelves are full of ball jars with dried flowers, stuffed animals, country bric-a-brac. The most original crafts are the saw blades painted with farming scenes by Jeanne's aunt Ardeth, and the quilts sewn by Neil's 94-year-old grandmother.

Six guest rooms with names like Betsy Ross and Benjamin Franklin range from small to spacious. All have bathrooms, firm beds, and pine floors or carpet. Some have fireplaces, some old hope chests. Furnishings are antique and crafts are authentic. Each room has a collection of books about its namesake and Civil War prints.

The place in fact is comfortable and friendly, and undeniably excellent value. It's 10 minutes from the heart of Pensacola on the Interstate. The only reason someone might not like it is because of an attitude you're not supposed to. Neil knows that love and warmth will take care of that.

The Homestead Inn, 7830 Pine Forest Rd., Pensacola, FL 32506. (904) 944-4816. Neil and Jeanne Liechty, owners. 6 rooms with baths (including tubs), AC, heat, ceiling fans, color TV, direct-dial phones (local calls free). Children of any age accepted, $5 extra. Can request crib or rollaway in advance. No pets inside, but fenced yard. No smoking. Chilled champagne for honeymooners. AmEx, MC, Visa. Year-round rates: $59-$79 single or double, 10% discount for seniors, military, and commercial guests, includes 5-course breakfast (served in bed on request) and evening desserts. $10 for extra person in room 12 or older.

Pensacola — NEW WORLD INN
Superior small hotel temporarily under corporate management.

New World Inn is a hotel named, designed, and furnished to tell the history of Pensacola. It delights a visitor's sense of discovery, and brings the city alive. Here you can tune in the intuitive hum that vibrates among the residents of America's oldest settlement (dating from 1559, though not continuously).

From the row of shiny red bikes for touring the nearby historic quarter to the detailing of guest rooms according to the city's history under five flags, New World Landing celebrates the time of its place.

The two-story hotel is built into a block of peaked warehouses next to the wharves and freight yard. It anchors the redevelopment of a downtown that had the good fortune to lie dormant until preservation began to be credible in the Panhandle.

With only 16 rooms and two suites, but three dining rooms, a lounge and meeting space for 1,000 under original warehouse roofs, New World Landing is a downtown meeting-and-greeting facility that also accommodates out-of-towners.

"Delight" sounds indulgent applied to commercial hotels. Plush, posh, opulent—we call them that. They satisfy our egos. Delight speaks to the spontaneous being inside us, supposed to be left at home when we're on business.

Why can't a hotel delight us, like exemplary architecture for even the most common purpose? Once we get past rudimentary shelter—even before—aren't our

39

homes our own reflections? Shouldn't hotels be more than shelter, and more than just "Style A" out of three options given to franchisees?

The best can be a combination of theater, gallery, club, library, and a window on the city. New World Inn is one of the best, and regularly attracts the likes of Ella Fitzgerald, Senator Bob Graham, Larry King, Charles Kuralt, Oliver North, Vice President Dan Quayle, and corporate executives whose travel agents book them here.

Oil geologist Arden A. Anderson and his wife, Kay, world travelers who look for hotels that interpret the places they travel to, built the inn in the early 1980s.

For all its faithfulness to Pensacola traditions, the hotel is utterly modern. Thick pile towels, the firmest beds, room phones, luxurious baths, cable TV unobtrusively present: guests want for nothing.

When the Andersons bought the property, it was a box factory. The land was filled during the 1880s when the waterfront was extended with ballast from ships under sail that had made Pensacola a rich Gulf port.

One photo mural shows horsedrawn carts collecting the scrap for fill discharged by ships ready to load West Florida lumber for Europe and the Americas.

The site became infamous as "Bay View Varieties." Early structures were built on stilts. Tall ships would anchor out, and the men would come in dinghies for the bar and 18-room brothel.

The Andersons traveled from Boston to Savannah to see what was happening with old warehouses. The small inns of Charleston gave them the idea for a hotel. They wanted guests to imagine that their rooms might have been built in 1890. Each is named for a prominent personality in Pensacola history. Each is furnished with Baker reproductions of museum pieces from Spain, France, England, and America.

One room, dedicated to Elias and Rebecca Durnford, is upholstered and quilted in wine reds, befitting the high office of Britain's lieutenant governor for West Florida. The wallpaper is blue with cardinals and hummingbirds sipping at tropical flowers, perhaps suggesting Gov. Durnford's earlier post in Tobago, or the Pensacola street he named Garden during his first assignment here as surveyor.

The room named Geronimo evokes the West where the Indian chief was captured before being exiled and imprisoned in Pensacola. The ceiling is period tongue-in-groove. The wallpaper is an early American stencil pattern carried out in bedcover and drapes. Desk lamps are gas-age replicas. The bathroom wallpaper is Indian blue with dim red flowers. The water basin, deep and oval, set in white marble, reflects the blue wall like a pool. Two small painted portraits are of an Indian boy and Indian girl.

Downstairs in public spaces are pictures of Pensacola's DeLunas, as they are known: prominent citizens who each year honor the first Don Tristan DeLuna y Arrelano, Spain's first governor, at the annual Fiesta of Five Flags.

Of three dining rooms, the most appealing overlooks the hotel's entry patio, with fountain and garden, from a bay window that conjures up a ship's stern captain's quarters.

Good as the hotel has been, its future is uncertain. Early in 1991, it was taken over by the First National Bank of Jefferson Parish, Louisiana, and turned over to a national hotel management company based in Gulf Breeze. New World Inn is the smallest property in their portfolio. Personal style is likely to suffer under institutional management. Policies early in the year were up in the air. Odds are that nothing will change in the guest rooms or facilities, and probably little in rates, though everything is subject to marketplace studies.

So far guests at the New World Inn have found everything offered bathed in the glow of wanting to be found out. Guests have had the sense that someone has thought about how they might like to explore before they actually partake.

It has been like entering a club of Pensacola, being made guest of an engaging inner circle. The hotel has been like an impeccable clubhouse or gallery offered on tour where you yearn to be allowed overnight privileges.

New World Inn undoubtedly will continue to embrace Pensacola's history. The only question is how well hotel hospitality will embrace guests.

New World Landing Inn, 600 S. Palafox St., Pensacola, FL 32501. (904) 432-4111. Managed by Highpointe Hotel Corp., Gulf Breeze, FL. 16 rooms and suites with AC, heat, color cable TV, ceiling fan, bathrooms with tub, direct-dial phone (also in bathroom), elevators. Restaurants, bar. Children of any age accepted, free in parents' room to 13. No pets. All major credit cards accepted. Year-round rates: single $70, double $80, suite $100, $10 each additional person. Corporate, military and long-stay discounts; weekends including 2 consecutive nights $65 per night. Includes morning newspaper. Breakfast $3-$5, lunch $4-$6, dinner $15-25. Off-street parking.

Port St. Joe – OLD SALT WORKS CABINS
Laid-back comfort in cabins in the woods.

It's easy to pass the Old Salt Works Cabins because the sign's so small. And if you do see the sign before you read the words, you might think you're already in the state park.

Truth is at one time the state sought to add this acreage on Cape San Blas to the park. They must have decided it was just as well left private, because with Don and Ardeth Schreck in charge it was going to stay park-like anyway.

Consider: There's no Coke machine and no ice machine. Walls of several cabins are covered in *National Geographic* maps. Interpretive signs are posted along paths, and everything in the little gift shop is locally made. There's even a miniature fort (built by Don) that depicts the site's history. Ardeth named it Fort Crooked Tree for the crooked slash pines that grow on the cape.

Don knew the peninsula when all of it was like this. He built a cabin and stayed 10 years. It was that long before anyone else built. When someone did, Don decided it was time to leave. He went back to insurance.

"I kept traveling, but I couldn't find anything prettier. I just saw a panther here two months ago, and I see bobcat all the time. A couple lady photographers counted 206 different species of birds when they were here lately. You've got fishing, hunting, beaches, safe boating. And you're only 10 miles from town, and they've got three good stores there."

Town is Port St. Joe, which is just across the head of San Blas Bay but by land is reachable only by driving back the length of the cape, then west along the shore again. Town is where a hurricane in the 1840s, followed by a tidal wave, fire and yellow fever, wiped out the population.

During the Civil War, Confederate soldiers came and hauled all the bricks from Port St. Joe to the cape. They used the bricks for the salt works, producing 150 bushels of salt a day until a Union force in 1862 stormed the site and routed the rebels. That was the end of the salt works.

Don and Ardeth think Port St. Joe is all the city they need. The cape has piped-in water, but no sewers—only septic tanks. The fear is that if sewers ever come, the developers will come right behind.

The cabins are all back in the bush except for one on the beach. All have four-burner ranges, toaster ovens, and refrigerators. They have enclosed showers inside and out. All cabins have screens, and the breeze cools, though all but one also have air-conditioning.

Decks nearly encircle the cabins, which have dining areas and sitting rooms with upholstered and straightback furniture. Every cabin has its own shelf of books. All have oil heaters, ceiling fans, and sliding glass doors to screened porches with pine picnic tables. Floors are vinyl and resemble grass mats. Beds are semi-firm.

Don's favorite cabin is the one far to the east of the property where, from the bed, you can look through double doors that open to the bay. On the other side a little pier extends to the pond.

The bay at low tide is a landscape of wheat-colored flats banded with blue ribbons of water, and to the far side the green bluffs of the mainland. Shell paths link the cabins with the rustic park-like office and the crafts shop. Cars are kept out of sight.

Less than a mile farther out on the cape is St. Joseph State Seashore, which has seven miles of natural dunes and few visitors in the winter and spring.

The cape is usually quiet, perfect for reading, communing with nature, and getting back in touch with yourself. Back here off the back road you're as far away as if you'd flown overseas. You might miss every sign that it's time to go home.

Old Salt Works Cabins, P.O. Box 526, Port St. Joe, FL 32456. (904) 229-6097. Don and Ardeth Schreck, proprietors. 8 cabins, all with showers (2 also with tubs), all AC but 1, heat, ceiling fan, 6 with electric kitchens, 2 with sleeping rooms only, screened porch. Color TV in 2 sleeping rooms and Lagoon Cabin. No phones but messages taken, and office has phone for free local and credit-card LD calls. Children of any age accepted, no charge for infant in parents' room, otherwise 3rd person charge of $5. No pets. No credit cards; personal checks OK. Rates: Palm Sunday through Labor Day: $42-$57 double; rest of the year $30-$45. Smoking allowed. Off-street parking. No handicap access.

Quincy — ALLISON HOUSE INN
First bed-and-breakfast inn in a town of
preservation treasures.

Quincy was a town waiting for a bed-and-breakfast to happen when, in June 1990, car dealer Bruce Thomas and his cousin Fred Fisher bought the A.K. Allison House.

The town, which is the governing seat of Gadsden County, is west Florida's crown jewel of preserved history. In 1980 its entire downtown and surrounding area of 36 blocks were placed in the National Register of Historic Places. Enhancement of the town's historical character quickly followed. Overhead utility lines were removed from around the courthouse square, sidewalks redone, period lighting installed, and trees planted in the four-block heart of town.

Visitors will come into Bell & Bates Hardware and tell the people there what a great restoration they've done—referring to the high casement windows, the brick, the chain-hung canopy, and the metal frame sign atop the squared pediment—and the hardware store folks will say, "Shoot, we never let the place run down. It's the original from 1902."

The Allison House Inn, two blocks north on Madison Street, was built in 1845, and is one of the oldest houses in Florida in use as a bed-and-breakfast.

About all that the house missed were the founding of the county and the town.

Gadsden County (named for an aide to the notorious Indian-killer Andrew Jackson) was the original site of Florida's capital until the first territorial legislature in 1824 carved neighboring Leon County and Tallahassee out of it.

The town of Quincy took its name from sixth President John Quincy Adams, who signed the papers establishing the county seat. The affairs of the territory of Florida at that time were largely governed by Washington.

The inn was named after A.K. Allison, who twice served as Florida's governor, neither time elected. His first tenure was while serving as speaker of the Florida House pending inauguration of elected Gov. James E. Broom. Allison served again after the suicide of Gov. John Milton, an angry secessionist who after the Civil War avoided trial for treason by taking his own life. Allison, more moderate in the cause of secession, nonetheless supported the Confederacy, served in its army, and later, for having served as Senate President and as Governor during the secessionist regime, was imprisoned for six months. He served a second prison term for intimidating Negro voters.

As a bedroom community for Tallahassee, Quincy has proven especially appealing because of its historical character. Oddly, the Allison House was virtually overlooked among those historical resources.

That's because in 1925 its original look was completely changed. What had been a Georgian double-parlor floor plan in the classical revival style was lifted off its tall brick pilings to become the second story of a new one underneath. Downstairs became a livestock pen (later office space), and upstairs, apartments. The entire new structure was stuccoed.

Once in possession of the Allison House, Bruce and Chris Thomas removed apartment walls that had chopped the house into cubicles and re-established five—potentially six—guest rooms along with manager's quarters on the first floor. Pine plank floors were refinished to show their natural deep red. Board and batten ceilings and big six-on-six casement windows were restored, nowhere more beautifully than upstairs in Ella's Parlor where, after the house was jacked up, eight of these windows were installed to form three sides. A continental breakfast is served here each morning on wicker furniture. Guests relax on two antique sofas. A 100-year-old, seven-foot-long highboy has been fitted into the room. There are a glass china cabinet and lace curtains.

Rooms have been redone in themes of light pink, green, and gray-blue. Chris says she first picked out comforters and dust ruffles, then painted accordingly. Rooms have a variety of cast iron, brass, and oak king beds. The downstairs Country Room has two doubles. Furniture throughout the house consists of English antiques. Most pieces are for sale.

Outside, the Thomases and Fishers have planted a flower bed in the circular entry. Though the yellow stucco exterior remains, the look has been enlivened by regimental striped awnings and shutters, white and gray trim, and a decorative folk art called rose mahling. Only the pedimented roof hints at the original look of the Allison House.

Guests enter through double-entry doors topped with beveled glass into a foyer of black and white tile with rose wallpapers. A floral runner in gray, black, and deep peach extends to the second floor.

The Allison Inn is a wonderful coming together of people, ideas, and history. It's unlikely the inn waits long for guests.

Allison House Inn, 215 North Madison Street, Quincy, FL 32351. (904) 875-2511. Patty and Fred Reynolds, innkeepers. 5 rooms with bath with AC, heat, ceiling fan, color cable TV in 3 rooms, portable phone (messages taken), no charge for local calls or surcharge on LD calls. Children free in parents room through 12 ($4 for crib or rollaway), $10 for additional person in room. Inquire about pets. MC, Visa. Guest access to hot plate and refrigerator. Cookies in kitchen. Tallahassee Democrat daily for each room. Year-round rates from $58-$68 include full uncooked breakfast. Off-street parking. No smoking in rooms. Antiques and collectibles shop on premises.

Seaside — SEASIDE
Stylish mix of past and present in award-winning new resort.

Seaside offers a variety of intimate lodgings in a little resort community of distinctive good design. Its layout as a village, rather than as a resort, would make Seaside special anywhere that tourists flock. Its singular impact is that it reminds us of how shoddy most everything else is.

Until Seaside, maybe developers could convince people that tasteful resort was an oxymoron. Look for miles around Panama City or Destin. One after another the hotels, motels, condos whistle, stomp, and shout as if they'd seen the future and it's been ground into the sausage of spot TV commercials, nothing shy of overkill allowed in the cause of getting our attention to spend a quick buck.

You drive along a nondescript stretch of beach road (the worst abominations of development have temporarily left off), and suddenly the buildings around compose themselves tastefully. Latticework graces your glance. The houses are pastel, and align themselves along sandy lanes with picket fences and little yards. The houses resemble a seaside neighborhood from a time when community values kept things orderly.

Robert Davis began developing the tiny town on 80 acres that his grandfather owned, where he had visited 35 years before as a child. The idea was to use the beachfront as a summer camp for employees of a family business. But that never happened, and the land lay but little used.

Davis over the years had become a small-scale developer in the Coconut Grove section of Miami where his projects were remarkable for how they kept to the scale and style of their neighborhoods.

Later, Davis engaged a pair of architects and city planners who defied conventional resort design. Andres Duany and Elizabeth Plater-Zyberk encouraged Robert Davis's dreams about re-creating the kind of sane village community he'd always been attracted to. Not only did they convince him that his instincts were right, but that by being true to his calm vision he would achieve his marketing objectives: that the world would beat a path to his doorstep.

The architects created a design code that called for cottages that had deep roof overhangs, ample windows, and cross-ventilation in all rooms. Cottages were to be built off the ground, to allow the breezes to flow under the house as well as through. Ample porches were required, and wood and other time-tested materials that with reasonable maintenance could last several generations. Buyers of cottages were encouraged to hire their own architects.

The result is a community, though far from built out, that resembles Charleston, Key West, Cape Cod, and such towns as have taken centuries to mature into their distinctive character. Best of all, the physical community seems to subtly influence behavior. People dress casually to walk from cottage to beach. They chat across fences and while walking the sandy lanes. They behave like neighbors rather than time-share owners. All feel commonly invested in their resorts, but at Seaside even vacationers who don't own the cottages they're occupying feel committed to a way of life that gives them common pride—not merely common ownership—with others.

The little town is divided into neighborhoods, each signified by a distinctive beach pavilion. The pavilions and wooden walkways over the dunes add to the visual amenity. They provide gathering places at the most popular recreation area, as well a way to get to the beach without trampling the dunes, which provide protection against sea surges.

The Honeymoon Cottages include six two-room houses just behind the dune. Each has a wood-burning stove-fireplace and steam bath. Two have an al fresco whirlpool on private porch. Quilts are down-filled. There's a kitchenette. Furniture is fine white wicker and upholstered pieces, all the colors pale, the walls pastel, brightness furnished by flowers and decorative accessories.

The eight rentals in Dreamland Heights enclose a roof garden. Five face the sunset and offer two-story living while three face the sunrise. Between the two sets is a public deck. These units are above a small shopping area that includes the estimable Modica Market, both gourmet and practical. There are several restaurants in the village now, a Saturday market, and numerous buildings of eccentric flair for visitors to discover.

Seaside attracts a large number of repeat visitors because people feel good vacationing here, not just hedonistic, but inspired as well.

Seaside, Seaside, FL 32459. (904) 231-4224. Bonnie Leigh, managing director. 6 2-room Honeymoon Cottages, 8 Dreamland Heights "cabins" (apartments) with roof garden, dozens of free-standing cottages, all with kitchen or kitchenette, at least one complete bathroom. Some units up/down duplexes, some with whirlpool, color cable TV, direct dial phone, robes, welcome basket of white wine and fresh fruit, coffee service, continental breakfast. No children in Honeymoon Cottages; accepted 12 and over in west cabins (5) in Dreamland Heights (no extra charge). No pets. No credit cards; checks accepted. Rates: Dreamland Heights (West Cabins) winter $160, spring/fall at least 10% above 1990 rate of $200; (East Cabins) $145, $140+, $175+. All units double. Free-standing cottages by the week: winter $308.44 for smallest units to approximately $1,200 for largest; summer $450 to $1,700; rest of year $371.80 to $1,375—all likely to increase in 1991 and 1992. Some units non-smoking. Off-street parking. Modica Market for everything from necessities to gourmet items. Several restaurants priced from inexpensive to high.

Tallahassee – GOVERNORS INN
Top style and service in a pair of storefronts
recycled for visitors to the state capital.

No surprise that in a solidly two-party state the finest hotel in the capital argues both sides of its case: that old is new and new is old, that preservation works but modern sells, that small hotels make money but you need more than one to keep owners happy.

Since 1984, the Governors Inn has occupied a niche in a two-block downtown historic district richly textured in wood and glass, with arches, awnings, shutters and planters. One feels instantly long-ago but comfortably contemporary in this updated brick lane of globe-lighted memory where street-level galleries and apparel shops mix with upstairs lawyer and dentist offices in a sampler of capital life that has persisted on Adams Street from Territorial time 150 years ago.

The hotel serves the district as well as its guests by top-notch concept, management, and service. Repeat business helps keep its 40 rooms full most of the year. Whether or not the legislature is in session, Florida government is a 12-month-a-year affair.

The Governors Inn might easily be mistaken for a quality jewelry shop—all glass, brass, and class. Elegant black awnings shadow a two-story lobby. Through the leaded glass double doors you enter as to the manner born.

To one side is a discreet registration desk, ahead a boldly geometric hallway, to the right the richly southern clublike Florida Room.

Guest quarters are accessible by the corridor that links two deep and old narrow storefronts converted to lodgings. In the days before gaslight and display windows, such office supply and hardware stores were essentially dark warehouses. Goods for sale were stacked outdoors, obliging customers until early in the century to share the dirt street with hogs and goats.

Today the high roofs are topped by skylights that draw in the sun, lighting up spectacular diamond-shaped trusses and muscular joinings. The walkway suggests an historic scaffolding or bridge, an extraordinary access to guest rooms that merit this kind of imaginative antespace.

Each room bears the name of a deceased Florida governor. Check the portfolio in the Florida Room where all (including Territorial governors) are pictured and told about. In each room a different story is encapsulated.

And each is different in a way that respects the ingenuity of architect and interior designer. Some feature sleeping lofts with lower sitting rooms that serve as offices. Corkscrew staircases impress circular walls in bathrooms.

Other rooms have wood-burning marble fireplaces, bars, a jacuzzi. All are furnished with antiques or quality reproductions. Locally milled armoires serve in place of closets and hide TV sets that feature digital clocks and AM-FM radios and come with remote tuners. Upper level rooms have soaring 15-foot ceilings and four-poster beds high enough from carpeted floors that a short person requires a mounting strategy.

A welcomed service is a morning choice of just about any metro Florida paper, the Atlanta daily, *New York Times* or *Wall Street Journal*. Who can resist the *Times* on Sunday? Weighty reason for weekending in town!

The caliber of the operation was set by an owner group that has had plans to open new hotels elsewhere in Florida. Lawton M. (Bud) Chiles, III, son of Florida's governor, heads the group. The hotel is managed by Charles Orr. His staff are mostly university students with an innate sense of the polite thing to do.

"If a manager is people-oriented, the employees take the same attitude," says Charles, called by his first name by guests but not staff. "There's a lot of stress for people on business in a capital city. We make it easy for them to concentrate on work. We provide 50-cent local calls and pass on our volume long-distance discounts. We never miss a wake-up or message call. When the legislature meets we keep four people on the switchboard. That's for 40 rooms! We provide free limousine service everywhere in the capital district, and we'll pick up and take guests back to the airport in our courtesy van. We never overbook. But we do send reminder postcards.

"If guests want, we'll provide introductions. Our guests tend to be good mixers. They can make valuable contacts here. During cocktail hour the Florida Room reminds you of an old-fashioned vacation hotel where people eagerly met each other because they could assume anyone staying there ranked prominently back home."

Tallahassee, like the legislated result of lobbying, is the story of compromise. Neither St. Augustine nor Pensacola would give way to the other as capital when East Florida and West Florida were united. The no-name place chosen—Tallahassee—was equidistant between. Win, lose, or compromise, Charles' guests are all winners. The standard at the Governors Inn is uncompromising.

Governors Inn, 209 W. Adams St., Tallahassee, FL 32301. (800) 342-7717 (FL). (904) 681-6855. Charles Orr, general manager. 40 rooms with AC, heat, bathrooms with tub, color cable TV, phone, AM/FM radio. Children of any age accepted, 12 and under free in parents' room. No pets. All major credit cards. Rates depending on time of year and type of accommodation from $70 and $109 single, $85 and $135 double, $170 and $215 double in suites. Includes continental breakfast, newspaper, afternoon cocktails, turndown service, mint, overnight shoeshine, round-trip airport service. Room service available from Andrews 2nd Act and Andrews Upstairs. Off-street parking at a charge.

Wakulla Springs — WAKULLA SPRINGS LODGE & CONFERENCE CENTER

Glorious nature preserve dedicated 54 years ago to comfortable family vacationing. Improved as state park.

There was always something state park-like about Wakulla Springs and Lodge and its administration even though it was a private sanctuary. Built between 1935 and 1937, the lodge was intended for conservationists and vacationing families. Its amenities have never been the sort to attract commercial travelers or those who flaunt wealth, even though its patron was one of the wealthiest men in America.

He was Ed Ball of DuPont, and here, where mastodon bones are clearly visible under water 180 feet deep and there are more than 150 varieties of wildlife, he set aside 4,000 north Florida acres of moss-covered forest for incorporation into a sweep of how early 20th-century captains of industry thought people ought to vacation.

Part of Florida's state park system since 1986, Wakulla Springs is 11 miles south of Tallahassee, and is a registered natural landmark of the U.S. Department of the Interior. Though now in a state park, the lodge as always accommodates overnight guests.

The show is outdoors, centered on a spring that pours forth more than 600,000 gallons of water a minute, filling a basin of $4\frac{1}{2}$ acres. Here forms the Wakulla River. Two miles of pathways penetrate dense woodlands. Swimming is encouraged during warmer months, and there is a 33-foot diving tower for plunging into the sub-70-degree water. Glass-bottomed boats yield clear sight of abundant marine life. Great shoals of fish and fantastic grottos appear among flagellate grasses. The stream remains one of the last "wild rivers" in the Southeast. In spring and fall the floodplain is home to many endangered bird species, as well as migratory stopover for huge flocks of geese and ducks.

Though the long, looping driveway from State Road 51 befits plantation style, the look of the lodge is rustic.

There are only 27 guest rooms, all with modernized private marble bathrooms, all on the second floor. These provide comfort without frills. Many rooms retain their original furnishings: brass beds, dressers with inlaid wood, and a few small antiques. In 1990, as part of a $600,000 renovation of the lodge, beds, spreads, draperies, upholstery, and area rugs were all improved and tubs reglazed. Asbestos has been removed from the attic, sprinkler systems installed, smoke detectors, and fire alarm systems improved, and the heating and cooling system replaced.

There are no TVs in the rooms, no computer jacks, no promotional materials. No alcohol is served.

Instead of a charged-up resort atmosphere, there are interpretive stations. These include a historical museum near the lodge and, in the lobby, a self-operated video program about the wildlife.

Special, too, are the native cypress paneling, the high-coffered lobby ceilings ornamented in Indian designs and scenes of the river, and the stuffed form of "Old Joe," a 650-pound 11-foot 2-inch alligator.

There is nothing Frenchified about the food, priced for families, served in a big-windowed dining room that overlooks the spring. All meals feature Southern favorites: grits, cornbread, oysters, blackeyed peas, pan-fried chicken. A house specialty is navy bean soup, thick with ham and potatoes.

The dining room is at one end of a vast lobby with hand-painted rafters of Aztec and Toltec designs, with a wood-burning fireplace and marble floors. At the other end is a souvenir shop and 60-foot marble soda fountain. Apart from confections, choice buys include the variety of books that feature Florida history, recipes, and restaurants.

In the half century since completion of the lodge, nature has begun to reassert its primacy over industry. All the more reason to appreciate Wakulla Springs for how it has always been.

Wakulla Springs Lodge & Conference Center, 1 Springs Drive, Wakulla Springs, FL 32305. (904) 224-5950. John R. Puskar, director. 27 rooms with AC, heat, bathrooms with tub, direct-dial phone. TV in lobby, restaurant and soda fountain. Spring swimming, boat tours, nature trails. Year-round rates: single $42-$49, double $50-$58, DuPont Room and suites from $65 to $230. Children of any age accepted. Rollaway bed $5, crib $5. Seventh night free. $5 for extra person in room. No smoking in hallways, bathrooms, elevator. No pets. MC, Visa. Breakfasts $3-$6, lunch $5-$10, dinner $6-$13. Non-smoking rooms available. Six conference rooms.

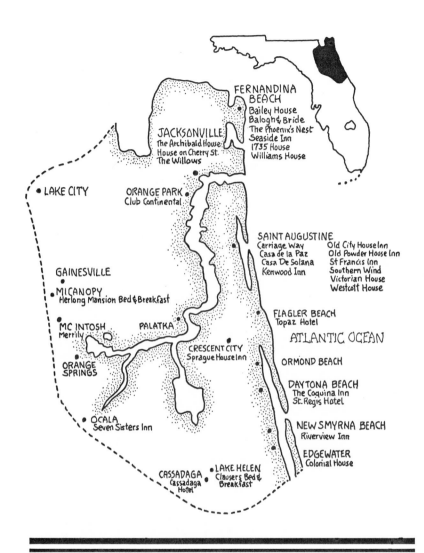

FERNANDINA
BEACH
Bailey House
Balogh & Bride
The Phoenix's Nest
Seaside Inn
1735 House
Williams House

JACKSONVILLE
The Archibald House
House on Cherry St.
The Willows

LAKE CITY

ORANGE PARK
Club Continental

SAINT AUGUSTINE
Carriage Way   Old City House Inn
Casa de la Paz   Old Powder House Inn
Casa De Solana   St Francis Inn
Kenwood Inn   Southern Wind
                      Victorian House
                      Westcott House

GAINESVILLE

MICANOPY
Herlong Mansion Bed & Breakfast

MC INTOSH
Merrily

PALATKA

FLAGLER BEACH
Topaz Hotel

ATLANTIC OCEAN

CRESCENT CITY
Sprague House Inn

ORMOND BEACH

ORANGE
SPRINGS

DAYTONA BEACH
The Coquina Inn
St. Regis Hotel

OCALA
Seven Sisters Inn

NEW SMYRNA BEACH
Riverview Inn

EDGEWATER
Colonial House

CASSADAGA   LAKE HELEN
Cassadaga   Clausers Bed &
Hotel   Breakfast

NORTHEAST COAST AND
NORTH-CENTRAL REGION

Openings far outnumber closings in this part of Florida where Fernandina Beach,
Jacksonville, and St. Augustine have seen steady expansion of their historic lodgings,
and others elsewhere have opened additional towns to inn-style overnights. Changes
of ownership have generally improved hospitality throughout the region.

53

New in Fernandina Beach are **Balogh & Bride, The Phoenix's Nest,** and the first floating bed and breakfast in Florida, three staterooms on the 82-foot **Yacht Bengal** [Fernandina Harbour Marina, FL 32034, (904) 277-3144]. Coming, but too late for this edition, is Bob and Karen Warner's **Florida House Inn,** to be 11 rooms and suites with baths in a pair of connected mid-1850s buildings. This is the oldest existing hotel in Florida and promises to be a prize piece of work [Box 688, Fernandina Beach, FL 32034, (904) 261-3300]. It is in the heart of the downtown historic district.

Scheduled to open before 1991 is out is the Nantucket shingle-style **Elizabeth Pointe Lodge,** 20 guest rooms directly on the beach on Amelia Island. David and Susan Caples, who turned the **1735 House** into a lodging and organized Amelia Island Lodging Systems, are owners of this venture. David is otherwise esteemed around Florida for his informed marketing counseling to many innkeepers [82 South Fletcher Avenue, Amelia Island, FL 32034, (904) 277-4851]. Also to open in 1991 in Old Fernandina is **Posada San Carlos,** an 1880 house of exquisite shingle and gingerbread [212 Estrada Street, FL 32034, (904) 277-2274]. Note on the island that as the **Seaside Inn** becomes more and more popular as a restaurant and night scene for rock and roll, its potential for overnighting diminishes, though rooms are still offered, and if you like staying up late and don't want to drive after, falling asleep upstairs makes a lot of sense. You'll wake up to look at the sea.

Four new lodgings have opened in Jacksonville: the exemplary **Archibald** in Springfield, and **The Willows** in Avondale: Bill and Yvonne Edmonds' **Judge Gray's House** in Riverside [2814 St. Johns Avenue, Jacksonville, FL 32205, (904) 388-4248], and Kathy and Jerry Ray's sumptuous eight-room **Plantation Manor,** where the one-time hippie pad that was the **Manor Inn** has debuted without a trace of the unsavory [1630 Copeland, Jacksonville, FL 32004, (904) 384-4630], are worth your attention also but have opened too late for detailing in this edition.

St. Augustine keeps changing—to be expected in a town that more than any other depends on vacationers. New are **Old City House Inn, Old Powder House Inn,** and **Southern Wind. Casa de la Paz** and **Kenwood Inn** have new owners. **Carriage Way** has been for sale. Also new and worthwhile in town though not detailed in this edition, are the little **Castle Garden** across the street from Ripley's Believe It or Not [15 Shenandoah, St. Augustine, FL 32084, (904) 829-3839]; Carole and Hal Schroeder's five-room **Cordova House** [16 Cordova Street, St. Augustine, FL 32084, (800) 247-8284, (904) 825-0770], and Terry Stover Rainey's 101-year-old **The 1890 Inn** [83 Cedar Street East, St. Augustine, FL 32084, (904) 826-0287]. In prospect is the **Old Mansion** [14 Joyner Street, St. Augustine, FL 32084, (904) 824-1975], likely to be a resplendent addition to the ranks if Vera Kramer sells her gift shop and turns innkeeper, as she's thinking about doing.

The **Ponte Vedra Inn & Club** dates from 1928, although none of the original lodgings remain [200 Ponte Vedra Blvd., Ponte Vedra Beach, FL 32082, (800) 234-7842, (904) 285-1111]. Just south is **The Lodge at Ponte Vedra Beach,** new but small with 66 oversized rooms and suites in a distinctly Mediterranean style. Neither of these properties is detailed.

Laid-back and idiosyncratic, the old-timey **Cassadaga Hotel** has reopened in its namesake town. Nearby are **Clauser's Bed & Breakfast** in Lake Helen, **DeYarman Inn** in an 1875 landmark building smack on the highway [300 South Volusia Avenue, Orange City, FL 32763, (904) 775-1177], and the **Deland Country Inn** [228 West Howry Avenue, DeLand, FL 32720, (904) 736-4244]. (The latter two properties are not detailed.)

New on the coast are the **Colonial House** in Edgewater, and the beautiful new **Coquina Inn** in downtown Daytona. Soon to open nearby is one of the most promising inn restorations in Florida, the **Live Oak Inn** to open across from the marina in the two oldest buildings in Daytona Beach [44-448 South Beach Steet, Daytona Beach, FL 32114, (904) 242-INNS]. Also newly revived is the **Topaz Hotel** in Flagler Beach.

A pair of inns have closed: **The Ritz** in Ocala, and the **Orange Springs Historic Country Inn** in its namesake town. Four others have had owner changes: **Sprague House Inn** in Crescent City, expanded and now offering all meals; **Herlong Mansion** in Micanopy, available again all through the week instead of only weekends; the **Riverview Hotel** in new Smyrna Beach; and **Seven Sisters Inn** in Ocala, where the very competent Norma and Jerry Johnson will be missed, having moved to Atlanta.

Some may still want to visit the **Alba Court Inn** in New Smyrna Beach [115 Washington Street, New Smyrna Beach, FL 32069, (904) 428-9193], where the look of yesterday remains in the glorious pine wainscoting that coats the splendid architectural atrium, and the best of the rooms might still appeal to the old-hotels aficionado for an overnight. Peggy and George Wolsfelt one day may bring their inn back to high style.

Among plainest overnights in the region are the **Thomas Tourist Home** in Gainesville, [835 East University Avenue, Gainesville, FL 32602, (904) 376-9394] where overnight rooms and apartments range from $17 to $25, and **The Yearling,** a cluster of fish camp cabins with an exceptional regional restaurant in Cross Creek [Route 3, Box 123, Hawthorne, Fl 32640, (904) 466-3033], where writer Marjorie Kinnan Rawlings' house is preserved as a state historic site.

Cassadaga — CASSADAGA HOTEL
Reprieve for old hotel in spiritualist community.

I was touring Florida with my older daughter and her then-husband Courtney, a Welsh artist who specialized in the Celtic style historically associated with mystical heroes and spirituality. Cassadaga was on our tour because of its charming gingerbread houses in the little town's up-and-down setting—and because of the town's link with spiritualists.

The hotel at the time had been turned into an adult congregate living facility. The Rev. Lillian Weigl, who was helping look after the place, showed us around. I let Courtney and Nancy follow right behind her, and I hung back slightly.

When we returned to the lobby after the tour, Rev. Weigl remarked to Courtney how much she enjoyed the presence of the tall, handsome gentleman who had followed us throughout. I felt flattered.

"Oh, did you notice him?" exclaimed Courtney. "He's my grandfather." I didn't understand. "He follows wherever I go," said Courtney. Whereupon the Rev. Weigl and Courtney had an animated discussion about spiritual beings and so on, and I, child of Western science, ever dubious about mediums and tarot readings and "all that stuff," stood by amazed.

Before the hotel became a congregate living facility, others had tried to keep it in the overnight trade, which in Cassadaga meant a lot of weekend business and generally good occupancy in the winter because it was right across the street from the grounds of the Southern Cassadaga Spiritualist Camp Meeting Association. Visitors from around Florida would come for readings by the mediums who live here, mostly in the winter.

The hotel dates from 1927. It replaced an earlier property that had been part of the little community incorporated in 1894 by a spiritualist group that George P. Colby led from upstate New York. The group built the wooden compound of classrooms and recreational buildings that remains largely intact across from today's hotel. Lake Colby and Spirit Pond, then as now, were popular for recreation, studded with gazebos and bandshells. On the surprisingly hilly grounds, members of the Southern Cassadaga group built their houses, most of which remain today and give the tiny town its charm.

In time, others not connected with the Southern Cassadaga group moved in. Some were merely exploiters of a public that seemed ever interested in communing with spirits. A certain friction has always remained between the outsiders and the insiders—and between the hotel and spiritualists, too, after its ownership was severed from the spiritualist community. The hotel's need to survive as a profitable business led to more raucous partying than the community wanted, and to some of the estrangement felt lately. The hotel's recent succoring of mediums not affiliated with the local camp hasn't helped.

In 1989, the news that the congregate living facility would become a hotel again was inspiring to any lover of the quaint and historical.

Joseph Stupar is now the manager for friends from Milwaukee who own the property. His experience in hospitality is limited to running a small cocktail lounge in Milwaukee. Nonetheless, he has since improved the property by stripping out the old green carpet and restoring the cypress floors. Metal beds and old wicker have been restored in the 30 rooms, each with its own small bath. Rooms have reverse-cycle air-conditioning, and will have ceiling fans as well.

The dining room has been re-established, and the lobby is being restored with antiques. Seneca Hall is used again for lectures, and the west porch serves as the Medium Walk, where mediums set up tables for guests who want readings (though none of the mediums accredited by the campground take part).

The charm of the hotel is its setting. Visitors should take advantage of the winter programs across the street at the campground. The Cassadaga Camp Bookstore has an extensive collection of spiritualist publications and others about the occult and about Florida. The camp maintains several meditative sites.

There is tension today not only between the camp and the outsiders but also within the camp itself. Some want to sell to developers who would end the camp. It's not clear where the hotel stands in all this. For the future, you probably need a crystal ball.

Cassadaga Hotel, 355 Cassadaga Rd., Cassadaga, FL 32706. (904) 228-2323. Joseph E. Stupar, proprietor. 30 rooms and baths, half with footed tubs, AC, heat, some with ceiling fans. Color cable TV in lobby. Pay phone. Children of any age accepted, free in room (cot available) to age 7. Checks, no credit cards. No smoking in public areas of hotel. 4 downstairs room with handicap ramps. Year-round rates: suite $75 (for up to 4), rooms $40 single, $45 double. For Race Week (February) and Bike Week (March) $75 single, $10 extra person. 3rd person in room $10. Restaurant with liquor license, has no-smoking section. Average meal prices: $4 breakfast, $4 lunch, $7-$13 dinner.

Crescent City — SPRAGUE HOUSE INN
Newly upgraded under attentive innkeepers.

Terry Moyer was an anesthetist, but now he's an innkeeper who shows his versatility at lulling folks into dreamland. Since 1989, he has turned this small-town inn into a little hub of good food and six rooms and suites.

The look of the 100-year-old place from the street is so intriguing you can't fail to stop. You see a balconied second story of hanging baskets under a sloping tin roof. There are gingerbread accents and an ornamental wood railing surrounding an entry porch that wraps around the side. A red and green leaded and stained glass re-creation of the street is installed in a front window.

The entry, at the side, leads into a woody dining room with ceiling fans, fretwork, stained glass, lamps, and odd-sized mirrors. The mirrors are Terry's, a collection that adds to the distinction of the inn and includes some that are for sale.

The little banquet room in the front gets set as a seafood bar on weekends. The Oyster Room, as Terry and wife Vena call it, has a wood-burning stove, and features a huge mural of Uncle John's Cane and Maple Sugar Syrup.

Until Terry came, these rooms were mostly the showrooms of glasscrafters Barry and Elaine Nord, who still have their studios across the street. The Nords revived the inn in the early 1980s. It's mostly their glasswork that guests find here.

Terry and Vena offer a mix of seafood and traditional American favorites—prime rib, grilled steaks and chicken, with a variety of luncheon salads and sandwiches. Breakfasts include the works: stacks of pancakes with syrup, bacon, ham, sausage, steak and eggs, omelets, biscuits and pastries. Terry and Vena bake their own breads. Inn guests have their choice of anything on the menu as well as special orders.

The action on Crescent Avenue is a big change on what used to be the main street of town but now is too easily missed because traffic flows north-south on Highway 17.

The Sprague House was built in 1892 by a Crescent City physician. Visitors used to come from Crescent Lake, where steamers docked on this southeasterly circuit off the St. Johns River. The boats came for citrus; the region is where groves were first planted in Florida before almost a century of freezes steadily forced growers south. Citrus was shipped out, tourists shipped in. Many, including Theodore Roosevelt, William Howard Taft, and William Jennings Bryan, stayed at the Sprague House.

Terry came from the Keys looking for the right place to develop his new career as chef. He bought the inn early in 1989. He and Vena married and began sharing the innkeeping load. "You have to have a partner with the same true love for innkeeping," Terry says.

Now Terry and Vena are working on the rooms. Each of the four rooms has its own clawfoot tub (suite bathrooms are fully modern) and sitting area. Furnishings are period antiques. Beds are firm. One room has antique maps on its walls. There are plenty of mirrors, most from the late 18th, 19th, and early 20th centuries, some French, some English, many from Art Nouveau and Art Deco periods. Additional rooms are in the works.

The upstairs porch has swings and rockers. You can read here and watch crabbers come up from the lake with their catch. The steady breeze sets the wind chimes playing.

While here, take time to read the various histories of the town and the hotel that have been etched into the sidewalk. These outline the growth of the town, of citrus, of the many hotels that once greeted guests. Today there's only the Sprague House Inn. You'll feel thankful that one remains, and that thoughtful innkeepers have charge.

Sprague House Inn, 125 Central Ave., Crescent City, FL 32012. (904) 698-2430. Terry and Vena Moyer, owners. Four rooms and 2 lakefront suites, all with private baths, AC, heat, ceiling fan. Telephone available, no TV. No children, no pets. Smoking restricted to outside porches, lobby, downstairs dining rooms. MC, Visa. Gourmet restaurant with beer, wine. Rates: $50 and $75, single or double, includes full breakfast. Special requests available. Lunch, $5 up; dinner, $9 up. Off-street parking.

Daytona Beach — THE COQUINA INN
Highly styled innkeeping evokes yesteryear Daytona.

For all the Floridians who put down Daytona Beach as has-been, blue-collar, cars-on-the-beach, and anti-environmentalist, please consider that one of the finest bed-and-breakfasts in the state has opened here. It's on a street of splendid town houses in a historic district that is at the heart of the city's redevelopment plans.

Whatever else does or doesn't happen, the Coquina Inn provides a wonderful reason for folks to make Daytona Beach a stop on the way north or south (it's very close to I-95, and conveniently at the end of I-4), or just for a weekend getaway.

This is a house of lyrical qualities, its curved arches set behind high mossy oaks on a corner of richly planted, divided streets. Memories of Daytona's early opulence, when Henry Flagler and John D. Rockefeller frequented the area, hover in the tropical atmosphere. About 100 years ago, this was as close to the tropics as Flager's railroad reached, and the area became the glory of East Coast winter resorts. Turn-of-the-century elegance here reminds one of Savannah and Charleston. But for hot summers, Daytona close by the Halifax River is heaven.

Jerry and Susan Jerzykowski have taken this one-time parsonage, richly textured in coquina rock, dormered, with an upstairs picket porch, and restored it to period elegance with an imaginative eye for color and a passion for acquiring the best of everything.

Jerry and Susan came prepared in more ways than one.

They knew Daytona from growing up, especially Jerry. His father has owned property in neighboring Ormond Beach since the 1970s, and his grandfather has been coming for more than 30 years.

Susan and Jerry were from Royal Oak, Michigan, a northwest Detroit suburb. They'd done well, she in retail management (with Dayton-Hudson at the end), and Jerry in industrial graphics and advertising. But both were burned out. They were still in early middle age when they decided to jump ship, head for Daytona, and start a bed-and-breakfast.

What the house gave them to work with were coquina walls, terra cotta tiles, push-out cottage windows, oak floors, working fireplaces, natural grain stucco walls, and multi-paned glass-topped doors.

The house was built in 1912, but Jerry and Susan took the 1920s-1930s as their guide for furnishing it. Because Jerry works in an antique shop, he was able to find the kind of luxurious pieces that would complement the house's built-in beauty. Their splendid inspiration was to enliven the house with colors of today's more liberal palette, fascinating guests with the sense of a century's gradual evolution of taste. Guests find here salmon walls, white with flax trim, mossy lime green, crushed raspberry, peacock blue.

Leather wing-backed chairs flank a hand-carved chess table in the drawing room. The oak floors have been stained with a red mahogany and the walls are a natural-grain yellow stucco. There's a working fireplace and an antique mahogany baby grand piano.

The parlor is done in white wicker with floral cushions, a wicker fainting sofa, half-sheer curtains, with a three-sided wall seat.

The formal dining room has French doors and a crystal chandelier. A hand-carved gold leaf mirror is set behind the buffet. Breakfast is served on Rosenthal and Lenox china by candlelight to guests seated on gold-leaf slipper chairs.

Beds have camelback headboards, waterfall headboards; a mahogany four-poster with canopied top and high parquet headboard. There are solid mahogany chests, French doors to bathrooms, and bathrooms with brass shower rings and porcelain shower heads.

Guests are likely to spend a lot of time in this house despite the attractions of the neighborhood. A great asset for a reviving Daytona Beach.

The Coquina Inn, 544 S. Palmetto Ave., Daytona Beach, FL 32114. (904) 254-4969. Susan and Jerry Jerzykowski, innkeepers. 4 rooms and baths (2 with clawfoot tubs and showers, all with tubs), AC, heat, ceiling fan. Floater TV (color) for guest use. Cordless phone for free local calls (no LD surcharge on credit-card calls), refrigerator for chilling beer, wine. Children accepted 12 and up. 3rd person in room $10. No pets. MC, Visa. Rates: Apr.-Nov.: $70-$100 (double); Dec.-March $80-$115. Special weekends, $95-$125. Rate includes full gourmet breakfast, beach cruisers, shuttle service to Halifax Harbor Marina, tea and cordial hour. No smoking inside. On-site parking.

Daytona Beach – THE ST. REGIS HOTEL
Restaurant's the thing; the rooms are good, too.

Rejoice! The St. Regis looks good for a second century. In a town trying to regain its bearings, this little hotel with the big history is heading straight ahead. Good news for vacationers and business travelers in Daytona Beach for a day or a week—or longer. Even for a meal.

This little hotel on fashionable Seabreeze Boulevard has attracted one of Daytona's top-ranked chefs and become one of the city's "in" restaurants.

It's the exception rather than the rule for Florida's intimate lodgings to rate for cuisine, chiefly because so few serve meals at all (though happily this is changing).

The St. Regis today rates equally for its management. It wasn't saved in the nick of time. But good luck has blessed the little hotel, and it now begins its third stage in a history that smiles like a protective big sister on it.

It was an inn right from the start. That was in the late 1880s when Regis de Montpelier arrived to seek his fortune along with other would-be millionaires drawn from the harsh northern climate to the still swampy peninsula by Henry Flagler's railroad.

De Montpelier was born into a boarding house family in the south of France. Hard times led them to settle in a Quebec village before the young de Montpelier came south.

Much to the skepticism of early settlers, he built his small inn in 1886 and quickly won a following by the haute cuisine he introduced. He called his place Regis de Montpelier Inn and Dining Room, but locals, who felt honored by his high style, affectionately referred to him as Saint Regis, a nickname which attached to his establishment.

A second principal phase of the inn's life began shortly after the Second World War when two sisters took over. For many years the inn had been a home for the elderly.

Dotty Cook and Frances Root bought the property for their parents who had been advised for health reasons to relocate in Florida. The family was wealthy from oil and retailing. After the house had been set up for them, they refused to remain unless their daughters stayed on.

The sisters looked after their parents until Mr. Root died in 1962 and his widow seven years later. A few guests were taken in before then. For a while, it ran like any other Daytona hotel. Everyone was elderly.

"Then a funny thing happened," Dotty says, laughing, "and everything changed. We had a fire. We had Oriental rugs all over the place. Sister was trying to pull the rug off the stairs. I damn near died laughing watching her try to drag that off the floor. The firemen pulled her out. But the place was so well built it didn't burn. We sold everything that was water-damaged. We just took some more stuff out of storage.

"We had a 13-star flag with a bullet hole in it. Frances mistakenly sold it for $25. Can you imagine? Two weeks later there was a story in the paper about John Wayne paying $1 million for it. Another one we had—it had more than 13, I can't remember—I accidentally put that in the washing machine. Ruined it, of course."

People heard about the sisters rebuilding the place and started coming—a younger crowd in their 30s, 40s, 50s. People told their friends. Storekeepers along Seabreeze—probably the most fashionable street on the beach—talked up the place.

With its wrought-iron look like an ice cream shop, with its grassy yard and white-trimmed green awnings, umbrella-topped tables, lyre-back iron chairs and davenport, it had a yesteryear look that fit with the two sisters.

When they lately retired, a small group of well established locals with good minds for trends acquired it. They saw the way that old was becoming new. Their timing was perfect.

Banker Anne Carlucci, who first took charge for the new owners, made the right moves. Daytona's famous Chez Bruchez had just closed. She talked their chef, Jimmy Means, into joining the new St. Regis staff. Then she enticed the best waiter from the best restaurant in Ormond, Jeffrey Swendsen, with a following to beat the band. Between Jimmy and Jeffrey they've built a reputation for French cuisine that's light in style, with plenty of Florida seafoods and fresh fruit. Breakfast, included in room rates, is croissants and fruit salad—and delightful leftovers from the last night's dinners.

Anne and crew pulled up carpeting, tore off wallpaper, repaired, and scrubbed. They took off all the window overhangs to let in light. The rooms were furnished with upholstered chairs, various sized beds, private baths and phones.

After Anne left, banker Jerry Glass took over, and more changes were made. In 1990 this included putting up new, livelier wallcoverings and adding antiques to the rooms. The restaurant has been expanded to 150 seats, spreading onto a patio. The look is early Florida with ceiling fans and open to the air in cool weather. The canopy is being re-established to the sidewalk. The front porch is being extended to accommodate a lounge with liquor service in addition to beer and wine.

Exuberant style is returning to the St. Regis. It's helped by an arrangement with Bethune-Cookman College which is providing the hotel with eager, competent young staff.

Over the parlor dining room the sign still reads *Parva sed apta*—Small but adequate. Regard that more than ever as understatement.

St. Regis Hotel, 509 Seabreeze Blvd., Daytona Beach, FL 32018. (904) 252-8743. Jerry Glass, proprietor. 9 rooms with AC, heat, bathrooms with tubs, cable TV, room phones, restaurant, full liquor service. Children not accepted. No pets. AmEx, MC, Visa. Call for new rates and policies about smoking, parking. Lunch: $6 up; dinner: $20 up.

Edgewater — COLONIAL HOUSE
Bed-and-breakfast European style; excellent value.

European machinations went on a couple hundred years ago near where Edgewater is today. Harold and Eva Brandner's arrival from Austria rates nary a blip on the historical record. Which, considering that most people choose a bed-and-breakfast because they expect comfort and hospitality rather than colonial intrigue, is just as well. Colonial House satisfies the way it ought to.

Yet the region's history can still be traced through the vicinity of the Brandners' B&B, and adds to the rewards of vacationing here.

The neighboring town of New Smyrna is rich in history. Its name is from Smyrna, Turkey. The region's first European colonizer, a wealthy Scottish physician, had married the daughter of a wealthy Smyrna merchant. Dr. Andrew Turnbull had the idea that people from Mediterranean climes could feel at home in Florida. When the British gained control of Florida in 1763, George III was eager to build up the colony. He issued royal grants to Turnbull and his co-colonizers, who brought Greeks, Corsicans, and Minorcans to the area. But Turnbull's colony collapsed in 1777 and five years later the Spanish regained Florida.

The coquina ruins of a palace begun in New Smyrna but never finished by Turnbull can be found along North Riverside Drive at Julia Street. If you go west along Canal Street to the old Mission Road, you'll come across the sugar mill ruins, where a plantation from the 1830s was destroyed during the Seminole War of 1835. Canal Street follows the paved route of the canal Turnbull dug to drain the lands that supported the plantation. Also in town is the old Fort Mound, an ancient shell midden and a coquina-block foundation for a late-18th century structure. Nearby on Riverside Drive, the Old Stone Wharf dates from the time of early river activities. The outlines of two of Turnbull's irrigation canals can still be seen running parallel to Canal Street and at the boundary between New Smyrna Beach and Edgewater.

Edgewater is where the Brandners settled in the mid-1980s. They came from Vienna, where they'd met at a dance during carnival season and married in 1972. Tired of the long winters of home, they traveled the United States by camper. They had liked bed-and-breakfast stays in Europe, and thought to make their place more European, with an emphasis on comfort and value more than on decorator sytle. Their fondness for B&Bs led them to their large colonial house in 1987. It was built in 1928, with a separate wing and a pool added 20 years before they bought. The addition includes a pair of guest quarters.

The spacious guest apartment has two bedrooms and a full kitchen (but for an oven). The space is funished simply in rattan. Living room and bedrooms are carpeted. Each bedroom has twin double beds with good reading lamps. Walls are veneer paneled. The kitchen has good enamelware pots, attractive chinaware, utensils, and a microwave. A central system cools and heats, and there are ceiling fans.

The little guest room is very European: all angled about like a ship's cabin. There's no excess. Twin single beds are set L-shaped to each other, each with its own good reading lamp. Furniture is scaled to fit this compact space comfortably. A dropleaf table with two chairs and a little refrigerator are opposite the bedchamber. There is a multi-speed ceiling fan, as well as central AC and heat.

European-style breakfast (for the guest room only) includes cheese, ham, cold cuts, and breads. If it's winter, odds are that Harold's mother, Uta, is vacationing here. To the breakfast she adds strudel of all kinds, and often there's some scrumptious Viennese dessert at night.

The apartment has its own entrance from the drive. Guests in the single room are more inclined to make use of the two-storied house with its large, comfortable living room. Harold and his brother operate a solar heating company, and in spare time restore antique cars. Eva speaks Italian and French as well as German and English. Little Harold is bilingual in German and English, and his younger sister is also likely to be by now. Europe in Edgewater is nowadays comfortably homey.

The Colonial House, 110 Yelkca Terr., Edgewater, FL 32132. (904) 427-4570. Eva Brandner, owner. 1 room, 1 suite, each with private bath, AC, heat, ceiling fan, color TV, kitchen in suite, direct dial phone. Pool and jacuzzi. Children accepted age 5 and over, included in rate. No pets. No credit cards; checks accepted. Rates: $45 single, $55 double for room (also $39 and $45 nightly for 2-night stay). Suite by the week: $250. Room rate includes full breakfast (no breakfast with suite). Free off-street parking. Smoking permitted. Daily newspaper available.

Fernandina Beach – BAILEY HOUSE
Exemplary Victorian in the historic district.

Just as Jack Daniels labels don't promise highs, Victorian guest house brochures don't promise swoons. But Victorian interiors are willfully seductive, and while liquor may be quicker, a place like Bailey House in Fernandina Beach starts with nibbles at the ear.

The Victorians, whom we label prudes, lived surrounded by barely contained sensuality. In their profusion of flocked wallpapers, plumped cushions, stained-glass windows, carvings within carvings, tassles, drapings and folds, they lived at the edge of ecstasy.

How un-self-conscious, this guest house in the historic district, one among a half hundred voluptuous structures casually consorting like concubines in a harem. Not that anything censorious is revealed. Everything is in order. Nothing quite touches anything. Everything is separated by its own border, frame, fringe. The barriers are never let down.

You might as well enter a tunnel of love, for all the provocations. It is the highest art of concealment that Victorian guest houses are allowably zoned in decorous neighborhoods. You would think someone hovers in the shadows of gaslight, penciling names of those who enter.

To the contrary, Fernandina celebrates the Bailey House—Effingham W. Bailey who built it, the McCranies who restored it, and the Hays who filled it, first with their collection of Victoriana, and since, more and more, with guests.

Nature and history are the attractions: broad white beaches, excellent surf fishing, the nearby National Seashore Park at Cumberland Island, and the protected natural deep-water harbor. Fernandina was the birthplace of the modern shrimping industry, terminus of the first trans-Florida railroad, and site of pre-Civil War Fort Clinch, now a state park, where the first weekend of every month rangers re-enact the 1864 occupation by the Confederacy in dress, actions, and speech.

Names of streets, families, and places echo the history that makes Fernandina the only place in America to have lived under eight flags: those of France, Spain, England, Patriots, Green Cross of Florida, Mexico, the Confederacy, and the United States.

In the city's halcyon era, it was a major shipping port for lumber, phosphate, and naval stores, and the prosperity of those years late in the 19th century brought the town wealth now preserved in a 30-block nationally registered historic district, which the Bailey House superbly typifies.

Fernandina's historic district never got run down as many others did. There was enough economic activity to maintain the town's small population even after its maritime commerce was shunted to Jacksonville and St. Augustine, and even after resorts south to Miami captured the tourist trade. Boom time ended early in the century so that newcomers didn't continue to come who might have bid up and bought the stylish houses. Families held onto their properties and maintained them.

Built in 1895, Bailey House never went unoccupied but also never took transients before Tom and Diana Hay bought the place in 1982. It was ideal for their antiques. If it was larger than what they personally needed for living, it was not too small for taking in guests. Today the house's Victorian effulgence outshines other Florida lodgings. We easily succumb to its lures.

Victorian patterning is wrapped in innuendo. It consists of miniatures within grand designs. Each is discrete, but precisely which "each" is in the eye of the beholder.

In the lobby a three-sided alcove nestles a triptych in glass. The flanking walls of dainty patterned papers stream in tribute to the reigning arrangement between them. Matched in the setting, lace-curtained windows surround a brawny six-foot-wide picture window, squared by generous frames of dark wood, topped by an equally wide stained glass panel of yellow and red, pink and green.

The beauty is tempered by utility. In front of the alcove is a table of neatly assembled brochures for other inns recommended by the Hays.

Distracting as the information is, the sensuality of the space carries us away again. There is a marble-topped table, painted gas globe overhead, gracefully turned legs, flanking chairs carved and upholstered on rollers. Is the background the setting for foreground, or is it the other way round?

Our contemplation is exhausted, we accept the bay corner and marvel at the Victorian capacity for exquisite containment of restless physicality.

In a corner stands a floor lamp, expressing the Victorian obsession with Araby. It is ramrod thin and extended, its slender brass shaft interrupted by a girdled carving, its shade flared down and out like a tent, the fabric of a flesh-colored undergarment, seductively fringed in black.

Temptation is everywhere.

Four wide steps of heart pine lead to a three-paneled, five-foot-high stained glass window. Stairs veer along the frou-frou wallpapering, the newel posts and balustrade with tiny applied moldings. Another window: stage-framed with lintel, cornices, half-turned, quarter-turned undulant modings, embracing 40 squares of stained glass, light streaming through, flooding the stairs in color.

The stairs ascend right again, your hands on well-rubbed banisters, posts carved with curls of falling turns. A gallery of Victoriana looms at the landing above, while below the panorama takes in trunks and love seats, set off by arches, mirrors, plants, flowers, doilies, carvings, turnings, and rugs a-riot in their own profusions, tensely held in their fringed containers.

"Steady, steady now; get a grip on yourself," you hear an imagined matron say, reviving a delicate young woman gone all aswoon over some pre-Freudian vision.

If you keep your balance all the way up, the second floor offers four dazzling bedrooms, each with private bath, at rates from $65 to $95 double, including expanded continental breakfast.

Bailey House, 28 South 7th St., Fernandina Beach, FL 32034. (904) 261-5390. Diane and Thomas Hay, proprietors. Four rooms with AC, heat, ceiling fan, TV, bathrooms, 3 with tubs, house phone for messages, free local, credit-card and collect toll calls. Bicycles available. Children accepted 10 and above. $10 extra each for 3rd or 4th person in room. No smoking inside the house. No pets. AmEx. Year-round rates: $65-$95 per night double, includes expanded continental breakfast. Check-in customarily not before 4 P.M.; check-out customarily by 10 A.M.

Fernandina Beach — BALOGH & BRIDE
Elderly owners, a lifetime of tales.

In a world awash in unconscionable fraud and corruption, John and Leila Balogh's little scam twinkles with charm.

They weren't sure about permission for their bed-and-breakfast, but they put B&B on their business card anyway. "And we could tell anybody we needed to that it stood for Balogh & Bride, because those were our names," explains Leila Balogh, who used to be Bride.

Neither of them is of an age where they need permission for anything. They are as much one-of-a-kind as the old houses they've lived in.

Their houses face across the street from each other on a shady street in historic Fernandina, a two-minute walk from Center Street shops. John lived in the one the bed-and-breakfast is in, Leila in the one they're living in together now, which they're also happy to show to guests.

John lived many years in the house with his wife. He'd been hotel chef at the old Penn-McKee in McKeesport, Pennsylvania, where he's from, and later at the Mount Vernon Inn at the Washington homesite in Virginia. His wife was supervisor of elections for Nassau County, where Fernandina is. After she became sick, Leila would send soups over to keep up John's spirits. When John's wife died, Leila was the first one over. She and her husband, Ray, took him under their wing.

Then Ray became ill. John would come and stay all night with him. After Ray died, a year later, Leila married John.

"I always admired him," says Leila of John. "He always had a smile. He walked with his shoulders so straight. We couldn't do without each other."

After they married and chose Leila's house to live in, a friend suggested they open a B&B in John's house, a subdued blue clapboard from early in the century, with red and white trim. Twin chimneys top the peaked roof. A bay and a wraparound porch help the house fit modestly into the preserved character of Fernandina. Its exceptional interior feature is the trifurcated staircase that goes forward, back, and up right behind the foyer. The house is homelike, comfortable, upholstered, and full of antiques. The dining room is mostly oak, with a sideboard, a buffet, and oak chairs around a circular little table. A baby chair converts into a stroller.

The living room has a piano where Leila will play if you ask. Enjoy an old spindle-backed juror's chair from the courthouse, an old radio, and a wind-up cylinder clock. A bedroom has a lady's bonnet chest with a drawer for gloves.

The four bedrooms range from small and very plain (with veneer paneling and a false parquet floor) to spacious. All beds are firm. There is one bathroom upstairs and a half-bath down. By now a shower should be ready outside on the patio for use in summer. The outdoor shower is part of improvements that include a little English-style structure for changing. A fountain and landscaping have been added, with crepe myrtle and allamanda.

Leila prepares the breakfast. She favors eggs scrambled and rolled with ham and onions, accompanied by juice, fruits, coffee, danish or toast.

Breakfast is a good time, if you'd like, for Leila and John to tell you about their neighborhood and town. You would have wondered about the big oak tree in the middle of Ash Street just to the south.

Seems that Mr. Bailey used to live in the house. He was the engineer who opened up Highway A1A. Leila's husband, Ray, saw that the bondholders for the road needed a comptroller. That's what brought Leila and Ray to Fernandina from Palatka. When the road was going in, there was talk of routing it down Ash Street. When Mrs. Bailey heard they were going to take down the oak, she said she'd shoot the first worker who laid a hand on it. Mrs. Bailey sat there an interminable time, Leila will tell you. The oak's still there and the road goes around, even if it's just Ash Street and not A1A.

A pleasure of staying at John and Leila's B&B is getting to visit the house across the street. Every antique has a story. The old English music box came by way of Barbados. An ancestor of Leila's had invested in Barbados from London, but found the weather in Barbados too rough. He petitioned the King for land in the colonies and was given the whole of St. Helena's Island in Georgia. That's how Leila's family came to be there, and how years later, in her own time, she would "put on one of Momma's old dresses" and turn on that little music box. It plays 20 tunes.

It is a charming old world that Leila and John live in. At rates of $30 to $45 a night, including breakfast, it is all the more accessible.

Balogh & Bride Bed & Breakfast, 20 S. 6th St., Fernandina Beach, FL 32034. (904) 261-3345. Leila and John Balogh, proprietors. 4 rooms and 1-1/2 baths indoors (including shower/bath), shower outdoors, room AC/heat, color TV in 2 rooms, B&W in one, none in smallest room, additional in dining room. House phone for local calls only. No credit cards; personal checks accepted. No indoor smoking. Driveway or street parking, except weekends when off-street parking. Hot spa with refreshments in patio. $30 single, $35-$45 double, includes full breakfast. Refrigerator for guests' use.

Fernandina Beach — THE PHOENIX'S NEST

Whimsical, comfortable, carefree by the beach.

Harriett Johnston Fortenberry has almost as many names as she has guest rooms. Or more precisely, guest apartments. She has four. She says her place is "in the bed-and-breakfast tradition." That's because she provides personal hospitality, but with a higher degree of privacy than most B&Bs assure. Harriett subtly leads you to rethink all your connections. It's her calling.

First you must understand the care with which she does things.

Harriett hasn't merely given you a selection of perfect places where you can regroup for a couple of days (one day is certainly too few). She offers her hospitality with such grace that regrouping seems worthwhile no matter how down your spirits. There definitely is a feeling of retreat at The Phoenix's Nest, something mildly therapeutic.

You see it in the quality of her literature. Though Harriett was not trained as an artist, she has produced a collection of graphics with the quality of souvenirs. Their artistry is Persian, Zen, and Native American. The pieces are the color of river stones in a shallow clear stream: brochure, letterhead, note paper. Several slips of various sizes tell about what's in your room, about blackbird songs you'll hear, and about horses, chocolates, and boats you may encounter during your visit. There are tapes from Betty Boop to Pavarotti, books by and about Bernard Baruch, H.L. Mencken, Robert Benchley, B.B. King, and Andy Warhol, videos of "Casablanca," Cousteau, gospel singing, healing, among a few hundred.

The house sits just enough by itself on the shore road to establish its independence. Across the road is undeveloped land, and beyond lie the beach and the ocean. In winter it's blowy and the house is cozy. In summer it's simply fun. You can see across that fringe of landscape to the sea from upstairs.

The house is a modified Cape Cod with traces of colonial, with wood boards, shuttered windows and a picket fence. Outside staircases lead to the upstairs apartments. The downstairs entry is through a little yard that has a hammock and slat-bench swing. The house, built in 1938, backs up to 200 acres of virgin hammock where bear used to roam.

Colors in one upstairs bedroom are charcoal gray and peach, mellow favorites of Harriett. The bed has a custom headboard made of scraps a Cajun man had accumulated for years. Pedestals are beside the bed. Harriett chose inlaid woods because she felt her house was too airy for wicker. The back room she calls the Heigh-de-ho. It has two studio beds full of pillows, a VCR, bookshelves, and grasscloth paper. There's a hand-carved wood screen that hides the space for

71

hanging clothes on the door. (Harriett had to sacrifice two closets for the bathroom upstairs.) There's a microwave, toaster, and coffeemaker. It's a respite from the beach, and cool even in summer (though there's always air-conditioning). French doors lead from bedroom to balcony and stairs.

Downstairs is more designed, with a trunkful of hints of faraway places: Roman busts on pedestals, zoomy Art Deco curves and colors in the full kitchen, a carved glovebox from yesteryear, Art Nouveau-styled wallpaper, and an alcove with Japanese lacquer screen. There are high-back wing chairs, and an iron bed under a deeply quilted bedcover in all colors of the seaside. Muted sea greens and an oaty carpet keep the feeling of the beachfront. Another downstairs space is full of doors into warmly distinctive spaces. The cottage out back is rustic-walled but detailed in sophisicated crafts.

Harriett breeds horses nearby, where you can ride. She lives in an apartment attached to those she rents. Proximity makes it easy for her to deliver fresh breads and juices in the morning, and otherwise to be available to guests for some time during the day or evening. A housekeeper also comes.

The Phoenix's Nest is a nest because you can fly out when you want to, come back as you need to. It is the kind of place you will want nearby wherever you live.

The Phoenix's Nest, 619 S. Fletcher Ave., Fernandina Beach, FL 32034. (904) 277-2129. Harriett Johnston Fortenberry, owner. 4 suites with private bath with AC, heat, ceiling fan, color TV, partial or full kitchen. Portable phone available as needed. Well-behaved children accepted 12 and up; pets sometimes (inquire). $5 per extra person. MC, Visa, checks accepted. VCR, outstanding videotape collection, library, boogie boards, bicycles, barbecue grill. Rates: winter: $55-$75, rest of year: $65-$85 double, $5 off for single. Includes continental breakfast and fruits. Smoking reluctantly accepted. Off-street parking.

Fernandina Beach – SEASIDE INN
Food, drink, nightlife – perchance sleep.

Travel the entire Florida coast and you will find only one inn directly on the beach with bed and board and open all year. Other interesting beachfront places offer only breakfast or mix long-term apartment guests with transients, but if by inns we mean intimate lodging and open-hearted hospitality, Florida's one and only is the Seaside Inn, since the 1940s on Amelia Island, at the top of the state.

The Seaside Inn brackets the post-War era of hoity-toity resorts as if it had dozed through a dull movie and awakened refreshed. It is a throwback to an era when people traveled a coastal road in need of overnight places to stay, and other people of friendly persuasion made hospitality their business. Such places are in vogue again, not for lack of alternatives, but because so many of the others are either frill-filled and expensive or lacking in style.

Today's times are unsettled. People are easily bored. Many demand unique experiences. Places like the Seaside Inn tingle the desire for wanderlust, nostalgia, romance, mixed styles—today's mood of restless uncertainty that seems satisfied less by credentials than caring. A place for one or two nights is okay, it's good. But it has to be "real."

The Seaside Inn nuzzles the dune in homey affection. Long and brick, full of windows with a third-story attic under its eave, the place draws attention away from its modest height by rows of sloping awnings. Their combined swoop suggests a huge, clumsy creature, its flaps extended, shyly settling into the sand, as if it might avoid notice among flocks of pelicans, pipers, pigeons, or gulls by folks just going about their business.

By day, the inn is for sitting on strapped PVC lawn furniture under a Cinzano umbrella with a beer and a paper plate of shrimp, or for pulling the roadside shower string and rinsing off salt and sand before repacking the car to head home.

The other three corners where State Road 108 ends at the beach don't amount to much. There's Halls, a bait and food store with beer signs in the window, fat-tire rental bikes, and a couple gas pumps; an ordinary motel on a weedy lot full of sandspurs; and a vacant parcel of sand they were asking a million dollars for but don't anymore because the coastal setback requirements mean that not much is going to get built here.

Nights the place is packed for dinners that feature local seafoods and "Wing it," all the chicken wings you can eat for $3.95, now an island tradition served with music. On weekends, a four-piece band plays classic rock-and-roll.

The inn is owned by Mitch Montgomery, a custom-home builder who held the property as collateral for a couple of Egyptian investors who had bought it from Valerie and David Pickett for redevelopment. The Picketts had bought the Seaside in 1980 and spent almost a year restoring it. They bought 10 rooms of furniture from the Fort George County Club when it was being renovated. They put in double beds, ceiling fans, quilts and comforters, stenciled the walls, and brought a homey look to 10 of the 20 rooms. Those are the 10 overlooking the ocean—the other 10 have never been put back into use. As general manager Bill Conrad says, "Nobody ever saw any use for streetside rooms in an oceanfront hotel.

"We just don't focus on the rooms in any case," he continued. "Our guests are principally younger folks because we have a lounge with live entertainment. We tell hotel guests that weekends the band plays till 1:30 in the morning and you can hear the bass and drum rhythms in the rooms. If that's a problem, we send them to the 1735 House or nearby motels. But I make sure to tell them to have some of this fresh seafood."

The rooms are a bit narrow. Someone else might have made two into one or three into two, upping the rate to $150 a night for velour robes and deluxe toiletries. That might have out-priced the Fernandina market where, but for the enclave Amelia Island Plantation and the Ritz-Carlton a mile and a half south, everything else is hoi polloi casual.

As is, the ambience is young and sincere. Air-conditioning helps muffle the weekend music. The rooms are like student compositions, clean, bright, in their way pre-pubescent. Downstairs the look and sound are Southern roadhouse. The mood, fun-loving adult.

Seaside Inn, 1998 Fletcher, Amelia Island, Fernandina Beach, FL 32034. (904) 261-0954. Bill Conrad, general manager. 10 rooms, including one suite, with AC, heat, ceiling fan, bathrooms. Downstairs pay phone. Sliders Oyster Bar Restaurant and bar. Children of any age accepted (no cribs available). Pay phone. No TVs in rooms. No pets. AmEx, MC, Visa. Year-round rates single or double, $65; $75 for suite. Continental breakfast with local newspaper, fresh fruit on arrival, bedtime mints included in rates. Restaurant meals: lunch (summer only): $3.50-$7.95; dinner: $5.95-$13.95. Off-street parking.

Fernandina Beach – 1735 HOUSE
Five suites on the beach in a shiplike old house.

On bright early mornings, the sun through a porthole concentrates an orange disc that slowly moves across a wall and sets in motion the mood of a coastal steamer. The captain's quarters are outfitted with barometers and thermometers, charts, and hurricane lamps.

An oil painting is askew on the wall as if a storm had rocked the night without interrupting sleep in beds firm as chopping blocks. No groan comes from the plank floors. A steamer trunk and red-painted tea chest hold steady. Outside the sea is disturbed only by porpoises teaching a breakfast lesson to a school of fish, signaling surveillant pelicans into dive attacks. For a few minutes the sea erupts in a furious patch like a faraway crowd of New Yorkers frenzied by a rave restaurant review.

At the shore the surf lazily churns gray sand, ending an ocean voyage upon the beach without ceremony.

Time for guests to breakfast. Handmade Italian picnic baskets with stout covers meant to withstand 30-knot winds are brought across open deck. Juice, fresh fruits, home-baked pastries, butter, preserves, coffee and cream—the pleasures of morning. Contentment fans out like the rising sun over Amelia Island.

The shiplike 1735 House sets a carefully put together standard for lodgings along Florida beaches. Much larger establishments with similar settings dull the caring edge here honed by exacting operators on only five suites. Old maritime photos could as easily be ordered by the thousands as selected by the fours and fives. Wicker sofas covered in Indonesian prints could be bought wholesale instead of found one by one. The nice touch becomes the glad hand when hundreds of guests are stacked in concrete and steel towers, but here only a weathered, shingled two-story clapboard house blends with the dune scrub and sand crabs.

A medical doctor named Baker built the house for leisure in the Twenties. Now it's owned by Gary and Emily Grable. Gary for 20 years had been controller for two major corporations.

"I had a strong desire to do something on a much more personal level," he says. "I'd traveled, staying all over in chain hotels. Pretty sterile. The last four years Emily and I lived on Amelia Island while I worked for ITT Rayonier in town and she was in real estate. We got to know the Caples and realized, when they were thinking of putting their business for sale, that this is what we wanted to go into."

David and Susan Caples had been chain-hotel managers when their wish for change led them to the Baker house. They liked historic Fernandina Beach and named their new place for the discovery of Amelia Island in 1735 by General James Oglethorpe. He had named the island for the daughter of his King, George II.

The nautical theme fits the location and the local economy. Fernandina had been a prosperous 19th-century seaport. Twentieth-century deep-water shrimp trawling began here before spreading worldwide. The fleet remains a mainstay of commerce that focuses a springtime heritage festival attracting tens of thousands. An expanding municipal marina on the Intracoastal Waterway draws boaters all year.

Each suite at the inn is different, drawing on the various eras in Amelia Island's history. Each has a private bedroom with bath, and on the oceanside, a living room furnished with wicker or rattan. In some is an alcove of sturdy built-in bunk beds, so that some suites can sleep six. Three suites have little kitchens.

Constant attention goes into maintaining the nautical look. Even the marine catalogs used for replenishing the inventory are stuffed in bathroom racks for perusal by visitors. Old shrimpers come by to tell about finds. Guests have put owners onto treasures, too.

There is a certain bustle at the 1735 House, which is also headquarters for Amelia Island Lodgings Systems, a referral agency for about 100 lodging units in everything from bargain to luxury accommodations. The extra staff ensures there are always people around who know about historic, dining and recreational pleasures of the area.

A down-home mood prevails. Although the inn serves only breakfast, a small public kitchen has all necessary utensils. Guests can boil a pot of their own freshly caught shrimp, bake cakes for birthdays, brew fresh coffee whenever they want, or make a whole meal—a nice touch appreciated by today's diet-conscious travelers.

Amelia Island is a place nobody's in a hurry to leave—or in a hurry, period.

1735 House, 584 S. Fletcher, Fernandina Beach, Amelia Island, FL 32034. (800) 872-8531, (904) 261-5878. Gary and Emily Grable, innkeepers. Five suites with color cable TV, AC, heat, ceiling fan, bath, phone for free local calls or third-party and credit-card LD calls. Children 6 and over accepted. AmEx, MC, Visa. Year-round rates: single, $55-$70; double, $75-$85; triple, $80-$90; quad, $85-$95. Includes continental breakfast and morning newspaper. Off-street parking. Smoking permitted.

Fernandina Beach — WILLIAMS HOUSE
Outstanding revival; fullest hospitality weekends.

Bud and Phyllis Lake are born-again innkeepers. They ask if guests would like to swing on the porch. Guests disappear for half an hour. Phyllis brings them iced tea. A couple shows up, checks in. "Mind if we get married here tonight?" they ask. "The notary said he would marry us anyplace in town we wanted." So Phyllis brings out a bottle of champagne, runs out for a cake, finds an orchid corsage that had been left in the refrigerator. Then she sends the couple to Allen's for dinner because she knows they'll make a fuss over them.

Bud and Phyllis run on intuitive energy. Their house looks like it was invented for innkeeping. Likely by Bud.

He'd never done anything like restoring a house before. In fact, neither Bud nor Phyllis had ever stayed overnight in a B&B until they bought the Williams House and decided to make it one. They got the idea after Bud retired from United Parcel Service. The idea of getting a bigger house than they could afford and taking guests just made sense.

Bud had all the technical skills—he just hadn't ever put them together before on a restoration. He learned about the house and how to restore it on-the-job, seeking advice from experts.

Although Bud had to completely rewire and replumb it, the house was in basically good condition. It proved a scrap yard for necessary replacements. There was a piece missing from the gothic cross-beaming that turned up in a bin in the yard. Same with a missing molding from the kitchen. Bud says he asks the guys at the plumbing wholesaler to let him go in back and find what he needs when it's not in stock. Invariably he finds the right part lying around because nobody calls for it anymore.

A grandly spindled and scroll-molded bifurcated stairway leads to the four guest rooms. Rooms are spacious, with completely restored features that put visitors in touch with the early times of the house.

Most windows have their original wavy glass. Cast-iron hinges appear throughout (except on a screened back door that still has even older spring-in-cylinder ones). There are elaborate Victorian fireplace mantels, brass beds, clothes racks, lace curtains, tulip lamps, heart-of-pine floors, and floor windows. Rooms are in pinks and yellows and peach tones, soft colors that curtsy to the bold Victorian wallpapers in the halls. One room does have a passion for Peter Max fantasy prints, but the look is much more of spindle mantels and bay windows, and altogether more country than elegant.

The house is set back behind a low black wrought-iron fence that Bud says is older than the house. There is in fact a graveyard look about it, a look that speaks to stern morality.

Profligately gabled, the house has a French mansard lower roof with fully enclosed pediment between gabled ends. A deep, all-around open porch extends in front of floor-to-ceiling windows. The roof is an elaborate undergirding of turned X-beams. Columns are turned from single solid logs with one-inch holes bored vertically to allow each column to expand and contract from the humidity. As one-time neighbor and woodworker J.P. McClennan said, "They spared no expense building this place."

On weekends Phyllis serves a full breakfast, something different each morning. During the week she's busy with a gift shop nearby. Weekends, guests gather in the kitchen. Maybe Bud's making popovers. He learned by doing and now knows to turn the fan off before taking them out of the oven. "Then run 'em out fast to the table." There the floors are walnut and oak alternating between heart pine. The three tables are set in front of Phyllis's lace curtains. Breakfast aromas waft out to the front porch under the magnolias and moss-hung oaks.

A touch from early Williams years is related by a granddaughter. She says that one of the Williams daughters, Miss Fanny, didn't like window screens, and slept under a mosquito net. But mosquitoes got so bad one summer that the family had to sit at dinner with legs wrapped in newspapers. Miss Fanny was ordered to like screens. Guests these days don't have to be ordered to enjoy themselves.

Note: the house was for sale early in 1991.

Williams House, 103 S. 9th St., Fernandina Beach, FL 32034. (904) 277-2328. Harold "Bud" and Phyllis Lake, hosts. 4 rooms with room AC and central heat, Hunter fans, 4 baths. TV in parlor. No children. No pets. Messages taken and house phone for credit-card and collect LD calls. No indoor smoking. AmEx, Discover, MC, Visa. Year-round single or double rates $50, includes full breakfast, round-the-clock tea and coffee, homemade goodies. $4 for second bed in room, $8 for extra person in room. Inquire if Jacksonville airport and Fernandina marina pickup and return still available.

Flagler Beach — TOPAZ HOTEL
Quirky hotel and excellent restaurant sandwiched between motel wings.

Flagler Beach has maybe more idiosyncracies than tourists—a good sign. For instance, the Flagler Beach fact sheet states that it's "The closest city to an exit on I-95 in the United States. 3.9 miles to Flagler Beach." Does I-95 going through West Palm Beach, Fort Lauderdale, and Miami not count?

It's a good sign, too, for those who think Florida doesn't really need to attract more people. The Flagler Beach Tourist Bureau may put out less information than any other in the state. Flagler Beach is so small that the tourist bureau generously lists all the businesses in town whether they're members or not. The list might be pea-sized otherwise.

And it's a nice oddity that the town named for Henry Flagler is one of the few along the east coast that his trains never came near. You, too, might find yourself missing it or driving right through, but that would be a mistake because you'd miss the Topaz Hotel. Or motel. Or whatever it is.

What we do know is that the mansion that became the Topaz was built by the 13th registered architect in Florida, Dana Fuqua, who lived from 1882 to 1970, mostly in Flagler Beach. Built between 1923 and 1926, the mansion was big enough that during World War II it became a Coast Guard Station housing 150 men. You might think it strange that there are only eight guest rooms today, but Coast Guardsmen slept in dormitories—today you get more privacy.

The house is a mix of prairie and Mediterranean styles in a finish of wood and coquina under stucco. Its appearance is odd enough that it may discourage some from stopping. Too bad, because inside is an utterly diverting lobby and one of the most satisfying moderately-priced restaurants you'll find along the coast. And though the rooms are mostly motel-like—and there are 20 sure-thing motel rooms to the north and 20 more to the south that are part of the property—at least two of the eight rooms upstairs are furnished in antiques.

You might have a good time playing here. Playing, because owners Bonnie and Paul Lee obviously have a playful streak. Their lobby is a hoot.

Look around. There's a silk floral tablecloth tatted and fringed, and early Edison and Victrola phonographs. In a staircase display is a model railroad with Lionel trains. An old L&N depot sign recalls when white and colored were directed to separate restrooms. There are wax recordings by Gene Autry and Lani McIntyre. There's an old Atlantic Coast Line menu offering 15-cent burgers, and 25-cent ham and eggs. There are antique Laurel and Hardy and Mickey Mouse toys, a player piano, and an Atwater Kent shortwave radio. A "Smokerette" brand tabletop radio has niches for pipes and humidors. Look through old photo albums, issues of "Country Gentleman" from the 1930s, and enjoy Deco-styled mauve drapes, a silk-upholstered loveseat, gilded mirrors, and case clocks.

The lobby cries out for costumes, and the costumes are supplied if you stay in one of two upstairs rooms. One room comes with a wardrobe supplied with an old tuxedo coat, high-laced shoes, and blue velvet jacket. The other has an old white cotton nightgown, old gloves, fans, corsages, and antique dresses.

Bonnie says she bought the Topaz because she had to be near the water. "I was born in a hospital room on the ocean in Portsmouth, Virginia," she says, "and all the time Paul and I lived in Nashville I had to keep telling myself I could smell salt in the air."

The building was structurally sound but had a nasty reputation. Police were after people here all the time, says Bonnie. So you know she and Paul have made a big turnaround when the only thing likely to draw police today is a cup of fresh coffee in the cafe.

The Topaz Cafe is run independently of the hotel/motel, though it's in the same building, just to the side of the lobby. It's wonderful. Food is made from scratch, breads baked, desserts made, and vegetables bought fresh. The room is pink and black in a Deco flamingo theme. Atop the bar are old Poohs, suitcases, a Royal typewriter, and old Mixmasters. There are excellent black and white photos of the area, including one or two of Frieda Zamba, the town's pride, a four-time world champion surfer (maybe five-time by now).

Catherine and Lisa Hampton, sisters from Illinois, run the restaurant, and it's worth making sure you come when it's open. It's closed Sunday and Monday and at lunchtime except on Friday. They'll feed you fresh crab and crabcakes, sauteed port tenderloin, country fried steak with mashed potatoes, and Italian-style chicken. It's home-cooking, and dinners go for about $20 to $25. Not gourmet, but home cooking. The best.

So stop. The stop is worth it.

Topaz Hotel/Motel, 1224 S. Oceanshore Blvd. (Hwy. A1A), Flagler Beach, FL 32136. (904) 439-3301. Paul W. Lee, innkeeper. 8 hotel rooms with private baths, 6 with balconies overlooking the Atlantic, some furnished with antiques. AC, heat, ceiling fan, TV. Direct-dial phone. Adults only. No pets. AmEx, MC, Visa. Checks for deposit only. $5 for 3rd person in room. Swimming pool. Year-round rates: single or double $55-$75, except for special events, when it's $75-$85. Smoking allowed. Off-street parking free. Inquire about motel units.

Jacksonville — ARCHIBALD HOUSE
Flowing hospitality in a scrupulously revived mansion.

It would be a shame if you avoided the Archibald House because you might have heard that Springfield is a bad neighborhood. The Archibald House is a sumptuous restoration of a turn-of-the-century judge's mansion. And the neighborhood is transitional, becoming gentrified while remaining racially integrated, and a model in many respects for Jacksonville.

Bed-and-breakfast operators who move into a neighborhood undergoing rejuvenation are a lot like airline pilots—they can't afford mistakes when it's them out front bearing the brunt.

Since the National Trust for Historic Preservation declared Springfield a national demonstration project, its turnaround has advanced far enough that you can not only feel good about being here. You might also think about investing in property while real estate prices still lag behind what's actually happening on the street.

Carolyn and Josef Molenda didn't invest in Springfield because they were looking to lose their shirts. They're solidly middle-class people. Josef teaches speech and film at the Kent Campus of Florida Community College. Carolyn owns a child-care business on Beach Boulevard. They felt that a B&B would let them take on a more substantial home than they could otherwise afford. Guests will be happy they chose the Archibald House. When the house was built in 1903 the **Florida Times-Union** called it a "very handsome dwelling...that would add another handsome residence to the Boulevard." The house was completed only two years after Jacksonville's great fire at a time when Springfield, spared the holocaust which did not jump Hogan's Creek, was becoming the neighborhood of choice for the city gentry.

While the neighborhood later deteriorated as prosperous residents moved into suburbs along the river, Springfield still has a great treasury of early 20th century buildings. You find examples of prairie school architecture designed by Henry Klutho, a contemporary of Frank Lloyd Wright, along with examples of Queen Anne and shingle style, and bungalows. The 1984 architectural survey and report done when Springfield was up for nomination to the National Register of Historic Places, observes that the neighborhood contains one of the largest concentrations of historically significant 20th century architecture in Florida. The district was entered in the register in 1987. Today hardly a block in the district isn't under renewal, including almost everything along 2nd Street where the Archibald fronts. More than 100 buildings are being restored.

The Archibald House is at the front of downtown Jacksonville. The city is replacing all the balusters that historically lined Hogan's Creek, renewing a virtual border around the landscape which distinctively frames the brawny skyline.

The house is a deep red with white trim, three stories of balloon frame construction with colonial revival influences. House interiors are marked by luxurious features immediately apparent in the grand entry hall, where Carolyn and Josef restored the decorative brick fireplace. The gas sconces again operate by gas. The fringed Oriental rug picks up the pale blue of the exotic paisley wallpapers and the fireplace terra cotta, as well as the glazed red of the patterned glass globes of the gas lamps.

All downstairs floors are polished-to-gloss heart pine. There are pocket doors with pine and oak, and wainscoting is topped by florid Victorian papers. Carolyn and Josef beautifully restored the coffered ceilings and added delightful touches even in nooks: for instance, the wall-mounted toilet tank in the little downstairs bath retrieved from the old Ponce de Leon Hotel. They brought lyre-bracketed planter tables and big bold brass chandeliers.

The stairs intriguingly trifurcate at the second floor. Bedrooms are off second and third floor landings which offer grand views of downtown. The house columns are trapezoids in the form of the letter "A."

Bedrooms are full of heavy, masculine antiques, lightened by the look of wicker in the third floor common room. Some beds are Eastlake. Another is brass over steel which puts you in mind of a mallet on chimes. The Judge's Chambers room contains exuberantly floral motifs in bedding and curtains, tile floor, a triptych mirror, and antique iron bed textured in paint-like wood. Skylights have been carefully fitted into the third floor rooms. A wonderfully textured carpet in plum color flows throughout this floor.

A brick courtyard has lately been completed between the house and a cottage next door that once was the carriage house. The little house has a two-story entry foyer, a clawfoot shower-tub and an upstairs sleeping loft. The porch is screened. A pool will be added between the mansion and cottage.

The mansion is a splendid restoration in a neighborhood now well into its own revival. Guests ensconce here in one of Jacksonville's treasures.

The Archibald House, 125 W. 2nd St., Jacksonville, FL 32206. (904) 634-1389. Josef and Carolyn Molenda, innkeepers. 2 rooms, 2 suites with private baths, refrigerators in suites, color cable TV and in common area on 2nd floor, AC, heat, ceiling fan in 3. Cordless phone for private use as needed. Game room in parlor. Children accepted 10 years old and over. No pets. MC, Visa. Rates: single or double, year-round: $59 3rd floor, $65 2nd floor suite, $65 carriage house. 2-night stays or longer receive 10% discount each additional night. 3rd person 20% of regular rate. Rate includes full gourmet breakfast, fresh flowers and ice, wine, cheese, afternoon tea, homemade dessert in the evening. Daily newspaper available. In-room mints. Smoking on porches. Off-street parking. Public tennis courts across street.

Jacksonville – HOUSE ON CHERRY STREET

For your collection of fine home-style overnighting.

Collectibles act like pollen for attracting guests to flowering hospitality. Carol and Merrill Andersons' brand is country-in-the-city in a Jacksonville house that slopes to the lower St. Johns where the river flows wide as a possible America.

The house is post-colonial. The hospitality is warm as houseguesting. The Riverside district is historic. Guests find the House on Cherry Street rich in lives worked out.

The place the Andersons chose is a federal-style clapboard at the quiet end of a tree-lined street. Guests who know the house from the drawing on Carol's blue brochure will be surprised to find it white-trimmed warm tan. The front is sideways off the street. Circular entry stairs are lined by pots of colorful flowers.

Right away guests notice the Andersons' two fullest collections: decoy ducks and old clocks. Guests play a game of finding all the different ways ducks accessorize the house. Their game is played accompanied by ticks, tocks, chimes, and gongs.

Rooms go off in all directions, like free will, including up stairs. This is more house than inn. One warms in the foyer to hospitality bestowed in bouquets of fresh flowers atop a round mahogany table, a crystal canister of porcelain, ferns, lamps, and framed drawings.

A selective display of American colonial design accompanies guests' adustment to the possibilities for satisfying different moods during their stay. Some notable pieces all comfortably set with appropriate accessories downstairs are an English Queen Anne chest of about 1720 in walnut veneer, a pair of American Queen Anne chairs about 1760, two Duncan Phyffe mahogany sofas in crushed velvet about 1850, a Martha Washington-type clipper chair, an English 3-corner country chair, a 1770 English hanging corner cupboard, a Chester County slant-front desk about 1760.

The tall case and shelf clocks are all about. "We buy houses by whether the 8-foot clocks will fit," says Carol, who repairs them, although only for herself.

Breakfast is sometimes set in a little room with family portraits and the charmingly mounted driver's license issued in 1919 to Carol's mother with a newspaper tearsheet of her engagement photo.

One guest room, the Duck Room, so-called because of its imprinted wallpaper, is small but complete and richly textured. It has its own sitting room across the hall, dusty blue in plaids with oatmeal-colored cotton rugs on shiny pine floors.

You feel comfortable crossing this carpeted common hall that further leads only to the Andersons' quarters. You want to dress in your best pajamas and robe, ready for maybe meeting over a cognac in a world where the most significant decisions are made by a benevolent elite comfortable with each other in fine bedrobes.

Guest rooms variously feature ceiling fans, crown stencilings, fresh and silk flowers, roll-up bamboo blinds, small TVs, digital clock radios. And all have hand-loomed Pennsylvania coverlets, mostly wool, some linen. "These are probably the finest buy in collectible American textiles," says Carol. "Quilts have gone through the roof."

Carol provides a full breakfast that includes goodies such as home-baked English muffins for her eggs Benedict and a variety of decaffeinated teas—served in duck-printed mugs.

Carol and Merrill have good stories about second careers as tennis umpires. There isn't a top-10 competitor that one or the other hasn't worked with.

Take the time to be at home with these hosts. Most appealing among their collectibles will be their stories about lives richly lived.

House on Cherry Street, 1844 Cherry St., Jacksonville, FL 32205. (904) 384-1999. Carol and Merrill Anderson, hosts. 4 rooms and baths with A/C, heat, some with ceiling fan, TV. House phone for free local calls, and collect and credit card L.D. calls. No pets; inquire about children and smoking. MC, Visa. Year-round rates $60-$70 nightly, $10 for extra person in room, includes full breakfast.

Jacksonville – THE WILLOWS
Gracious hospitality in a riverside manor.

Mary Collins did not need to open a bed-and-breakfast for income. She needed something to do, people to meet, to entertain, in a beautiful home with not too many guests.

Her house, called The Willows, is on Willow Branch Terrace in the Riverside section of Jacksonville. The Willows is the second B&B in this historic district, and elevates an already high standard. Willow Branch Creek empties into the St. Johns River just across from its namesake road. At road's end, the yard reaches to the river. To the northeast are the skyscrapers and spans of Florida's great river city, and to the southwest, the Ortega Bridge and the splendid residential district by that name.

The setting is Venetian, inspired by stone balusters lining the waterway. The house is languidly Mediterranean, with textured stone walls that trap grains of soil and sprout ferns. Much of the outside is covered in vines. From a cast-iron seat in the yard one can see the three-story house, fortress solid, arched, and balconied. Stone urns decorate a walkway where on a still summer evening Hunter fans coax the breeze. There are glass-topped tables in wrought-iron patio sets for a drink or conversation. Wicker loveseats hang above a tiled porch behind stucco arches. Stone planters are red with geraniums. Magnolias, water oaks, and palms frame a lighted swimming pool with diving board.

The house was built during the Florida boom in 1925 by a lumber businessman. Marsh and Saxelby, the architects, are renowned for their design of Epping Forest, the Dupont estate in Jacksonville. Mary and her husband, Clyde, bought the house from children of the original owner.

Guests enter up stone stairs through a massive Palladian portico. Inside has a viceregal character with high ceilings, broad and high fireplace, and iron drapery rods. Moorish serpentine furniture adds to the mood as do high lamps and tile floors extending beyond the Oriental rugs that overlay carpet. Furniture is high-backed and imposing. There are ornate mirrors and frames, much brass, and a grandfather clock. The room is pecky cypress, with an 18th-century English bench from an old church and a hand-painted German piano. A French tapestry hangs. There are brass torchiers surrounding a huge fireplace that is used frequently during winter and always at Christmas.

The dining room furthers the Mediterranean theme with an original chandelier, iron axes and curtain rods, and tile floors. Breakfast is served here on Mary's grandmother's china, silver, and crystal.

Guest rooms are composed of treasures accumulated from estate sales and auctions. One room has twin beds that once stood in Flagler's Ponce de Leon hotel in St. Augustine. Crocheted lace coverlets are on the beds, Chinese rug on the floor. There are twin reading lamps and night tables, a cane rocker, and cane-backed armchairs. The bathroom is a garden of tile, green and marvelous as a grotto, with a complementing green shower curtain beneath the high ceiling.

An upstairs room has a porch and rose-vined porcelain chandelier. There is a shiny brass table fan. The entire bedroom suite of seven pieces is in ormolu. The rug is a French-weave floral; the bedspread, 100-year-old lace. The porch is enclosed with glass, but its windows open between serpentine columns. A low wrought-iron railing connects the columns.

In another room roses twine around lamps. A blue tile and blue bath pick up the blue that is only hinted at in the rug and in daybed pillows. The little porch is tile with two chintz-covered chairs, tables, and potted plants.

Guests receive fruit, liqueur, chocolates, ice, and fresh flowers when they arrive.

Mary also operates M&M tours in Jacksonville, planning tours to Europe and all over the United States. She takes up to 30 at a time. Most people who go with her just like to travel and plan trips. They talk about where they'd like to go and leave it to Mary to work out the details.

Her bed-and-breakfast is like that, as if we'd all asked her to adapt a mansion for our use when in her city. We feel like guests on a select list, entertained and entertaining.

The Willows, 1849 Willow Branch Terr., Jacksonville, FL 32205. (904) 387-9152. Mary M. Collins, proprietor. 3 rooms with private baths, AC, heat, 2 with ceiling fan, color TV, direct-dial phone, swimming pool. Adults only. No pets. Visa, checks accepted. Year-round rates: single or double $65-$80, full breakfast included, fresh flowers, fruits, ice. Newspaper available. Smoking allowed. Off-street parking.

Lake Helen–CLAUSER'S BED & BREAKFAST

Like Grandma's house down a country lane.

This is a place you want to stay because the hospitality never stops. It's no surprise that Marge instinctively knew she wanted this house the moment she saw it. Fate surely runs on the side of someone as dedicated as this, so that even though the house wasn't available that first day, Marge confidently told the woman to be sure to call if it ever were for sale.

Marge Clauser drives anywhere and looks at houses, saying to herself, "That one would make a great bed-and-breakfast, not that one, not that one—but that one there would."

She has guests on her mind all the time. Now she is thrilled that she can serve guests farm fresh eggs in the morning. She brews a decaffeinated coffee from beans she keeps in the freezer and grinds fresh for each serving.

She doesn't have dieting on her mind—only hospitality. Show up, and you're greeted with iced tea and cookies or fresh fruit or pie—"always something fattening," says Marge. Winter Sundays bring English tea with sandwiches and scones.

Serving guests isn't enough. Marge brings muffins to the ladies at the Cassadaga Camp and to the DeLand Chamber of Commerce. Her desserts are famous at the Copper Cove Restaurant, where waitresses deeply apologize when they're out of Marge's bread pudding and cobbler.

Guests get into the spirit. Marge is known to offer a beer to those who like it, and one guest lately replaced the offering with a Harp of his own.

You might expect that one room is called Peaches and Cream, the other Lavender and Lace. They're both over-decorated for effect. No surface is without its crochet rugs or flower-beribboned straw hat, floral print, and heart wreath. Beds are firm. Here, as throughout the house, polished pine floors almost show your image. Pegs on a wall rack are for clothes. Stenciling highlights windows and doors that all have bull's-eye surrounds. Windows are high single-pane casement type, and there are ceiling fans, air-conditioning and heat.

Each room has its own bath. Since Peaches and Cream's is in the hall, guests here have robes—and there's a little dressing room that used to be a kitchenette when the house was used by the military during World War II (when neighboring DeLand was a Navy base).

Like Marge, you will fall in love with this place when you first see it. It *looks* like a bed-and-breakfast. Below its steep-pitched tin gables under cedar shake shingles the house is white clapboard with gray-blue shutters, picket railings, gingerbread bracketing, spindles, and low-to-ground lattice baffling. Wraparound porches upstairs and down have rockers and wind chimes. There's an American flag on the downstairs porch, and begonias in hanging baskets. A little shingle under high oaks and magnolias tells you this is Clauser's. In the evening, electric candles glow from all the windows.

Right away your eye is caught by a canister full of canes and walking sticks, the oak rolltop desk, a bent-glass china cabinet, and the pair of crushed velvet wingback chairs that face the wood-burning stove. Burled pine wainscoting rises up the stairwell.

Marge will show you the old table radio and spectacles of a deceased brother, along with his coal-miner certificate, upstairs in the sewing room. Framed photos of husband Tom's family include one of George Armstrong Custer and of Anne Custer, who married Ephraim Hiram Kresge (who founded the first store in the chain that later became K-Mart in Bethlehem, Pennsylvania). Tom's more recent family have been steelworkers. He's a computer communications consultant, while Marge—until finding her soul's work—was in hospital administration..

The house was built in 1882 on land owned by George Colby, who founded the town of Cassadaga next door. All the land around here is wooded. One of Tom's sons by a previous marriage says he saw a rare Florida panther within two miles of the house.

Lots of stories get told in this house, especially in the living room evenings when the fireplace is burning, and a glass of port or sherry warms on sparks of conviviality. This is high hospitality, and not to be missed.

Clauser's Bed & Breakfast, 201 E. Kicklighter Road, Lake Helen, FL 32744. (904) 228-0310. Marge and Tom Clauser, innkeepers. 2 rooms and baths with AC, heat, ceiling fan, screened porch, petting animals, TV in reading room, house phones for free local calls and LD credit-card calls with no surcharge. No space for 3rd persons in rooms. No pets. MC, Visa. Rates $60-$75 per room, $10 less for single, and mid-week discounts. Includes full breakfast, afternoon tea, fresh fruit, use of house refrigerator. Off-street parking.

McIntosh — MERRILY

Rocking chair hospitality in a town of Victorian memories.

Squinty eyed jack-o-lanterns line the grassy lanes of McIntosh on a chill Hallowe'en night. A narrow street divides around an ancient oak arthritically gripped by vines. Long trails of Spanish moss hang limply patient for an inviting breeze to set a-dancing.

A few corners toward Orange Lake from the lone caution light on Highway 441 run the remnant tracks on the faint hump of leveled land that bends beyond sight among enshrouding high weeds. Twenty scant feet of rail remain between the long, peak-roofed tin packing shed and the old white screened-in board station. At the absent north end the sign beneath the eave still reads "McIntosh." A marker cautions, "Close clearance ahead. Will not clear man on side or top of a car." Two pots of yellow mums hang like the homage of consoled loved ones from the old black iron and glass lamp.

History, like knickered kids who once made it, runs across lawns to the lake and up to the places for overnighting, these days only one open. In McIntosh, population around 300, north Marion County's past is reviving.

Four years before the old hotel opened in 1895, the trains arrived to start shipping out citrus. Later, everyone would traipse to the depot to see who was coming to stay. After the freeze of '85, vegetables prospered the town, and buyers and tourists came.

When the Depression hit, south Florida produce had already captured the early market. McIntosh lost its economy.

It happened so fast while Ocala just south grew rapidly on ranching, and Gainesville just north developed its university, that people just forgot about McIntosh. Business moved out, and then the Seaboard decided to pick up its tracks.

Realtor-preservationist Marge Karow, though she came only in 1970, thought that was a shame. The look of the town hadn't changed, all those gabled old houses, narrow and uncrowded, with yards all around. The depot and the tracks and the railroad history were part of it.

Just the way tourists once came for fishing, they might come again for the look of an old town. Not many like McIntosh left in Florida, she knew, and though the old hotel would be a big project to fix up—too big to start with—she had a mind that the old-timers, eager for extra income and once used to tourists, this time might want to put them up in their houses.

The way things happen it's Marge who started that, in the pretty little yellow clapboard house with the rocking-chair porch all set around with flower beds she calls Merrily.

Getting that going was easy compared to saving the railroad relics.

At first she tried with bake sales. Too slow. So Marge organized the Friends of McIntosh and started the annual 1890s Festival. By signing a promissory note, the first two festivals raised just enough to move the depot off the railroad property and save the section of track. Later events have kept the old depot maintained. As for the old hotel, the Florida Trust for Historic Preservation has committed matching funds to repair it, but the local share has yet to be raised.

The hotel stopped taking guests in 1964, just before the railroad closed down. Sisters Betty McKoone and Helen Schorfaar, long-time owners, have stayed on with their memories. They love to show visitors around.

They can remember the first night a nephew stayed.

"At two in the morning the train came to the crossing and like it always did gave a blast that frightened the poor boy right out of his bed. You could hear it first down at Orange Lake. And then here, then up in Boardman, all down and up the line. Our grandson used to come from Ocala by train and they'd drop him off right here. Oh, if we could only still ride the train to Jacksonville!"

Meanwhile the roof falls in.

"I wish we could have it fixed," the sisters sigh. "We have to just close off another room upstairs every time some more ceiling falls in. But we live very comfortably downstairs."

"Not a lot of time left to save the place," says Marge, who makes sure her guests at Merrily learn about the old hotel and the sentiments that keep the town alive.

Her own place is all guests have for now. There are three comfortable rooms, one with its own bath, the other on the first floor—small inconvenience in a place that's purely authentic.

Upstairs ceilings are only 8 feet high. Marge thinks it's because postmaster W.E. Allen, who built the house in 1888, ran out of money.

Best room in the house is her living room with its yellow wallpaper, formal curtains, mix of armchairs, fireplace (another in the parlor), rolltop burl-inlay desk, wood hutch, drop-leaf tables, and scroll-armed sofa.

She serves a light breakfast and afternoon tea, and there's always a kettle on for guests in the kitchen. Every few months, when the spirit moves her, Marge puts on a Victorian high tea. Friends Betty and Helen from the old hotel serve at the dining table, Mitzi sings, Jane plays violin, and grandsons recite from the 1890s. "We are all in costumes," says Marge. "We have a great time in our make-believe party." She charges $10 per person, and limits the event to 15. You might ask when's the next event.

Marge disclaims anything special about the house.

"You can't really call anything here antiques, 'cause they've just come down from the family. I'm only trying to turn a liability into an asset," she'll tell you. "There's just me and my dog, and at least I like company."

There's also a town full of memories—"preservation power," Marge calls it—that may keep it all going.

Merrily, Ave. G at 6th St., McIntosh, FL 32664. (904) 591-1180. Marge Karow, innkeeper. 3 rooms and 2 baths (both baths detached, both with tubs), AC, gas heat, ceiling fans. Telephone messages taken. Well-behaved older children. No pets. Private off-street parking. No credit cards. $55 single or double year-round, includes continental breafast and afternoon tea. Smoking discouraged.

Micanopy – HERLONG MANSION BED & BREAKFAST

New owner redeems promise of unstinting hospitality.

Sonny Howard is making a lot of changes at the Herlong Mansion, but almost all to start on the outside. He bought the place in 1990 because he loved it the way it was.

The big change inside will be finishing off the third floor space which Kim and Simone Evans never got to after they restored this most striking house in Micanopy in mid-1987.

One change many non-guests will notice is that the mansion is open seven nights a week again. When the Evanses owned it, the demands of family and other jobs led them to close it midweeks. Weekends got reserved for weddings and other special occasions. It was easier to make a go of the mansion that way. The result was that many who tried to book rooms were frustrated either because there was no space or because calls never got returned.

Sonny Howard, on the other hand, has raised a family, is tired of looking for things to do, and has always loved small towns. He'd stayed in bed-and-breakfasts for 12 years, and had spent five years looking for one of his own throughout the South. He was one of those who tried to stay at Herlong Mansion but gave up after calling four times.

The Herlong Mansion is just 12 miles south of the University of Florida and provides a preservationist's alternative to the nondescript accommodations offered in Gainesville.

The house was built about 1875. Forty years later the original L-shape was encased in a symmetrical wraparound. Its four white Grecian pillars front a sturdy brick facade. An American flag hangs from the upstairs porch, visible through moss-hung trees that shade a wide grassy yard. That yard is a large part of what's going to change.

Sonny wants formal gardens out front with a gazebo, a fountain, reflecting pool, and flower gardens. He wants a scented garden to the side, walkways, Charleston benches, a grape arbor in back, and a rose garden on the south side.

That started, he'll then turn to putting an additional four rooms in the third floor space. A daughter who's an architect is already working on those plans.

Kim and Simone Evans had bought the place on impulse and turned it into one of the finest specialty lodgings in Florida. Simone perfectly captured the restrained yet confident era of the house's origins. Its proud dimensions and expensive materials are graced by tempered selections of antique furniture and fixtures placed to complement rather than outdo what was here to begin with. Guests right away sense its dynamic era when craftsmanship was freed from excessive ornamentation, and quality was the badge of a reforming America.

Oak, maple, walnut, and mahogany are used lavishly in floors and mantels. Pine appears in the earliest section. In the living room, a crown molding squares off wood beams and a dramatic ceiling. Color is subdued. Pale peach and rose brocades, a reserved Oriental rug—color and decor are secondary to function downstairs.

Bedrooms are brighter, more floral, rich in quilts, needlepoint, wicker, and cane. Antique beds include two wood sleigh frames salvaged from the old Ormond Hotel. The headboard in the master suite is unapologetically Victorian, carved with a dentate frieze.

Named for an Indian chief, Micanopy is a town where footpaths are worn through grassy swards on the fully rented main street, and where dirt roads meet downtown.

Frame and brick buildings are ungussied relics of a time just after the Indians, and of a place where late in the 18th century William Bartram visited and remarked of the vicinity that it "stands on the most pleasant situation that could be well imagined or desired, in an inland country."

At that time, a large lake opened north of town. Its most recent subsidence, in 1892, yielded the vast marsh known as Payne's Prairie, now a state nature preserve. Other nearby attractions include author Marjorie Kinnan Rawlings' house at Cross Creek, and the composed landscape of Marion County's horse ranches. The region is best explored by bicycles, which can be rented in Gainesville.

Sonny Howard's changes aren't all that's happening in Micanopy. In the last year, for the first time, houses on Cholakka Boulevard got street numbers. Herlong Mansion's is 402. And if you call before you arrive, odds are excellent a live person will answer.

Herlong Mansion Bed & Breakfast. 402 NE Cholokka Blvd., Micanopy, FL 32667. (904) 466-3322. 6 rooms and baths with AC, heat, color cable TV in Master Suite only, ceiling fans in 2 rooms, 3 baths with tubs (2 also with shower), 3 with shower only. Color cable TV in Music Room. 2 direct-dial phones available for guest use, free local calls, no surcharge for LD calls. Messages taken. Gas log fireplaces in Master Suite and Amber Suite (terry cloth robes in these suites). Well-behaved children accepted. No pets. $5 for 3rd person in room over age of 2. Rollaway and playpen available at no charge. MC, Visa. Year-round rates: midweek: $75-$95; weekend: $85-$115, single or double. Includes full breakfast weekends, expanded continental breakfast midweek, and wine and cheese on weekends.

New Smyrna Beach – RIVERVIEW HOTEL

Tested professionals take over from bankers,
restoring old-time hospitality.

You can tell Florida innkeeping is coming of age when experienced hoteliers downshift to smaller, more intimate places. For Christa and Jim Kelsey, taking over the Riverview Hotel means finding their niche after having proved themselves in bigger leagues.

For eight years they ran Faro Blanco, an ocean-to-bay resort in Marathon that they'd built from 32 rooms to more than 120. They made the place famous with service and Christa's super desserts.

But for an offer they couldn't refuse, they might still be in the middle Keys instead of making their subtle changes at the Riverview, where the previous owners ran the inn well but without flair. No question that the right people make big differences out of small opportunities, and inn guests always spot the change.

After Faro Blanco, Jim and Christa decided they wanted something smaller, a bed-and-breakfast. They wanted a marina nearby. In the Riverview they found a property larger than they'd looked for, but the marina convinced them. From the Riverview, Flagler Avenue spans the old downtown from the Indian River to the Atlantic. The weathered wood shops display breeze-blown T-shirts and summer dresses that garland the sidewalks.

Some stores refer to Coronado Beach. That was the name of the settlement when the bridgetender replaced the ferryman and was lodged in a little riverside house in the late 1800s. In time a drawbridge replaced the flat bridge and the house became a little hotel, a forerunner of the Riverview. In time the little hotel closed. Years later John Spang bought and updated it, and it became the Riverview that the Kelseys eventually bought from his successor.

The hotel is old Florida stylishly updated, while Riverview Charlie's, its restaurant next door, is made mostly of 100-year-old brick. The hotel is warm and homey in yellow clapboard and cream-colored trim. It has three stories that slightly lean to the main street they front on, surrounded by picket porches under a tin roof. The porches are all canopied under khaki awnings.

Inside is cool as white linen under paddle fans in a setting of creamy white rattan set off by overstuffed floral cushions and green planters.

There are 18 rooms, tropically styled, rich in natural woods. Ceilings are made of wood planks. Bed head- and footboards are wood, and furniture is made of sturdy natural and white-painted wicker. Color comes in accents: in striped upholstery cushions, quilts in red and green, and Haitian wall art. Three third-floor rooms have four-poster beds. The entire floor can be closed off for a single party.

Christa wants fresh cold fruit and cereals added to the continental breakfast. But otherwise she and Jim don't plan to interfere with the restaurant which has been leased successfully since the day it opened. Riverboat Charlie's draws a clientele that comes from as far as Orlando for a seafood dinner on the water.

The Kelseys plan to add 10 rooms by the pool in back by 1992 . Christa says the look will be same as the existing building. That will still leave the number of guest rooms under 30, but will add conviviality to the inn, Christa believes. People will feel there's more going on and will be attracted, she says.

Unlike the recent owners, Jim and Christa will live in the house behind the coral rock wall across the avenue. It's likely they'll become key players in a town that enchants them. Visitors are likely to benefit.

Riverview Hotel, 103 Flagler Ave., New Smyrna Beach, FL 32169. (904) 428-5858. Jim and Christa Kelsey, owners. 18 rooms and suites with AC, heat, ceiling fan, bathroom (15 with tub), cable TV, phone (charge for local calls, surcharge for LD calls). Older children accepted. No pets. All major credit cards. Pool, restaurant, bar, library. Year-round rates $70 to $150 single or double (honeymoon suite includes champagne). Rate includes expanded continental breakfast and newspaper. Inquire about 3rd person in room. Lunch $7 and up; dinner $12 and up. Off-street parking.

Ocala — SEVEN SISTERS INN
New owners likely to keep up rave-worthy reputation.

The night Bonnie Morehardt took over as innkeeper at Seven Sisters she had to move out. The place was overfull. That was on the transfer of this prize-winning house from restorers Norma and Jerry Johnson, who turned it into one of the most talked-about inns of Florida.

For Bonnie, moving on short notice was no big problem. She's been a flight attendant and pilot for 25 years.

For her and her partner, Ken Oden, Seven Sisters was meant to bring stability into lives of urgent moves.

No sooner had they decided on Seven Sisters than Ken got assigned by United Airlines to Los Angeles.

"We hope he gets transferred to Chicago," says Bonnie, "and then to Orlando."

Orlando is where they first looked for their B&B. Both had been bumped from their careers, Bonnie after flying for Braniff, Ken after 20 years of flying for Eastern. They were in Fort Lauderdale. Orlando looked good, only there weren't any houses available that had the right zoning.

Bonnie was familiar with taking in guests. For a time she had run a boarding house for pilots in Kansas City. She is from New England and was familiar with the concept there. She likes old houses and renovated one a hundred years old in Indiana.

Little will change at Seven Sisters, the three-story Ocala landmark built in 1888. The house had been in the same family for 78 years before Norma and Jerry bought it in 1986, the same year the house was voted best restoration by the Florida Trust for Historic Preservation. It's taupe and dusty blue, prominent for its angular cupola, gables, bays, red brick chimneys, sweeping baluster porch, latticework, slopes of shingles, wicker, bough wreaths, and border gardens.

Guests on entering trace trails of delight. From the pillowy duchy of quilt and brass in Loretta's room, you look across to a far wall at the country armoire, hand-painted by an itinerant artist Norma happily gave free rein to. Great froths of lace-bordered bow-tied curtains show off their ruffly bottoms like starched crinolines aflutter on a washday line.

Sylvia's room, dazzling as a stage behind hung pocket doors, has five distinct sitting areas and ornaments near giddy with excess: a baby teddy at play with a bubbly mouthful of remnant lace, fresh daisies clarion yellow in a bowl atop a bird-and-flowers painted porcelain pedestal.

Loretta's room is country English in peach floors and stripes, shady, cozy, with an old four-poster, an heirloom armoire, and a hand-painted jelly cupboard for treasures.

The room Norma named for herself is all white: white walls, wicker, lace curtains, paddle fan, accessories, and fringed cotton rugs. There's a hand-painted trompe l'oeil rug on the heart-pine floor. The sliding pocket door to the little bathroom with its solid brass fixtures and four-foot tub is so perfectly mounted a feather can move it.

The third floor is completely given over to Lottie's room, a 1,000-square-foot suite with bare pine floors, handmade pleated space dividers of whitewashed pine, a white plastered eave to reflect the skylight, and everything else green or hinting of green. Evident as everywhere through the house is great sophistication with childlike notions. Framed wall mountings from children's books describe the history of vegetable soup, the pleasures of orchards, and the story of Noah's Ark. A wicker basket has a ceramic bunny rabbit for a handle. An antique child's chair is stacked with green books. The bathroom is unusually spacious—except that the space goes up. It's otherwise odd-cornered, high and angled (white and green, of course). One change here: Bonnie has installed a king bed. Luxury!

The second floor also boasts a parlor in hunt-club tartan that offsets the tropical wicker of the breakfast room, and the sisterly rooms and suite embowered in flowers and lace.

By now, that breakfast room is likely relocated downstairs to part of a living room that was Norma and Jerry's and outfitted with a baby grand piano, gas log fireplace, tables with white Battenburg lace and floral print tablecloths. Walls are cheerful yellow, warm and inviting, French cafe-style with Monet prints. The full gourmet breakfast for which Seven Sisters became famous is faithfully served by Bonnie.

Other changes coming include extending Loretta's room into the former breakfast room to make this a two-room suite, and adding another room on the first floor with hook-up for laptop computer and private phone.

At last Seven Sisters will have seven guest rooms!

Seven Sisters Inn, 820 SE Fort King St., Ocala, FL 32671. (904) 867-1170. Bonnie Morehardt and Ken Oden, innkeepers. 5 rooms and suites, with complete baths, AC, heat, ceiling fan, color cable TV. Telephone messages taken, portable telephone available. Children 12 and older accepted. No pets. No smoking indoors. Guests' refrigerator. Private off-street parking. AmEx, MC, Visa. $75 to $105 double year-round. Includes complete gourmet breakfast and basket of fresh fruit and soft drinks at any time.

Orange Park – CLUB CONTINENTAL
Great riverfront estate with mansion-scaled rooms, excellent
recreational facilities, a privileged setting at bargain rates.

Sandra vacuuming the carpet makes the only sound in the grand stone mansion. Otherwise the house seems lifeless. It is Monday and the place is closed.

Sunday was busy. There had been the regular brunch and at least one wedding. Some Sundays there are three or four: one or two at Club Continental, another outside Winterbourne, maybe one at the River House.

It is off-season, which means winter in north Florida. The newlyweds are staying in the bridal suite. None of the other six showcase rooms of the old Johnson villa are occupied.

There is life aplenty nearby on this riverside point off I-295 in Orange Park. In the Seventies, part of the 30 acres was developed for condominiums, and that four- and five-story block with marina beyond can be seen from the lawn.

But the mood of the place—a world set apart by its style and history that hang in the air—is such that you wish away intrusions of modern times. Old times and nature prevail. By early morning the river to the east has turned so pink one marvels to contemplate the source of such blushing.

The view from the Mexican Room is across a barrel-tile roof, a lawn with a gazebo, a giant oak, a stone balustrade with intermittent planters, and a few palms, all the way to the broad St. Johns, more a river than anything else the scant Florida uplands seem able to produce.

It took the wealth of the Palmolive Soap king to bring it in view, and the will of his heirs to preserve it.

Club Continental has become one of Florida's finest guest accommodations, comprising Mira Rio (also referred to as the Club Continental) for overnight guests. Winterbourne mostly for longer stays, and the River House for informal socializing.

Mira Rio was the winter home of Caleb Johnson, who built his Italian-style villa in 1923. If the lower St. Johns seems oddly northern for the wealthy in winter, Johnson chose Orange Park because that was as far south as the railroad went in the 1870s. That was when a great wooden mansion, Winterbourne, was built where his kin later wintered. He liked that so well that he built Mira Rio, his own retreat nearby.

Winterbourne remains as attractive as it was more than 100 years ago, resplendently gabled and columned. The house was threatened first by neglect, then by sale for razing. What a loss was averted!

Its ceilings are 11 feet high, and its rooms are filled with Queen Anne antiques, Oriental rugs, fireplaces, a grand piano, a library. Blue and white elegantly predominate, along with wood tones and brass hardware. A fantastic large-patterned bird-in-bush wallpaper contributes to a look of country sophistication.

Mostly weekly and monthly guests reside here now, though rooms are occasionally available for overnight lodgings and visitors should ask about them. For a while after Johnson's last surviving daughter moved out, the family lost interest in the place. Winterbourne was scheduled for auction and demolition. The current Mrs. Massee, Fredericka, convinced her late husband Jon, Caleb Johnson's grandson, of an alternate plan to syndicate and restore the properties.

She did more. She added a concept that would make Winterbourne, Mira Rio, and the antebellum River House part of a social facility for Jacksonvilleans and those of nearby counties for meetings, luncheons, French dinners, catered affairs, and overnighting.

The little frame River House was about to be sold at $1,000 for its lumber. It was without electricity, plumbing, or a functional roof. Fredericka relocated the house downstream. Today it has been repaired, modernized, and extended with decks on pilings into the river between Winterbourne and Mira Rio where it is the popular clubhouse for Duval and Clay County yuppies.

Mira Rio is ornate and formal, marbled and gilded. Its grounds include swimming pools, tennis courts, lounges, bars, dining, banquet and meeting rooms, a beauty salon, marina and apartments nearby.

Fredericka's husband revived Mira Rio at her urging. Their daughter, Jean Patterson, then added the guest house concept by giving each of six decorators an equal budget, and having them design the five original bedrooms and suite in styles to accommodate the collections of furniture and antiques her great-grandmother had shipped home from world travels. (The tower suite has been designed as a family collaboration.)

Now managed by the Massees' son Caleb, the Club has its own schedule of fees and dues, but most facilities are open to overnight guests. Overnight rooms and suites are $55 to $70 per night double—one of the best buys in Florida—and include TV, telephone, and breakfast. Historic and contemporary, unquestionably luxurious, but modestly priced, Club Continental is an excellent choice for business or vacation travelers in the vicinity of Jacksonville.

Club Continental on the St. Johns River, 2143 Astor St., Orange Park, FL 32073. (904) 264-6070. Caleb J. Massee, Jr., manager. 5 exceptionally large rooms and 2 suites with AC, heat, bathrooms with tub, color TV, direct-dial telephone, pool, restaurant, bar, lighted tennis courts, gardens, riverwalk, plus additional rooms occasionally available overnight in Winterbourne. Children of any age accepted, free in parents' room. Cots $5. No pets. AmEx. Year-round rates $55 to $70 double, including continental breakfast. Suites $350 by the week. Average meal prices: lunch $5-$9, dinner $10-$16. Sunday brunch $5-$9. Beauty salon on premises. Marina. Off-street parking.

St. Augustine – CARRIAGE WAY
Expanding house, growing family, overflowing hospitality.

At Carriage Way, art imitates life–joyous, playful, reborn life. Good times pop like the cork on champagne. You will not leave without celebrating.

It has to do with trust and intuition, and how Karen Kovacik, formerly Karen Burkley, helps people accept the good in life. It is why guests can get all those "special touches" Carriage House has come to be known for.

Karen ran the B&B by herself before she married Frank. They met when he was a guest here.

Karen recalls, "I thought nothing special about him. Then when he called to book a second time, I flashed. 'He was the one!'

"I said to myself, 'No. Don't be ridiculous. You don't know him.' So he shows up with a rose. I couldn't believe it. It was Valentine's Day. I was so struck by his thoughtfulness he thought I was reacting like he had the plague.

"We had everything the other wanted. I showed him my pictures of whitewater rafting, of fishing, of the mountains. He had a piano, a guitar, two violins.

"It was after midnight and I was giving him a tour of St. Augustine. At 4:00 in the morning he was cooking breakfast for me."

One evening when he was back again as a guest, Frank was in a tee shirt. Guests were having dinner in the house. One said, "Ah, we only need a strolling violin."

"So in comes Frank, a tie on his tee shirt, strolling with his violin playing 'Edelweiss,'" tells Karen.

She had never had a proper wedding. This time the carriage came to Carriage Way with champagne.

Now Karen and Frank Kovacik, together with baby and Karen's daughter from a previous marriage, dote on guests with honeymoon breakfasts in bed, candlelight dinners, gourmet picnic lunches and other such special touches. Spring flowers in the room? Roses? A cheese board and fruit basket? Champagne? Special-occasion cakes? All can be had at a reasonable charge with a little advance notice.

Karen and Frank have been busy. Four new rooms bring the total to nine. For the first time, each has its own bath.

Most rooms are still the straightforward late-Victorians that Karen crafted for the house when she restored it in the mid-1980s, though the new Rebecca Rose in the addition has a 13-foot cathedral ceiling with skylight gables, crystal sconces, and brass plumbing.

The house had been four apartments and was collapsing. The abstract shows a two-story house under construction on the site in 1883. Dust-catchers in stair corners are dated the same year. A lot of original window panes—the kind with wavy glass—are still in the high start-at-the-floor windows.

When Karen first saw the house she knew it was the place she wanted, though she didn't know how much was wrong with it. But she was a contractor and knew how to make wrong right.

"When I first moved here from Tampa I was so impatient, geared up, I'd tap my feet while the pharmacist was on the phone. Now I'm probably just as slow as everyone else here. I find when I go back to Gainesville I have trouble crossing a four-lane highway.

"Here, when I come home and I'm on the porch fumbling for the door key, by the time I get inside I've said hello to half the town.

"When I went for a loan to start the project they laughed at the bank. I said, 'Okay. I'll get a couple rooms ready so I have something to show.' Finally I found a finance company. I paid 18 percent! But after I'd stripped all 73 of those spindles going up the staircase, rebuilt ceilings, fixed the upstairs porch for guests—many mornings, still working when the kids got up to go to school—I had done it. The bank stopped laughing long ago."

Though plain, guest rooms are up to date. Karen's style bridges the divide between fantasy and ordinary. Minimalist Victorian. Rooms have full carpets, no moldings, stenciling or other vivid coloration. Open space is preserved. Guests moving around aren't likely to knock over anything precious. Colors are soft. Beds have dust ruffles. Some, cane headboards. Dressers and tables are passable antiques. Here and there she has placed baskets, shells, bowls of dried flowers, potpourri, wreaths of woven twigs and vines. No phones, no TV (though you can ask for one), no clocks (though you can borrow an alarm or Karen will knock on your door in the morning).

The dining room is favorite indoor public space. Six chairs are set around a covered table, two cupboards behind. A cuckoo clock ticks but doesn't tell time. Newly added is a parlor with European wicker and Key West-style paddle fans, books, and games.

Guests have made the adjustment to Karen settling down. Used to be they'd catch her coming back early in the morning in her jogging suit with headphones on. Nowadays they find her pushing the baby carriage with headphones on. And Frank is preparing breakfast.

Guests feel at home here as they always have.

Carriage Way, 70 Cuna St., St. Augustine, FL 32084. (904)829-2467. Karen Kovacik, innkeeper. 9 rooms, 9 baths (4 with clawfoot tubs, 5 with showers), with AC, heat, 1 with ceiling fan, TV in parlor and portables on request (no charge). Extremely well-behaved children accepted under constant parental supervision, free in parents' room. Baby-sitting (extra charge). House phone for incoming messages, collect or credit-card outgoing LD calls; no charge for local calls. No pets. Smoking on veranda. Sherry, brandy, wine, liqueurs provided. Bicycles at no charge. CB, MC, Visa. Honeymoon and anniversary packages, picnics, flowers and candlelight dinners arranged with notice for added charge. Year-round midweek rate: $49-$79 (Sun.-Thurs.) single or double. Weekend and holidays: $59-$99. Seniors discount. Expanded continental breakfast included. $10 for third adult in room; free if family member.

St. Augustine – CASA DE LA PAZ
New owners add plantings, courtyard, lighter look.

Sandy Upchurch had never stayed in a bed-and-breakfast, and she certainly had no ambition to run one. But she found herself cut off from the museums and theaters of New York in a small town and needing to do something.

She found Casa de la Paz.

Her predecessor as owner was a university professor frustrated by academia, looking for change. It was he, Harry Stafford, and his then wife Brenda who decided to convert this Mediterranean revival house into a B&B. Its good looks and waterfront location on the Avenida Menendez quickly established its success.

The house had been built between 1910 and 1917, together with its like-looking neighbor, by father-in-law and son-in-law bankers. The Staffords bought it from a couple in their 90s and made the place home-like with a living room full of upholstered furniture and walls of books set among beautiful wainscoting and elaborate moldings. Sandy and Kramer Upchurch moved from New York to St. Augustine in 1986 and bought the house four years later.

"You might say that Kramer and I have always had a banking relationship," says Sandy. "We met at the Sun Bank automatic teller machine in Gainesville, Kramer is a banker, and when we moved back to Florida we wanted a good investment. That's what brought us to B&B. We loved this house."

Sandy has redone the house inside and out. She's done especially well with plantings. The front lawn has been grassed behind ligustrum bushes. The back, once an afterthought, is now a colorful year-round garden with azaleas, camellias, roses, hibiscus, night-blooming jasmine, and large white hydrangeas. There are also impatiens, heather, day and hurricane lilies, rose of sharon, and sago palms, ferns, and honeysuckle. The back gate that leads to Charlotte Street, though latched, is always unlocked. There's another at the side of the house.

A new sign out front tells the name, Casa de la Paz. The wrought iron has been removed from the windows, making the house more friendly to passersby.

The dining room now sports a rich yellow-gold paisley print wallpaper and a large Federal bull's-eye mirror. Six monkey prints are framed on the opposite wall.

Sisal rugs have replaced the Orientals in dining room and living room. All the furniture has been changed, lightened in look. There are two teal couches, club chairs with large colorful prints in rose and cranberry as well as rose, royal blue, and emerald green, and two little antique tables. Ornamental Costa Rican pottery was collected by Sandy and Kramer in travels.

The little sun porch that guests enter has been redone with a large black-dot-in-white-octagonal tile. The room is otherwise white, with wicker furniture cushioned in a red ticking fabric and more colorful prints. All the architectural detailing remains.

Upstairs, a fourth guest room has been added in what was once the library. All rooms have been brightened with striped and chintz prints. Swedish rag rugs let the heart of pine floors show through. Blanket covers are alternately Marseilles-styled and in pretty applique and pique prints. Window treatments are new, some with swags, some with Belgian lace. Some of the beds are new, too, some iron, some black iron, some pewter.

Breakfasts are much expanded from what they'd been. Instead of just continental items, Sandy serves egg dishes and casseroles. Baked treats are her own inspirations. Fruits and juices are included. A decanter of sherry goes in each room. Chocolates are iffy because Sandy doesn't like to clean chocolate off the beds. Though she was looking for things to do in St. Augustine, this isn't one of them.

Casa de la Paz, 22 Avenida Menendez, St. Augustine, FL 32084. (904) 829-2915. Sandy and Kramer Upchurch, proprietors. 4 rooms and 2 suites with baths (all but one with tubs), with AC, heat, ceiling fans, TV available, phone for incoming messages, collect or credit-card outgoing LD calls; no charge for local calls. Older children accepted, younger when suitable accommodations available. No pets. Smoking outside only. Sherry and chocolates in rooms. Full breakfast. Tea, coffee available during day. AmEx, MC, Visa. Year-round rates from $65 to $125 double, $10 for extra person in room.

St. Augustine — CASA DE SOLANA
Early Spanish house in spacious compound;
most formal of the St. Augustine guest houses.

Ancestral, inward, and ordered, Casa de Solana is like an island. Not merely Spanish, so inclined by history to grandeur, the house is the 14th oldest in St. Augustine.

It is one of those places surrounded by a high wall breached only by a latched gate that puts you in mind of a portcullis guarding a moated castle. Such a scene might not have been far in memory for Don Manuel Solana, who completed his house in 1763.

Like its proprietors, the house reveals itself by stages.

First the grassy yard, a miniature field, secure in its compound. The clip-clop on cobblestones outside the walled intersection at Cadiz and Aviles streets echoes the separation between spectators and insiders. The structure is thick-set coquina, solid; the door, imposing; the knocker, obligatory. The foyer establishes the lodging's formality.

Interior walls are sculptural, each recess or forefront having a door, a shadowy fireplace, a glassed antique breakfront. Frames are gilt, whether wall art or mantel mirror. There are marble hearths, solid brass and irons, cut-glass chandeliers, hand-hewn beams and hand-pegged floors. Modern details incorporate digital clock radios, quilted ice buckets, wrapped chocolate mints, antique bottles of sherry. Nights are passed in four-poster or brass beds. From the balcony of the colonial suite guests look behind the wall to the Ximinez-Fatio House, built in the late 1790s and operated as a boarding house in the 1800s. It is frequently open to the public without charge. The McMurrys are the first to take overnight visitors into their own 228-year-old house.

Morning is a stage for Faye McMurry, who at 8:30 serves a meal of eggs and cheese and a sausage casserole, homemade fruit-nut bread and a variety of muffins, and fruits, juice and coffee. In the ornate dining room with its 10-foot-long 10-seat mahogany table, Faye presides.

Each guest house is its proprietor's concept. Faye's is rooted in her Richmond upbringing and a career as a juvenile court lawyer with the Commonwealth of Virginia. She radiates when talking with guests.

"I think breakfast is a peak time of experience here," she says. "Guests arrive in the afternoon and rush to see the sights. They come back, change, go for dinner, come back, sleep. They wake up and now for the first time see where they are. They come to breakfast and meet people. They are not here as spectators. They are engaged. This is the high point. They don't want to leave. This breakfast time is quality time."

She makes it so, not just by talking. Guests talk among themselves. That is a big part of it. At most guest houses breakfast is served at guests' pleasure during a span of maybe two hours. At Casa de Solana breakfast is served at 8:30.

Almost everyone shows up, partly, to be sure, because the meal is included in the rates ($125-$135 double), but also one senses the occasion. Breakfast is an assembly. People want to know why others are here.

Faye has made it a new career, assisted by one servant. While she no longer practices law, she draws from it.

"I always knew how important a house environment was for youthful offenders. I spent so much time counseling. Here I'm combining education and trade. The inn gives us tremendous opportunity to interact with people."

She counsels visitors on what to do, where to go. She packs lunches for them, makes dinner reservations. She makes bicycles available. Faye is also president of the Aviles Street coalition, with its five museums, three restaurants, some of the older houses and the oldest street in America.

"I've made myself an innkeeper," Faye says, "because nobody seems to do it like you want it done. It's been seven years of learning to apply the same principles of dealing with juveniles to dealing with overnight guests. Everyone responds so well to care."

Casa de Solana, 21 Aviles St., St. Augustine, FL 32084. (800) 771-3555, (904) 824-3555. Faye L. McMurry, owner. Four suites with AC, heat, color cable TV, baths with shower and tub, digital clock radio. Children 13 and up accepted, $10 (as all additional persons) in parents' room. No pets. No smoking inside inn, only in courtyard or on balconies. Gas log fireplaces. House phone for messages, free local, and credit-card and collect calls. AmEx, Discover, MC, Visa. Year-round rates: from $125 to $135 (double) per suite. Includes full breakfast, chocolates, decanter of sherry, and use of bicycles. Paid parking lot behind the inn.

St. Augustine - KENWOOD INN
Young family extends personable hospitality.

The Kenwood is a charming, small hotel with ship-like intimacy. Perhaps it's the pineapples on the gateposts, or the hint of a widow's walk in front of the third floor dormer. The pineapple is a welcome-home sign; the widow's walk, where seafarers' wives stood watch for signs their husbands were returning.

It's a hotel, but definitely in the bed-and-breakfast tradition, not just because a continental breakfast is served, but because common space is so conducive to guests meeting each other. Intimate, too, because a family is in residence again, youngish and eager to mix.

The house has been a lodging for more than 100 years. It was built in 1865 as a private home. By 1886 it was taking guests and, with a new wing added in 1911, the Kenwood became a hotel.

Elsie Hedetnieme, who's now a broker in historic properties in St. Augustine, owned the inn early in the 1980s. Then Dick and Judy Smith ran the place for some five years. They added a lot of nautical touches, as in the Captain's Room, renamed Captain Charlie's Room for a frequent guest. It's all blue and white and woody, with steam and sailship prints, a steamer trunk, and a ship's desk with a brass lamp among its jaunty blue nautical notions.

Mark and Kerrianne Constant, the current innkeepers, came in 1988 from New Hampshire, where they'd been innkeepers for nine years. They remembered St. Augustine from when they were kids. They liked that the town feels friendly, that it's one of Florida's younger-in-age communities, and that it's a lot like New England in its historic age and well-lived-in style.

The Smiths, who had retired once from the automotive parts business only to come to St. Augustine and go into the inn business, were ready to retire again. The Kenwood hadn't even been on the market when Mark learned it could be bought. The Portsmouth inn was under contract. In a twinkling the Constants sold it, bought the Kenwood, and moved.

What appeals is the homey look of a building big enough to have 15 guest rooms. It's three stories with wraparound porches behind spindle balusters and gingerbread bracketing, close by narrow Marine Street and just a block from the bay. The east- and north-facing dormers, the clapboard construction, and the wood gates that lead to the pool yard all keep it looking like country in the city.

Mark will tell you that he and Kerrianne think of the Kenwood as a little more Victorian than country, but changes from how the inn looked with the Smiths are barely noticeable. Returning guests might notice that the former dining room is now a third sitting area. Also, guests can choose where they want to enjoy the continental breakfast that Mark and Kerrianne serve.

They might choose the sun porch, where there's a TV and a supply of puzzles, books, games, and magazines. They might choose the larger sitting room, where there's a good mix of antiques and comfortable pieces in blends of pinks.

The rooms are a wonderful mix of sentiments, full of antiques chosen to accent the best features of the rooms. Many have bare pine plank floors. Numbers 8 and 9 upstairs have access to a veranda that overlooks the pool and Marine Street. Number 9 is smallest in the house and at $55 is a good value.

The Honeymoon Room, #10, is off by itself overlooking the pool. It has what must be the smallest bathroom in America. By now the third floor has been renovated as a three-room bridal suite with Victorian wicker and chintz. One room, #11, is country Victorian with an Eastlake bed and soft floral prints. The Country Suite has an Adirondack cedar bed with quilts in Shaker motifs. It's carpeted in blue, has oak rockers, a drop-leaf antique pine table, and an old pine chest from Kerrianne's mother. The Shaker-built little cart with Shaker toys was Mark's toy.

A favorite is #17, done in the softest foam green. It's a room almost for convalescing because it's so soft in mood. Downstairs, #1 has a four-poster with a fish-net canopy, and lovely little double doors to a bathroom with a clawfoot tub.

All the rooms have baths, but the baths in the west wing are more modern.

Kenwood is one of the warm small hotels of St. Augustine. With its pool and its walking proximity to everything in the old city, it's a wonderful place for being welcomed.

Kenwood Inn, 38 Marine St., St. Augustine, FL 32084. (904) 824-2116. Mark and Kerrianne Constant, innkeepers. 15 rooms with AC, ceiling fan, heat, private bathrooms (some with tubs). Color cable TV in sun room. Swimming pool. Digital clock radios. Refrigerator and ice downstairs for guest use. House phone for messages and free local calls. Children accepted 8 years or older. Extra person in room $10. No pets. No smoking indoors. Discover, MC, Visa. Year-round rates, $45 to $125. Two-night minimum stay Fri. through Sun. Continental breakfast. Free off-street parking at Oldest House Museum, 1 block south (as well as complimentary admission)

St. Augustine — OLD CITY HOUSE INN
Comfortable rooms, exceptional meals supplied by two-generation hosts.

It makes sense that in this popular family vacation city a family should operate the town's only combined bed-and-breakfast and restaurant. Both businesses are first rate, which makes a compelling reason to visit.

These are ideal family quarters for overnighting because they're clean and uncluttered. Each of the five rooms has a private entrance. The restaurant is gourmet on a family budget.

Mom and dad Alice and Bob Compton run the B&B, son John and his wife, Darcy, the restaurant. Bob is a retired executive computer specialist with AT&T who now in addition to looking after the B&B does computer consulting and substitute teaching. Alice was a church secretary in Pearl River, New York, near Nyack. Their idea was to retire and operate a bed-and-breakfast.

From the start their idea was a place that could accommodate a restaurant for the kids to operate. John and Darcy had met while students at Johnson & Wales in Providence. After graduation Darcy managed a restaurant there, while John worked with a company that catered seasonal parties in Newport.

The senior Comptons checked things out in Missouri, Virginia, West Virginia. They had a place in mind in Crescent City but that was too off the beaten path. The first day Alice and Bob saw what became the Old City House Inn, they made an offer.

The building was put up in the early 1870s and served as a stable for the Ammidown Mansion. It was renovated in 1896 and became one of three winter cottages rented to wealthy northerners who came in winter. Later, it was used for a hat shop, antique store, apartments, and offices.

Though it's more than a hundred years old, the building today has a look that's called post-1930 St. Augustine revival architecture. An owner in the 1930s, when the building still had its clapboard siding and tin roof, encased the sidings in stucco. So much was later lost to termites that major reworking was necessary.

Original heart pine rafters show in some of the guest rooms. When the contractor proposed to trash remnants, John and Darcy salvaged these for attractive table edges and air returns and vents in their restaurant, adding a noticeably rustic sentiment to an otherwise bright, open, airy, clean-surfaced dining room.

Neither Alice nor Bob are antique people, though they have included family heirlooms in their guest rooms. So the B&B, like the restaurant, is light-colored, clean, and airy, efficient looking more than period. Beds are queen-sized firm.

Baths are modern with slip-proof marble showers.

Yet the touches are here. Look in Cordova (one of the rooms) for tintypes by Lionel Barrymore, and a huge 1936 dictionary Bob paid 50 cents for in high school. The Flagler room has a walnut piece from Alice's great-great-grandmother, and an 1873 family Bible. The Lightner room has a side-opening drawer with a secret compartment.

There's an upstairs veranda where guests can relax in lounge chairs and catch the bay breeze.

Breakfast is served at 9 A.M. in the bed-and-breakfast except Sundays, when house guests are served in the restaurant downstairs. That's the only morning the restaurant is open. While breakfast other days is a set menu, Sunday fare includes omelets, quiche, pancakes, and fruit salad with all kinds of side dishes. Not to be missed.

John is chef, Darcy dining room manager. John's menu policy is to serve the freshest of what's available. Hence the menu changes daily.

The result is top reviews by critics and guests alike. Guests will appreciate the attention to details: a Sam Smith pale ale among beer choices; California wines in the $10-$18 per bottle range, with five available by the glass. The young, alert staff is informed about wines and food ingredients. Homemade salad dressings are piquant: poppy seed-maple and creamy garlic (the poppy seed-maple is also sold for take-out). Sour cream and poppy seed dinner rolls are made in-house. The coffee is locally roasted and made fresh many times a day.

Menu items may include a grilled seafood pizza, a seafood pasta, baked grouper with smoked bacon, mustard, horseradish and sour cream sauce, or grilled dolphin with cajun marmalade. There's a vegetable Alfredo for vegetarians, and a good daily selection of beef, veal, and fowl. Entrees range from $10 to $19.

Turns out that Old City House Inn is more a family operation than is first apparent. The maple syrup that John favors in his cooking is supplied by two sisters who live in Vermont. A third sister looking to relocate in Jacksonville was quickly hired by Darcy.

Out of these good family connections comes warm, caring hospitality that guests relish.

Old City House Inn, 115 Cordova St., St. Augustine, FL 32084. (904) 826-0113 (B&B), 826-0781 (restaurant). Alice and Bob Compton, innkeepers; John and Darcy Compton, hosts. 5 rooms with bath, AC, heat, ceiling fan, color cable TV, alarm clock, private entrance each room, use of portable phone for free local calls (no surcharge for LD calls). Messages taken. Children of any age accepted, $6-$8 for crib. Inquire about pets. AmEx, MC, Visa. $65-$95 per room, reduced rates weekdays. Includes full breakfast, wine and cheese on arrival and otherwise, together with fruit, on request. Meter parking, free on weekends. No smoking indoors.

St. Augustine — OLD POWDER HOUSE INN

St. Augustine native returns with family, opens family house to guests.

"We've kissed a lot of frogs," says Michael Emerson—to which an outside observer can add, "on the way to becoming first-rate innkeepers."

It's not just that Michael grew up in St. Augustine, that his stepfather managed the glory that once was the Ponce de Leon Hotel, or that Michael and Connie's house has its own rich history. It's that the Emersons care about innkeeping with a fervor that benefits guests.

Those frogs of Michael's metaphor are the trial and error of getting established, though frogs there surely were, happily ribbiting in this vicinity when the original Spanish powder house was most of what stood in the swampy tract before it was developed in the late 1800s as part of Henry Flagler's revival of St. Augustine.

Beginning in the 20th century, the tract attracted more modest investors who settled into the mix of mostly late Victorian houses that characterize it today. History has bequeathed a comfortable urban neighborhood of landmark distinction because of the conversion of the Ponce de Leon Hotel to Flagler College, and because of the maintenance of Grace United Methodist Church in the Spanish Renaissance style.

The house had been converted to guest use around 1904, five years after it was built, and later became apartments. In the 1960s, the house became the family dwelling for Michael's mother and stepfather. Michael lived there from his 10th through 17th years.

Michael remembers the little city as more charming then, less commercialized. Young people could engage in innocent hi-jinks in a setting of antiquity. Michael recalls an occasion throwing water balloons by the fort, one tossed into the window of a police car. The police never found who did it, but Michael's mother did. So ended the tossing of water balloons.

Michael met Connie after the family moved to St. Louis. They married and in 1983 gave St. Augustine a try together. Connie didn't take to it. But when the first of their three sons was born, the city seemed perfect for raising a family. They returned and bought the old Emerson place.

Rehabbing the house took four years. Michael and Connie had trained in St. Louis where they lived in a border house, a middle class dwelling built for the 1904 World's Fair among those meant to buffer the mansion district.

The bed-and-breakfast idea came easily to Michael. Partly that was because he'd grown up in the hotel business. Partly it was his love for St. Augustine and wanting to share the city more intimately than he could in other lines of work. Mike had been in hospital administration in St. Louis. Too much stress.

They've restored many of the best features of the house, and filled it with antiques. In Grandma's Attic, the tub is one of the first built-ins after the clawfoot style, and features the rolled edge carried over from the previous era. There's an original whisper-flush toilet from the turn of the century. Crown moldings, door and window casements were all replaced, and wainscoting added to the dining room, all accentuating the house's Victorian provenance.

Rooms have Jenny Lind beds and bentwood furniture. Quilts, some hanging, others on beds, were crafted by the women of Mike's family. The Garden Room is a deep green with white trim with a floral bedcover and bough wreaths. Appended is a day room with built-in beds and floral papers. White-curtained windows offer three exposures.

The house displays a certain eagerness, a trying out of ideas finding their own harmony. The living room, for example, has floral upholstered pieces, swagged curtains, and a federal look to the moldings, all somewhat formal. Yet a hooked rug lends informality.

The outside of the house is tan with white trim, and green- and plum-bracketed window boxes. Brass rails lead up the five front steps and hint at elegance which is only partially realized inside. To one side is a fire escape reproduced from a ship by Michael's stepfather, hence its steepness. The fire code no longer requires it, and it's chained off, not in use, adding a quirky aspect.

An upstairs porch has a glider, rockers, and outdoor furniture that for a time was neglected. Under the white open-beamed roof and the added shade of a pecan tree, this is a pleasant place for breakfast. That breakfast is a full meal, with egg souffle, homemade granola, fruits, muffins or croissants, and brewed decaffeinated coffee. Wine and hors d'oeuvres are served before dinner or a carafe is placed in guest rooms after dinner. There is afternoon tea.

A lot of rewards from the one-time frog kissers.

Old Powder House Inn, 38 Cordova St., St. Augustine, FL 32084. (800) 447-4149, (904) 824-4149. Connie and Michael Emerson, innkeepers. 9 rooms and baths, AC, heat, ceiling fan, guest refrigerator in hall, 10-person jacuzzi, 1 room with kitchenette. Children accepted 2 and older, $6 in parents' room. No pets. MC, Visa, checks accepted (on FL banks). Portable color cable TV available. Hall phone for free local and credit-card calls. Messages taken. Coaster-brake and multi-speed bikes available at no charge. Year-round rates: $65-$98 (weekends and holidays), $50-$75 (Sun.-Thurs.). 10% senior citizen discount (65+). $9 extra adult in 1 room where extra bed. Afternoon high tea, wine and hors d'oeuvres and fruit juice evenings. Rate includes full breakfast. Smoking limited to verandas. Free off-street parking.

St. Augustine – ST. FRANCIS INN
Down-home hospitality in Florida's oldest inn.

Entrusting the oldest city in America to Florida is like bestowing credit on a spendthrift. Florida's patrimonial urge has been to knock down, uproot, and pave. Antiquity has been celebrated more for emptying the pockets of tourists than for preservation, though that finally has come, and why harangue the past.

St. Augustine's beauty is that real people live workaday lives in a setting of four and a half centuries of history. Laundry flutters in courtyards freshened by ocean breezes that blew explorers landward. In Castillian Spanish, humble gossip across fences sounds like puissant narrative. Secretaries gather at water coolers in offices across from the Plaza de la Constitution laid out in 1598.

The town is county seat of a vast farming area where crossroads settlements are named Spud, Fruit Cove, and Molasses Junction. King Philip may have colonized the territory, but cabbage is king today. Cabbage and tourists.

The European history of St. Augustine begins with Ponce de Leon in 1513. A brief period of French rule followed before the Spanish returned for nearly 200 years, impressing the dominant architecture that inspired Henry Flagler and Yankee imitators to turret, tower, and tile the state.

Much of what they built was wasted as early as the late 1500s, when English raiders stormed ashore pillaging. Vernacular buildings were lost to the torch, replaced by fortifications. These, too, survived only to limited extent. Even city gates were destroyed by Flagler era progressivists.

Fires further reduced the old city in 1887 and 1914. What remains is an architectural gumbo of frame, brick, coquina, tabby, and gingerbread, and a combination of original, rebuilt, and adaptive styles now used by a comparably polyglot population.

Monumental sites abound: the cathedral, the Castillo de San Marcos, and two of Flagler's remaining great hotels: the Ponce de Leon, now Flagler College, and the Alcazar, now a mall of antique shops called the Lightner Museum.

So far the bayfront is clear. Early before sunrise the Bridge of Lions sleeps. The slapping halyards from the municipal pier are heard more than trundling cars. A crescent moon yields to the solar crescendo in the celestial routine of a grandfather clockworks marking time for a favored town. Tourists walk the streets slowly with cups of coffee in hand, contented by boat putterings and seagulls.

For every historical attraction, someone has dreamed up a tourist come-on. But who cares? The best attractions are the old buildings themselves. They assume no taint just because they are used by tourists.

The Inn

The St. Francis Inn sits right-angle solid at the corner of St. George and St. Francis streets with no space at all left over for even imagining it hasn't always been here. Its shield-like shingle set over the sidewalk on St. George Street mocks modern notions of setbacks. Guests stepping out of horsedrawn coaches are right in character. The old plank and stucco inn fits so well on its cobblestone street that it's the rest of us, in today's modern clothing, who appear to be in costume.

This is one of the oldest inns continually in use in America. It dates back to 1845. That was the year that Mary, widow of Col. Thomas Henry Dummett, conveyed the house and lot to their daughters Anna and Sarah.

Col. Dummett was born to British parents in Barbados. He held rank in the British Marines. When the English abolished slavery and uprising followed, the Colonel fled with his family, slaves, and movable property on three cargo vessels for Florida.

After establishing plantations south of St. Augustine in Tomoka—parts of a sugar mill he built on the property still stand—the family got chased again, by the Second Seminole Indian War in 1835. This time they resettled in St. Augustine.

Two years later the Colonel purchased the house built in 1791 that his daughters turned into lodgings for visitors.

Dummett House prospered through a succession of owners, name changes, and improvements. In the late 1880s a third floor was added. In the 1920s central heating and bathrooms were installed. In the late 1940s Dummet House, later Dummett-Hardee House, then Graham House, became the St. Francis Inn.

The inn faces a courtyard and tropical gardens and has a variety of single and double rooms, two- and three-room suites with kitchenettes, a three-room apartment, and, best of all, a five-room cottage once the slave quarters. Fireplace, wainscoting, and stairs are all original. Downstairs there's a full kitchen, a comfortable sitting room that opens onto the courtyard and direct to the little lap pool. There's also a full playroom with games for children all screened in next to the living room. An outstanding value at $98 a night for up to four. The living room in the main house has a great walnut and beveled glass Regency mantel. The room is full of art, Civil War photos, and a Civil War library.

More than anything, guests return for the at-home comfort, the accumulated look that comes from a succession of owners who flourish their enthusiasm more than they dispel their predecessors'.

Marie Register has added more color, more Oriental rugs, more antiques. She picks flowers daily. Lately she has reopened fireplaces in the downstairs lobby, sitting room, and living room, and three guest rooms and the upstairs sitting room now also have working fireplaces.

"Christmas Eve we had all 12 fireplaces going," she says. "What a festive glow came over the old inn! But all year there's this feeling of 'Come in. I'm here for you.' That's the inn talking, and you know, as old as this place is, folks abide by what they hear."

St. Francis Inn, 279 St. George St., St. Augustine, FL 32085. (904) 824-6068. Marie D. Register, manager. 11 rooms/suites, cottage, with AC, heat, most with ceiling fans, cable TV (some black and white), private bathrooms (some tubs, all with showers, two baths private but down the hall), some with refrigerator, range tops and toaster oven. Small swimming pool. Pay phone and house phone for messages, local calls; free credit-card and collect LD calls. Children welcomed. No pets. MC, Visa and checks. $8 for additional persons above double (or 4 in cottage). Year-round rates: $47-$110 (cottage for 4). No smoking in guest rooms. Coaster-brake bikes. Includes free admission to The Oldest House, and continental breakfast. Free off-street parking.

St. Augustine — SOUTHERN WIND
Beautifully decorated rooms with cottage perfect for families

Get with Jeannette and Dennis Dean if you want to save weeks of combing east coast Florida for where the living's best. They traveled it all, and liked little before reaching St. Augustine.

Though they wanted to sail, the Deans after they got to Florida realized they wanted to work. For Dennis it was a contract security service with guard contracts he services around America from a computer. For Jeannette it was bed-and-breakfast.

She wanted something "artistic." She likes to entertain. Both had worked with old buildings, and Jeannette is an interior designer. For four years in Hollywood and New York she did all the lobbies and executive offices for Motown Records. In St. Augustine she wanted to make a home for people traveling awhile and show how much she liked the city.

The house they bought was built in 1916 by Henry Flagler's physician. It's two and a half stories, masonry vernacular. For a while, when it consisted of 15 apartments, it housed descendants of the Minorcans who arrived in St. Augustine after giving up their colony in New Smyrna Beach in 1777.

Porches on the first two stories were enclosed on the south side in the Thirties. They now give the two rooms there, one upstairs and one down, attractive bays. The house is built of gray-brown stone, with white trim and teal shutters. A two-story bay to the north houses the dining room, where a full breakfast is served in the morning, and teas and coffees throughout the day.

Jeannette's mastery of colors and accents shows in the five rooms and suites of the main house, and in the four rooms and suites lately added in a guest cottage a block and a half away. She has chosen richly patterned fabrics, complemented by crown borders in furniture. She has hidden TVs or dispensed with them altogether. You feel relieved more than deprived. Ask if you want a room with one.

Jeannette has used the bays in south-facing rooms to furnish charming seating areas that make suites of rooms. In the bathroom of the Crystal Suite she has set two eye-catching panels of parquet flooring above the all-around pine.

Two rooms at the back of the house share a common foyer off the landing. One is flowery pink and green chintz and features twin cane-backed little armchairs with chintz cushions at a lace-covered octagonal table. The other is blue—blue doors, blue carpet and walls, blue ceiling fan, along with blue accents in the furnishings.

The non-Crystal Suite is floral, the bed with its bamboo headboard centered in a seven-sided room set among five windows covered in lace. The room is rose, green, blue, and white, and the colors mesh like the harmonies of a Schubert quartet.

A little dream setting in the Veranda Suite upstairs is composed of French doors to the closed-in porch. There is an Oriental tea-canister lamp close to the queen bed.

All beds in the house are firm, all towels thick as bumpers on dodge-'em cars. Downstairs is a combination living area, parlor, and dining room. Colors are pale sea-green and deep reds. There are formal drapes, lace curtains, and a red Oriental rug on green carpet. Green napkins play their color against a floral centerpiece where the reds and greens stand out. Accenting the crown molding is a band of green-draped wallpaper with red tassles. Wing chairs are deep red, side chairs red-on-red brocade.

Jeanette and Dennis acquired their cottage in 1990 and opened it at the start of the following year especially for guests with children. The suites can accommodate from two to six persons in settings of antiques from the turn of the century through 1920. Notably, the Fireplace Suite (with a working fireplace supplied with pressed logs) has an antique Victorian bed, oak draw-leaf table with Queen Anne lace; the Raspberry Room a high varnished, gold-trimmed, French walnut Louis headboard; the Garden Room a Chippendale day bed (as well as a queen). These lodgings all have wet bar, microwave, coffeemaker, and small fridge, as well as outside deck, and guests here can have either a continental breakfast or come to the main house for the full buffet breakfast.

The full breakfast includes ham and eggs, fresh fruits, and baked goods such as homemade muffins or banana nut bread. There's also tea and coffee (including decaffeinated), all self service-style at little tables in the second story hall. Wine is in decanters downstairs. All very civilized, caring, well done. Very much the work of people very happy in their new Florida home.

Southern Wind, 18 Cordova St., St. Augustine, FL 32084. (904) 825-3623. Dennis and Jeannette Dean, innkeepers. 4 rooms, 3 suites, all with private baths. AC, heat, ceiling fan, color TV. Hall phones for free local and credit card LD calls. Refrigerator in main house hallway. No children, no pets in the main house; children of all ages encouraged in cottage (7 more rooms and baths). AmEx, MC, Visa. Checks accepted. Additional person in room more than 2 (including cot or rollaway) $10. Year-round rates: $60-$95 (weekends), $50-$70 (Sun.-Thurs.) (except holidays and spring, apply weekend rate), includes fresh flowers, decanter of wine, full gourmet breakfast. Bicycles available at no charge. Smoking on verandas.

St. Augustine — VICTORIAN HOUSE
Country-bright fixed-up old house full of colorful stenciling and friendly cheer.

It was Daisy Morden from Niles, Michigan, who started fixing up St. Augustine's old houses and turning them into guest quarters. Doubtless hundreds of others have had the idea during the centuries that St. Augustine has had old houses to fix up. But Daisy freshened the idea, and others have followed.

She didn't want to be bored. She had "meandered up" from Fort Lauderdale in 1980, part of a trip she had promised herself once her three children were grown.

The house she chose was wood frame, built in 1890 with impervious heart pine floors, a block and a half from the Plaza de la Constitution, in the nationally registered historic district.

But what a mess!

"Anybody who's ever been through a tornado knows what the place looked like—rotted wood smashed into splinters, concrete blocks blown through walls, a porch with its steps ripped away, shutters blown down. The columns had been stripped of their decorative moldings down to bare pipe.

"It was an ugly duckling, but I love pitiful things. Can you imagine? People pose for pictures in front now."

It's not surprising because now it's a boxy, plenty-windowed, two-story gabled house painted "Philadelphia cream" and "Jamestown blue"—approved colors—with woodturnings and latticework, hanging plants, and a white picket fence.

The carriage house made it feasible. It gave Daisy two suites with private baths, the mix she felt she needed with the four rooms that at first shared two baths upstairs in the main house. Now all have their own bathrooms, though all rooms remain attractive to people on budgets.

Guests have the pleasure of a country Victorian setting and farmhouse hospitality.

Daisy's stenciling sets the pattern. Her bird-in-the willow logo shows up on walls, floors, in trim above draperies. She favors small-patterned wallpapers, upholstery, and rugs, colorful contrasts to solid wood floors.

Be sure to have a look, if you're not bedded down there, in the upstairs room at the end of the hall with the vanilla ice-cream floor stenciled in red and green like a strawberry sundae, with colorful quilt embroidered in flower sets on the little iron-framed bed from Kentucky, and crown stenciling that flows like a frolic 'cross a summer field.

She has filled the place with antiques, less for design than comfort. There is nothing couldn't-you-just-die about the place.

She has always collected things. She has always liked older people, "and they'd give me things to re-upholster, and sometimes just give me things. I love weird, eccentric people."

Some notable pieces inlude an extended parson's bench, a carved love seat covered in sky-blue velvet, a 10-foot-long spindle-backed bench, an art glass chandelier, and an 18th century grandfather clock with moonface and chimes. "You could buy things like these from Sears in the 1890s," says Daisy. "We used to swap for them in Niles."

She's at home and so are her guests.

They can sit in the Victorian living room, play Trivial Pursuit in the dining room, swing on the porch or rock in rockers. Most people spend their days sightseeing after starting with Daisy's homemade breakfast.

"I've made muffins almost every morning since opening. Had no guests those days. I'll tell you, they're the same every day. But then, the people keep changing. It's like having children. You have to feed them every morning."

Guests also get Daisy's granola and quickbreads, fruit, juice, and coffee or herbal teas.

It's good to let Daisy know when you expect to arrive, though many guests just show up. Apart from finding the place full, you might not find her at all. If she is out, she leaves notes on the door, though often there is a guest around to let others in, and nowadays a helper.

"I don't at all mind leaving guests alone in the house. I'm certainly not worried about anything being taken. One person who broke an ashtray wouldn't leave without glueing it together again. More people leave things than ever take things from guest houses."

Since she opened Victorian House there are now a dozen bed-and-breakfast inns in St. Augustine.

"We get tons of people coming through who say they want to buy inns," Daisy says. "Very few actually do. But it's a way of saying they love St. Augustine."

Victorian House Bed & Breakfast, 11 Cadiz St., St. Augustine, FL 32084. (904) 824-5214. Daisy Morden, innkeeper. 8 rooms and suites in main and carriage houses with AC, heat, ceiling fan, some with TV, private bathrooms (all but 2 with tub, 4 with showers). House phone for messages, free local calls, credit-card or collect LD calls. Children accepted only in carriage house. No pets. Smoking requested on porch only. Color cable TV in parlor. AmEx, MC, Visa. Year-round rates $55-$85 single or double, including continental-plus breakfast. $10 per extra person regardless of age. Limited off-street parking.

St. Augustine – WESTCOTT HOUSE
Richly appointed rooms in a superbly revived
100-year-old house on the bay drive.

A collector of stamps commemorating gourmet achievements, notified driving south that she has inherited an unduplicated set of unperforated 150-Groshen Austrian issues honoring Viennese pastry chefs, could hardly do better than celebrate the occasion by overnighting at the Westcott House in St. Augustine.

Westcott House is the preservationist equivalent of an unashamedly high cholesterol experience.

It begs to be discovered and yielded to, all creamy peach, blue, and white, banistered, tiled and gingerbreaded along St. Augustine's romantic waterfront. At overnight rates of $75 to $135 per couple, the architecture will be savored by many less the ensconcing. But celebrations are not for stinting. Westcott House says let yourself go.

One imagines the Dennison families did just that, once having spied the bleak structure and deciding on impulse to restore it *a la mode*, hoisting no ordinary brew when they celebrated completion of their six-month labors with

700 St. Augustinians.

You approach a friendly low stone wall and more-decorative-than-necessary wrought-iron gate from Avenida Menendez, then cross a walkway of 8x8 peach diamond-shape tiles. Step up alongside an iron railing to a portico with carved balustrade, hanging ferns, potted palms, and white wicker.

An equally spacious second story balcony graces the house, Creole style. Yet a third porch wraps around a portion of the south side and rear, tunneled under a bay apartment, giving the appearance of a covered bridge a few steps up from the flowering yard.

The house is clapboard finished, with colonial-framed, fan-lighted windows, shutters, and transom above the French entry doors, their upper portions in "WH" monogrammed glass. Curtains and shades drawn just-so right away establish an impeccably maintained lodging.

It is hard to imagine the place run down as it was when the Dennison brothers came upon it. They were fresh from impressions of Charleston and Savannah, and suitably engaged in real estate and furniture retailing to stoke their impulse when they found the house for sale.

Dr. John Westcott had built it more than 100 years before, in 1886. Horse-drawn passersby even then would have remarked on its Victorian embellishments of colonial style along the bayfront that Henry Flagler's railroad had made accessible to vacationing northerners.

Dr. Westcott had his own innovative ideas about transportation. After moving to St. Augustine in 1858, he was a promoter of the St. Johns Railroad, which linked coastal and riverfront settlements of the time. Though his railroad became merged with Flagler's, his more enduring legacy was conception and early development of the Intracoastal Waterway.

Over the years his house fell into disuse. When the Dennisons came upon it, the house still existed almost without plumbing or electricity.

Sheena Dennison Florin, first innkeeper for the family, recalls, "It. was in very poor shape, old, neglected, decayed. We put in 11 bathrooms. I'd wanted to re-do an old house and live in it. I'd been working in my father's furniture store in Orlando. I like working with people. I like old things. I guess I was misplaced in time. It's kind of like entertaining full-time here."

Her successor Ruth Erminelli indulges that penchant by providing a complimentary bottle of Liebfraumilch from a temperature-controlled cellar Uncle George converted in a closet under the inside stairs. Further indulgence includes terry cloth robes, pillow chocolates, and bedside sherry, with croissants, pastries, juice and coffee for breakfast.

That breakfast can be enjoyed in a brick courtyard on wrought-iron furniture, on the wicker-set porches, in one's room, or in the opulent parlor in front of an 1865 European cast-iron fireplace.

Each of the rooms is a showcase of antiques, reproductions, and choice detailing, with high-polished pine floors or rich carpeting. Brother Jim and each of the brothers' wives decorated two bedrooms; brother George did one, and Sheena did one as well as the innkeeper's apartment.

Upstairs, Isabella is blushing pink and green, green carpeted. The imaginative bath arrangement has the WC behind a narrow 10-paneled glass and curtained door, stall shower opposite, lavatory between, all in a narrow alcove.

Esmeralda is emerald green and white with a built-in glass cupboard in boxcar-siding white that shows off a mounted collection of green-glass tableware. Green balloon curtains cast a spell over white shades. Three walls are papered in exuberant country bouquets.

Anastasia is an Eastern European memory in the New World. A great mahogany vanity is topped by triptych mirrors, the center a five-foot oval. Heirloom lace covers an organ pipe bed with inset orbs of painted porcelain. A steamer trunk recalls a shawled fugitive forced to abandon plenipotentiary privilege, barely time to pack but a few portraits of loved ones, now hung on these walls. One steps down to an alcove bedchamber beyond surveillance.

All rooms have private baths, some with claw-footed tubs, and all the expected amenities. They also include information packets with words about "Midnight Sympathy": being considerate when closing doors, drawers, etc. Ah, thoughtful.

But you know what?

Celebrate anyway!

Westcott House, 146 Avenida Menendez, St. Augustine, FL 32084. (904) 824-4301. Ruth Erminelli, innkeeper. Eight rooms with AC, heat, ceiling fan, color cable TV, direct dial phone (no charge for local calls), bathrooms (some with tub). Inquire about children. No pets. MC, Visa. Year-round rates: $95-$135 weekends, $75-$110 midweek, single or double, continental breakfast included, wine on request, turndown service with brandy on request, robes. $10 for 3rd person of any age in room. Street parking.

THE GULF COAST: CEDAR KEY
AND SOUTH

Renewal of two grand hotels and the net gain of more modest lodgings leaves vacationers with choices up and down this coast, though not as varied as might be, given the large supply of historic housing.

The big news is that the Vinoy Park, first opened in 1925, will reopen in 1992 as the **Stouffer Vinoy Resort.** It will be the cornerstone of a $92 million new golf and tennis resort in bayside St. Petersburg. Across and north on the Pinellas County peninsula, the Belleview in Belleair, formerly the Belleview Biltmore, is now the **Belleview Mido**, acquired by a Japanese international hotel chain, which, with a $10 million infusion, is refurbishing and adding restaurants, tennis courts, and shops while maintaining the Belleview's *belle epoque* grandeur.

Two excellent new bed-and breakfasts are **Harrington House** in laid-back Holmes Beach, and **Inn By The Sea** in Naples, where owner Elise Sechrist Orban spent two years convincing that city that bed-and breakfast in a good idea in a historic neighborhood where there already are many attractive small motels.

Newly described in Pass-A-Grille, a magical little appendage of St. Petersburg Beach lately entered in the National Register of Historic Places, is **Island's End**, a bijou cottage colony. Also in Pass-A-Grille, is **The Inn on the Beach**, which includes 11 efficiencies and apartments in a house that, though added onto more recently, dates from the 1930s [1401 Gulf Way, St. Petersburg Beach 33706, (813) 360-8844].

Also new are the little **Pointe Pleasant Inn** in Bradenton, the warmly hospitable little Art Deco hotel called **Palm Pavilion Inn** in Clearwater Beach, the rustic and seasonally available **Ivey House** in Everglades City; and, opened too late for review here, **Pepperberry House** on the Hudson Bayou in Sarasota [1898 High Point Drive, 34230, (813) 951-0405], in Bradenton Beach, **Duncan House B&B** [1703 Gulf Drive, Bradenton Beach, 34217, (813) 778-6858], and **Ruskin House B&B** [120 Dickman Drive, S.W., Ruskin, 33570-4649, (813) 645-3842].

The **Crown Hotel** in Inverness has new owners, Welsh hoteliers Nigel and Jill Sumner heading a partnership that acquired this railroad-era prize from its Scottish restorer. **The Heritage** in St. Petersburg has gone through Chapter 11 to emerge more financially secure. **Bayboro House** in St. Petersburg, the **Cabbage Key Inn**, and the **Izaak Walton Lodge** in Yankeetown have all added rooms.

Charming though only obliquely historic is **The Boat House** at the Olde Marco Inn [100 Palm Street, Marco Island 33987, (813) 394-3131]. On this island where almost everything from the late 19th-century fishing community was relocated nearby to Goodland to accommodate a sterile modern resort "paradise," the restaurant of the inn dates from 1893 when the W.T. Collier family began taking guests for $1 a night. The Boat House offers 20 luxurious guest rooms.

On Siesta Key there are new owners at the **Crescent House**, but the **Grey Dove Inn** has closed, as has the **Eagle Point Lodge** north of Venice.

Big opportunities exist for would-be B&B operators in Fort Myers and Tampa, where nothing exists today, in towns like Brooksville and its vicinity along Highway 41, and along the barrier islands, especially in Sanibel and Captiva where many ordinary lodgings draw visitors to these popular shelling beaches and wildlife bays. **'Tween Water Lodge**, although the oldest lodging on Captiva

[Beach Road, 33924, (813) 472-5161] has only a few of its original cabins remaining, and today, greatly expanded, is more of a motel and convention facility. **Thistle Lodge** on Sanibel [2255 W. Gulf Drive, 33957, (813) 472-3145] is a restaurant re-creation of the original lodging compound called The Sisters. Farther out on Sanibel, the **Island Inn** [P.O. Box M, 33957, (813) 472-1561] dates from 1896, but none of the original structure houses guests. The **Clearwater Beach Hotel** has none of its original structure remaining, but its new enlarged version is architecturally interesting, and original artifacts are displayed [50 Mandalay Avenue, Clearwater 33515, (813) 441-2425].

In Tarpon Springs, the rustic **Livery Stable** [100 Ring Ave., Tarpon Springs, 33589, (813) 938-5547] that dates from 1904 sometimes takes overnight guests.

For those who like to look at old hotels even if they can't any longer stay in them, consider **The Edwinola** in Dade City, now a retirement home; the **Inn in Bowling Green,** now a drug rehabilitation center; the **Mason-Princess Martha,** the **Manhattan,** and the **Soreno** in downtown St. Petersburg; the **Floridan** in downtown Tampa, and the exquisite **Tampa Bay** from 1891, now part of the University of Tampa, though with ground floor spaces on view to visitors. In Gulfport, the **Rolyat** since 1954 has been part of Stetson University; and the **Fenway** in Dunedin and the **Fort Harrison Hotel** and **Gray Moss Inn** in downtown Clearwater have lately been occupied by religious institutions. In downtown Bradenton, the **Manatee River Hotel** [309 10th Street, West, 34205 (813) 748-0434] for several years has been a retirement home, though sometimes with a room available for overnighters. Inquire.

Boca Grande – GASPARILLA INN

Old and elegant inn that rambles through a quaint town on a quiet island with one of Florida's most beautiful beaches.

In a hostile age that erects hedonist resorts behind fortified perimeters and, for the sake of security, treats outsiders tough, sourness curdles hospitality like the twitch of repugnance one feels on discovering that a prominent citizen kicks cats.

How different the tradition at the Gasparilla Inn, conceived in an age of civility, that willingly embraces the quaint little town it rambles through and keeps vacationing in touch with local life.

The inn is a spread-out resort, centered by a two-story white-trimmed yellow wood structure with a high Georgian facade set a few blocks from Boca Grande's wondrously long sandy beach. The look is old worldly, the clapboard style favored from when the town was a 19th-century fishing port.

There are accommodations in rooms and cottages for about 225 guests. They enjoy use of an 18-hole golf course, tennis courts, a beach club with two pools and exercise club, and croquet lawns. Inside the inn are drawing rooms and sun parlors furnished in old polished wood, wicker, and chintz—same as guest rooms—that in their graciousness and order remind us that the *sine qua non* for getting away from it all is not to substitute the stress of go-go stimulation for the stress of work, but to help us relax.

Not only are there no walls around the property, but the resort is indistinguishable from the surrounding town. Its cottages mingle with ordinary houses. The inn is on a side street. It doesn't dominate.

The same intelligent attitude extends to the peak-season staff of 220, who are treated better than many guests on vacation elsewhere. Most are housed two to a room with private bath and three meals a day.

For guests this means that everyone who lives and works in Boca Grande feels an investment in the well-being of people at the inn. Guests feel at home everywhere they walk. No one vacationing here fails to understand the difference between life in Boca Grande and at more typical chain resorts.

General manager Steve Seidensticker came from the renowned Stanley Hotel in Estes Park, Colorado. A Coloradan, he wasn't eager to leave. "But my wife was a ski instructor, and she was pregnant," he says, "and moving to Florida was the only way I could keep her off the slopes. We fell in love with Gasparilla Island and haven't left."

Caring extends to every aspect of the operation. All meals are prepared from scratch with freshest ingredients. The kitchen includes its own butchery and uses the bones for stock. A new menu is prepared every evening throughout the social season (as winter is referred to) that includes homemade breads and pastries and home-frozen ice creams.

Time stirs slowly in Boca Grande near the end of the road on Gasparilla Island. Streets are named Dam If I No, Dam If I Will, and Dam If I Care. "They don't have any house numbers," says a fireman. "They just say it's so-and-so's house, and we know where to go."

Railroad tracks have been replaced with a bike path, the lighthouse is to become a historical museum. Fewer than 1,000 live here year round, and the last of Florida's private bridges, with a $3.20 toll, discourages the merely curious.

Guests have come since 1913, first to an 11-room hotel called the Boca Grande, purchased in the Thirties by streetcar tycoon Barron Collier, who added and added until the inn reached its present size of 140 bedrooms with 38 added living rooms, including 20 cottages.

"We have pretty much built the inn out to the right size for Boca Grande," says the inn's manager. "It's right for our guests, right for the town. Now all we have to do is maintain the status quo."

An altogether proper attitude for a place where civility remains the standard.

Gasparilla Inn, 5th & Palm, Boca Grande, FL 33921. (813) 964-2201. Steve Seidensticker, general manager. 140 rooms and cottages with AC, heat, ceiling fan, bathrooms mostly with tubs, cable TV, direct-dial phone, swimming pools, exercise club, golf course, tennis courts, beach club, croquet lawns, complete water sports, dining room, restaurants, bars, elevator. Children of any age accepted, $15 crib charge. 3rd person in room high-season rate $75 (AP). Pets accepted in cottages. No credit cards. Winter rates: $268 to $312 per room for 2 persons, AP; $344 to $420 per cottage for 2 persons, AP; $150 to $189 for 1, AP; spring rates: $135 single, $198 double, $248 cottage, all MAP; summer/fall rates: $80 to $120 for 2, EP. Off-street parking.

Bradenton — POINTE PLEASANT
Top value with a well-traveled retired couple.

It is a redeeming fact of bed-and-breakfast travel that a place can suffer towering locational imperfection and still satisfy because the quality of hospitality draws guests into the lives of the people who provide it, imperfection and all.

That said, behind Pointe Pleasant looms a towering Alp of an apartment house with none of the grandeur of a snowy peak. Of course that's only an aesthetic evaluation, because what's behind is a 20-some-story condominium with 210 units all occupied by elderly people. And as Audrey Bach likes to say, she is happy that so many others are enjoying the view.

Audrey and Joe Bach live at Pointe Pleasant, a bed-and-breakfast inn. Bradenton is no compelling tourist destination. More likely, guests are passing through, or have to be in town and like getting to know people. Audrey and Joe will satisfy.

Their intention from the outset was to provide the kind of tourist lodging they remember from when they traveled in the Midwest where, in the days before motels became prevalent, travelers who didn't want to spend for fancy hotels could get a decent room for the night and a meal.

"We aren't doing this because we need the income," says Audrey. "We didn't want to be doing nothing."

Joe and Audrey are retired from Michigan. Joe was a steel fabricator and erector in Detroit. They knew about bed-and-breakfast from England where they have offspring and grandchild. They'd come back after their first experiences with B&B there and realized it was a topic of conversation back in the States. They liked the family aspect. "We'd been six in the family and only one bath," recalls Audrey about growing up.

Their idea was to find a retirement life where the weather was good. They traveled coast to coast. California was too busy—"too busy even to talk to you," the found. "Californians are only concerned with how fast they can get from here to there. "Florida was more laid back. "The natives here made us feel at home," says Audrey about Bradenton. "The community has everything I need. We met a lot of people through Unity Church."

Their house was built in 1935 by B.H. Pope for about $6,000. Pope was a banker who was instrumental in expanding an old-line appliance company, DeSears, into the grocery business. He became wealthy and lived into the mid-1980s. Joe and Audrey bought the house from his estate. This section of Bradenton juts into the river and was where the wealthy lived around 1900, early in the history of the town.

The huge condo was already behind the house when Joe and Audrey moved here. And yet for all its bulk, it doesn't generate much noise. You can sit in the front-yard gazebo and hear yourself think. None of the traffic spills down the slope to Joe and Audrey's. The loudest noise might be a window shade flapping in the breeze or the wind chimes on the screened porch.

The house is a southern-style Palladian, peach with white trim, on a street of live oak trees hoary with Spanish moss and royal palms. It has gray shutters and copper gutters and downspouts. Joe has added a cast-iron bench out front for the comfort of the old people who sometimes walk along this street. He has planted bougainvillea, azaleas, and split-leaf philodendron. People from church bring him their plants that aren't doing well. Podocarpus pines are from Mr. Pope's time, as are the many fruit trees that Audrey uses for preparing her continental breakfasts.

Guests enter through the screened sun porch on the west side of the house. Joe has filled the porch with diffenbachia, caladiums, and small almond and ficus trees that threaten to outgrow their confinement. Floral cushions cover wicker.

The living room is homey, with peach-painted walls and a mix of furniture on oak floors with Oriental rugs. There's a gas log fireplace.

Audrey refinishes furniture. Joe cuts glass (a Tiffany-style lamp shows) and takes photos. Several of his photos from Baja California are mounted on walls.

The house has two homey guest bedrooms, the Victorian (which isn't very) and the Rose (for its dhurry-style rug). The Rose has two twin four-poster beds of cherry wood. The bath is a fruity pink-purple. Joe and Audrey are considering adding four more bedrooms, two up and two down, all with private baths.

Breakfast is served in a dining room furnished in antique oak pieces. Guests leave satisfied that they've made new friends.

Pointe Pleasant, 1717 1st Ave. West, Bradenton, FL 34205. (813) 747-3511. Joe and Audrey Bach, hosts. 2 rooms with hall bath (shower and tub), AC, heat, ceiling fan, color TV. House phone for free local calls and credit-card LD calls (no surcharge). Well-behaved children welcome. No pets. Inquire about 3rd person in rooms. No credit cards. Rates per room: Oct.-Apr. $45; rest of year $35. Includes expanded continental breakfast. House refrigerator for chilling wine or beer. No smoking indoors. Off-street parking.

Cabbage Key — CABBAGE KEY INN
Rustic island hideaway that boaters and birds flock to.

Cabbage Key is Florida's only year-round full-service inn on its own island. No bridge, no airstrip, no 7-11. Just six rooms and four cottages, bar and restaurant, docks and boathouse, plus a few private dwellings tucked into the bush. The end of the world without passports.

Up and down the Mississippi, boaters by the time they reach New Orleans have heard of it. Their charts show Cabbage Key at Marker 60 on the Intracoastal Waterway between Fort Myers and Punta Gorda. The vagabond stops of these inland sailors for grog, gab, and a bucket of shrimp give the place the wayward allure of an old Bogart-Bacall flick. The mood is aged in layers of legend and a patina of spirituous amber.

More than any place else in Florida, Cabbage Key is worth an overnight stay. The guest register is rich in testimonials to every circumstance. "Enjoyed celebrating my divorce," reads one. "Can't wait to bring my lady here," another. "We keep coming back," a third.

The attraction is a place without pretense in a privileged setting. Pine Island Sound surrounds large and small islands of dunes and rookeries, isolated beaches, broken-down docks of squatters and millionaires gone other places long ago.

Nearby are beaches so secluded behind stands of mangrove that they urge acts of utmost intimacy, leaving memories that defy camera shots.

Better to stay overnight and let the inn arrange ferry transport from Pineland Marina than come by excursion boat from Captiva Island. Day-trippers arrive for lunch in a parabolic surge. If that's the only way for you, fine; but for most of us, at least 24 hours is required to fully savor the offerings of Cabbage Key.

Mary Roberts Rinehart built the house with her family starting in 1927, and her writing prospered for almost two decades in the seclusion she created for herself here. Writers have kept coming, from Hemingway to John MacDonald, as well as artists and celebrities. Along with less celebrated visitors, they have signed their names to dollar bills patched to walls of the bar, where notable signatures recently added include Jimmy Buffet, E.G. Marshall, Walter Cronkite, Melanie, Ted Koppel, and Neil Young.

Rob Wells came with his family from North Carolina in 1976. He had been admissions officer for a liberal arts college but was looking for an adventure in private enterprise. He bought the place, brought the family, and they became part of the staff. Now it's more of a place for visitors than it ever was. The six rooms are comfortably rustic in cypress and pine. They have private or shared baths, firm beds, a dresser, tables, lamps, mirrors, closets. Four cottages have kitchens, living rooms, and porches, two on the water.

"It's hard to get across to people what the atmosphere is," says Rob. "The place is so sensitive, you can tell if there's a new housekeeper or when anything's disturbing the ospreys nesting atop the water tower. You can sit outside the bar, look down the hill, and see a wild pig swimming to the island, or a pileated woodpecker or red-shouldered hawk. It's very special.

"But it may not satisfy everybody's need for complete privacy because in nice weather there's always a crowd that boats over for lunch, and nighttime—especially weekends—people come for the bar. They might get to singing. You don't know. Even the ones who like it quiet during the day for painting or writing, they usually join in at night.

"It's not going to get any busier than that because the state and federal government own most of the Pine Island-Charlotte Harbor Aquatic Preserve. I own 90 percent of the island. And there aren't going to be any bridges over here."

From atop a 35-foot Indian shell mound long grassed over, you look from the inn past the palms and oaks and cedar across the sound to Useppa Island. The sun is bright early. The throttle is on slow. There's a breeze. You can imagine cold early mornings in winter with fireplaces lit. People re-establish their natural selves in such places. These islands make you believe you have gone backward in time. Why shouldn't you feel rejuvenated?

Cabbage Key Inn & Restaurant, P.O. Box 200, Pineland, FL 33945. (813) 283-2278. Rob Wells, owner. Judy Natale, manager, Joleen Forgie, reservations. Six rooms plus 4 cottages with AC, heat, private or shared bathrooms, some with tub, some with fireplace. Restaurant, bar with TV. Children of any age accepted, $5 extra in room with parents. No pets. MC, Visa. Year-round rates: $65 rooms, $145 cottages (for up to four). Breakfast $6.25; lunch, average $6.50; dinner about $17.95. Free parking, Pineland Marina. Round-trip transportation $12.50 per person.

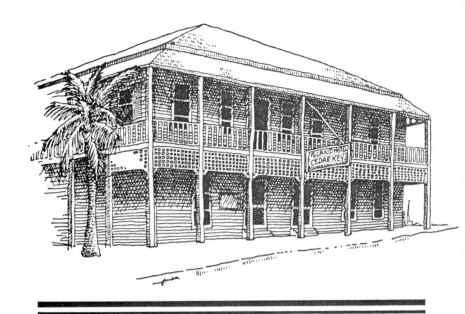

Cedar Key — ISLAND HOTEL
One-of-a-kind pre-Civil War frontier hotel at the
end of the road.

Winter in Cedar Key it's every tern for itself. Late afternoon a few fishermen
are out on the pier. A bundled-up child tells her sister, "Kirsten, we're freeeeeeeez-
ing!" A couple of fisherfolk move off and the gulls move in to check out their
refuse. A woman lets her line be, moves back six paces, takes out her camera for
sunset. Someone asks, "Howdja do today?" "Fed 'em a lot," she mutters. The sun
bulges as it sets as though it were a water balloon threatening to burst. But it just
slips into the sea, semicircle, sliver, slurp. "The sun's over!" Kirsten's sister cries.

The Island Hotel is meant for unbundling. The furnace-heated old cedar and
cypress lobby greets you warmly (coolly, you'll be happy to know, in the summer,
when the French doors are open to the street). Odd benches and uncushioned
chairs, remnant tables, oil lamps, old photos and prints, and barrel planters make
the place old-salt friendly. A hanging stuffed manatee is hugged by a stuffed child.
Potted plants green up the edges. A model boat builder works behind a lattice
partition next to the front desk.

The Island Hotel, listed in the National Register, antedates the Civil War by
12 years. If Cedar Key were nearer the mainland instead of 27 miles at the end
of a swamp road, the hotel would probably have been torn down for condos. Or
maybe not. They are strong on history here.

Apart from Spanish settlements, hardly anyplace in Florida goes as far back.
David Yulee linked the Cedar Keys (as the place was called) to Fernandina at the

start of Florida's railroad age. The cedar was used for pencils. But a literate America was a moving-on America, and when the trees were cut down and the railroad extended to Tampa, Cedar Key, along with its Island Hotel, was left in a backwash. In time, history became the chief resource. Fish, too. History, fish, and nostalgia.

Badly neglected for many years, the hotel has revived on the strength of preservationist claims on tourism. Instead of down and out, these days it looks up-and-at-'em. Revival is in the air and neatens the rooms. Marcia Rogers has turned the corner, and people are flocking to her place.

She bought the Island Hotel in 1980. She offers good value for money. She is sincere and evokes the whole grain in us. She has fixed up the guest rooms so while all are still rustic, all are now air-conditioned, but the mosquito netting still types them as old-time.

Marcia's restaurant is more than just the typical waterfront fish house. Hers offers superb cuisine, the work of Jahn McCumbers, served in a romantic setting of high chocolaty wainscoting topped by a gallery of local art. Tiny starlights turn dark rafters heavenly. Tulip lamps glow from cypress knees hung on the walls. French-glass smoking lamps cast soft light onto pink and brown tablecloths. Seafood comes poached or steamed on top of a bed of raw vegetables or brown rice. The scallop ceviche is silky fresh. The homemade poppy seed bread is served with homemade hummus. You can also get a half order of almost anything, or even just tastes. But no red meats or fried foods.

Marcia learned her priorities as a gestalt psychologist who operated a natural foods restaurant in Vermont, and who naturally attracts artists and writers around her. Therapy combined with wanderlust brought her to Florida for the sun and water. She wanted a "beautiful place."

The Island Hotel resembles a Western adobe outpost, a second-floor balcony (wonderful for afternoon relaxing) and extended roof supported by rough-hewn posts forming a frontier colonnade around the street corner. Much of Cedar Key looks like this, more off-beat than trendy.

Though there are changes in town, they are mostly agreeable. At least four restaurants are now built on pilings. There is a small beach, a historical museum, and many attractive shops with distinctive merchandise have opened in historic buildings.

On the other hand, a bank has gone in where the Gallery at Cedar Key used to be; you hear that oysters are being taken from polluted waters, and that the Seafood Festival and crafts show are getting too much flea market stuff.

Whatever, the Island Hotel fits the way things have always been and is not likely to change.

"I've reached an age and stage where I'm not going to compromise with values," says Marcia. "With all the craziness in the world, I want a place that feels good."

Island Hotel, 2nd & B Streets, Cedar Key, FL 32625. (904) 543-5111. Marcia Rogers, owner. 10 rooms, six with private baths, some with tubs; heat, AC, ceiling fan. Restaurant, cafe. Children of any age accepted. No pets. Smoking outdoors only. Discover, MC, Visa. Year-round rates: $70 weekdays, $78 weekends (share bath), $80 weekdays, $93 weekends (private bath). Full gourmet breakfast included. Dinner around $25 (served only Thurs.-Mon.). Guests can stay throughout the week, but hotel phone answered only by message machine Tues. and Wed. Pay phone in lobby.

Clearwater — THE BELLEVIEW MIDO
Florida's *belle epoque* glory.

They say the Belleview Mido is the largest occupied wooden structure in the world. If so, until 1986 it was also the largest such *unoccupied* structure eight months of the year. For most of its near 100 years, from late April through mid-December, the hotel closed. The grand tradition.

When it opened in 1897, visitors were more concerned with staying warm in winter than cool during Florida summers. Each of its original 145 rooms had a fireplace. Wooden hotels and fireplaces, as newspapers from Fernandina to Key West excitedly headlined, were made for each other.

"Survivor" is written all over the hotel outside and in. It is worth its girth in history.

The Belleview (before Biltmore was added to the name in 1919, replaced by Mido in 1990) was the last great achievement of Henry B. Plant, whose railroad empire opened the west coast of Florida for commerce and tourists. Every room had three electrical lights. Here golf was introduced to Florida hotels, and the Belleview was first in the state to pave an asphalt track for the newly popular sport of racing bicycles.

If the Belleview didn't introduce orotund language into hotel brochures, neither was it first to eschew it. Upon opening, the hotel proclaimed, "The caprice of wind and wave seems to have anchored here . . . . Nature's wondrous charm lies on this pink-shelled, sun-kissed coast . . . . The freshest ring of the true metal of real romance seems to hover between land and sky."

The Belleview Mido remains the treasured hotel of Florida's *belle epoque.*

The hotel's lofty gables are surrounded by thousands of acres, spreading over two 18-hole golf courses and a third a mile away. Its five stories of white clapboard, now preserved under aluminum siding, are stacked like the sloped roofs of alpine chalets. Each of its eight great east- and west-facing gables harbors clusters of eaves, dormers, bays, and windows that resemble villages set in a hillside of green tile.

Seen from the Gulf road two miles across Clearwater Bay, the peaks of the structure suggest dreamy places stamped in passports, maybe some re-creation of homeland facades meant to ease the exile of a sportive monarch.

The structure alone is vast enough that the 20 minutes it takes to stroll around is less a walk than a circumnavigation.

By the time several expansions were completed in 1925, there were almost 400 guest rooms plus 200 for staff, and slightly more than two miles of walkways under the roof. Shops and conference rooms radiated along corridors which opened onto wraparound porches.

The majestic Tiffany dining room is so long that a green 12-foot-wide runner almost dissolves in perspective like the merging rails of a far-off Plant track. The room has the columned, arched formality of a great 19th century railroad terminal: high, wide, its handsomely vaulted ceiling clad in 96 panes of Tiffany glass. Great fanlight windows rise behind louvered shutters, surrounding banquet guests in coats and ties and dresses with the attentive spirit of a military guard.

Chintz, brocade, and damask give the new east lobby the ambiance of a great living room where introductions are made and appointments kept. Commercial transactions are discreetly removed to the side. The suggestion is that all such business has been taken care of elsewhere by factotums. Only some tidying of accounts may be necessary.

Public spaces are set apart one from the other by stained glass partitions. Here are staunchly striped wallpapers in galleries like the reticulated guard of a diplomatic phalanx. Great high-ceilinged meeting rooms and salons are introduced by anterooms that elsewhere would be meeting rooms, and these distinguished by chintz upholstery seemingly trained to climb walls made rosy floral as the insides of cherry cordial candies.

In the early days the privileged came in their Pullman cars, those Disstons, Fords, Newberrys, Whelans, and some first by steamer from New York to Jacksonville, whence by Plant's trains direct to the property.

Then as now, their rooms were wood wainscoted, high-ceilinged, furnished with antiques and reproductions, and graced with lovely watercolor prints. There are deep, wide closets, large uncluttered bathrooms with old-fashioned hexagonal floor tiles. TV and telephones were added later.

Guests golfed with celebrities Rex Beach, Irving S. Cobb, Judge Kenesaw Mountain Landis, and Grantland Rice, as well as all the sport's great names of the day: Babe Didrikson, Walter Hagen, Tommy Harmon, Bobby Jones, Francis Ouimet, Gene Sarazen, among others.

Tennis courts were added, and a 200,000-gallon swimming pool(since closed) that took imported Italian tile-setters two years to build. In 1920 a cabana club was opened on the Gulf beach across Clearwater Bay with private launch service for guests, since discontinued.

Twice the hotel nearly succumbed. During the Depression it fell into receivership after the Bowman chain had acquired it from the Plant family. Although successful seasons were enjoyed again in the early Forties, the property was taken over by the Air Force in 1943 and 1944, then remained closed for two more years while the more recent owners, a group from Detroit, went about its refurbishing.

Adaptations to changing times have resulted in concrete condominiums now flanking the hotel toward the bay. Group business has become necessary to fill the rooms even though the hotel enjoys a large repeat clientele. The mix is about 50-50 between conventioners and vacationers, and as on the great transatlantic liners, one learns to repair to private alcoves when crowds appear.

Recent concens for the hotel's future was resolved by purchase of the property in 1990 by MIDO Development, Inc., an Osaka-based company which also bought the Pelican Country Club Golf Course and the Cabana Club on Sand Key beach. Some $10 million in renovations have already resulted. There's a new lobby and entrance to the east side. A first set of guest rooms has been renovated. The new owner has increased the number and mix of hotel gift shops, added an olympic-sized pool where the south tennis courts were, replaced the old pool complex with five terraced tennis courts, tripled the seating capacity of the Terrace Cafe, added a new kitchen, and repainted and installed new air-conditioning in the Candlelight Dining Room. Other rooms will be refurbished in two subsequent phases, each likely during the summer seasons of 1991 and 1992, at which time a Chinese and a Japanese restaurant will be added. All renovations should be completed by June 1993, according to Christopher Reyelt, general manager since 1983.

Withal, the Belleview Mido endures ever charming, endowed with the spirit of some Christmas workshop, guests ever coming upon next sections of foil and ribbons, the fantasy pleasures of a child endlessly rearranging a cache of fabrics and furnishings for illustrating precious imagination.

As with the great remaining transatlantic liner, the Belleview Mido is an experience not to be missed.

The Belleview Mido, 25 Belleview Blvd., Belleair, Clearwater, FL 34616. (800) 237-8947 (national), (800) 282-8072 (FL), (813) 442-6171. Christopher J. Reyelt, general manager. 350 rooms and suites with AC, heat, bathrooms with tubs, cable TV, phone, dining room, bar, shops, elevators, swimming pools (indoor and out). Whirlpool, and sauna, tennis courts, 18-hole golf course, putting green, beachfront cabana club with complimentary transportation, splendid lawns. Children of any age accepted. Infants free in parents' room; 3rd person in room $15 EP. Small pets accepted with $100 deposit. All major credit cards. Winter rates approximately $155 to $175 double EP; off-season approximately $135-$150 double EP. Suites: add approximately $100 to room rate. A la carte breakfast $7 up; lunch $18 up; dinner $19 up. Off-street parking.

Clearwater Beach – PALM PAVILION INN

Family-friendly Art Deco invention on the beach.

Clearwater Beach, like most of Pinellas County along the Gulf of Mexico, is packed with tourists and hotels. Visitors come who prefer a hustle-bustle vacation scene, with souvenir shops, inexpensive restaurants, and rides with Captain Memo's Pirate Cruises. The scene is more cluttered than honky tonk, and it's popular with families. Though there are beachfront bars, these don't feature competitive boozing or wet T-shirt contests. The broad safe beach holds the scene together—that and the mostly spring-like weather in winter.

The busyness of it all does not necessarily produce anonymity. Larger hotels like the Clearwater Beach have had guests return for generations, so that even in its cavernous new reconstruction a family atmosphere prevails. The same tradition begins in the more intimate Palm Pavilion Inn, an appealing Art Deco-styled property that offers good value and a caring family management.

The hospitality seems especially warm on one of those cold nights that sometimes blow winter in across the Gulf. Kaye and Terry Reinhardt, new parents, run the place family-style for the four Hamilton brothers. The brothers' dad is a Clearwater native who has operated the little Palm Pavilion restaurant on the beach since 1964. The landmark was built in 1926.

The hotel, with its 24 rooms and two efficiencies, is a recent acquisition of the Hamiltons. It was the Sea View Hotel, built in 1947-48. It was rundown but not an eyesore in 1988 when the owner's wife died. The brothers thought it a prudent investment, considering that the property stood across the parking lot from their restaurant.

Ken, the oldest brother, saw that though plain, the hotel's boxiness lent itself to Art Deco embellishment. What guests today might deem a perfect Deco charmer is actually a make-over contrived from Ken's research in Miami Beach. He took 150 pictures of everything that appealed to him there and remodeled the hotel as it now looks from those photos.

Hence the streamlined glass-bricked pylon outlined in vertical bands that mount in tiers at the top and horizontally flair in fare-thee-well overhangs at the bottom. The combination of horizontal accents that interrupt the vertical glass shaft suggest a rocket ascent through layers of clouds.

Colors that might at first seem red, white, and blue turn out to be peach, cream, and aqua. Ken was attracted by the pinks and purples of Miami Beach, but felt something more subdued was appropriate to Clearwater Beach.

The lobby is aqua with rattan furniture in chintz accents that toss the theme colors around in forms and textures. Shell-encrusted lamps, potted palms, and viney plants give an air of the beach and the tropics.

Cream-colored vertical blinds are used in the lobby and throughout the property. In guest rooms the blinds substitute for curtains and drapes. The blinds promote a sleek aspect that highlights the cleanliness of the rooms, though they emphasize the absence of warming textures.

Guest rooms are harmoniously aqua and peachy pink in patterns set by quilted bedspreads in an abstract philodendron design and by a Bermuda sailing scene centered above headboards of bleached pine. Rooms are trim and neat. Beds are firm. The bathroom is modern-tiled with a stall shower and a light above. A little entry foyer also has a plain enclosed overhead light. Another is centered in the ceiling of the bedroom. A rattan chair at the desk extension adds a touch of texture to the otherwise smooth surfaces.

The roof of the little three-story structure has been outfitted with chaises and chairs. It's perfect for viewing sunsets.

Kaye and Terry keep a pot of coffee going all the time in the lobby. They keep daily copies of the St. Petersburg and Tampa papers. There's a TV in the lobby and in each guest room.

Kaye and Terry came from Atlanta to this coast, looking to manage a motel property. Instead they found the Palm Pavilion, where Terry started working in the snack bar. When the Hamilton boys bought the hotel, they asked the Reinhardts to manage it. When the Reinhardts had a baby girl in mid-1990, the Hamiltons promptly took two of their efficiencies out of service to extend the Reinhardts' living space. Guests sense the caring that marks this little property, and they return.

Palm Pavilion Inn, 18 Bay Esplanade, Clearwater Beach, FL 34630. (813) 446-6777. Kaye Reinhardt, manager. 28 rooms and baths, with AC, heat, and in the 2 efficiencies, ceiling fans, and complete kitchens. Color cable TV, direct-dial phone. 50¢ for local calls, no surcharge on credit-card calls. Children of any age accepted, free in parents' room through 12. No charge for crib, cot, rollaway. $8 for third person in room. No pets. AmEx, MC, Visa. Rates: April 4-Sept. 5, $49-$74; Sept. 6-Jan. 31, $42-$60; Feb. 1-April 3, $70-$110, all single or double. Includes complimentary coffee in lobby. Daily newspaper available. Swimming pool, roof sundeck. Smoking permitted. Free off-street parking.

Englewood — MANASOTA BEACH CLUB
Comfortable family-run cottage-style inn on unspoiled Gulf beach.

For many, the Manasota Beach Club is a quest for something in the imagination we know must exist, something that retains the congeniality of a camp without the spartan aspects for building character in children.

You cross from the mainland by bridges north and south to the narrow seven-mile island, the southern end of which lies in Charlotte County, has a public beach, and the beginnings of condo-itis. Even with easy access, the northern portion of Manasota Key, which is in Sarasota County, is remarkably free of commercial intrusion. Like most of the set-back houses it resembles, the Manasota Beach Club can't be seen from the narrow, bush-bordered road. A small sign the size of a couple of rural mailboxes says you have arrived, and you turn toward the Gulf through the scrub.

Here are 18 shingled, peak-roofed wood cottages, the clubhouse, and a variety of recreational uses compatible with nature. The site actually occupies the width of the island on both sides of the road with the buildings on the Gulf, and docks and trails along the mangrove-lined shore of Lemon Bay.

Each cottage is different with a mix of bedrooms, living rooms, baths, and screened deck. Each feels beachy, outfitted in subdued wood and sea tones, pale like driftwood, comfortable and well-lighted, carpeted but not wall to wall. Each is heated, but without telephone or TV.

In the multi-winged, many-peaked clubhouse there are tables for bumper pool and ping-pong, and there's one TV. A piano has a sign that says, "We enjoy your playing of any music except for Chopsticks." A comfortable reading room is served by what must be one of the only resort libraries catalogued by the Dewey Decimal System. There is no bar, but a bottle club.

There are two airy dining rooms, brightly lit by day, illuminated by table lamps for evening. The plainest, green doweled chairs and white-covered tables provide a flattering contrast for guests who come for meals tanned and dressed in plaids and bright colors. In everything the guests are distinct in a setting marked by restraint.

Days are given to sailing, water skiing, windsurfing, fishing, and operating the canopied motor launch on the Intracoastal Waterway. There are courts for bocci, shuffleboard and tennis, a heated swimming pool, miles of beach and trails for jogging and walking. With accommodations for only 50 guests, most of whom come for extended periods during the December-to-April season that the resort is open, the facilities are never strained.

The seasonality is part of an all-but-forgotten tradition in American innkeeping. The same staff that works winters here travels north in spring with owner Bob Buffum and his wife, Sydney, to prepare for the summer season at the Weekapaug Inn in Rhode Island.

Bob's family has been in hotels for three generations. "By keeping the family in the business," he explains, "you nurture a consistent innkeeping style that guests keep returning for. On the other hand, generations multiply and one inn can no longer support all the families."

When Bob looked for his own inn in Florida, he knew what he wanted and he found it in 1960 along what then was a dirt road with only the 100-year-old main buildings and two cottages. The property had once been a nudist camp and later was used by a Long Island couple for their friends.

"It had been closed for two years when we bought it but was in excellent condition," Bob says. "We made improvements and invited a few guests from Weekapaug. They liked it. We worked harder. We set up the kitchen, added resident cottages. We stayed 100 percent within the zoning. We don't battle nature.

"There is no question people are looking for places out of the way, less cement, more natural habitat. How much more pleasant the back roads are! We don't advertise. We write letters to people."

In case you don't get a letter, rooms at the Manasota Beach Club when available during the winter are $140 and $150 per person per night double occupancy including three meals, with 15 percent service and tax.

Manasota Beach Club, 7660 Manasota Key Road, Englewood, FL 34223. (813) 474-2614. Robert and Sydney Buffum, proprietors, assisted by Buffum family management. 18 cottages, 25 rooms with heat, ceiling fan, bathroom with tub-shower. Dining room, heated outdoor pool, lighted tennis court, windsurfing, sailing on Hobie 14 or aboard 38-ft. trimaran, 12-ft. fishing skiff, bicycles, bocci bowling, shuffleboard, croquet, Buff Ball miniature tennis, horseshoes, game room, library, motorboat for water-skiing, nature trails. Children of any age accepted. No pets. No credit cards. Rates winter season only: $140-$150 per person, double occupancy, AP. Inquire for opening and closing dates and off-season EP rates and for rates for additional persons in cottages.

Everglades City – IVEY HOUSE

Rustic and congregate, seasonally available, in the Everglades.

Ivey House is the closest you'll get to a hostel in Florida's bed-and-breakfast trade. Guests mix in easygoing informality in the common room and the bench-set dining room that's more like an indoor picnic area.

The best the house can boast is make-do construction with straightforward unfussy furniture. The 10 rooms line up across from each other like double rows of buttons on a seaman's pea coat. Men's and women's bathrooms are down the hall. And if you can't exactly prepare your own meals in the kitchen, it's sure a place to stand around while Joan or David is preparing the meal of the moment, and you are reliving the day's adventure—or getting ready to live it.

Call it double B&B: bed-and-breakfast back to basics.

People meet easily anyplace in Everglades City because most are here for the same reason: to go touring in Everglades National Park or to fish. Canoeists are likely readying to shove off for a week in the Glades. Most of them outfit at North American Canoe Tours. They paddle waters warm with the ooze of life in a fecund ecology of mangrove swamp, wild beaches, and teeming bird rookeries. Campsites on stilts provide viewposts for everything from alligators to zoom-shots of bald eagles.

The Ten Thousand Islands area here might have made 10,000 resort condominiums, but fortunately the national park was established in 1947 before developers had yet figured out how to get rid of the mosquitoes. If you want a look at how developers scalped nature in this setting, have a look at Marco Island just west of Everglades City off the Tamiami Trail toward Naples. Nothing is there that wasn't built. Marco Island is an ill-fitting toupee on bald land where there used to be luxuriant growth.

David Harraden operates the canoe tours as well as the Ivey House. After nine years of renting the rundown house, he was ready to buy when it came up for sale in 1989, 60 years after it was built for workers on the Tamiami Trail that cut across the Everglades from Tampa to Miami. The house had been a recreation hall, a bowling alley, and a theater. Earl Ivey, who ran one of the steam dredges on the Trail, turned the house over to his Mrs. to run. She earned a reputation for homemade meals.

The house looks and feels like an elongated double-wide, up on block mounts, made of grain-finish Southern pine. You enter up a few open stairs that were added once the structure was in place. The common room is full of sofas and upholstered chairs. People read the magazines, talk, and watch the videos that David rents for entertainment.

A lot of map work gets done here. People talk about their cameras and camping gear. Guys checking out on their way back to New Mexico are talking to women just in from New Hampshire. They're swapping tales about kayaking the Nantahala or the Colorado, about hiking the Appalachian Trail or cycling North Carolina's Outer Banks. All B&Bs make it easier than in hotels for people to meet each other, but at Ivey House guests are into the camaraderie of the shared search for adventure.

There's no smoking or drinking allowed in the house. There are quiet hours from about 10 o'clock on. The TV gets turned down, but you still might want to consider rooms at the far end of the hall if you're a light sleeper.

Each guest room has twin beds with firm new mattresses, a night table, and a mirror on the door. There are room air conditioners, but not heaters. During the few chilly nights a year, you can pile on blankets—and there's wall heat in the halls. When it gets down to 40 degrees or below, guests leave their doors open.

Though David began B&B operations serving only a continental breakfast, he's thinking about making that a full one and adding dinner service. If he hasn't, eat at the Oyster House Restaurant. Whatever grows in the sea, they serve. There's beer and wine and full bar service. A superior hangout. You'll probably see most everybody from the Ivey House at dinner. Everglades City is a movable feast. Ivey House is at the heart of it.

The Ivey House, 107 Camellia St., Everglades City, FL 33929. (813) 695-3299. David Harraden, proprietor; Joan and Howard Hopkins, managers. 10 rooms, with men's and women's bathrooms down the hall (3 shower stalls men's, 2 women's). AC, fan, no room heat. Heat in hall. Color cable TV in living room with phone for free local calls and credit-card calls. Children accepted 10 and over, same charge as adults. No pets. MC, Visa, checks accepted. Closed May-October. $20 per person. Includes continental breakfast. No smoking. Free off-street parking.

Everglades City — THE ROD AND GUN CLUB

Once-famous frontier lodge in a swamp town.

The ghost of big-time haunts Everglades City. Illusions are the devil to get rid of. There's no limit to what you might believe, once you've seen streetcars in the swamps, then the railroad, and the almightiest jetport in the world. . . . Almost.

You can sit out a storm on the screened porch of the Rod and Gun Club. Have a drink. Look out to the swamp across the Barron River. Frontier lodgings, but damned fine for that.

They couldn't have been finer at one time. Barron Collier hired Kaiser Wilhelm's chef to cook for a parade of notables chauffeured in, after arriving by yacht, or piloted onto the landing strip. Zane Grey and four Presidents came, John Barrymore and Gypsy Rose Lee.

Mr. Collier was a Chicago millionaire who poured money into southwest Florida land. By 1923 he owned more of the state than anybody else—almost 1.3 million acres of the county he carved from two others and named for himself. He was itchy to do something big. Something bigger.

He dreamed up a coast-to-coast road across the Everglades. He set his command post on the high ground nearest his route, a farming ridge called Potato Creek settled in 1883 by W. S. Allen, who built himself a mansion there. By the time Collier finished the Tamiami (Tampa-Miami) Trail five years later in 1928, he'd already put up a bank, railroad station, supermarket, and theater, and made it headquarters for his diversified empire. Grandly, he called the vegetable patch Everglades City. He made it the county seat and added a Grecian courthouse.

Along with everything else, Collier acquired the old Allen mansion. He added rooms and transformed it into the luxurious club it was to remain for three decades.

How important was the Rod and Gun Club?

"Without it, this wouldn't have been nothing," says former mayor Sammy Hamilton, a native of Chokoloskee Island, who used to boat over and back to school, 40 minutes each way, before they built the causeway. "This was everybody's living. You were either working in the hotel or charter-boating. The hotel fed the whole town."

It might have lasted if Hurricane Donna hadn't rampaged in 1960. But probably not. The trains had already quit coming. East Naples was about to capture the county seat. That was okay with Collier heirs. The old man had died and none of the brass cared to stay on in the Glades. When they left, they took the bank. The hurricane had blown down the movie house.

The Rod and Gun Club continued but it wasn't the same. Opening to the public didn't help. Bankruptcy wiped out one operator. Another added a screened pool, patio, and 42 motel rooms. A 1973 fire destroyed the rooms, but the water-filled pool saved the lodge.

The dream was revived in the early Seventies when a jetport loomed in the swamp nearer to Everglades City than downtown Miami. For a while the lodge was filled with Federal Aviation Agency and airline people. A retired oil company man put $3 million into a marina, restaurant, and modern motel. But nature lovers nixed the jetport. The motel died with the dream.

Then Everglades City folks dazzled by riches snatched at even wilder schemes. Some good ole boys, savvy as gators, took to boating in bales of Colombian Gold. The law couldn't track them in the swamp but zapped 'em when high living showed up in town. Mighty suspicious without any Colliers around!

People of lesser dreams took over the Rod and Gun. Pull-top beer cans, no BS, quiet. That's what guests say they like about it now. With its white clapboard exterior with bright yellow and white canvas awnings, some mildewed, the place seems to be waiting. All the rooms upstairs where the swells used to stay are shut. Guests nowadays sleep in clean, efficient cottages with standard amenities.

When not fishing, they hang out in the lodge, all dark red cypress with ceiling fans, the walls mounted with tarpon, paintings of the sea, ship models, mounted lures, and fishing rods and chronometers.

The high-ceilinged dining room, the dark corner bar, a larger one chummy in winter, the huge lobby fireplace and billiard table—all good. Enough guests come in winter to pay the bills for all year.

Sammy Hamilton says the future lies with promoting the place as a gateway to Everglades National Park. You can doubt it a little because he has the tour concession, but the Rod and Gun, the fishing, and the boat tours do fit together. Maybe, after all the busts, the place will make it on the natural features that started Everglades City more than 100 years ago.

Rod and Gun Club, 200 Riverside Drive, Everglades City, FL 33929. (813) 695-2101. Martin Bowen, owner. 25 rooms with AC, heat, bathrooms, some with tub, cable TV, lobby phone, swimming pool, tennis courts. Children of any age accepted, free in parents' room to 5. 3rd person in room $6. Pets accepted. No credit cards. Year-round rates: $47 single, $50 double. Restaurant and bar. Breakfast $3.75 up, lunch $7 up, dinner $12 up. Off-street parking.

Holmes Beach – HARRINGTON HOUSE BED & BREAKFAST

Excellent quality on a bridged island amenably low scaled.

The sea, the little beach, and Harrington House compose a serene order. The house inside and out balances distinctive structural features with good taste in color and furnishings. Betty and Walt Spangler and Jo and Frank Davis supply unobtrusive care. Vacationing well here takes no effort.

The good prospect begins with seven-and-a-half-mile-long Anna Maria Island that curves a sensuous lip of beach to the mouth of Tampa Bay. From the lee side of the island you look to the sculptural Sunshine Skyway that vaults long-distance traffic north and south over the bay. Immediately you feel forgotten—the condition of choice. Anna Maria Island is a cluster of three little communities of unpretentious houses and stores where bicycles are the way to get around. Good, small seafood restaurants and convivial bars rim the Gulf of Mexico.

The house, which takes its name from Betty's family, sits back from a shell-spread drive behind a picket fence. Its look is curiously Tudor, with steep eaves and a mossy green color. A latched gate gives way to a courtyard, whereupon the beach and the Gulf appear. You sense how right the setting is, that you've brought yourself to a place where the pieces fit. You feel *you* fit.

The satisfying look is no accident—the house was reworked to produce it. A beach house when built in 1925, it was smaller then and had less texture. The house deteriorated during two years when no one lived in it. Neighbors were delighted to have the house remodeled and put back into use. No one objected to the Spanglers taking in guests. Anna Maria Island caters to vacationers in small, mostly old-fashioned shoreside apartments.

The third story was added to the house, as was the pool between the house and beach. Another newer feature is the distinctive slat railing around the upper two stories. The slats, the textured stone of the lower level, and the boldly paned French doors that lead from guest rooms to the porches give the house a virile texture matched inside by elegant spaces and thoughtful hospitality.

Most striking is the 20-foot-high living room. The height easily accommodates a big stone fireplace. A paddle fan turns high above. Wrought-iron sconces add to the manorial aspect. Furniture is amply proportioned and mostly in subdued chintz that balances the grandeur with the don't-take-anything-too-seriously look of the tropics. Elegance is tempered for leisure.

A sure hand has chosen the greens. Green harmonizes with white and wood tones. Lambent variations please in the subdued chintz, in leafy patterns, in forest-quiet solids that cover arrangements of sofas and side chairs.

Second- and third-story rooms, all but one overlooking the sea, are reached from inside by a pair of staircases that hug the high walls. Furniture styles mix Chippendale, Georgian, and Empire. Gauzy pink curtains are stylishly swagged to suit. The soothing greens combine with soothing rose. Door knobs throughout are floral porcelain.

Beds are firm, some four-posters, some kings, queens, some brass. All have night tables and lamps to either side except in the small Primrose Room. Porches are under pines and seagrapes, and guests can descend from them to the pool and beach without having to pass through the house. A nice touch throughout is the decoratively arranged hats, homage to the possibility that famed milliner Lilly Dache may have stayed here once.

Betty serves a full breakfast in the dining room. Guests can dawdle mornings and still be served at 10:30. She will provide a cheese platter for those who bring their own wine. On cool evenings guests can enjoy hot chocolate by the fireplace, and pop corn.

Betty and Walt have obviously become masters of this style of hospitality. Guests will feel well rewarded. Harrington House is one of Florida's best.

Harrington House Bed & Breakfast, 5626 Gulf Dr., Holmes Beach, FL 34217. (813) 778-5444. Betty and Walt Spangler and Jo and Frank Davis, innkeepers. 7 rooms with private baths, AC, heat, 6 with ceiling fan. Cable color TV, phone on desk in living room for free local and credit-card calls. Pool, beach. Children accepted 12 and over. No pets. MC, Visa, personal checks accepted. Rates: May-Nov., $79-$99; Dec.-Apr., $95-$115, single or double. Includes full breakfast, rose in room for special occasions, free use of kayaks, floats, chairs for the beach. 3rd person in from $10. Newspaper available. Free off-street parking.

Inverness — THE CROWN HOTEL
Excellent value at the crown jewel of Florida's historic re-creations.

Carrie Ella Mountain's earliest recollections are of Sunday dinner after church at the Orange Hotel. "We all went, didn't we? Sunday dinner was from noon to 2:00. You couldn't tell any difference from dinner to supper. They always had so much food!

Now the Orange is the Crown, and it had to do some moving around before becoming the pride of Inverness and one of Florida's finest hotels.

Carrie's Aunt Tom took over the property early in the century, soon after it was moved the second time. First was when they made a hotel out of what had been the first commercial building in Tompkinsville. They called it the Orange Hotel and it was two stories on the north side of Main Street. That was as far as the paved road went before it turned to limerock if you went to Crystal River or Homosassa Springs.

As part of the hotel's second move, new owners jacked it up and added a new ground floor. They put in stores along the street, and enough rent money came in that after Aunt Tom's steady management for 55 years, the place wasn't torn down.

After Aunt Tom's death in the late 1950s, the hotel kept turning over. Everybody would think it was a good idea to run it. So they would open—and close again.

By then the Orange had become the Colonial Hotel, and it could easily have gone up in flames. But in 1980 a Scotsman visiting the west coast on a deal that fell through saw the old place and revived it. Nearly a century before, a Scotsman had renamed Tompkinsville because its lakes and hills reminded him of Inverness. The second Scot renamed the hotel the Crown.

The hotel was closed and gutted. Nothing remained but bearing walls. Estimates are that $2 to $3 million went into turning the place around. Late in 1990, Welsh patrons bought it.

Today the Crown occupies the same compact site as the Orange and the Colonial before it. Its wood exterior is white and its windows are set off by white-trimmed maroon awnings. The old sun porch has become a pair of banquet rooms called Buckingham and Windsor. A canopied archway protects guests entering from cars on Seminole Avenue.

But for its attractive architecture and a red antique double-decked London bus stationed out front, the hotel does little to announce itself.

Inverness has not gone all Tudor and Anglophile trendy, even though the hotel is a piece of England transplanted. The entrance is through leaded glass doors into a lobby where replicas of the Crown Jewels are displayed in illuminated wall cases. A circular staircase sweeps grandly under a chandelier to a second-story sitting area and fireplace, the steps flanked by portraits of British monarchs.

Guest rooms on the second and third floors—there are only 34, and they rent from $40 to $70 a night, $115 for the suites—are individually furnished in the refined style that marks the hotel throughout. Brass headboards, fine patterned wallpapers, reproductions of Queen Anne chairs and desks, and gold-plated bathroom fixtures distinguish the interiors.

The restaurant is Churchill's, the tavern the Fox and Hound. There is a pool in a diminutive patio garden. It is all quite modest, as if by its compactness and good taste The Crown absorbs the patronage of the surrounding population who spread its word, while the hotel itself remains intensely concentrated on its little Seminole Avenue site.

As for the locals, Carrie Ella says, "We love the place. It's become a center of activity again. We can remember when the mines closed. The mill had already shut down. Turpentining was finished. The fishing industry on the west side was about all there was for payrolls. We used to make an evening's outing out of going down to the station to watch the Southland go through.

"Now we've been discovered, and we're growing fast. Like that or not, so many hotels that were the centers of country and community life have not come back. This one has. We love their British accents and manners."

The Crown Hotel, 109 N. Seminole Ave., Inverness, FL 32650. (904) 344-5555. 800-82-CROWN. Nigel and Jill Sumner, managers/owners. 34 rooms and suites with color cable TV, AC, heat, direct-dial room phone, bathrooms with tub. Restaurants, bar, pool, elevator. Children of any age accepted, $6 for rollaway or third person in room. AmEx, MC, Visa. Year-round rates: $40-$60 single room; $70 double room; $115 2-room suite. Average meal prices: breakfast $6, lunch $6, dinner $20. Off-street parking.

Naples – INN BY THE SEA
Exceptional lodgings in a quiet, historic old town.

Thank heavens Elise Sechrist was willing to go through hell to get her bed-and-breakfast opened. She spent three years at hearings before finally getting permission.

The house, built in 1937, initially had boarders, and later became single family. When owners let the house deteriorate, it became an unlicensed flophouse. The city didn't want anything remotely like that. Over the years Naples had changed from a quiet fishing village to what Elise calls "the heart of Southern affluence."

True enough. At Inn By the Sea you're amidst one of the choice leisure communities of Florida. Posh estates extend south to the end of the barrier island. Charming cottages once owned by Vanderbilts punctuate streetscapes. The elegant shops of Third Street are two blocks away.

You might miss the sign for Elise's inn because it is just above a fast-growing hedge. The two-story house is faded pink with white shutters and trim. Out front are coconut palms in a sandy drive where a few Adirondack chairs and a glider sit.

You can come in with sand on your feet and it's no crisis. The place is casual but not utterly. It feels like a substantial old beach house, rich in good ideas.

The sun parlor is coral pink with white wicker, full of plants, a vermeuil lamp, coral paddle fan with tulip lamps, and white tiered shades. A stone fireplace warms guests on chilly days. The ceiling and borders are pine. There are wicker pieces and a gaily painted straw chair. A loopy ribbon stencil, chintz cushions, ruffly throw pillows—all colorful yet controlled.

The breakfast room is country French with awning windows and venetian blinds. Guests in the morning are more likely to talk about the good book they read the night before than about any night out. There are many good restaurants, but otherwise Naples closes down early.

Elise's rooms are full of exceptional features, in many cases left from a designers' benefit that featured her house when it reopened. Hence the circus-tent green and white-striped ceiling and wallpaper in the room called Captiva. The headboard is made from repainted 18th-century armoire doors. A nona chair is reproduced in green.

The room she calls Gasparilla has an ornate brass and white iron bed that fits with the wicker furniture. There's a lovely little carpeted bath with a hot ceiling lamp that you will appreciate after a winter evening on the pier.

The Sanibel room has a pencil-post queen bed with patterned sheets, botanical prints, and a little desk and chair. A striking feature is the wood ceiling and floor.

Upstairs, the Bokeelia room has swagged curtains tied with blue ribbons, twin maple beds with tatted sheets, and dhurry rugs. The Useppa has a double brass bed and wicker, with charming little window-top theater curtains. Keewaydin is a suite with a pullout brass bed painted white, and a seafoam pine bed with matching seafoam rug, pillow linen, frame trim, and stenciling. The bathroom is also seafoam mixed with pine butterfly cushions on wicker.

Naples is a town for walking or bicycling to restaurants, boutiques, and art shops. Stores have neatly symmetrical shutters. The Naples Mercantile Company that dated from 1919 is now Wind In the Willows, a gift shop behind lovely tan with black wrought-iron porch and benches below. The Chef's Garden and Truffles are two of the best restaurants. Also, the Palm Cottage is on 12th Avenue South.

A bed-and-breakfast makes so much sense in Naples, where the motels are low-rise, dignified, and not part of chains, where commercial uses are kept away from a beach that is still lined with elegant houses under groves of palms.

The pleasure of it all is now easily available, thanks to Elise's ordeal.

Inn By the Sea, 287 11th Ave., S., Naples, FL 33940. (813) 649-4124. Catlin Maser, innkeeper. 5 rooms, 1 suite with 4 private baths, 1 down the hall shared by 2 rooms. All with AC, heat, ceiling fan. Cable color TV in living room. Phone in dining room for free local and credit-card LD calls. Children accepted 16 and older. No pets. MC, Visa and personal checks accepted. Rates: Dec.21-Apr. 30, $70-$115; May 1-Dec. 20, $45-$85, single or double. No extra charge for 3rd person in suite. Includes full uncooked breakfast. Newspaper available, coaster-brake bicycles free. Free off-street parking. No smoking indoors.

North Captiva Island – SAFETY HARBOR CLUB

Townhouses and full houses on an island not too fussed over.

The test of a good vacation place is whether on gray and rainy days you can still have a good time. Not with bowling alleys, mall shopping, projection TV, saloons, tanning salons, and video arcades.

With a book.

Suppose there's little else. An island without a bridge. Beaches, boating, shelling, swimming. Paradise, sure. But on a $100 day the sun never shines?

How well does it satisfy in a stuffed chair under a rain-tattooed roof with a book you've been meaning to read but haven't because the weather's been too good to be inside?

If you're like rental agents Gary Walker and Mary Jane McKnight, it's something you look for. You don't ask for the rain, but you take what you get when you're helpless with nesomania. Island fever.

After visiting islands around the world, the pair settled on North Captiva. A barrier island but not exactly pristine. There's talk about a contract post office for the 25 folks who live here year-round. There already are three tiny restaurants that stock personal items and Safety Harbor Club tee shirts.

Until a 1921 hurricane there was only one Captiva. A wind- and tide-driven channel split the island. Of 650 acres separated to the north, the state preserves almost three-quarters undeveloped. The upper quarter with a grassy airstrip and safe harbor has been platted in a mostly cheek-by-jowl series of subdivisions which probably won't get built. Real estate speculation cooled when the state ruled against bridging Florida's remaining unconnected barrier islands.

Only the 37-acre Safety Harbor Club has been laid out with imagination. Shell roads exclusive for golf carts or walking explore through native vegetation from Gulf to Pine Island Sound. Houses are sited to curve around a freshwater lake, a clubhouse, two tennis courts, and birding tower. A cluster of townhomes and the Over The Water Restaurant make up a village at the landing.

The few houses so far are raised old-Florida style on structural pilings with spacious screened verandas, open decks, lofty cathedral ceilings, wide overhangs, rough cedar trim, and expanses of windows and sliding doors.

These are owned by a wealthy international clientele who in 15 minutes boat over from Pineland Marina to dress down in T-shirts and flip-flops that hint at the eccentric life squatters on the island once enjoyed among the herons and coots, sea grapes and pines, nowadays colored with hibiscus and bougainvillea.

When not in use, their houses are available from Gary and Mary Jane. The lodgings are decidedly comfortable, rich in wood, tile, metal, and glass. Kitchens are stocked with quality cookware and dishwasher. Clean white plaster walls are typically brightened by museum posters and ornamental crafts. Furniture groupings are designed for comfort and easy care in spacious living rooms. Beds are the firmest with night tables and bright lamps on either side for reading. Baths are smartly tiled, supplied with plush towels and digital scales. There are ample deep closets, plenty of extra linens in decorator patterns, and a washer and dryer. These houses want for nothing.

Maybe it's their uncluttered aspect—completeness without the accumulation they'd bear if anyone lived here steadily—that makes them so appealing and so library quiet on one of those days when inside makes more sense than out.

But even on those days, gloomy dark before the rain, North Captiva's pleasures are deeply satisfying.

On such uncompromising mornings maybe no one else shows along miles of beach, as if the island had been evacuated and one's eccentricities have daunted even Gary and Mary Jane from intruding. What's left of green sea and blue sky are thoroughly grayed. All is ready for the appearance of submarines. On such a bleak day the shore remembers nothing of yesterday's easy pleasure. The sea has the look of a growling dog.

Downwind from the twittering telegraphy of a flock of orange-billed gulls, two couples forage for shells on a sandspit with flocks of sandpipers in high-stepping ballet. Thick gray clouds lower an imprisoning sky. The force-tickled tops of the cabbage palms resent the breeze.

Rain gusts in. The beaten sea still stalks the stilted sandpipers. A beachcomber waits out the shower as others might ascend some peak for the mystical word of a hermit guru. Chill settles in bones.

Now the sheets streak the near sky, urging beachcomber onto the boardwalk across the dune, quickly down a path and up stairs to sanctuary.

One dries in luxurious pile, sets the kettle to boil, settles in—yes, why not—with *Florida Tropic*. The right place, the time. Better than home.

Safety Harbor Club. Arrange overnights through Islander Realty, P.O. Box 334, Pineland, FL 33945. (813) 472-3000. 25 homes and 33 townhouses complete in every respect. Children accepted. No pets. No credit cards. Rates: townhouses $160 (summer), $210 (winter) (for up to 4 or 6); houses $170-$235 (summer), $220-$350 (winter) (for up to 8). Rates are per night for 3-night stay. Call or write for other rates. Lunch at Over The Water Restaurant, Grady's Store, or Barnacle Phil's: about $8-$9; dinner $15-$20. Limited seating, reservations advised. Beer/wine at Barnacle Phil's and at Grady's. Supplies available at Grady's. $3 a day parking at Pineland Marina.

Palmetto — FIVE OAKS INN
Riverside with frilly hospitality.

Bette and Chet Kriessler, who retired from careers of looking after people, are looking after people. When they opened their Five Oaks Inn in Palmetto early in 1987, Bette and Chet were a rarity: a retired couple running a Florida inn. Soon they'll be joined by their daughter Pam and her husband, Frank Colarito. Together they helped find the place.

"You see, we wanted to be around people, but in a more friendly way than motels allow," says Chet. "Sure, when we were kids there were guest houses and tourist cabins. But all that died. We didn't know about bed-and-breakfasts. Then we saw how much closer to guests you can get with a B&B, and we knew we'd gotten the right concept. After that we just had to find the place."

The place they found turned out to be looking for them.

"Well, yes," says Jo Harrison, president of the Palmetto Historical Society. "We couldn't imagine who was going to buy this beautiful old house on the river. It's too big for modern families. We were just sick at what might happen. You know there are condominiums that started moving in just as close as across the street. When Chet and Bette bought this and asked the city's cooperation for turning it into a bed-and-breakfast, we knew at last the house would be preserved."

What a landmark it is! With Bette and Chet's Five Oaks Inn, the property came full circle after 136 years.

The site is nothing less than the original settlement of Palmetto. It's where in 1851 Joseph and Juliann Atzeroth from Bavaria, who first looked at the area eight years before, moved into a partially completed log house. After they built a larger house nearby, they took overnight guests at the log house and served them breakfast.

After the Civil War, the Atzeroths sold the riverfront site to an interim owner who stayed little more than a year before selling in turn to Samuel Sparks Lamb. There were fewer than 10 families living in the area then, but it wasn't long before S.S. Lamb became the leading merchant and one of the largest landowners in the rapidly growing farm area around Manatee County.

It was one of his sons, Dool, who with his wife, Lillie, chose the site of the original log house for their home. They built that with a set of plans ordered from a Sear's catalog. Today, the house two generations of Lambs lived in until 1987 is in a quiet residential district listed in the National Register of Historic Places.

It's a terra cotta and white landmark on a low rise at the river, five miles from the Gulf. You can sit on the lawn or the enclosed porch—where Bette likes to serve breakfast—and look across to bustling Bradenton. About the only noises are an airplane drone, crow caws, gull bleats, maybe a boat motor.

The only crime in this kind of setting is stolen moments.

Four guest rooms are all on the second floor, each with its own bath, each fully carpeted. If anything, the all-over carpeting somewhat detracts from the rich craftsmanship of the interiors. It's the way Bette and Chet found it, to which she has added lots more frills and heavy drapes.

The place looks like a retired couple's wish to have somebody to look after again—and look, they're saying, how we're ready to lavish care.

Aunt Lillie's Suite overlooks the river that can be seen better in winter when the oaks lose their dense foliage. What was Lillie Lamb's sewing room is a comfortable sitting room. Miss Evelyn's is five-sided, and the Cap'n's Quarters has twin beds and good desk space.

But the beguiling choice is the Palmetto Room. It's a closed-in sun porch. Where it narrowly edges around back of the upstairs, Bette has fitted in a vanity and a rocker that are part of a room full of wicker. There are eight windows and three exposures. The room is pink and white and bright. At starting rates of $55 double the five summer months, $65 October through April, it's a bargain. Full breakfast for two comes with it.

The living and dining rooms feature high shelf-topped wainscoting, geometric open-beamed ceilings, and a variety of antiques. Bette loves to point out the rocker with its own rocking footrest she thought was a pincushion.

The library is a separate dark room full of books about American presidents plus cassette tapes of old-time radio shows like "The Shadow," "Amos 'n Andy," and Arch Oboler's "Lights Out Everybody."

Prized, too, are some of the pictures Bette and Chet have collected from years in the hospitality trade. Chet was a bartender, Bette a hotel hostess. (Bette makes a welcoming rum-based Manatee Sunset, Chet serves it.) One or the other is pictured with Dorothy Lamour, Cesar Romero, Broderick Crawford, Martha Raye. There's one of Bette with Helen Hayes where Bette is showing off the pendant she bought at auction that Helen Hayes wore in "Victoria Regina" in 1927.

Palmetto remains a quiet town in one of Florida's agricultural regions. If you're nearby on business or idly vacationing, Bette and Chet want to look after you.

Five Oaks Inn, 1102 Riverside Dr., Palmetto, FL 34221. (813) 723-1236. Bette and Chet Kriessler, innkeepers, with Pam and Frank Colarito. 4 rooms and baths (2 with tubs), with AC, heat, 2 rooms with ceiling fan, TV in library, house phone for incoming messages, collect or credit-card outgoing LD calls, no charge for local calls. No children, no pets. No smoking in guest rooms. Evening complimentary cocktail, and welcoming Manatee Sunset. Fresh flowers and complimentary wine for special occasions. MC, Visa. Rates: May-Sept.: $55 to $90; Oct.-April: $65-$100, single or double. 3rd person in room $15. Includes full breakfast. Off-street parking.

St. Petersburg — BAYBORO HOUSE
Victorian flair without fussiness, close to downtown,
across the street from Tampa Bay.

Is it really possible to be in a neighborhood of turn-of-the-century houses facing the unblocked Florida shore—Tampa Bay in this case, a surprisingly clear body of water for swimming, shelling, crabbing?

The idea takes getting used to, but Bayboro House persists in an attitude of open access to the waterfront. With the gross weight of experience otherwise, how remarkable that out front of a small guest house—certainly defenseless against zoning lawyers—there is only this two-lane waterfront street, a sensible sidewalk, a strip of grassy park, sandy beach, and the flats of the bay.

Instead of monumental structures, the scene is populated by a parade as eclectic to the visitor as it is predictable to Gordon and Antonia Powers, husband and wife proprietors in middle age, all children away at school or married.

At turn of the tide, fisherdogs champ the water full of darting pinfish. A woman steps out of her shorts in a swimsuit for a noonday tan. The "advertising air force" flies over from nearby Whitted Field. Late afternoon motorists dressed in coat and tie, steadying the wheel with both hands, drive to the Polish-American

Club. Oscar the snowy egret flaps to a landing in the grassy yard for his late afternoon feeding of whatever he's trained Gordon and Antonia to provide.

The scene is enjoyed from slatback rockers behind white pickets on a wraparound porch. Two stone lions flank the six steps behind the little semicircular drive centered by a grassy plot. Each stair has a conch shell marking its sides. From across the bay an easterly breeze blows the American flag. (Sometimes, you learn, the wind can blow fiercely, and protective screens drop over the porch.) Hanging baskets sway. The large new sign seen from the street tells visitors: 1719, Bayboro House, Bed and Breakfast, Guest Lodging.

1719 is of course the address on Beach Drive. The many-gabled house was built between 1903 and 1907. Bayboro is one of St. Petersburg's oldest sections. This is the most attractive house on the street.

Gordon and Antonia share your pleasure to be here. Bayboro House is as much their stage as their living. They seek to delight while maintaining a backstage presence. Their hand is not meant to be seen.

They have put in place their collections of treasures with so practiced an eye that visitors hesitate to compliment them. Will their hosts be flattered by guests who marvel that anything can be so contrived, so curled to the lip of bursting—but in a succession of last minutes utterly checked?

Without question, everything is in place. You want to spend time pausing place to place in these rooms. No rush. How blessed to be here at leisure, not on tour. No guide wanted, thank you. You feel like trying out every chair, every antimacassared loveseat, the ruby red fainting sofa. Good that nothing is cordoned off like in a museum. You remember other times in life when you have felt invited to touch but couldn't.

Antique marble-topped tables, side tables, gas lamps, rockers, wingback chair with footstool, plants, cameo scenics and staid family photos, player piano, fabric flowers in hanging pink pitchers, miniature wicker atop the runner atop an extended wall heater, decorative wall wreath, a miniature straw hat hanging by a red ribbon, a lacy sachet strung from a pink one.

Here is a teddy bear in a lace collar of dried baby's breath seated at the foot of an ornate trunk topped by a hand fan, baby boots, a rose-ribboned little wreath. Everywhere are straw baskets and pedestals, cut-glass candy dishes rimmed in lustrous rose, windows, columns, carved frames, a little stone Cupid.

In the quiet of a sunny Sunday you have found yourself alone with a grandfather clock tending the quarter hours. How many have passed? Is this old time, or merely time?

There are three rooms for overnight guests: the Rose with its baffling entry to the bathchamber, the Yellow, and the Captain's, a little more plush. There is also one seasonal rental apartment. After six years, Gordon and Antonia feel at home with people who come and go, and want to spend more time with their guests. Gordon continues to teach in the county school system.

There is more of everything than you can ask for. A sign in the Yellow Room says, "This room is equipped with Edison Electric Light. Do not attempt to light with a match. The use of Electricity is in no way harmful to health, nor does it affect the soundness of sleep."

Rates are $65 to $75 year-round and include a continental breakfast, newspaper, and the satisfaction that you have done something good for yourself by having found this place.

Bayboro House on Tampa Bay, 1719 Beach Drive, S.E., St. Petersburg, FL 33701. (813) 823-4955. Gordon and Antonia Powers, proprietors. 3 rooms with AC, ceiling fan, heat, TV, bathrooms with tub except the Yellow, shower only. Inquire about apartment. House phone for messages, free local calls, and credit-card and collect LD calls. Children, pets not accepted. MC, Visa. Smoking on veranda only. Year-round rates: $65 to $75, includes continental-plus breakfast and newspaper, use of laundry facilities for $1. Inquire about rates for carriage house, seasonal apartment. Weekly and monthly rates on request. Off-street parking.

St. Petersburg — THE HERITAGE
Civic-minded restoration in the heart of downtown.

The cargo-cult invocations of St. Petersburg's elders are about to pay off. When that happens, good fortune may finally bless The Heritage. Anyplace else, a property as good as this wouldn't have to wait for a baseball team to fall from the sky. And lately, it's been doing pretty well without one.

There was much sniggering in the early Eighties about "senile" city fathers in this city known as a haven for the elderly. They were likened to cargo cultists, Pacific Islanders abruptly dislodged from the Stone Age during World War II when construction of airstrips suddenly brought from the sky a great bounty of material goods. When war ended, the islanders—by then completely dependent on outside ways of life but with the stuff of life no longer divinely dispatched—sought to re-invoke the gods by rebuilding their airstrip temples.

Skip east a half world and by nearly a half century to the city of St. Petersburg, where a baseball-crazed population eager for economic revitalization decides to build an ultramodern baseball stadium, convinced that a stadium would attract a major league franchise.

Bill Bond Jr. was one of those much-maligned city councilmen who put St. Pete's money where his vision was. But by the time his vision comes to pass and The Heritage becomes a beneficiary (it's less than a mile from the already-built stadium), Bill won't be reaping the hotel's rewards. A third-generation hotelier who tried to recycle the leading hotel of his grandfather's time into the leading hotel of a revived St. Petersburg, Bill was forced out of The Heritage when the bills got way ahead of the income. The Heritage went into Chapter 11, and a team of Holiday Inn franchise owners then took over operations for the bank.

Things could be worse.

Indeed they were. Service had run down to bottom. Guests drove up—and waited. There was no bell service. Management turnover left guests uncertain about what they'd find. Plans for a restaurant in the beautifully converted Victorian house attached next door were slow to materialize.

Now the Heritage Grille has become one of the best restaurants in town. Guests checking in get snap-to-it attention. Weekday evenings they mingle over complimentary wine and cheese in the lobby. The rooms are beautifully redone, quiet, and well kept. Landscaping out front and around a little swimming pool and spa won a chamber of commerce beautification award in 1990.

The Heritage is again a deluxe low-rise hotel convenient for downtown business and vacation travelers.

At one time, plans had called for converting the 1928 property into a congregate living facility. That was when Bill Jr., approached to consult on the project, wound up acquiring it. One of the breaks was that one family had owned the property since its inception. All the original furniture remained. Though Bill thought it was ugly, his designers prevailed on him to let them restore one piece. That turned out so well that it set the tone for the entire restoration, and hence the name, Heritage.

Even knowing nothing of the hotel history, guests are quickly impressed by an intuition of quality. Even if the pass through the lobby is quick and transactional, once in their rooms guests will admire the work of the restorers: the mirror-topped dressers, desks, armchairs, brass ceiling fixtures with flame-shaped bulbs, and oval tables with drop leaves extended by brass hinges.

Colors are exceptional: greens, mauves, rose, soft blues, whites. A lot of exposed wood and soft white curtains and royal green drapes with multiple mauve motifs.

Sofas are plum-colored in pinpoint upholstery. Walls throughout are papered in a threaded hint of beige-white that stripes upward from low white baseboards to crown moldings, above a circumferential border of blue-green.

Inside the pair of double front lobby doors are ceiling panels of stained glass in rosy glow and blue-green borders that hint at the colorations that ensue. The lobby is unusually open and combines sitting areas to one side with a brass-rail bar to the other. Large dhurry rugs further introduce visitors to the soft greens and mauve.

The lobby is also where guests are served a complimentary continental breakfast that comes with copies of USA Today. Maybe before long guests will read the box scores of that St. Pete team that fell from the sky.

The Heritage, 234 3rd Ave. North, St. Petersburg, FL 33701. (813) 822-4814. (800) 283-7829. Sergio F. Ortiz, general manager. 76 rooms and suites with AC, heat, bathrooms with tub, color TV, direct-dial phone. Children of any age accepted, free in parents' room 12 and under. No pets. All major credit cards. 3rd person in room $10. Rates: April 15-Dec. 31: single $58, double $66, suites $85-$95; Jan.-mid-April: $75, $85, suites $95-$110. Includes evening turndown with chocolate chip cookies, continental breakfast, wine and cheese reception Mon.-Fri., USA Today. Outdoor pool and jacuzzi. Lunch $5-$8, dinner $10-$15 in Heritage Grille. Free off-street parking.

St. Petersburg Beach — DON CESAR BEACH RESORT

Absolutely first-class revival of fabled pink
beachfront resort on the Gulf Coast.

The Don CeSar floats on the beach between Boca Ciega Bay and the Gulf of Mexico like an elaborate ornament atop a cake, wedding Florida dreams of yesterday with Florida dreams of today.

Only a box of custom Crayolas in 64 shades of pink could capture the dreamy drift of the Don between make-believe and believe-it-or-not.

In morning the easterly sun creams the pink walls with splendor that rings imaginary bells in imitative belfries. The setting sun bathes the pink Moorish towers a shimmering rose till a stealthy mauve rises from the tented beach and purples the dreams of Arabian nights.

Once such pink, pastry-like palaces patterned both Florida coasts. Pink sidewalks were poured, and when summer showers cooled hot pavement, nature released a pinkish vapor that rose like a coquette's blush.

But the Don's summer dalliance with nature was private. Visitors came only for the two months a year that the hotel was open. January and February. In that bare seasonal span beginning in 1928, when rooms were $12 and $14 single, $24 double, and all rates included meals, Thomas J. Rowe's palatial pink Don was an audacious success.

Such dreams as the Don are not lightly spun. Mr. Rowe overcame bad health, bad marriage, marginal means, bust of the Florida land boom, and the incredulity of ostensibly wiser heads who advised against his site for a 110-room, $450,000 hotel that, when completed more than two years after construction began, had grown to 200 rooms at a cost of $1,250,000.

Mr. Rowe insisted on his own site but freely borrowed from the Mediterranean stylings of Flagler, Deering, Merrick, and Mizner. Theirs was a coast of sunrises, brilliant but unobserved over the Atlantic except by early risers. At a time when pale skin was the badge of good living, Mr. Rowe's guests could indulge in the glow of twilight, lengthened by crystal evenings, secure that by morning their natural porcelain would be unmarred.

F. Scott Fitzgerald and Zelda came, along with baseball heroes and department store barons. Their luminous tenancy kept the Don busy if not always full when the Depression closed other hotels. Rowe more than once lost cash reserves when banks and others he trusted failed. In 1940 he died. There had been only the few good years. Three lean decades followed.

Mr. Rowe's estranged wife blundered through a season's mismanagement before returning the hotel to more experienced hands. War in December, 1941, foreclosed the future. One year later the army took over. The Don became a hospital, then a convalescent center, finally a regional office of the Veterans Administration. Its ornate furnishings were sold or purloined, and what was left was ruined. Maintenance suffered. Eventually the VA moved out, pigeons and vermin moved in. The hotel by 1971 was an eyesore and bruited for the wreckers.

Don Caesar, the operatic pirate for whom the hotel was named, led a charmed life. Condemned to execution by firing squad, he miraculously survives when the guns misfire. Mr. Rowe gave a name to history he could hardly have imagined repeating, but fate intervened to save the latter-day Don in the form of resolute preservationists led by June Hurley, whose booklet, "The Don Ce-Sar Story," describes in detail the three years it took to rescue, rebuild, and re-open the Don, revived (but for the hyphen in its name) to original glory and then some.

Of course there was risk. A tawdry resort strip had spread north along the beach, and St. Petersburg had become known as a retirement city for the poor. Disney World had captured the family trade. No two-month season could attract good help, and summer trade was assured only along north Florida beaches.

The success of the new Don required a commitment to absolutely first-class revival and a marketing plan that mixed business guests with vacationers. Vacationers share the *luxe* that only expense-account living can fill in for, while businessmen conduct their affairs in a setting that could only have been conceived for the leisurely privileged.

Today there are 277 rooms and baths, including 50 suites with balconies, four restaurants, three lounges, shopping hall, meeting and conference facilities for up to 500, health club, tennis courts, heated pool with jacuzzi, and the spacious beach with its variety of water sports. Everything inside is air-conditioned. The roof, plumbing, wiring, paint, windows, and furnishings are all new.

The enchantment is unchanged. The flattering pinks shade again into rose and lilac, into beige and cream. Guest rooms—renovated with meeting rooms in 1987 at a cost of $8 million—feature reproductions of imperial Spanish furniture, often with open beams, lightened by print fabrics, adorned by oil paintings and watercolors.

On the inside, the elaborate exterior architecture shapes sloped ceilings, distinctive carved corners, corridors of light and shadowy movement. Upper-story views span the bay of islets and extend between pink wings that stretch to the sand at the edge of open waters. Splashing fountains enliven the moment. You imagine yourself on a devil-may-care voyage in the arms of the magical Don.

Don CeSar, A Registry Resort, 3400 Gulf Blvd., St. Petersburg Beach, FL 33706. (800) 247-9810, (813) 360-1881. Jerome Thirion, general manager. 277 rooms and suites with AC, heat, cable TV, bathrooms with tub, room phone. Restaurants, bars, pool, complete outdoor recreational activities including watersports, lighted tennis courts, golf course privileges. Elevators. Children of any age accepted, free in parents' room to 18. No charge for crib, $15 for rollaway bed. AmEx, CB, En Route, DC, MC, Visa. Rates based on location. Off-season rates: $115 to $750 (the highest rates are for penthouses). Winter rates: $180-$1,000. MAP $55 additional per person per day, inclusive. Restaurant meals at varied prices. Free parking on property.

St. Petersburg Beach — ISLAND'S END
Little cottage colony in a delightful village.

Most fantasy getaways reduce to a few elements: alone with a lover on a tropical island, endless sailing into sunsets, cycling at sunrise.

When instead we accept that the best to come is going to be compromise, we should know that at the estimable end of what's possible is Pass-a-Grille. Island's End fits right in.

The spirit of good times past is present here for visitors browsing the one-block downtown, walking the undeveloped beach, tarrying over a meal in a palm-canopied yard by candlelight.

The urban sprawl of St. Petersburg has bypassed this part of Pinellas County. The barrier islands have been relentlessly built up, an ugly scar on the beach. But where the Bayway elbows north to become the mind-numbing strip, a quiet little two-lane street drops off the other way.

For 35 blocks this appendage is Pass-a-Grille, a charming garble of Passe-aux-Grilleurs, named for the fishermen who once grilled their catch here. The village is mostly one block wide from beach to waterway. All else is swallowed at the end by the wide mouth of Tampa Bay. Beyond, the soaring Sunshine Skyway bridge arches south.

Island's End is so definitely at the end of the island that the last block and a half of the property is under water. The remnant that's dry is a walled compound of five cottages and two houses that are about 50 years old. It shares the curve at island's end with a bleak condominium which falls out of mind about the second day.

The compound is sandy and weathered with criss-crossing board walkways. Slats, shingle, latticework, a few palms: everything is wooden. Hardy plants add minimal color. The salty breeze blows all the time. There's a gazebo, a little fishing dock, a comfortable cushioned porch beside the small office, and strapped casual furniture on the private deck of each cottage. As many pelicans as people occupy the setting.

Jone and Millard Gamble have equipped their lodgings with comfortably casual sofas, armchairs, glass-topped tables, floor lamps, straw rugs on terrazzo and wood floors. Beds are twins, but there are hide-a-beds in the living rooms that open into either queens or doubles. Bathrooms have showers. All have complete kitchens, AC and heat, cable color TV. Laundry machines are available. The guest house has three rooms and a private screened pool.

The Gambles live in a two-story house marked 1 Pass-a-Grille Way at the head of the compound.

The look of Pass-a-Grille quickly establishes itself south of the Bayway. The

169

garish gives way to garden apartments, and these to houses behind picket fences and big bushes of pink and white oleanders. What a miracle to have the banal banished! Bicycles become as numerous as autos. The houses are an unpretentious mishmash, many with tin roofs. Sandy walkways run between rows.

From 22nd Avenue south, Gulf Way runs along the beach. The few businesses are nondescript guest houses, two or three unattractive condos, and a few bistros. Most popular is the lately hugely expanded Hurricane Seafood Restaurant. People nurse a plate and a brew for hours because sitting is as good as walking.

Otherwise, 8th Avenue is the diversion. The market serves fresh deli food, sandwiches with names like Cindi Lauperwurst and Barbara Pastreisand, salads, wines, danish, and ice cream. The Lighted Tree outdoor bar and restaurant is island magical. Evander Preston is the grandly self-promotional jeweler whose high-priced shop you're admitted to only after you've pressed the bell.

Changes come slowly. Old-timers will tell how Cubans and Bahamians were here more than 200 years ago. British and Spanish came later. Civil War veteran Zephania Phillips is revered as first settler. Early in the century ferries brought picnickers from Tampa. Hotels sprang up, a causeway was built, the hotels burned, but people kept building beach houses. At one time Wanamakers were here, the towel Cannons, August Busch Sr. The town was consolidated with St. Pete Beach in 1958, probably a blessing because sewerage had become a problem, and so had garbage. By the Sixties hippies were showing up, then tough bikers, later gays. Each group has troubled the old-timers for a time before layering in its own legacy. The overall accumulation has been recognized in the National Register as a historic district since 1990.

Come late afternoon, everybody's out on the beach. Anhingas dry their wings like fringed black shawls. A blissed-out sun-worshipper slung in a canvasback chair slowly sinks in sand lapped by a rising tide. In the setting sun a fat woman like a hope casts a long lean shadow. The flashiest scene is sunset. Night falls quietly.

Island's End, 1 Pass-a-Grille Way, St. Petersburg Beach, FL 33706. (813) 360-5023. Jone and Millard Gamble, proprietors. 5 1-bedroom cottages with private baths, and 1 3-bedroom house with private pool, with AC, heat, color cable TV, pushbutton phone, fishing pier. Children of any age accepted, $3 for crib, $6 for 3rd person. No pets. No credit cards. Checks accepted. Rates: Dec.15-June 1, $61 to $75; June 1-Sept.15, $55-$64; Sept. 16-Dec. 14, $52-$60, all single or double, includes continental breakfast 3 days a week, and fresh fruits on arrival for stays of 5 days or more. Year-round rate for 3-bedroom house: $135 daily, single or double. $6 per additional person. Smoking allowed. Off-street parking.

Siesta Key, Sarasota — CRESCENT HOUSE

Simple style, international milieu across from the beach.

Crescent House satisfies a vacationer's need to be part of a scene, yet able to withdraw into an intimate space.

Buildings in Siesta Key's village district of pleasant shops and restaurants next to Beach Road keep low to the ground, casual, informal. The attraction is a powdery white beach that the gulf most early mornings tests with a mild surf, a feeble roar. Sun-up walkers and joggers stir the strand with energetic strides.

The sand squeaky soft, pelicans bruising loud, gulls stridently fishing, striders with fists of weights; the southerly breeze seems to blow—does one hear right?—an itinerant preacher's urgings. He in his low black socks, black shorts, black windbreaker is overtaken by a boy in a ribbed white undershirt on a mountain bike, followed by women in warm-up suits of coral pink, lavender, soft blue. Their shadows are Bill King sculptures lankily stretched by a lazy sun.

From across the street, Crescent House is oddly wood-shingled above, jalousied below, colorless—suggestive of weathered beachfront—but for blue accents: a Crescent House shingle at the sidewalk, two shutters at dormer windows, and a puckered canopy over the entry. Next to nondescript neighbors the house assumes character. Sprightly colorful flowers adorn a small yard below palms and rubber trees, strewn with broken shells used for a car park.

The house was built in 1914 and was one of three like it moved from the Venice-Englewood area. A Siesta Key rehabber fixed it up for bed-and-breakfast in 1985.

Light and airiness flood your impressions of the entry, streaming from outside in with you. Colors are pastel, muted, the hues of shallow water and sandy bottom. The subtropical tone is set by a Syd Solomon gallery poster, he the abstract colorist of the Gulf Coast.

Downstairs is best, compressed fore and aft, decidedly vertical. The fireplace dominates parlor and living room with its parquet wood chimney face rising the full nearly 25 feet of room height. Fresh and silken flowers, some in baskets, some vases, adorn the room together with musical bric-a-brac, rows of trophies, a selection of lamps, tables, upholstered pieces.

Furniture is well arranged for conversation.

The small dining room is set for breakfast with a lace cloth showing a blue cover beneath, six almost all matching chairs and place for two more. Tie-back full curtains frame two double-hung windows, surrounded by an all-around beige, blue, and muted red fall-colored wallpaper, and on the polished pine floors found throughout the house a woven Persian-style rug. Here mornings between 8 A.M. and 10 A.M. Paulette Wolf and Robert Flaherty serve breakfast of fruits, juices, cereals, yogurt, home-baked specialties, tea and coffee.

Here guests chat about histories from all over Europe, Australia, the Americas. They are an international clientele attracted by previous owners Jean Marc and Patricia Murre, who had bought in 1986. The Murres had given up high-profile lives in pre-crisis Saudi Arabia to reimmerse in Western life. For four years, until Disney enticed Jean Marc to France to help prepare Europe's first Disney World, they developed Crescent House as a nest of cosmopolitan pleasures. Paulette and Robert, who acquired the property early in 1991, have changed little.

"A couch," says Paulette. "It needed reupholstering. And we've added a fourth bedroom where Patricia's son lived," a room light green and beige with a wall of windows that looks toward the village and a closet large enough for another bath.

Otherwise returning guests will find the three guest rooms as before: comfortable in their furnishings if not distinguished. Beds are firm, some kings, some twins, all with unusual headboards. The larger rooms could each do with another upholstered chair, and without the air-conditioner hum guests in rooms closest the street might some nights be bothered by traffic noise. The downstairs room with bath opens directly onto the deck out back with its jacuzzi and Adirondack chairs.

The casual tropical look immediately appealed to Paulette and Robert when, after too many cold winters in Chicago, they opted for Florida. They'd been coming twice a year to Key West, Fort Myers, Sarasota. It helped make up their minds for a permanent move when headhunters approached Robert to join a stock brokerage firm in Sarasota. Paulette, who had thought about running a bed-and-breakfast, one day called telephone information hoping to find a B&B association that could advise her. The only reference proved to be Jean Marc and Patricia's listing. When Paulette explained her interest, Patricia let her know that Crescent House was for sale. Paulette came down, looked, and bought.

Now as before, there is no place as welcoming, unshowy, and modestly priced on these playtime islands off Sarasota.

Crescent House, 459 Beach Rd., Siesta Key, Sarasota, FL 34242. (813) 346-0857. Paulette Wolf and Robert Flaherty, owners. 4 rooms, 3 baths (2 with tubs), with AC, heat, ceiling or table fans, TV in all rooms (cable, color). Children of any age accepted, free in parents' room to 10. Pets of reasonable size accepted. House phone for incoming messages, collect or credit-card outgoing LD calls, no charge for local calls. Fresh flowers in rooms winters. No credit cards. Smoking allowed. Rates: Dec. 15-Jan. 31, $50-$75; Feb. 1-Mar. 22, $65-$90; Mar. 23-Apr. 5, $75-$100; Apr. 6-June 30, $50-75; July 1-Nov. 30, $40-$60 (single or double). 3rd person in room $10. Off-street parking. Rate includes full uncooked breakfast.

Tarpon Springs – SPRING BAYOU INN
Comfortable and walking convenient between the bayou and the little downtown.

If tough guys don't eat quiche, you wouldn't think they'd thrill about people gushing over doll houses set up in their living rooms either. Or sure-enough take to making beds and washing dishes.

No sexist, Ron Morrick is endearingly given over to his wife Cher. Likes the idea of her keeping an inn in their large turn-of-the-century house. Even was ready for a weekend commuter marriage to buy her the Georgia house she first wanted for B&B while he stayed midweek running his Tampa construction company.

Didn't come to that. Tough guys go for good looks, and the Morricks' Spring Bayou Inn in downtown Tarpon Springs is an easy walk from one of the most beautiful townscapes in Florida.

Compact Tarpon Springs' attractions include the revived and pedestrian-scaled downtown, the Universalist Church famed for its landscape paintings by George Inness Jr., and the sponge docks where the town's Greek heritage is gaudily on sale among souvenir shops, restaurants, and the Spongearama.

But it is the hauntingly historic Spring Bayou with its natural contours outlined by rising tiers of serpentine paths, stone walls, and sheltering palms, pines, and oaks that draws and awes visitors.

The beauty of the setting compels people out of their cars. Those who drive north or south where brick-paved Tarpon Avenue divides at the bayou slow to an Edwardian pace. Eras mix. Bicycles at times outnumber cars, as they once did, while joggers in shorts train for leanness in front of extravagant mansions.

Each Jan. 6 the Epiphany Day parade sweeps by the inn to the bayou where young men of Tarpon Springs dive into the chill waters to redeem the sunken cross and win glory.

The town began as a health resort more or less 100 years ago. It's that salutary disposition, you realize, that lingers and so marks this setting sanely apart.

A short walk north along the bayou is the church established by the town's widely traveled founder Anson P.K. Safford and his sister Mary, first woman M.D. in Florida. The liberal Universalist community set the early tone for Tarpon Springs, as they shared their house of worship with other denominations, built a library, and raised up imposing homes, steadily attracting a like-minded Northern gentry who came on the Orange Belt Railway for winter's salubrious climate.

Compare the heritage mood west of the inn with the bustle of the downtown business district just east, concentrated between Alternate U.S. 19 and the old rail tracks. Successful work by the Main Street Program of the state and city has brought back restaurants that specialize in the exotic marine fare and sweet pastries beloved by the Greeks, while shopkeepers offer antiques, apparel, art, flowers, housewares, market foods, and services that keep the little district a place for practical shoppers and often indulgent visitors.

The Morricks' inn is obtrusively round, not all of it, but two boastful bays, so much so that the rest of the house hangs diffidently back, the whole behind a brick wall as if to forestall anyone's finding the switch that might set the huge rotunda spinning like a top, or launched and leaving a void like a rocket split from its casing.

Cher Morrick's stylings are vintage intuition. She has added good imagination to a house that was structurally sound and featured built-in beauty.

The combination is immediately apparent in the foyer entered through an oval glass and wood door, her own perfectly Victorian sentiment, whereupon guests are struck by her choice of an electric blue wallpaper that seems to twinkle with inexhaustible inner blueness like a starry night far from any settlement. Rising alongside is a staircase in a patina of glowing burl-like paneling achieved by curly pine cut on the bias to give a watered silk effect.

The same wood treatment cloaks the living room fireplace. Wood dominates, up from the shiny heart pine floors through trim topped by kingly arches with their split crown moldings. There are a baby grand piano and comfortable twin sofas in an amiable L, squared off by an Oriental rug and wing-back chairs.

Cher has accessorized with various cabinets of collectable ivory carvings and her doll-house general store, as well as an ornate cast-iron Victorian hat rack and much else worth discovering.

There are four guest rooms, one each downstairs and up in the rotunda, each with its own bath, and two more upstairs with a hall bath between. Their signature feature is an antique girl's dress on a hanger, a hint of time past, in one of the shared rooms extended by an armoire piled atop with antique hat boxes and gloves, as if mother and daughter might have arrived on the train, unpacked hastily, and irrepressibly launched themselves sightseeing into the quaint little town. The same room features antique furniture all with elaborate wood turnings.

Cher for breakfast serves home-baked breads, cheese, fruits, maybe granola, juice and coffee in a dining room distinguished by an elaborate carved sideboard. It's here where Ron helps serve weekends, at 8:30, three hours after he's normally gone. For a hard-driving businessman, it's a welcome change. It ought to be all that and more for others who come as guests.

Spring Bayou Inn, 32 W. Tarpon Ave., Tarpon Springs, FL 34689. (813) 938-9333. Cher Morrick, innkeeper. 4 rooms and 3 baths (including tubs), AC, heat, ceiling fans, 1 portable TV (first come, first served) (B&W), house phone for incoming messages, collect or credit-card outgoing LD calls, no charge for local calls. No small children. No pets. No credit cards. 3rd person in room $10. Digital clock radios. No smoking. Rates: Dec. 16-Apr. 15, $55-$75; Apr. 16-Dec. 15, $50-$65 double (single deduct $5), includes full breakfast. Usually closed September. Off-street parking.

Useppa Island – USEPPA ISLAND CLUB
Florida's patrician island resort, accessible to day-trippers, and overnight to financially qualified membership prospects.

If maps were charts of endeavor, the barrier islands and inland waters of Florida's Gulf Coast would stretch from Do-It-Yourself to Don't-Lift-A-Finger. Between Gasparilla and Captiva islands lies a shallow basin of deep possibilities.

No one has fathomed these better than Garfield Beckstead, who in his first career pulled companies out of the morass of mismanagement, and began his second rescuing a beautiful Florida isle from the jungle of neglect. We might regret that at the time he didn't renew lodgings for the public. Access to Useppa Island today is limited.

For a half century after the island was colonized, guests were welcomed as long as they were prominent. Chicago streetcar magnate John M. Roach built 20 guest rooms in 1902, and when his nephew Barron Collier acquired the island 10 years later, he doubled the rooms, built nine holes of golf, and added a fishing club acclaimed as America's foremost—amenities that attracted presidents, the wealthy and powerful, and film stars.

Today in a way Useppa is more open than when it was public, when Collier's personal likes and dislikes had a lot to do with who came ashore. Then as now, somebody had to bring you by boat—or you captained your own. And given the chic of the crowd who came, Useppa was public in the way that the Concorde doesn't discriminate against anyone either.

So the fact that Useppa is private today and you come as a club member, guest of a member, or as someone interested in membership, limits access in a new way, but no more decisively than once upon a time. You also can come on the tour boat from Captiva Island, enjoy lunch, and spend a few hours visiting.

Useppa is exquisitely proportioned. A mile and a half long by a half-mile wide, the island is slender and rounded. Cresting at 38 feet, Useppa, given its width, is proportionally higher than any place in the Carribean. Nearby green tufted islets in a painterly blue sea impress how the island, though inhabited, is vouchsafed from gross intrusion that would despoil miles of idyllic composition.

White latticework borders the cottages here and there edging the shore. They further resemble each other with sloping tin roofs, and most are built on criss-crossed pilings. Their structural similarity respects hard-bargaining nature, whose side Gar Beckstead has taken. He also has subdued any inclination toward manic display on the part of owners by imposing deed restrictions. Cottage interiors are inventive. Outside, conformity reigns.

Look is enhanced by mood. The island is just long and hilly enough for changing vistas. No cars, no billboards break into view. You relax assured that their absence is intended. You are treading a pink, flower-canopied ridge path wide enough only for people to walk. The land slopes on either side to a shore of palm and sea grape. It takes awhile for the novelty of an uncluttered landscape to take hold. Why isn't the rest of the world like this?

Gar Beckstead was part of a group that acquired the island in the early Seventies. He later bought out the others and gave up his globe-trotting career as a McKinsey consultant for two years without electricity, water, or telephones while he re-established Useppa's elegance of the Thirties, the last period Collier lived on the island.

He used old photographs to locate buildings covered by forest. The structures had been built of Dade County pine which withstood the rain, the vermin, the salt, sun, and scavengers. Only the old inn had succumbed. In its place Gar restored Collier's own residence to serve as a formal dining room, lounge, recreation and meeting area. He also built a museum featuring original guest registers and memorabilia from the Izaak Walton Tarpon Club that Collier established in 1912.

Most of the work has been done. Today all of the 100 planned cottages have been built. The membership hovers near 600, about the number Gar wants. As intended, 80 percent of the island has been kept in open space. A putting green has been installed. There are tennis courts, a swimming pool, a life-sized chess set, croquet lawn, and shuffleboard courts.

Other features include a reception center with a general store and the Tarpon Bar—where two palm trees have been preserved by building the roof around them.

Useppa remains outstanding and intriguing. Archaeologists lately unearthed a pre-Calusa Indian site described by University of Florida researchers as one of the most important archaeological finds in the state. It dates back more than 7,000 years.

Today's arrivals who qualify financially are housed in member cottages generally used by owners only a few weeks of each year.

Useppa Island Club, P.O. Box 640, Bokeelia, FL 33922. (813) 283-1061. Vince Formosa, V.P. 100 homes for up to 6 persons each "complete just like a fine home" including washer and dryer, pool, rental bikes, sailboats and dories, croquet lawn, lighted tennis courts, basketball court, putt-putt course, beach. Children of all ages accepted. No pets. AmEx, MC, Visa. Rates: Dec.15-June 15: about $100 (room) to $500 (4-bedroom house); June 16-Dec. 14: about $70 (room) to $340 (4-bedroom house). (Houses can accommodate up to 6). Continental breakfast at the Tarpon Bar about $4. Full breakfast weekends at the Collier Inn, under $10. Lunch at the Collier Inn about $7.50, dinner about $25 and higher. Round-trip ferry from Bokeelia Marina on Pine Island $9 per person one way. Restaurants and bar plus convenience store.

Venice — BANYAN HOUSE
Victorian interiors in a residential Mediterranean neighborhood.

You could hardly imagine the colorful past of the Banyan House just by coming upon its decorous setting where today it appeals to visitors who like quiet vacationing near the area's recreational and shopping attractions.

The house fits into a residential neighborhood attractively set on both sides of a boulevard with a grassy median strip and a low speed limit. Front lawns slope up from sidewalks to houses with a Mediterranean look. Banyan House alone has a sign out front indicating guests are welcomed. It is a privileged use.

Hardly revealed in this well-to-do neighborhood is an oddball house history in a town that, while not flooded by canals like Italy's Venice, is awash in half a century's vicissitudes of south Sarasota County.

The city was developed in 1925 by the Brotherhood of Locomotive Engineers, investing its heyday treasury. They boasted of spending a million a month to build their "model city" in less than four years. But as their work neared completion, the Depression swallowed it. The union, as well as its town, was finished.

Venice then bobbed on the tides of a hurricane that destroyed Eau Gallie across the state, and so brought a relocated military academy; a mammoth land sale in Sarasota that delivered the Ringling Brothers, Barnum & Bailey Circus to a new home nearby; and the war, whose aftermath left the city an airbase that became the airport and the site of a vast trailer park that boomed the population.

In 1926, the house at 519 South Harbor Drive opened as a retirement home for the president of the Brotherhood of Locomotive Engineers. It was the town's first hurricane shelter. The first pool was built here, and the first solar heater installed.

178

With the Bust of 1929, the house was abandoned. Hobos came. They cooked in the fireplace. Later, when the town got a schoolteacher, she taught classes in the house and opened a teahouse here and the first taxi-cab business.

During World War II the house became the unofficial USO headquarters, and afterward, a museum for an owner who bought it while writing a book about shark teeth. (These and other fossils are widely found along the beaches.) She threw her rejects into the pool. The gardener made a compost heap out of it. Later came a trapeze artist, whose ropes lately dangled in the banyans that gave the house its name when it began taking guests.

The recent succession of owners has included a retired Air Force colonel turned financial consultant, a couple of medical technicians, and now Susan and Chuck McCormick, she a nurse full-time into looking after guests, and he a would-be commercial fisherman lately full-time into expanding their little warren of accommodations.

Susan and Chuck have reassembled the property as it had been before a parcel was sold off in the Sixties, and they've fully developed it into a mix of guest rooms, suites, and adjacent apartments. All share the expanded outdoor spaces that now, in addition to the pool, include a jacuzzi, and brick and wood decks.

Indoors is a sparkling solarium of green and black checkered tiles, and white wrought-iron chairs and tables with peach cushions and tablecloths where guests enjoy breakfast. An original cypress ceiling here has inspired adaptations.

Chuck has introduced the cypress to ceilings upstairs where—surprisingly— the generally softer, more homespun character set by the guest room furnishings adapts well to the informal woody and rustic look.

Downstairs, Chuck and Susan have blended the house's Mediterranean architecture, which has a lyrical quality, with a rococo Italianate scheme in the redone living room.

These changes are the result of an earnest do-it-yourself approach which works for guests here for good times.

A more experienced intuitive or altogether professional hand might have done the house differently. Ah, but the B&B essence is people doing their own thing. For Susan, that means excelling in the business of looking after guests. She is a home-baker. Her morning breads and muffins, combined with a crackling fire set chill mornings in the living room, scent the house for happy awakenings.

Her guest quarters in the main and adjacent houses are done in a mix of furniture that suffices for comfort. Some rooms include kitchens. Views are over the pool and patio, to the banyans, and onto Harbor Drive, all pleasant.

For a house that has gone through the changes of this one, Susan and Chuck have added their own independent style. Grandfathered into privileged status, the house remains harmonious for all vacationers who seek the pleasures this American Venice serenely approximates.

Banyan House, 519 S. Harbor Drive, Venice, FL 34285. (813) 484-1385. Susan and Chuck McCormick, innkeepers. 2 rooms (that share a bath, no tub), 3 efficiencies in main house, 4 next door, with AC, heat, ceiling fans, bathrooms (with tub), color TV, house phone for messages and outgoing credit-card and collect long-distance calls, local calls free. Outdoor pool, hot tub. Children over 12 accepted, $15 in parent's room. 3rd person in room $15. No pets. No credit cards. Checks accepted. Rates: Dec. 15-Apr. 30, sleeping rooms $65, efficiencies $79; May 1-Dec. 14: $45, $59 (all double). Weekly and monthly rates available. Deluxe continental breakfast. Off-street parking. Coaster-brake bikes free.

Venice — EL PATIO HOTEL

A plain little hotel for guests who like each other's company
in the heart of a town with plenty to do.

Small hotels on the main streets of small towns, close to the bus station. These were transits for people from the country come to test the town, for men forced out of breaking-up marriages, for salesmen traveling to downtown accounts trying to save a few bucks.

They were different from the fleabags because their neighborhoods were still decent. Bums didn't hang out, and the lobbies felt something like the "Y" or a hostel or a retirement home. The lights were dim, the furniture plain, and the desk clerk, who was street-smart and courteous, would look after your suitcase while you got a haircut or bought food for the ride between the time you checked out and your bus or train came.

They were still respectable before malls superseded downtowns, and before newer hotels prideful of chain affiliations were built with urban renewal grants.

Some of the small ones on main streets remain. Sometimes great will, foresight, and dollars lead to their remodeling and re-emergence in the European style. Their new popularity is helped by never having changed their location.

Faye Miles' El Patio could become one of these but probably won't. Land is too valuable in downtown Venice, so when Faye retires her son will likely replace it with shops or offices.

Despite alterations that have removed its namesake patio and busied its look, the little hotel fits well in the bustling downtown which, thanks to the wide pleasant grassy mall that divides Venice Avenue, and the resurgence of downtown retailing, has become a popular pedestrian area.

The hotel's large plate window on the avenue fits with the looks of bakeries, boutiques, and the drug store. The building is not set back with a circular drive. There is no special No Parking zone. Guests are no more fashionably dressed than for an appointment with the optometrist.

The lobby is set like the stage of a play about a main street hotel: original rattan from 1926, TV, landscape print on the wall, mirror, magazines on tables. The desk sits in front of stairs that rise out of sight. No one is here. You ding the bell, and momentarily Faye descends.

She looks faintly stagey, a petite woman treated well by her years. She and her late husband have been the only owners since 1948. A certain style has settled in with an appreciative clientele that returns winter after winter.

Sedate as the first floor is, the second is lively. Guests share a long lobby that is more like a living room that bedrooms open onto. Coffee perks all morning.

Guests bring breakfast foods from their refrigerators and chew over plans for the day. It is a place for bridge or for reading, watching TV, tending the plants. Some evenings the crowd pitches in for a potluck dinner using Faye's kitchen. A few guests are retired. Some work for the Ringling Brothers and Barnum & Bailey Circus. There is a little the feeling of a congregate living facility. That's because familiarity prevails. But the hotel is open only eight months a year, and everyone is gone by June 1st.

Originally there were gardens on either side of the downstairs lobby. These have been replaced by shops. The 25 rooms are still set in double rows to either side of the upstairs lobby, the outer rows opening onto overhung side porches, with corridors that turn from the outer walkways into the upstairs lobby. On the east side upstairs is a sundeck for guests.

Rooms that were small and plain have now been reconfigured so that from 27 there are now 16 units, some with two bedrooms, some with one, but all with private baths. Rooms have white spreads and green carpet, simple furniture acquired as needed. Venetian blinds give privacy to rooms that open onto the lobby. All have color TV, phones, small refrigerators, heat, and there is air-conditioning in all. Some have floor fans. During 1990 the exterior of the hotel was restuccoed and repainted, and a new roof was put on during the winter of 1990-1991.

El Patio is the only remaining in-town hotel, and the only of those that in the Twenties gave Venice its upscale reputation. The other three great hotels, all built by the Brotherhood of Locomotive Engineers who founded the town, have either been razed or converted to other uses.

The liveliness at El Patio reflects Faye's own lifestyle. Active and vivacious, she uses part of the four months each year that the hotel is closed to compete around the world as a gold medalist on the ballroom dance circuit.

During the season she gets out evenings to dance, and gets her guests out as well for everything from aerobics to knitting clubs and lectures at the Civic Center. Her son Bob says, "When the season's at its peak, it's like a giant three-month party among the guests."

It is reasonable, too.

El Patio Hotel, 229 W. Venice Ave., Venice, FL 34285. (813) 488-7702. Faye Miles, owner. 10 units with 2 rooms and bath, 5 single rooms with bath with heat, most with AC, color TV, cable TV in lobbies, small refrigerator, switchboard-connected phone in rooms. Free local calls. Children of any age accepted; rollaway $8. No pets. No credit cards. Seasonal rates: $22 single, $40 double. $8 for extra person in room. Open October-May. Off-street parking.

Yankeetown — IZAAK WALTON LODGE
In a river town that looks barely carved out of the woods,
new owners revive and add to the hospitality.

Hallelujah! Clap hands! Revival down by the river!

After a decade of frightful mismanagement, hospitality has been renewed at the Izaak Walton Lodge. Where doors before were kept locked against the possibility of welcome, new owners have opened them onto new dining rooms and 10 restored guest rooms. Cottages have been spruced up, and rebuilt boat docks are busy again.

If the change seems abrupt, that's also partly because development in this backwater has crept along rather than marched, even though Yankeetown from the beginning was meant for drawing outsiders. But low-keyed hunters and fishermen, as they settled and built houses, did nothing to attract the fun-seekers who populated much of the rest of coastal Florida.

Lack of beaches kept them away. This is a coast of forest and marsh. Mosquitoes and sandfleas can make summer evenings outdoors miserable. In winter it can freeze (though rarely does).

Left unpressured, Yankeetown settled into mossy slumber. It was never meant to be a big deal. A.F. Knotts had already had his fill of big-time. As attorney for U.S. Steel he founded Gary, Indiana, and became its first mayor. When in 1922 he decided to make a town out of his camp on the Withlacoochee River near the Gulf of Mexico, he set about avoiding the mistakes he associated with Gary.

We can be thankful his new place wasn't built for a steel mill, that the proposed Cross-State Barge Canal never turned the town into a busy harbor, that a World War II oil storage plan failed, and that Elvis Presley, who made a movie here in the Sixties, never put it on the map either.

Another mistake A.F. avoided was land speculation. To get their deed, purchasers had to build within a year. Hence nobody came to get rich quick. Later, when land booms collapsed elsewhere, nobody was left with thousands of heavily mortgaged acres in Yankeetown to importune politicians about rezoning for mobile home parks.

A.F.'s only indulgence of tourists was a rustic lodge he put up to house Midwestern friends who were overwhelming his privacy. He had come to Florida for an early retirement of hunting and fishing. His nephew, Eugene, and Eugene's wife, Norma, said they would look after the guests. So in 1923, four years after he had arrived, A.F. started the Izaak Walton Lodge.

He built it on an abandoned river site where a pre-Civil War cotton and sugar plantation had reverted to jungle. The kind of swath-clearing done elsewhere in Florida was avoided in Yankeetown. That would have been pointless and expensive for people who at first were building houses for only seasonal recreation, nothing fancy.

"It was the most wonderful life anybody could have," recalls Tom Knotts, Eugene and Norma's son, who came when he was 5 and grew up in the lodge.

"Of course there were the insects then, too. They used to have infestations of hopping fleas. The houses were built on stilts as protection from when the river flooded. Wild hogs would get under the floor at night and their fleas would find their way up. We'd carry a can of Dee Brand Powder and just shake it on us every time we went by someplace where the flies were particularly bothersome."

Linda and Wayne Harrington have taken over and pulled the lodge out of years of neglect. They've repaired the tin roof, repaired the cypress planking, fixed up the old window frames. The broad porch, held up by old palm trunks, has been stabilized, repainted hunter green, and planted all around with red geraniums in red planter boxes that offset the black-painted planks. These were originally a near-black creosote. Under the tall trees and grassy lawns the lodge looks—and is—welcoming again.

The two dining rooms are the more dress-up Izaak's, with its starched pink napery set behind the etched glass portrait of its namesake, and on the waterside, the seafood restaurant they call The Compleat Angler.

The riverfront cottages are wall-to-wall carpeted and have complete kitchens. The small rooms upstairs of The Compleat Angler have been redone using the original metal furniture. Bright new colors and fabrics coordinate duck and quail themes. Air-conditioning and heat, as well as ceiling fans, are in. All rooms have their own lavatories but share two big bathrooms in the hall. Don't avoid the lodge for that. The spiffed-up hospitality in this rustic lodge in its remote setting—and the very reasonable rates—make the Izaak Walton a must for enjoying the compleat Florida.

The lodge is back. Praise the Lord!

Izaak Walton Lodge, Riverside Drive at 63rd St., Yankeetown, FL 32698. (904) 447-2311. Linda and Wayne Harrington, owners. 10 rooms, ceiling fan, lavatory, 2 hall baths; and 2 efficiencies equipped with AC, heat, kitchens, bathrooms with tub. Pay phone. Children of any age accepted, free in parents' room under 16, free rollaway available. MC, Visa. Color cable TV in efficiencies. No pets. River boat dock. Year-round rates: $34 single or double, $69 for efficiencies. 3rd person in room $15. 2 suites available, one with 1 bedroom (the Honeymoon Suite, done Victorian style), the other 2-bedroom. $79 each (ask about combined rate for both). Average lunch price $6 in The Compleat Angler, dinner $11.95-$16.95. Izaak's higher. Complete bar service. Off-street parking. Scenic boat tour $35 for 2, $40 for 3, $45 for 4. Inquire also about cypress outpost, stilt cottage 20 minutes by boat. Sleeps up to 4.

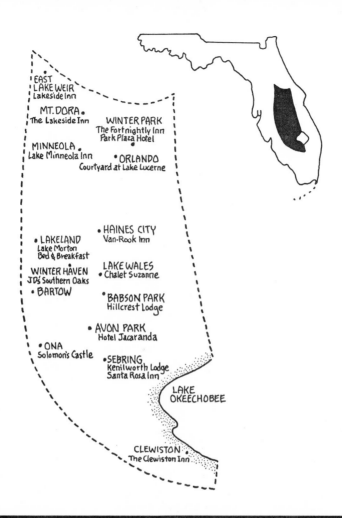

THE PENINSULAR HEARTLAND

The **Fortnightly Inn** has opened in Winter Park across from Rollins College, and the **Norment-Parry Inn** has expanded with acquisition of two adjacent historic buildings, the entire compound now called the **Courtyard at Lake Lucerne**. Alas, **Meadow Marsh** in Winter Garden has had to stop taking guests because of harsh licensing requirements of Orange County, and similar tribulation caused **Fugate House** to be sold.

To the west of Orlando, the **Lake Minneola Inn** is a splendid old-timey addition to B&B ranks, as I suspect farther west is the **The Son's Shady Brook Bed & Breakfast** operated by Jean L. Martin [P.O. Box 551, Coleman 33521,

(904) 748-7867]. Jean has four rooms and baths. Her husband was a pastor, and she thinks of her place as a Christian B&B, no smoking, no alcoholic beverages. Her site is on a spring-fed creek that flows into nearby Lake Panasoffkee, and affords good freshwater fishing. I have not personally visited but am intrigued.

Also new and to the northwest of Orlando is the **Lakeside Inn** in East Lake Weir. The other **Lakeside Inn** in Mount Dora came out of Chapter 11 status late in 1990, and with a new manager should be first rate again by the time readers review these notes.

Just north of Mount Dora in Umatilla, the **Umatilla Hotel** almost made it back as De Hart's Country Inn. The De Hart brothers ran out of money and lost it in foreclosure.

The **St. Cloud Hotel** continues in its namesake town, though mostly it operates for long-term tenants. It is worth a look as part of the historic downtown off Route 192: 1004 New York Ave., St. Cloud, FL 32769, (305) 892-2313.

Southwest of Orlando are the **Lake Morton Bed & Breakfast** in Lakeland, the **Van-Rook Inn** in Haines City, and **JD's Southern Oaks** in Winter Haven. Both are convenient to Cypress Gardens. In Lake Wales, the **Grand Hotel** [115 N. 1st St., Lake Wales, 33853, (813) 676-944], is worth noting only because it's historic. Guests who stay north of town at the **Chalet Suzanne** are convenient to the Bok Tower, where free carillon concerts are presented every afternoon throughout the year, and where the gardens are a Florida pride, and the views exceptional, some days almost from coast to coast. The **Palm Crest** in Haines City remaines boarded up.

In Avon Park, the **Hotel Jacaranda** has been taken over by South Florida Community College. Once moldering, the Jacaranda is happily revived, full of college students as well as some seniors, and overnight guests who enjoy being buffered by young and old alike. New restaurant upgrading has made the Jac very popular.

Next town south is Sebring, where the **Santa Rosa** has completed its second- and third-floor renovations. Next to come on line as a B&B is the **Nan-Ces-O-Wee Hotel** [139 N. Ridgewood Drive, 33870, (813) 385-0131]. In 1990, this historic brick hotel (since 1922, with application in for listing in the National Register) was acquired by Detlev Borgeest, a German traveler, who is upgrading its 60 rooms, 28 with connecting baths, and with restaurant and bar operating again. You might have a look. The old pink **Harder Hall** west of town is still closed for overnight guests.

Between Sebring and Avon Park is the old **Pinecrest Hotel**, most recently used as a teaching center by the Transcendental Meditation people. What a prize for someone to bring back to guest use!

Finally, to the east in this part of the state at the intersection of Highways 60 and 441 is the **Desert Inn** in Yee Haw Junction [Yee Haw Junction, 33472, (407) 436-9936, 436-1054]. Not much here. As locals say, "For excitement you go down to the gas station and watch the grease rack go up and down." The inn is a two-story motel with bar and restaurant that has been around in one form or another since the roads were dirt.

Avon Park — HOTEL JACARANDA
A fortress of nostalgia on Main Street — that's not the main road.

Bikini-clad coeds perch tanning above Main Street. Bathrobed 100-year-olds putter in their motor carts. The yin/yang leaves downstate lawyers speechless. Yet they wouldn't trade the place for a Hyatt. No worry about that.

This is the Jacaranda Hotel in Avon Park, where Main Street drops off high-speed Highway 27 like a silting meander into downtown. Commerce trickles through until winter, when nostalgia floods the route with traffic of snowbirds looking for places like they used to be.

Avon Park qualifies. There's talk that if industry comes, the people who pick citrus will leave for jobs that pay better. Others say the good ole boys also like what the Northerners come for—the quiet, easy pace—and they won't give it up for newcomers who don't deserve a second chance at the expense of local folks still enjoying their first.

Slow's the word. If nobody's in the hardware store, you can take what you want and leave the cash or write it in the book.

When Peggy Willis at the Chamber was sweet-talked into giving up Naples for Avon Park, her husband told her they had a mile-long mall.

"I thought I'd died and gone to heaven," says Peggy. "Turned out to be a landscaped mall. The ice cream store didn't even have chocolate. I wouldn't say there's anything to threaten Disney around here."

Just any notion that one way fits all when it comes to running hotels.

Don Applequist, who runs the Jacaranda, is working on his Ph.D. in herpetology. He won the orange-bricked, hulking Jacaranda as a prize for being an ace fund-raiser. President Catherine Cornelius of South Florida Community College gave it to him to house the college foundation he heads.

For years the hotel had already been housing old folks, secure in the relic style of the Jac that they and their times were growing old together.

Applequist added students, in their own dorm wings, and transients to the hotel's population. A charm of the Jacaranda today is watching the youngsters read to old-timers in the lobby library while hearing stories of when citrus was king and Avon Park was the prince of places.

That was the Twenties. The boom was on. Babe Ruth played golf nearby at Pinecrest. The Orange Blossom Limited chugged its Pullmans of wintering socialites into town.

When prosperity crashed, the Jac emptied. New Highway 27 bypassed the town. The train stopped calling.

Traveling salesmen still came, retired folks, people whose cars broke down while passing through Avon Park, civilian workers at the Air Force Bombing Range, and tourists who wandered off the highway and couldn't resist inquiring if the place was for real.

It was and is, though you think maybe something was forgotten. It cries out for gargoyles or a fanged, caped creature aswoop from its turrets and parapets. It has the look of a fortress meant to withstand an assault against architectural zealotry. Its orange brick bulk occupies almost a block of the town.

When the college bought the place, the last owner was touting bounties to people who signed up new guests.

The Jacaranda is in transition today. South Florida Community College's hotel school serves home-cooked meals in two restaurants here, one with full linen. The lobby is spruced up with new track lighting and brass ceiling fans. But much of the original wicker remains, and has been prettily reupholstered. Other features of the past remain: the crinkly skylight, the water cooler, the exposed pipes attached to the high ceiling. A person still operates the little elevator.

Patched onto one side of the building is a large screened swimming pool and hot tub where locals, for a small fee, can join "aquabics" classes. Others come for the low-priced meals. They love to look at the original china displayed in cases of old objects, some of antique quality, that give the lobby the look of one of those country museums set up in a vacant space once used for other things.

Upstairs is changing slowly. Rooms are getting redone, though they're small as ever, still with their original fireproof metal furniture. The barrel vault of the dark halls still feels like a subway tunnel during emergency drill, with ponderous fire doors that seal on weighted pulleys.

"Hey, that's why we come," says Miami lawyer Bob Dady, who makes a night of it at the Jac whenever he visits his son. "You come to a small town, why not stay someplace unique instead of a Holiday Inn. I have friends who stayed at that fabulous Hyatt in Hawaii. They came back and said they might as well have been in Orlando."

An ice cream parlor is new. A bar and French restaurant are in the works. The Jac's not likely to become anybody's version of posh. You just feel grateful that it's still around.

Hotel Jacaranda, 19 E. Main St., Avon Park, FL 33825. (813) 453-2211. John Naylor, general manager. 60 rooms and suites with AC, heat, private baths, color cable TV, direct-dial phone. Pool, elevator, library. Children of any age accepted, free in parents' room to 12. No pets. MC, Visa. Year-round rates: single: $30, double: $35. Mini-suites: $35, $40. Master suites: $45, $50. Weekly discount: 14%. Meal prices: lunch: $4 - $7, dinner: $4 - $10. Smoking permitted. Free off-street parking.

Babson Park — HILLCREST LODGE
Long established, family-run, mid-Florida lakeside lodge.

Hillcrest Lodge has had no change of owning family in 66 years. You might think it's had no change of guests.

Near Eastertime, at the end of each season, guests begin putting down deposits on their rooms for the next winter, just to ensure they'll be back. In turn Bob and Martha Wetzel keep saying, "Well, sure, let's do it one more year."

The lodge is tucked off Alternate Highway 27 in a subdivision started more than 70 years ago on a hillside south of Babson Park on the way to Frostproof. It is a quiet place where Wetzel daughters talk about *their* daughters growing up with their grandparents next door. Grandchildren at the lodge become third-generation table-crumbers. They exist in an amiable country order of freckles, mud turtles, and afternoon swims in the lake.

Guests have supplied a large part of what makes a hotel into a tradition. Hospitality is renewed each fall. The annual return of guests teaches kids growing up here the sentiments of fond hellos and goodbye hugs, and it makes of the seasons something that deepens kids' quarterly turns.

In the lobby and living room there are jigsaw puzzles, wicker, upholstered furniture with slipcovers you sink into, shelves of old books, a new carpet, a grandfather clock on the landing, wire hangers on a wooden coat rack, casement windows screening out the bugs but letting in the breeze, the sounds of crickets and boats on a lake, the colors of snapdragons and petunias in simple cut-glass vases on white-clothed tables in the dining room.

Hillcrest Lodge has been in the family since Martha's father bought it in 1925. Before that it was a community clubhouse for the well-to-do who wintered in Babson Park on Lake Calusa in the central Florida highlands. It burned in 1921, again in 1927, and was rebuilt each time.

The building is two-story stucco, tidily shuttered and symmetrical, with wood trim, and don't worry, now it more than meets the fire code. That's Bob's doing. He wants to be sure the insurance is renewable. That's his way. He is not only chairman of First Federal of Lake Wales, he is also chief electrician, plumber, engineer, accountant, and baker at Hillcrest Lodge. As guests like to tell newcomers, "The meals are superb, and they're all cooked by the owner's husband!"

Vacancies are rare for the nine air-conditioned apartments in four duplex buildings, and three air-conditioned self-catering cottages with 22 rooms as well as the eight bedrooms and baths on the second floor of the lodge. All are plainly furnished. Bob built all the outlying buildings, kind of the way Martha and he kept adding to the family.

There are nine children, 38 grandchildren, and 10 great-grandchildren—at recent count. Martha's first husband was killed in World War II after they'd had four. Bob and Martha had five more. All nine are close as can be. All grew up working in the lodge after Bob and Martha started operating it in 1946.

The lake is still clean for swimming and you approach it down a slope from the lodge to a sandy beach. On the other side is Webber College, whose students double as waitresses at the lodge.

The lake is large (though lately shrunk from drought), but there are no other hotels on its 45-mile shore. Hillcrest is hardly larger than many of the houses that rim the lake. Families are out in motorboats and sailboats, splashing from floats, fishing from wooden piers.

People who run hotels of this sort make a mark. They have influence. Their places are centers for activity. Such innkeepers become the focus of memories for families in the vicinity and others from far away.

Hillcrest Lodge, Hillcrest Heights on Alternate Highway 27, P.O. Box 67, Babson Park, FL 33827. (813) 638-1712. Bob and Martha Wetzel, managers. Lodge with 8 second-story rooms, three garden buildings with 22 single and double rooms, and 4 villas with 3 duplexes and 1 triplex, all with heat, private baths (except Gateway Hall with connecting), some with AC (including all apartments). Private beach. Dining room (Christmas to Easter only). Children of any age accepted. No pets. No credit cards. Villas with kitchens. Winter rates: rooms from $35 to $44 per person by the night; from $179 to $230 per person by the week, AP; apartments $44 by the night, $225 by the week, $575 by the month. (Apartment guests are expected to take a minimum of two meals each per week in the lodge dining room.) Off-season rates on request.

Clewiston — THE CLEWISTON INN
Old South hospitality in the finest lodgings around Lake Okeechobee.

There's no reason for the Clewiston Inn to be sitting all white-pillared and gentrified on the south plain of Lake Okeechobee but for sugar. Nor any other reason for the town itself, leastwise not for the prosperity that brings a country club, landing strip, and all else the planters calculate as benefits against costs increasingly totaled by environmentalists.

Sugar's demands have roots in 19th-century visions of empire when land was everywhere tempting beneath shallow basins of water. When Hamilton Disston began draining the Everglades in 1881, paying the state 25 cents for each of 4 million acres, there was no Palm Beach, no Fort Lauderdale, no Miami.

Sugar became dominant after 1921, when the first commercial plantings began to replace diversified vegetable crops. Intense cultivation after 65 years has severely depleted the soil and despoiled the lake. Vast regional wellfields that supply drinking water for coastal inhabitants are menaced, so that the debate is part of a larger argument about the future of the Everglades that will increasingly determine the future of investment in south Florida.

The inn is owned by the U.S. Sugar Corporation and sits aside US 27, locally known as the Sugarland Highway, near the Cane Court Motel and the Sugarland Shopping Center, in what is called the Sweetest Town in America.

The town was founded in 1921 as a construction camp during the extension of the railroad from Moore Haven. It was named to honor A.C. Clewis, a Tampa banker who had arranged financing for the line.

The inn was built five years later by the Southern Sugar Company and was meant to impress. Early visitors were surprised to find rooms with baths.

Though the hotel burned in 1937 (it was built of celotex, a flammable byproduct of sugar), it was immediately rebuilt, and the old-time feeling was kept.

Its colonial look puts visitors in mind of more ordered times when white pillars, whitewashed brick, circular drives under high porticos, French doors, and fanlight windows were everywhere symbols of welcome in Southern towns.

The hospitable lobby is cypress paneled, open-beamed, modestly chandeliered, attractively outfitted with reproductions of colonial furniture in front of a fireplace and set upon paver tiles and area rugs. To one side is the reception desk with a selection of local souvenirs, and to the other, the entrance to the Old South room where three meals a day are served in a setting of ladderback chairs, white cloths, hanging baskets, and windows with New Orleans shutters.

The Everglades Lounge is a popular cocktail bar for locals and visitors. Even teetotalers ought to see its wildlife mural.

Rooms are pleasant with firm beds, carpets, double-hung windows with venetian blinds, bed lamps, and simple decor. They were all refurbished with the dining room, in 1989, and remarkably with no increase in rates, making overnighting here a remarkable Florida bargain. Box lunches, boat rentals, and fishing guides can be arranged. Nearby is an 18-hole golf course, tennis courts and a public swimming pool.

Clewiston also features the Old South Bar-B-Q Ranch, a regional landmark renowned for its hokey hand-hewn rhyming signs that line the highway for miles in both directions. Nearby to the northwest is the Cypress Knee Museum.

Clewiston is a part of old Florida under intense pressure for change, and worth a visit away from the turnpike.

The Clewiston Inn, US Highway 27 at 108 Royal Palm Ave., Clewiston, FL 33440. (813) 983-8151. Joseph Rollin, manager. 53 rooms and suites with AC, heat, color cable TV, direct-dial phone, bathrooms with tubs. Restaurant, bar, municipal pool and tennis courts across the street, nearby 18-hole golf course. Children of any age accepted, free in parents' rooms to 12. AmEx, DC, MC, Visa. Winter rates: single $55, double $65, full breakfast included. Family rooms (for up to 6) $60, also with breakfast. Balance of year: single $45, double $50, family room $50. Meals in Old South room: lunch $4 to $8; dinner $7 to $13. Off-street parking.

East Lake Weir — LAKESIDE INN
Revived hunting and fishing lodge, a woody hideaway.

Y ou wouldn't think that in Florida today you could get so out of the way as at Bill and Sandy Bodner's Lakeside Inn. East Lake Weir is miles from any superhighway. As a consequence, back roads here offer some of the best bicycling in the state.

Though you can see the inn from the road, its best side is the one facing the lake. From there it looks grandly northern, but with pinched architectural features that make it feel hidden and inaccessible.

The Lakeside feels like a secret waiting to be opened. That secret is revealed in stages, like the unlayering of an artichoke. It helps that there's so little organized activity in the vicinity that you gladly spend your time visiting with this blue-trimmed gray house and its grounds atop a hill in a former orange grove. The place holds you like the memory of a grandmother.

What drew the early Canadians is still here: the lake and the mild climate. They outfitted their hunting lodge in heart cypress, and installed fireplaces to warm those who spent chilly afternoons fishing the lake or hunting the woods.

The place was built in 1882. Citrus was prospering in those years. The train from Ocala carried the fruit north and brought tourists south to the towns that rimmed Lake Weir. Paddlewheel excursions were popular. From the lake, visitors could see the great homes of the prominent growers, Captain John Carney's "Grand View" and his brother Ephram's "Emerald Hill."

The great freeze of 1895 slowed things, but didn't end the good living here. The lakeside town of Stanton was on the Chautauqua circuit. For 30 years, the yearly assembly attracted prominent lecturers and performers to the auditorium and amphitheater.

Train, Chautauqua, heyday citrus—all are gone now but for the remnant grove and the dock of the Lake Weir Yacht Club next door. And the lodge.

Sandy and Bill Bodner had come to Florida when an opening in the food business moved Bill to Jacksonville. After Jacksonville, Bill joined Certified Grocers of Florida in Ocala. Sandy had become a realtor, but it was Bill who took to the old inn as a place to live.

"It smelled so bad," recalls Sandy. "All the tile was falling off the kitchen ceiling. The paint was all peeling outside. I was in a state of shock. The first time I saw it, it was so overwhelming. We spent 10 weeks just restoring the kitchen."

But the inn is now a prize again—comfortable, meant for relaxing in with a newspaper or a book. The living room is all cypress walls and ceiling, and pine floors with patterned rugs. The recently redone parlor is the bright room of the house, where a lot of white rattan adapts Victorian furnishings to modern comfort.

There are five guest rooms, two with adjoining bath, three that use the bath at the end of the hall. An apartment with its own bath is planned for the north wing. Rooms are furnished with antiques Bill and Sandy have collected. The rooms feel cozy in cypress and pine.

Guests enjoy home-baked breakfasts of pancakes or egg dishes, fresh fruits in season, and orange juice squeezed winters from trees on the lawn. Roosters on the property provide a built-in alarm clock. The dogs and cats are just for the pleasure. A horse that sometimes grazes at the bottom of the hill belongs to the neighbor.

Canoes are available for guests to use on the lake. They explore by car, typically up to Oklawaha or down to Leesburg for dinner.

Mostly they ease themselves into the mood and stay put. For guests who want to indulge in the mood of long ago, Bill and Sandy's satisfies like few places can.

Lakeside Inn, P.O. Box 71, East Lake Weir, FL 32632. (904) 288-1396. Bill and Sandy Bodner, innkeepers. 5 rooms, 2 baths (with showers and tubs), color TV in one room, color TV in the parlor. Children accepted 5 and up, $10 in parents' room. Small pets accepted, no charge. House phone for free local and credit-card calls. No credit cards, checks OK. Smoking outside only. Off-street parking. Canoes available at no charge. Year-round rates: $45-$50 double, $30-$35 single.

Haines City – VAN-ROOK INN
In-town, frilly, with tea room.

Year after year, freezes have pushed citrus farming south. Where mid-state once was thick with groves, freezes in recent years have led owners to sell in a market ever prime for retirees.

Trailer parks are replacing citrus.

For towns like Haines City, the adjustment has been difficult. Change not only has uprooted a familiar and easygoing way of life, but also has brought a demand for more services. Whereas groves required only limited populations and were easy to manage, their replacement by residential communities brings a need for expanding parks, recreation, hospitals, and police.

"We don't have a broad enough tax base," says Ernest Vandiver, a former mayor of Haines City and a current member of the city commission. "We can't keep up with the growth."

Ernest frequently sounds off about the state of affairs at the little Van-Rook Inn, where he's at home because his wife, Frances, runs it. The Van-Rook is an early and so far happy sign of change in this crossroads town along the I-4 corridor in an area under pressure to grow.

Vacationers who happen to come upon the town typically remark on its landmark feature, the Palm Crest Hotel. Unfortunately, the hotel has been boarded up for almost 20 years. The Palm Crest and Haines City prospered together in the 1920s during the land boom. But these days nobody's eager for out-of-way hotels in cities with uncertain futures. So the Palm Crest, its multiple stories visible for miles around, seems to stand for Haines City's questioning about what's next.

Haines City is more favorably known as northern terminus of Florida's Scenic Highway. State Road 17 runs south from here 68 miles through groves that roll along the hilly and lake-studded spine of mid-state Florida to Lake Placid. Haines City's little downtown is undergoing a historic revival, though most of the growth continues at the fringe, where shopping centers and other nondescript sprawl dominate.

The Van-Rook is a happy change because it's one family's attempt to make a go of staying put. Frances Vandiver–who owns the inn with Diane Rook, her sister in Texas–has lived in Haines City since childhood. Her grandmother worked at the first citrus plant.

The inn was built in 1921 as a private house. Then it became a CPA office and an antique shop. Frances and Diane got the idea for opening a tea room and an inn.

"Till we opened it was either fast food or truck stops," says Frances. "There was no place in Haines City where women could come and feel comfortable by themselves."

The Van-Rook has changed that. Since mid-1989, the sisters have served a daily lunch and afternoon tea Tuesdays through Saturdays, with fashion shows on alternate Fridays. A little dress and jewelry boutique has opened opposite the inn's sitting room. Locals drop in for a visit. It's not unusual for women of the town to offer their recipes, often bringing samples for Frances to try.

Guests take to the inn because of its stylish looks—green trim on white stucco with a giant oak in front.

The tea room is all very pink, pale, and chintz with cushioned lyreback chairs on polished pine floors. Frances has made the drapes here and throughout the house. She has swagged these with rosettes that amenably combine with rosy bough wreaths, chintz napkin holders in fabric rosettes, and rose and lily prints.

Her five rooms are all different, from the open and airy Southwest Room with exceptional bent willow pieces, to the theatrical bath of the Country Room, where anyone emerging from the shower virtually debuts. The Peach Room has an elaborately constructed 1910 triple-mirror dressing table in mahogany. The French Room is named for its massive French sleigh bed, antique French bench chair, tryptich vanity with satiny chair, and striped provincial paper. Wood tones warm the downstairs Green Room, with bentwood rocker on glossy pine floor.

Now that the inn is successful, Frances has opened an antique and crafts shop in back, and has leased space to a balloon specialty shop. She has become active in the Haines City Main Street program, begun in 1990, and in reviving the Community Theatre building. Guests at the Van-Rook are at the heart of what's holding Haines City together.

Van-Rook Inn, 106 S. 1st St., Haines City, FL 33844. (813) 421-2242. Frances Vandiver and Diane Rooks, proprietors. Five rooms and baths with AC, heat. Ceiling fan, color TV in sitting room. Phones on front desk for credit-card LD and local calls. No cot or rollaway available. No pets. MC, Visa, checks accepted. Rates: $65 per room single or double Jan.-April, $55 rest of year. Rates include full breakfast, fresh flowers in room. Lunch available: $5.95 up. In-house dinners can be arranged. Smoking only in tea room and on front porch. Off-street parking.

Lakeland — LAKE MORTON
BED & BREAKFAST
Architecturally rich town, intellectually rich hospitality.

Bryce Zender is a former Fulbright Scholar in the Soviet Union who once started a "school for living" for the inner city poor in Kalamazoo, Michigan. Mary Ann Zender started the Head Start program in Polk County. Their social activism adds an unusual dimension to the world of innkeeping.

Lakeland, where they live, is regarded by uninformed Floridians as a town of little interest because Tampa overshadows it to the west, and Orlando to the east. Yet Lakeland's architectural heritage, remarkable only in part because of the legacy of Frank Lloyd Wright, and its reviving downtown make this a worthwhile stop on any tour of Florida. The Zenders' Lake Morton Bed-and-Breakfast is the place to stay.

For all their commitment to their causes, Mary Ann and Bryce are warmly hospitable. You want to set aside the time to get them talking. They'll stoke your own idealism. You'll likely drive away with more than you expected from a night on the road.

Lakeland has been a railroad town and a citrus town. Its prosperity at the turn of the century was due to the aggressive pro-railroad stance of its founder, Abraham Godwin Munn. Thanks to him, 20 trains a day were stopping in Lakeland by 1893, only eight years after the city's founding. The decades of the early century saw successive building booms that have left Lakeland today with a clear architectural trace of its history.

Much of the best is accessible by foot from the Zenders' bed-and-breakfast.

They are a block from their namesake lake, three from the heart of downtown with its wealth of landmark buildings, and only slightly farther from Florida Southern College with its treasury of Frank Lloyd Wright designs.

Wright came in the late 1930s because he was invited by the college president, and because he was intrigued by the challenge of Florida. He later summarized his work at the Lakeland campus with the pithy, "Out of the ground, into the sun." Some seven of the buildings and much of the overall campus design and landscaping are Wright's contributions.

If you can work out your visit to suit their schedules, the Zenders will give you a tour. But they do stay busy. Bryce nowadays teaches gifted kids at McLaughlin Middle School in nearby Lake Wales. Mary Ann started the Head Start agency in the county, got eight day-care centers going, and was then promoted to grants writer for the county for a range of social action programs.

The Lake Morton Bed-and-Breakfast, a beige bungalow, was built in 1925. Mary Ann discovered that for a time it was called the Tourist Rest Apartments. She named the three guest suites of the house (all downstairs) for three longtime residents: Bessie Willis, an owner; A.T. Phillips, a resident manager, and Ethel Eicker, who lived here for 28 years. Mary Ann and Bryce have decorated the suites with furniture of the period, which is to say, with a mix of what would have been accumulated by householders of the time. Each suite has its own bathroom, sitting room, and private bath.

Furnishings consist of items like an Eastlake mirror from an old theater in St. Petersburg, and half an oaken ice box thrown away in Wisconsin and salvaged for a vanity and sink. Bryce and Mary Ann have found old doors by running ads, and have come up with an Amish cherry loveseat, maple dressers, a mahogany country armoire, and a little two-thirds-sized tub. There are oak obelisk dividers between living and dining rooms. A handmade needlepoint was made by an 85-year-old aunt.

Mary Ann and Bryce think of their house as vaguely northern because it's dark. And so it is. They've pledged to lighten it. The house is constantly changing. No surprise for a couple given to stirring things up.

Lake Morton Bed & Breakfast, 817 South Boulevard, Lakeland, FL 33801. (813) 688-6788. Bryce and Mary Ann Zender, proprietors. 3 suites with private baths, AC, heat, kitchenettes, 2 with ceiling fans. Color cable TV, house phone for free local and credit-card calls. Children of any age accepted, $5 includes bed. No pets. No credit cards. Personal checks accepted. Rates: Nov.-June $50 single or double, July-Oct. $30, includes continental breakfast. Newspaper available. Smoking permitted. Free off-street parking.

Lake Wales – CHALET SUZANNE
Florida's most imaginative small hotel and gourmet restaurant, mid-state in the citrus belt near Disney attractions.

Hidden among groves down a side road off the back road at the end of a bumpy brick lane three miles north of Lake Wales lies an elfin kingdom where grown-ups spin in the air and defy the law that location is everything.

Chalet Suzanne is Florida's most imaginative small hotel with a reputation that has reached to the moon.

Its business depends on closer markets, however. People for more almost 60 years have found their way to this implausible site for lodging and gourmet meals by following fanciful road markers almost as well known as the pastel version of a Tyrolean duchy they point to.

In 1931 Bertha Hinshaw chose to stay on in rural Polk County after widowhood, the stock market crash, and a fire. She created the Chalet Suzanne and survived by her flair for cooking and entertaining. Since then the Chalet has grown in popularity despite major changes in tourism patterns.

Bertha's legacy has been to trust whatever happens, bad breaks and good, see where they lead. Innocence like that is why the Chalet is whimsical storybook fare. Its success has been never to vary the mix of theatrical illusion and country hospitality that have made it one of Florida's notable places.

Food is what most people know the Chalet for. Whether breakfast, lunch or dinner, a Chalet meal is as much setting as food.

Five dining rooms have risen from an early fiery disaster that left Bertha only the chicken house, the horse shed, the rabbit hutch frames, and a game room over the lake. She played a hunch that the quirky shapes would charm rather than dismay. Thus the child in her was inspired toward ever more fanciful constructions until the entire place became fantastic.

Hinshaw family recipes have become the traditional entrees served every night of the year. Most popular is chicken Suzanne, a much-basted, amber, baked delicacy that flakes from the touch of a fork. The best food story has to do with chicken liver hors d'oeuvres that were readied so late for a group of guests that the baked grapefuit appetizers were already at their tables. So the livers were lightheartedly placed on the grapefruit halves, in one of those "accidents" now traditional, part of all meals that also feature Chalet-famous soups, hot potato rolls, salad, vegetables, potato, a palate-clearing ice, dessert, and coffee.

The dining rooms are on 14 levels, and no two tables are alike. No two settings are alike! Some are set on wrought iron with rustic tile borders, some with inset tile murals of medieval scenes, others with lace cloths. The eclectic collection of hanging lanterns, Persian lamps, and stained glass dapple the room bewitchingly. By the end of the meal you are likely still scanning the variety of silver, china, pitchers, chairs, and costuming, feeling good that you've hardly found two of anything.

One dining room that resembles a sumptuous Viking longboat is overlooked by an interior balcony of the honeymoon suite, as if royal heirs of the Principality of Marzipan might appear to wave Godspeed to their explorers about to discover realms of riches on winds of gluttony.

It is hardly a surprise to learn that Astronaut James Irwin took Chalet soups on his two voyages to the moon, and even on the Apollo-Soyuz link-up.

Carl confirms that "the place was put together by accident. My mother tore anything down if it didn't look just right after it was built. There were no plans. It's been hell on us ever since with leaks and maintenance. She just loved to create. Then she'd lose interest. She'd go travel around the world and bring back everything she thought would make it look more like a storybook."

Like the restaurant, the Chalet's 30 rooms make eclecticism seem patentable. Carl's wife, Vita, says that anything added is still Bertha-style: by eye and feel, though these days they are a little more planned when artisans carry it off.

The cottages line up like roll call at a tipsy masquerade alongside a petunia-lined greensward. The exteriors are gingerbread and pastel with carved belfries and sloping pink awnings, with gables, hips, chimneys, turreted peaks, and spires. Antique lanterns of stained glass and wrought iron are strung from baroque stanchions and palms with drunken sways.

A typical atypical room has a country Swiss bed with knobby head- and footboards, rusticated chests and planked odd-shaped desks fitted into sharp-angled corners. Area rugs accent sometimes sloping parquet floors. There are plenty of mirrors, all different. Tiles are everywhere. Throw pillows and drapes, quilted spreads and door sashes—all make you want to curl up and read someone small a story.

A Carl-project is to expand the fly-in facilities which already include a 2,450-foot sod airstrip within walking distance of rooms and restaurant. In the old days the strip was a country road with gates at either end, and pilots still sometimes radio ahead to ask if the gates are closed. Today they fly in looking for Carl, a former P-51 fighter pilot, to be air-bobbing in his one-man gyrocopter—"like flying on a kitchen chair," he says.

Next to the airstrip is the soup cannery, for 40-some years a mainstay for a worldwide mail-order business that also includes the distinctive bowls the soup is served in, plus sauces, preserves, crafts, and other goodies featured at the restaurant and its gift shops.

Before the Florida Turnpike and the Interstates, lunch was the popular meal at the Chalet to spell the drive for motorists bound to and from Miami. Today the trade is mostly dinner, for people from populous mid-Florida cities and tourist attractions.

Withal, the same once-upon-a-time hospitality.

Chalet Suzanne Country Inn & Restaurant, US Highway 27 & 17A, 3 miles north of Lake Wales, FL 33859. (813) 676-6011. Carl and Vita Hinshaw, owner-managers. 30 rooms with color cable TV, AC, heat, direct-dial phones, bathrooms (27 with tubs). Restaurant, bar, gift shops. Swimming pool, lake. Airstrip on premises. Children of any age accepted. Extra person in room $12. Pets $20. All major credit cards. Year-round rates: $95 to $185 single or double, except summer special: dinner, lodgings, breakfast for 2, including gratuities, for $239. Breakfast $7-$14; lunch $25-$36; dinner $50-$69. Off-street parking. Smoking allowed. Restaurant handicap accessible. 1 guest room handicap accessible.

Minneola — LAKE MINNEOLA INN
Friendly, big-porch hospitality.

If there were saving grace from the greenhouse effect warming the earth, it's come too late for citrus growing in central Florida. You can climb the Citrus Tower on U.S. 27 in Clermont and see for miles around where recent freezes have wiped out the crop. They'll be able to call this the RV Park Tower one day soon, when all the groves have been converted to the next wave of use.

From atop the tower, you also may be able to spot the Lake Minneola Inn.

The lodge was built early in the century on the site of an old hotel that had burned. Before the Depression, this area around the lakes boomed. There was a golf course, a country club, a yacht club. A lumber mill was next door, and an ice house and a train depot. People came through looking for land. They could catch the train from Minneola Station to Sanford, and later, could take steamboats from the St. Johns River.

After the Depression, Clermont and Minneola dwindled almost to nothing. The lodge was made into apartments. The owner opened some doors, locked others and added a few bathrooms. He ran it like an apartment house from about 1964 to about 1980. There were no overnight guests.

When new Highway 27 was engineered to curve around town, that left the old Main Street and everything in its sharp angle forgotten by the speedsters. Time settled in, and that was what captured the willing soul of Steve Parrish, an electrical engineer by profession but a preservationist at heart.

Steve would trailer his boat down to the lake from Ocala until one day, on his first date with Shari when they came waterskiing, she fell in love with the look of the area. He first thought about rehabbing the old Straker place before she did. "I thought, 'What a neat place,'" recalled Steve, rocking on the porch with his mom looking at old pictures of the town. "Shari looked and said that it needed a lot of work."

The building's look—as much as anything inside—anchors the past in place. It has big overhangs that slope to cover a big open wraparound porch. Even on a hot summer day, the breeze is cool. Baskets of lime green ferns and violets add color in front of the butterscotch siding with vanilla trim. A big grassy field tumbles to the lake. Mossy oaks shade the lawn.

Inside the inn, the look is country plain, with a lot of timber and framing cypress. Thick beams solid as square trees that tell you the house is going to be here a long time. The parlor has tongue-in-groove wainscoting. Steve and Shari have brought in Victorian pieces and added theatrically swagged curtains. It's not a connoisseur's house, but it's comfortable.

Rooms have Eastlake beds, some tiger oak with scrolled head- and footboards.

There are cane chairs, and oak and mahogany pieces. One bed has spoon-carved ornamental hex-like signs. Most of the rooms have near-ceiling-to-floor windows. Beds are firm. Steve and Shari are still adding to the rooms. They only opened in 1990, and hadn't yet looked at a lot of other inns for ideas.

History is the real pull here. It's hard to find places this quiet and friendly. Steve and Shari and Steve's mom, Nell, tell how people had their mules pull buggies right into the lake so they could fill barrels with water.

Guests like to eat breakfast on the porch, which has a galvanized tin roof and cane and wicker chairs. The meal includes juice, homemade coffee cakes, hot and cold cereals, coffee, and maybe croissants, bagels and cream cheese, and bran muffins.

From down the slope you can see, across the lake, a golf course and clubhouse coming back where there used to be groves. Beach rockers tip back and forth in the phantom gusts, moss whipped by the wind hisses through the oaks, and white caps rush at the little beach. History gets all blown about, but you feel safe in this inn that bobs surely and is likely to stay around.

Lake Minneola Inn, 508 Main Ave., Minneola, FL 34755. (904) 394-2232. Stephen Parrish and Nell Parrish, innkeepers. 10 rooms with 9 baths (1 bath for 2-bedroom suite on 3rd floor), AC, heat, ceiling fan. Color cable TV. Radios in some rooms, otherwise available. Living room phone for free local and credit-card LD calls. Kitchen refrigerator available. Coolers available for room or picnics. Children accepted 5 years and up. $6 for rollaway. No pets. MC, Visa. Year-round rates: $45-75, single or double occupancy; up to 4 in suite. Includes continental breakfast. Newspaper available. Lakeside swing, picnic table, dock, cane poles (license required), electric fringe-topped lake launches, 10 covered boat slips. No smoking inside. Free off-street parking.

Mount Dora — THE LAKESIDE INN

Graciously restored 107-year-old resort in one of central
Florida's most beautiful small towns.

Hospitality hugs the slopes and livens the hopes of lakeside Mount Dora, a town
named for a welcoming pioneer. The 107-year-old Lakeside Inn, already revived
once in recent years, in late 1990 emerged from its Chapter 11 handicap and
remains the center of town life.

The Lakeside was started the year the settlement took the name of Dora
Ann Drawdy, a settler with her husband in 1846, a year after Florida entered the
Union as 27th state. Two wilderness surveyors she helped provision named a
nearby lake for her. When later settlers chose to change their place name from
Royallew (briefly commemorating three children of another pioneer), they
enshrined the hospitable Mrs. Drawdy as their town's namesake.

Without doubt Mount Dora is one of Florida's fairest small cities, population 7,000, beautifully set amidst lakes and hills that rise 184 feet. Its towering oaks and magnolias shade grand and humble homes, and green a tidy low-rise downtown. The entire panorama inclines from the surrounding highland down to Lake Dora as if it were a spacious amphitheater for lakefront performance by the gods.

Mount Dora is blessed to have been bypassed by Highway 441. From the east and south, the town route slips away from four lanes past a citrus packing plant and over a little railroad overpass before entering a neighborhood of modest stores and the ubiquitous antique shops constantly replenished from the estates of well-to-do retirees.

From the west and north, the old highway and lesser roads skirt the lake. A railroad track from the county seat of Tavares—a smaller town than Mount Dora—runs down the middle of an old connector road in the fashion of inter-urban lines of the Twenties. The route is along an historic bicycle path of the last century, and twice a day freights rumble by the old Atlantic Coast Line station that now serves as attractive quarters for the chamber of commerce.

Other landmark buildings intact or in part survive with new uses. The ice house is now the Ice House Theater. The everything-you-ever-wanted-to-know-about-Victorian-architecture Donnelly House has mellowed into a Masonic temple. The old jail is the Royallew Museum of the historical society, one vignette per cell. Pillars of the Guller House, once a hotel, later City Hall, have become part of the new City Hall, and a once waterside post office, later a landed cottage, has returned to the water as a boathouse that served the Lakeside Inn.

Everyone was thrilled with revival of the hotel when it reopened in 1985 after it had missed its first winter season in 101 years. At that time not a single hotel was left operating in town. The Simpson had become a boarding house. The Villa Dora and the Grandview had been torn down. The city manager vowed to refuse a demolition permit to a group seeking to replace the inn with con- dominiums. But happiest when new owners announced plans to save, upgrade, and reopen the hotel year-round was Richard Edgerton.

His family had owned the property for more than 50 years, from the time former President Calvin Coolidge and his wife stayed for a month one winter, until forced by retirement to sell to an interim group which proved unable to make a go of a bargain too dilapidated to maintain its market.

"The hotel performed a vital function in bringing families of substance to live here and help form Mount Dora's present quality of life," he said. "I know at least 150 families who came here the same way.

"And we need new residents. In an average town," he explained, "about five percent of the houses will change hands in a year. Here, close to 20 percent change because of age and job transfers."

The hotel's revival at a sum of more than $5 million was carried out by a genial lover of the old and charming, Ellison Ketchum. Ellison brought back 87 rooms and the $4^1/_2$-acre grounds. He so wedded the hotel to the town again that voters saw fit to elect him to the town council. But a falling out with majority owners forced his departure. After that, despite good efforts by a succession of managers, the hotel lost its luster. Faucets leaked and chipped tiles went unreplaced. Service in the dining room was eager but sometimes amateurish. Trade slipped. The hotel was holding on. Now all is likely to be improved again by mid-1991 under new general manager W. B. "Bill" Smith.

The hotel is ever worth visiting. Guests find a spacious yellow, white-trimmed Tudor-style resort with touches of old Florida, full of gables, bays and windows, covered walkways and flower gardens in broad yards. There is a large heated swimming pool and sandy lakefront beach—though the lake is not fit for swimming—tennis courts, and a putting green. Within walking distance is an overwater boardwalk to Palm Island, inhabited by owls, ospreys, and waterbirds, and where barbecue pits and picnic tables are provided.

Rooms are done in Laura Ashley papers and fabrics. Beds are extra long. Closets are walk-in. Tubs are deep. Windows are sealed shut, an unfortunate concession to overbearing insurers.

Ellison Ketchum says that the hotel is a marriage of old Mount Dora and new Mount Dora. He expects that locals will continue to support the dining room and lounge, and that guests will continue to love the place and the downtown shopping. He sees a lot of commitment in town. Everyone is betting that the Lakeside will make it into its third century.

The Lakeside Inn, 100 North Alexander Street, Mount Dora, FL 32757. (904) 383-4101; 800-556-5016 (national). W.B "Bill" Smith, general manager. 87 rooms with AC, heat, bathrooms with tubs, color cable TV, direct-dial phones, dining room, bar, meeting rooms, pool, tennis courts, putting green, lakeside beach, fishing. Children of any age accepted, free in parents' room to 12. No pets. All major credit cards. Rates: Jan.-April, $80-$120 single, $95-$135 double; May-Dec., $65-$95 single, $80-$120 double. Special mid-week packages. $10 for each additional person. Breakfasts $1.75-$8 (available only on weekends), lunch $5 to $10, dinner $11-$19.25. Room rates include morning newspaper and continental breakfast. Off-street parking.

Ona — SOLOMON'S CASTLE
One room in the one-of-a-kind wonderland of a
one-lining genius.

Howard Solomon dropped like a Coke bottle out of an airplane into the backwash of DeSoto County. The gods must have been crazy. The tilt sign lit up and has been on ever since.

Consider Howard's son Benjamin. At age five, Benjamin has never lived anyplace but in a castle at the end of a yellow brick road. When Benjamin goes visiting people, he lifts up their rugs to look for their dungeons. He has one. Doesn't everybody? Then again, nobody else has a dad who never grew up.

Howard skewers life on a shish-ka-bob of sight gags.

He had just come back from seven years of creating flashy interiors for tourist boutiques in Freeport, Grand Bahama. He'd heard land was cheap near Arcadia. For $350 apiece he bought 54 acres, the deal of a lifetime. Except that Howard had bought his acreage during a drought. When the rains fell again, his property turned into swamp.

"I made lemonade out of the lemon," says Howard.

Would you believe a castle out of scrap aluminum? In season now, 500 people a week come by bus and pay Howard $3.50 a head to see the place.

The moat came first. Or what others might call a drainage canal. He drained water off the land into a ditch. Since he was born with imagination, his ditch was a moat, and moats come with castles.

Howard's good luck was seeing an ad for aluminum plates, good for fixing your roof and patching chicken coops, at 4 cents a square foot. "I said to myself, 'Hey, a lot of people live in Airstreams,'" Howard recalls.

Today he and his wife, Peggy, Benjamin, and Howard's mom and dad all live in an aluminum-clad castle with a 45-foot spired bell tower as conspicuous in dour DeSoto County as an elephant in a tutu. Howard, who likes nothing if not abrupt juxtapositions, has programmed his electronic bells to play "Follow The Yellow Brick Road," "If I Were A Rich Man," and "Hava Nagilah."

The bell tower and the family domain are connected by a set of galleries where Howard's drollery has given physical form to the one-liner humor he grew up with in the Forties and Fifties. Out of scrap metal Howard has created galleries of mechanical jokes. He has a pistol without a trigger for a man without a finger, thumbscrews for pressing wine grapes one at a time, and a flying lawnmower for tall grass. There's an entire gallery of clothes-hanger art, and another of cars made from 300 empty beer cans.

Howard got the idea for creating an attraction in the middle of nowhere thanks to the independent ways of southwest Florida cowboys. Until 1957, DeSoto County was open range, and the cowboys would round up their cattle every October. When a fence law was enacted, oldtimers continued open ranging on their lands, so that in 1972 cowboys were still rounding up out in the woods. Word spread that a castle was being built in the swamp. Curiosity spread. Folks asked if they could visit.

That worked out fine for a daughter who was living with Howard at the time. She didn't want to go out to work, so she volunteered to show people around. Then a tour bus operator from Sebring invited representatives from 40 attractions —including Solomon's Castle—to plan new tour circuits. Tourists come 25,000 a year now. Hardly a day's blip at Disney, but enough that after nearly 20 years, Howard is thinking that maybe some nice person would like to come from Japan, buy his collection of junk-turned-to-jewels, and let him retire to a life as sculptor.

Out back in the only structure not clad in aluminum, he has his iron shop and wood shop: "The only serious part of the operation, where my heart is," says Howard. It's where he'd like to retreat to become a serious artist.

Yes. The bed-and-breakfast. It's under a high-sloping ceiling that pulls in the sunlight through stained glass windows. There are French doors, a large bedroom with queen pull-out beds, and carpeted floors. There's a full kitchen with tile floors, and a huge bathroom with towels thick as castling armor (albeit softer) and the sulphurous smell of the local water. All perfect. Except don't rely on the clock. It never keeps time. Howard says he can never get things right.

The East Wing at Solomon's Castle, Rt. 1, Ona, FL 33865. (813) 494-6077. Howard Solomon, proprietor. 1 efficiency private bath, kitchen, AC, heat. TV for rent $4. Direct-dial phone available for free local and credit-card LD calls. Fishing, canoeing. No credit cards, checks accepted. Children accepted 12 and up. No pets. Rates: $100 for up to 4 persons, includes fruits and ice in efficiency, and tour of Solomon's Castle. Gift shop on premises. No smoking. Free off-street parking.

Orlando — COURTYARD AT LAKE LUCERNE
From unrestrained bravo to standing ovation.

Surreal like a monorail through Yesterland, the East-West Expressway dips a downtown ramp by Orlando's oldest house, easing descent of travelers soon bound for the 21st century into plum-pudding cozy lodgings of the 19th.

A ticket-taker out front would qualify the old Norment-Parry House turned inn as a downtown extension of the main mouse at Disney. Orlando in-the-reviving is still up for grabs, juxtaposing cheapo hotels with shimmery skyscrapers, railroad boxcars with Ferraris.

But there's nothing unfinished about the Courtyard at Lake Lucerne, a three-house compound developed from the Norment-Parry House, at 107 years the oldest house in Orlando. And not that the going has been easy. From its pioneer prominence as a judge's house (Norment), later owned by a tax collector (Parry), the Norment-Parry House across the expressway from Lake Lucerne slipped as a rooming house, slid as a Salvation Army dormitory, crashed as a halfway house run by the city.

Attorney Charles Meiner, who bought the heap for an office, got talked into bed-and-breakfast by his preservationist son Sam. The father made a game of it. He made seven trips to England, shipped back containers of antiques. After restoring the Queen Anne architectural dignity, he invited a group of friends—interior designers, architects, artist, carpenter—each to visit his warehouse to pick out what he or she wanted for doing a room.

Like inviting Craig Claiborne into the kitchen of LeCirque for "doing" a meal.

As if the staged theatricality weren't enough, Charles and Sam have since added to the compound the Wellborn Apartments, one of Orlando's best examples of Art Deco, with 12 one-bedroom suites, each with its own living room, bedroom, bath, kitchen, phone, and TV. They also added the I.W. Phillips House, which has three large Edwardian suites upstairs (jacuzzi and steam shower in the Honeymoon Suite), and a downstairs used for wedding receptions and other occasions.

Pleasure, barely whispered outside the Norment-Parry House in pale blue and white, bursts in blue brilliance from the Jay Crawford Suite to the right upon entering. Of course it's the wallpaper. Its lick-me-candy-blue bands, unrelenting in their tickle, so putting you in mind of feather-to-foot laughter, shamelessly surround the room, extending to behind the bath set conspicuously in an alcove. Truth to tell, the delicate curtain left open suggests a person (dear reader, one leaves the gender to your own mature imagination) affording a naked presence.

The suite combines Victorian order with harlequin humor in a statement utterly stylized, so that satisfaction with the rooms' decor hangs like the grin of a Cheshire cat. It is the sort of arrangement that makes you want to practice your penmanship, the application of Victorian control—teeth-clenching control—to an otherwise unrestrained Bravo!

Consider the Steinbaugh Suite directly above. Guests immerge in green that extends from the green-carpeted bedroom into a green glassed-in sunparlor with striped green-cushioned classical wicker sofa and armchairs curved to resemble the questioning bent of a Boston intellect. Cool mornings, the warming sun upstairs cloaks guests at breakfast who enjoy views to the lake.

Never has so much been done with so little as in the Gena Ellis Suite. The space is small but the concept arresting as a bright bulb suddenly lit on a dark night. The bathroom has been simply stripped into the bedroom, separated more by imagination than by construction.

First the space is zoned apart by texture. The bedroom is blue carpeted. The "bathroom" is white tiled from floor up to height of the sink. Separation is furthered—and whimsy extended—by a 4-panel decoupage screen illustrated with turn-of-the-century variations on the theme of happiness. Behind is a molded shower stall.

Next along this strip of a bathroom is the sink. Then, at the far end after a stand-out striped tufted-in-satin side chair, and behind the narrowest white paneled door, is the commode.

No less praise for the remaining guest quarters.

Miss Baby's Boudoir features a church-style rounded window that, unlatched, falls forward braked by chains. The Honeymoon Suite is faintly martial, suggesting retreat to an encampment beyond reach of some nemesis. Here at last romantic respite crowned by a 6-foot walnut Victorian headboard. The Clippinger Suite (best in the house for families because of its large spaces) features a frenzied floral wallpaper and fabric design—red flowers in dense green jungle—that remains utterly wild though caged in perimeters of upholstery.

What guests find throughout are virtuoso ensembles of furniture, wallpapers, fabrics, and accessories that perfectly elaborate an essential Victorian concept that prescribed abstruse order for justifying private overabundance. Here are kilim rugs keyed to draperies accenting carpets, hand-knit coverlets contrasting embroidered cushions on fainting sofas, wall-mounted Staffordshire china complimenting cabriole chairs with enamel inlays. The living room is a tour de force of silks and satins on elaborately turned, bent, and beaded furniture, and toasting forks and make-up-preserving face shields, all set among bursts of flowers freshly arranged in ornamented porcelain.

Throughout the courtyard are superb tropical plantings and low brick walls. The twinkling lights in the great shade trees make the entire place Christmas cheery year-round. Truth is, this place amounts to a gift you'll want to give yourself every time you visit Orlando.

The Courtyard at Lake Lucerne, 211 N. Lucerne Circle East, Orlando, FL 32801. (407) 648-5188. Charles and Paula Meiner, innkeepers, Jo Ann Dearing, manager. 22 rooms and suites, all with baths (most with tubs as well as showers), AC, heat, some with ceiling fans. Color cable TV in Crawford and Clippinger suites downstairs in the Norment-Parry, all in Wellborn and the I.W. Phillips House. All rooms with pushbutton phones, 50¢ for local calls. Children accepted. No pets. AmEx, MC, Visa. Complimentary wine on arrival. Rates: $85-$150 double, year-round. $25 for persons more than 2 to a room. Extended continental breakfast. Off-street parking.

Sebring — KENILWORTH LODGE
Once grand hotel now provides comfortable lodgings at bargain rates.

Winter used to whistle in with the Orange Blossom Special and jauntily withdraw with a trainside musical farewell. In between, the news of Sebring was always full of comings and goings at Kenilworth Lodge. From winter to winter, the hotel's season surged with the railroad's, powered by the Powerful escaping the North.

Northern winters are still for escaping, but railroads and the Kenilworth are only slightly involved. Hotel and railroad today draw fewer patrons in 12 months than they once easily attracted in four.

The hotel remains conspicuous even if diminished in aspect. Its 138 rooms in use on two of its three floors stretch in long arms that overpower a site once surrounded by miles of orange groves. Grandeur, lost when cows were set grazing on the golf course, will not revive from a K-Mart shopping center built to replace it.

The dimensions remain impressive. An immense flat canopy between symmetrical towers shelters a broad staircase. Public rooms extend through the entire first floor of the south wing: a lobby, nightclub, area for musicales, another for billiards, small function rooms, vast pillared ballroom and bay-windowed bar, and a restaurant that seats 300 with private meeting space. Only limited use is made of these.

Things were different in 1924 when the National Governors Conference was hosted here, and the following year when the president of Seaboard Air Line Railroad arranged a special party of more than 500 guests, including Governor John Martin, who came for the railroad debut of through-service to Palm Beach. Guests received constant attention from more than 100 in staff who provided the service expected by those Pullman travelers.

The hotel had been one of the first major promotions of the Sebring Development Corporation after Ohioan George E. Sebring and his brother founded the city to prosper in citrus cultivation. Kenilworth with 250 rooms opened in 1916, the year that the Atlantic Coast Line Railroad extended its service south to the coast. For half a century the railroads and the hotel kept pace with each other.

For the 1926-27 season, the Seaboard distributed a special folder exclusively featuring Sebring and the Kenilworth, as a newspaper report of the time announced, "showing the mileage from Quebec over its entire line, and displaying Sebring in most prominent letters."

As another report described the relationship, "The fact that George E. Sebring and the Seaboard president, Davies Warfield, were close personal friends, may not have influenced the special services enjoyed by Sebring, but at least it did not hurt anything."

The hotel was sold for the first time in 1925 for $1 million. Typical recreation included sailing and motor boating, golfing, bathing, and horse riding. As late as 1967 the property included two golf courses, a beauty salon and barber shop, tennis courts, boutique, and an orchestra nightly in the ballroom.

By 1972 it was sold for $1 million again, but this time to become a retirement hotel. Only 120 rooms were in use. New purchasers talked of putting in townhouses, garden apartments, villas, condos. In fact, a swimming pool and cabanas were added. New owners in 1973 decided to stay open for summers, but five years later the hotel was closed altogether.

Most recently have come the Wohls, wealthy in cattle and banking, who reopened the property and have leased it to their young managers, Mark and Madge Stewart.

Though the elegant furnishings that once rated the Kenilworth's claim as "an exclusive resort and one of the most splendid hotels in the South" are long gone, the homey rattan now in the lobby is more suited to the hotel's use as a bed-and-breakfast establishment, a format that allows for minimal service while keeping the premises in good repair.

Sebring itself is growing again, and the Kenilworth is enjoying new popularity among groups attracted by its low rates and congenial new managers. Without its patrician setting or current guests' memory of it, the hotel appeals like a curiosity because of the generous space that elsewhere would likely have been carved up.

Here guests seem oddly independent of management. Family reunions, lodge outings, square-dance and bicycle clubs use the space as if engaged in a bareboat charter: the facility is theirs, and it is up to them to best use it. As Mark says, "We can arrange every kind of package, whatever people want." Mostly that translates to limited service, and the special camaraderie that stems from groups finding they are all improvising together.

Rooms are comfortable with modern baths, firm beds, TV, and refrigerators. There is a laundromat and beauty shop. Two trains a day, northbound and south, still call at the station a mile and a half away. It is not as it was, but with rates starting at $35 double off-season, and $47 on, the attraction is obvious.

Kenilworth Lodge, 836 SE Lakeview Drive, Sebring, FL 33870. (813) 385-0111. Mark and Madge Stewart, operators. 138 rooms with AC, heat, refrigerators, color cable TV, bathrooms with tub, villas, efficiencies, elevator. Children of any age accepted, free in parents' room to 12. 3rd person in room $5. No pets. Swimming pool. MC, Visa. Winter rates: single $42, double $47; villas $53, efficiencies $58; off-season: single $30, double $35, villas $37, efficiencies $42. Continental breakfast included in room rates. Off-street parking.

Sebring — SANTA ROSA INN
Newly upgraded in-town favorite with toney restaurant.

How do you run an inn with your banker looking over your shoulder?

You call him Sweetie, add his name on the brochure, and when somebody asks whether it's inhibiting to have a banker around all the time, you let him thunder, "Hell, no!" then sweetly add, "She gets whatever she wants."

"Then I have to go find the money," says "Farmer Don," as Jan likes to call her banker husband.

He also goes to the market, is known to rake leaves, tend shrubs.

Well trained.

When Jan Bowden ran the Sandwich Depot in nearby Avon Park, Don the bank president would often take lunch break to run the register.

Now in Sebring Don helps run the remodeled Santa Rosa Inn, and say what you will about bankers (Bertolt Brecht said robbing a bank's no crime compared to owning one), when it comes to running small hotels, at least this one's all heart.

At first the question was whether to bid on the place. The widow McGee had run it—hold on to your hat—for 60 years till she died early in 1987. They say it wasn't in the best of shape, but early on her husband for 10 years had been mayor of Sebring, and nobody ever got around to writing her up about the wiring or plumbing.

Her nephew wanted rid of it. The bidding began at $200,000.

Jan had just sold the Sandwich Depot after five successful years. She was a little bored and thinking about a new restaurant. Banker Don asked if she really wanted the Santa Rosa, and when she said she did told her to bid $201,000.

Score one for bankers.

Score two, because how Jan and Don went about it was to remodel as much as they needed to get the cash flowing their first year, then finish the job over the next two.

That's done now and, in a kind of celebration that never stops, they keep the Christmas tree up and lit all year in the lobby.

The Santa Rosa is a chunky brick three-story place behind tall oaks awash in moss just where State Road 17 southbound becomes Ridgewood Avenue and opens to four lanes entering downtown Sebring. Its Cafe 24 is named for the year the hotel was built.

There hasn't been a place for a little dress-up celebration in Sebring since Harder Hall's heyday, and that grand pink stucco palace when open wasn't quite in Sebring anyway, west beyond the limits on Highway 27 toward the state park at Highlands Hammock. But the Santa Rosa is downtown, where the hotel's revival is a big score for the comeback of Ridgewood Avenue.

The Santa Rosa's lobby is full of bright silk flowers in brass pots, reflecting in gilt-framed mirrors on pale flocked walls. Deep sofas sit to the side with a tableful of "Architectural Digests."

Don's the greeter. He learned that skill in banking. When you're a food success in a small town, lunch is where you hear it all, from stories about gramp's boll weevils to tut-tuts about the fried food—which here hardly any of it is. Don coaxes a laugh from an elderly fellow moving slowly by chiding his wife, her foot newly in a cast, about how "You sure slow Sam down, you know that!"

Jan works the kitchen, where she turns out fine American and continental meals.

The best rooms are the first-floor suites. They're done in a classical post-colonial American style: dark bedroom furniture, comfortable upholstered armchairs, rockers, and large sofas in chintz. Rooms are lit by lamps with white fluted shades atop crystal. Ceilings are high. The feeling is spacious, generous, well-appointed.

Second-floor suites are modest. They have double beds, some pencil post, with white curtains, floral quilt spreads, and upholstered chairs. The individual rooms are a little dressy, with carpeting and dust ruffles that match drapes.

A sun porch on the second floor is full of wicker and warmed by the rising sun. A console TV sits in a corner. You're up in the oaks, like a child secretly sheltered in dreams above the busy wakened world of Ridgewood Avenue. The Santa Rosa feels like Christmas most any time of year.

Santa Rosa Inn, 509 N. Ridgewood Avenue, Sebring, FL 33870. (813) 385-0641. Jan and Don Bowden, proprietors. 21 rooms and 4 suites, all with baths (most with tubs), AC and heat. Color cable TV. House phone for messages, and outgoing credit-card and collect calls, free local calls. Children accepted 12 and over. No pets. MC, Visa. Year-round rates: room $46, suites $90. Higher during Race Week (March). Weekly and monthly rates available. Off-street parking. Breakfasts must be eaten out. Lunch average $9, dinner $15.

Winter Haven – JD'S SOUTHERN OAKS
Finest country bed-and-breakfast in Florida.

"Who deserves such care?" you hear yourself asking as you contemplate Juanita and Dallas Abercrombie's JD's Southern Oaks, a mansion in near wilderness. You travel up an oak-lined drive from the brick and cast-iron entry gate, seasonally bordered by blooming azaleas or impatiens, to the outstanding country bed-and-breakfast in Florida.

The Abercrombies did not have to do this. They even admit they wouldn't have if they hadn't been a bit bored, Juanita with more than 20 years as a Winter Haven florist, Dallas retired after 32 years with the Winter Haven post office.

To do it they had to save an old cypress and heart pine house from vandals and decay. They had to find a new site for it quickly, because otherwise the developer could still knock it down to use the land he'd bought beneath it.

Moving the house to its new 37-acre site meant flatbedding it through two miles of pastures and 28 cattle fences that all had to be taken down and replaced. Then began 18 months of restoration that culminated at the end of 1990 with a party for neighbors and friends.

Today the house sits behind a glorious front lawn overlooking a fishing pond through massive moss-hung oaks. Swings, rope hammocks, and a gazebo promise easy country living—though not swimming, because there are alligators in the pond.

The house is three stories, a white clapboard colonial. The lower two stories have porches wrapped behind antebellum-style pillars. The brick porch is full of white Kennedy rockers.

Juanita and Dallas tell how they found letters in the house dated November 12, 1925, that must have been dropped by accident in the soffit when the roof was put on. One attic plank has written on it, "When you see this remember that it was put on by J.B. Blalock from Decatur, Georgia, Jan. the 9th, 1926. Saturday and it is raining."

When the Abercrombies moved the house from Dundee Road, that was its second move. Thirty-one years earlier the house had been moved from Lake Roy, near Cypress Gardens, where it was home to one of the region's old citrus families.

With Juanita and Dallas, or on your own, you'll want to tour these country acres where cattle graze. Soon horses will be quartered here, maybe for riding. Nature trails are planned, too. Among abundant wildlife guests might see are eagles, sandhill cranes, North American horned owls, hoot owls, and dusky woodpeckers. Dallas has spotted fox, raccoons and opossum.

In the fall, the fields are full of goldenrod. In cooler weather, sunsets are gorgeous. Close around the house are camphor trees, maple, bay magnolias, and Florida pine. Dallas has planted a vegetable garden in the back.

The house has splendid public rooms, large enough that together with the outside spaces and the three bed-and-breakfast rooms (two more are in a nearby new house Juanita and Dallas call "the barn") guests will never be in each other's way. They can easily meet if they want, and a small group traveling together would feel the entire house their own, a dream privilege.

The living room, the library, the great parlor are beautifully furnished with antiques, the living room in wicker, the cypress-paneled library with stained glass windows, the parlor with stately white walls and Italian rose marble. The mantel in the living room is of poplar with five-mold trim and two rosettes. It came from the Mary Jewett House in Winter Haven.

Two guest rooms are on the second floor. One is mauve and black with a Karastan rug that picks up those colors. It has an antique cherry bed with a spread crocheted by Dallas's great-great aunt. The east bedroom, maize and blue with twin pencil post beds, overlooks the pond through the pines. The suite, on the third floor, has a king-sized sleigh bed, pickled floors, crank-out windows, Victorian papers, and antique wicker. The old brick chimney shows behind the cast-iron footed tub in the bath. The suite has its own door leading down by a circular staircase.

The house may be new as a bed-and-breakfast, but the hospitality is old southern tradition. The Abercrombies extend that tradition to our time.

JD's Southern Oaks, 3800 Country Club Rd., Winter Haven, FL 33881. (813) 293-2335. (800) 771-OAKS. Three bedrooms and baths, plus 2 in the new carriage house, with AC, heat, ceiling fan, TV in great parlor, phone for guest use (free local calls, no surcharge for LD calls). Messages taken. 3rd person in room $5. Swimming pool possible late in 1991. Southern Oaks not appropriate for children or pets. MC, Visa. No alcohol allowed in house. No smoking inside. Off-street parking. Year-round rates: $65-$85-$115, includes fresh flowers in room, coffee mornings at 6:30, fruit basket in kitchen of parlor, expanded continental breakfast.

Winter Park – THE FORTNIGHTLY INN
Exceptional overnighting in college town.

The newest place for lodging in Winter Park is The Fortnightly Inn, five bedrooms and baths, some with parlors, on busy but well-buffered Fairbanks Avenue.

When Judi and Frank Daley, after more than a year of restoration, decided to make this a bed-and-breakfast instead of their private home, they knew they had a market among the affluent parents of students and alumni from Rollins College across the street.

Their first thoughts of making a home of the house are largely responsible for the special quality of the place as a lodging. "It feels like a home," says Judi, a Disney manager. "We weren't trying to address someone else's taste."

Care reaches to the china shower heads, the hand-painted little pot-metal bulb fixtures (on $9\frac{1}{2}$-foot ceilings), the original hardware and wavy glass restored or replaced.

The house feels like authenticity revisited.

Though it comes across as a spacious home, it's obviously a B&B. Yet because owners live elsewhere and only guests share the space, it feels like an inn. There's a staff person who checks guests in and out, but is otherwise unobtrusive.

Other guests are likely to be worldly and on the move. Breakfast in the formal dining room will probably include talk about the town's theater of performing arts, its fine arts center, its museums, quality shops and restaurants, and about excursions on town lakes.

The hoops and hassles you go through to open a B&B in Winter Park—zoning is only the start of it—ensure that no one is going to bother who isn't as intrigued by the idea of hospitality as by profits.

The restoration took 18 months. Because it went back to the 2-by-4s, the Daleys were able to put in the sound baffles that keep the house quiet on its busy street.

There are imaginative colors (much teal and cantaloupe) and sometimes florid fabrics. Spatial arrangements are inspired.

In a small second-floor room, the double four-poster bed occupies almost the entire narrow recess, while the wider foresection has been outfitted with burl wardrobe, hat and coat rack, and five-foot tub in front of a striped silk settee. Bed and settee are from Jacqueline Lenfest, the elderly surviving grandniece of the doctor who built the house in 1922. Look closely at the low walnut headboard to see carvings as subtle as if naturally in the wood. Also, close the little desk lest you miss the exquisite inlay in its top. Colorful balloon valances are made of bunched Laura Ashley sheets.

In the adjoining room, the sleeping porch has been converted into a many-windowed bathroom. Colorful antique rugs appear like bright canoes on a spring run of reddish pine floors. Wall decor includes a Wagnerian alto referred to in-house as "the mad lady with the axe."

A feature of the Honeymoon Suite is a full-sized antique mahogany sleigh bed. French doors lead to a sun porch with an elegant three-seat empire sofa and windows all around. Work the antique walnut desk to appreciate its near friction-free mechanics.

One spacious room is "where I'd put my mother," says Judi. "It's the only room with white walls, whereas everything in her house is blues and greens. I know there's another person trying to get out."

In the spacious, comfortable living room, period tables, sofas, and upholstered chairs are set in conversational groupings on a large Oriental rug. Romantic scenics are framed on the walls. A baby grand piano, and a dulcimer and guitar (played by Frank, a realtor, who comes by every day), fill out the room.

The downstairs suite has a full-sized iron bed, antique oak corner armoire and matching dresser, a tiny bath with tiny sink and tiny (but deep) clawfoot tub, and adjoining sun porch.

The house was built by seventh-generation American Dr. Charles E. Coffin, whose forebears bought Nantucket Island from the Indians. For a time, he was president of The Fortnightly Club, which played an important part in the social and intellectual development of Winter Park.

On the outside, the house is marked by graceful three-on-two windows, rosy clapboard in white trim, a second-story front porch, and low shrubs and geranium beds. A scrolled shingle beckons welcome.

The Fortnightly Inn, 377 E. Fairbanks Ave., Winter Park, FL 32789. (407) 645-4440. Judi and Frank Daley, proprietors. Five rooms and baths with showers and tubs, AC, heat, 2 rooms with ceiling fans, color TV. Telephone for free local, credit-card calls available. Children of any age accepted, $10 including breakfast (and crib or rollaway). No pets. AmEx, MC, Visa, checks accepted. Rates: $75-$95 year-round, double or single, includes full breakfast, sherry in rooms, and multi-speed bikes. Free off-street parking.

Winter Park — PARK PLAZA HOTEL
Top service in an elegant small hotel in the heart
of one of Florida's stylish small cities.

Recently one morning, an occasional visitor to Winter Park had to take the train from Miami to Palatka before the newsstand opened. That meant missing the *New York Times*. At the Miami station, he called the Park Plaza to ask if someone might pick up a copy from the news box across the street and, when the train stopped, bring it to him on board. He alerted the conductor. As the train pulled out of Winter Park, an attendant asked for him by name, then handed him the paper.

Small hotels can do this for clients. Clients know they can ask at the Park Plaza. The staff all know how Cissie and John Spang like things done. It is the ordinary way of hospitable people. Only that in many hotels staff are left guessing if they are really to make the effort, use their own judgment, or just not volunteer for anything. "It's not my job," is what you hear. But not at the Park Plaza.

The reward is hearing a guest in the lobby tell a friend that "Central Florida has more hotels than anyplace else in the world. I wouldn't stay at any of the others anymore. I like the charm, the unique street, the good food at this place. The balcony breakfast. It's relaxing."

The Park Plaza is the kind of hotel you find in cities like London, Paris, Buenos Aires, cities that over centuries have expanded and absorbed what once were towns of the surrounding greenbelt with their distinctive places for overnighting. The towns retain their charm as they become locales of special character within the metropolis, and their small hotels become "finds" in the city. In a hundred years Winter Park may be absorbed by expanding Orlando and one can imagine guests of the 22nd century newly discovering the Park Plaza. One wishes they might still arrive by the train that stops in the park and be assisted with bags by someone sent to accompany them the few hundred feet past the flowering shrubs and fountains under the oaks 'round the corner to the hotel.

The Park Plaza, which would be outstanding anywhere, fits in perfectly on this low-rise, tree-lined street of brightly painted European-style shops and galleries. Its two-story roofline is trimmed by hanging baskets and flower boxes under striped awnings that make a garden of a long balcony. The awninged entry is set off by a brick arch, colorful flags between palm trees, and flower-filled stone planters. The facades of a chocolatier and florist on either side are topped by miniature awnings. You enter the hotel as if discovering an arcade of delights off an already enchanting street.

The lobby is dark and cool in tile, wood and brass, suggestive of a gentlemen's club for the privileged clientele of its 27 rooms. The reception desk has a brass bowl of shiny red apples surrounded by brass pots of corn-plants, ferns, and gladioli. Sherry is available in the sitting room where the fireplace is lighted in winter. A wide rose-carpeted staircase winds its way up beside a small elevator.

Guest rooms are decorated but not to death. They are a mix of restored 1924 furniture from the hotel's initial inventory, and new wicker with floppy-bowed floral cushions, brass beds, carpets, and in the suites showing hardwood floors. Chocolate and beige stripes, first seen on outside awnings, repeat in draperies, bed covers, and shower curtains. There are swivel-mounted TVs with AM/FM radios. Old-fashioned hexagonal bathroom tiles and four-knobbed sink handles are originals in the small bathrooms. The suites have sitting rooms and the balconies overlook Park Avenue's posh shops.

When they bought the Hamilton Hotel in 1977, "all the activity was north of the park," says Cissie. "They called that Little Europe. Every store on this block was closed or going out of business. The hotel had soap on its windows. But John's a great visionary. He has a history of succeeding with things he's never done before."

They had restored properties in Racine before moving to Tampa in the late

1960s. John opened an antique shop with a bar in it that became the most popular hangout near the University of South Florida.

A trip to Winter Park with its chain of lakes, gracious homes, museums and theaters convinced them to move. In the shuttered Colony Theater John first opened the East India Ice Cream Company (since become a market).

Typical of John's ingenuity, the a la carte Palm Gardens Restaurant used to be an overgrown patch with a short-cut through the weeds. It is where hotel staff hung out the mops. Now there is a brick floor, brick walls to varied heights, and small twinkling ficus trees because the guests so liked the Christmas lights one year they were never taken down. The restaurant is partly under a soft rainproof roof, partly in the open. It stays busy with locals when business visitors thin a bit in summer.

Chocolate mints accompany the turndown service. *The Wall Street Journal* is delivered with continental breakfast, and copies of the *Orlando Sentinel* are free at the desk. Lately the *Times* has been available, too.

Park Plaza Hotel, 307 Park Ave. South, Winter Park, FL 32789. (800) 228-7220, (407) 647-1072. Sandra Spang, owner-manager. 27 rooms and suites with AC, ceiling fan, heat, color cable TV, bathrooms with tub, direct-dial phone, elevator, restaurant, bar. Children accepted 5 and over, free in parents' room to 10 (cot $10). No pets. All major credit cards. Year-round rates: $70-$110 single and double, $125-$165 for suites. Continental breakfast included and turndown service, free New York Times, Wall Street Journal, and Orlando Sentinel. Restaurant and bar under separate management. Off-street parking.

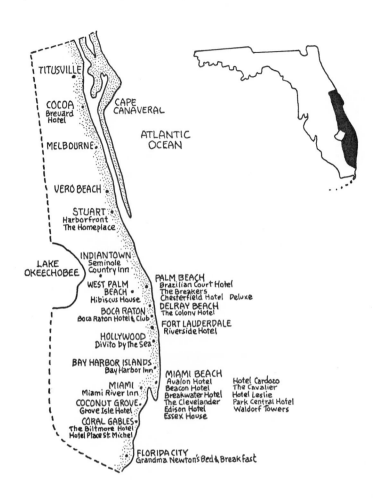

The following locations appear on the map:

TITUSVILLE

COCOA
Brevard
Hotel

CAPE
CANAVERAL

MELBOURNE

ATLANTIC
OCEAN

VERO BEACH

STUART
Harborfront
The Homeplace

INDIANTOWN
Seminole
Country Inn

LAKE
OKEECHOBEE

WEST PALM
BEACH
Hibiscus House

PALM BEACH
Brazilian Court Hotel
The Breakers
Chesterfield Hotel Deluxe

DELRAY BEACH
The Colony Hotel

BOCA RATON
Boca Raton Hotel & Club

FORT LAUDERDALE
Riverside Hotel

HOLLYWOOD
DiVito by The Sea

BAY HARBOR ISLANDS
Bay Harbor Inn

MIAMI
Miami River Inn

COCONUT GROVE
Grove Isle Hotel

CORAL GABLES
The Biltmore Hotel
Hotel Place St. Michel

MIAMI BEACH
Avalon Hotel
Beacon Hotel
Breakwater Hotel
The Clevelander
Edison Hotel
Essex House

Hotel Cardozo
The Cavalier
Hotel Leslie
Park Central Hotel
Waldorf Towers

FLORIDA CITY
Grandma Newton's Bed & Breakfast

THE SOUTHEAST COAST

The most populous part of the state sees the least growth in bed-and-breakfast inns. Tourist promoters only think big league, not yet in touch with the shift in the martketplace toward smaller, more intimate lodgings.

But make an exception for Broward County, with its program of Superior Small Lodgings. Subject to independent inspection/review administered by a representative of the Nova University hospitality department, so far 38 properties all with less than 50 rooms are described in a free 24-page directory available from the Greater Fort Lauderdale Convention & Visitors Bureau [200 East Las Olas Blvd, Fort Lauderdale 33301, (305) 765-4466]. Though not historical, the properties are clean and some have character. Too bad that the one B&B that was in the program, Casa Alhambra, has closed since told about in the previous edition of this guidebook.

Otherwise, starting north, Dan Haddad has lately opened the **Colonial River House B&B** in Brevard County in a 1910 house directly across from the Indian River with its own landing [607 N. Indian River Dr., Cocoa 32922, (407) 632-8780]. Just a couple blocks away, Garry Clark has opened **Clarament Inn** in a 1921 house [11 Olive St. 32922, (407) 632-7594]. Both are worth your attention, though Dan has said he's not sure he will stick with the business. In the heart of Cocoa, new corporate owners have taken over the **Brevard Hotel**. Once bruited for demolition, the Brevard is now under restoration. You can read about it in these pages.

Two new properties have opened in the very smartly reviving waterfront town of Stuart. These are **The Homeplace** and **Harborfront**, both described in detail.

The Seminole Country Inn in Indiantown has a new owner, Charles Miner, who has the stick-to-it commitment that ensures that whatever it takes to satisfy the market, he's remaining in business.

Newly reopened in Palm Beach is the **Chesterfield Hotel**, a few years ago a standout when it briefly reopened (then closed) as the Palm Court. Exceptional beauty and value. Also new in Palm Beach is the **Plaza Inn** of Ajit Azrani and Sharon Knickerbocker. From the crown lobby moldings of cupids and flower garlands to the pecky cypress little dining room, this is an oasis of sane pricing truly in the heart of Palm Beach [215 Brazilian Ave., Palm Beach 33480, (800) BED AND B, (407) 832-8666]. In West Palm Beach, Raleigh Hill has added rooms to **Hibiscus House**, ever surprising with unstinting hospitality. Ask Raleigh about other B&Bs in the Old Northwood section for when he's filled up. Others are planning to open.

Not as historic as most places told about in this book but exceptionally well sited and offering exceptional value is the **Sea Lord Hotel** in the south end of Palm Beach. It runs from the ocean to the west side of A1A abutting the Intracoastal Waterway. Very friendly, very set apart, with return guests all year and a tiny restaurant that engenders hospitable interactions among guests who might not know each other [2315 S. Ocean Blvd., Palm Beach 33480, (407) 582-1461].

In neighboring Lake Worth on the other side of the waterway, the Twenties-pink **Gulfstream Hotel** reopened in 1990. The canny Finns in charge have Scandinavian tour groups coming throughout the year. Don't let the groups scare you off. The scene is very easygoing. Nothing at all pretentious about the place, and excellent value [1 Lake Ave., Lake Worth 33460, (407) 586-9250].

Too bad that the little **Tarrimore Bed-and-Breakfast** opened and closed in Delray Beach before we could tell about it. The property was a struggle to open because of nay-saying from otherwise inspired city officials who have done an excellent job of restoring the historic scale and charm of this town, extending its civic improvements westward toward the interstate. Tarrimore is closed to guests and the house is for sale, but who knows, new buyers might keep it in the trade. Inquire: 52 N. Swinton Ave., Delray Beach 33444, (407) 265-3790.

Another fine property not as historic as others we describe is the The Seagate on the beach in Delray Beach. It's partly a private club, but guests are afforded full use of the romantic restaurant and bar directly by the water. Value is excellent here, too, with beautiful garden apartments and rooms around a pool on the other side of Highway A1A (just two lanes here). Inquire at 400 S. Ocean Blvd., Delray Beach 33482, (407)276-2421, (800)233-3581, or in Canada (800)521-1226.

Best news in Miami is the reopening of the Miami River Inn, Sallye Jude's exceptional 40-room lodging directly across from its namesake river. This is country in the city less than a 10-minute leisurely walk from the heart of downtown. You can't imagine how unlike the rest of downtown Miami this is, and the rates are as gentle as the look of the place. Detailed in these pages.

North near the beach in metro Miami is the Bay Harbor Inn in the snazzy little town of Bay Harbor Islands. Again, top value in stylish townside or creekside rooms, with two fine restaurants and a pool. Read about it.

Opened too late for review in outlying Miami is Pinelands, a suburban B&B [18600 SW 157th Ave., Miami 33186, (305) 253-3059].

Other worthwhile alternatives in metro Miami, even though they don't fit the format of this book, are the toney Grand Bay Hotel [2669 S. Bayshore Drive, Coconut Grove, 33133, (305) 858-9600, (800) 221-2340 (worldwide), (800) 327-2788 (in Florida)], and Mayfair House [3000 Florida Ave., Coconut Grove, 33133, (305) 441-000, (800) 433-4555 (national), (800) 341-0809 (in Florida)]. For those who want to avoid their price and who can't get into the Grove Isle Hotel because of its priorities for members and their guests, there is the Doubletree Hotel in Coconut Grove [2649 S. Bayshore Drive, Coconut Grove, 33133, (305) 858-2500, (800) 528-0444], and nearby in Coral Gables, the residential-looking but sophisticated David William Hotel [700 Biltmore Way, Coral Gables, 33134, (305) 445-7821, (800) 327-8770].

Aficionados of the historical will at least want a look at the old pink Hollywood Beach Hotel [101 N. Ocean Drive, Hollywood 33019, (305) 921-0990], mostly now used by time-share owners, and on Highway A1A near US 1 in the next town north, the Dania Beach Hotel [180 E. Dania Beach Blvd., Dania 33004, (305) 923-5895] and its affiliate, the Hotel Poinciana [141 NW 1st Ave., Dania, 33004, (305) 925-8541], though neither will suit the needs of mose guidebook readers.

Meanwhile we're holding our breath about the reopening of the Biltmore in Coral Gables, one of the great hotels of Florida that temporarily closed in 1990. As this book goes to press there is news that the Biltmore has been bought by a European investment group which will reopen it in the summer of 1991.

Bay Harbor Islands — BAY HARBOR INN
Nifty compound much admired in its community.

Sandy Lankler is a great bear of a man, and Celeste a frail reed. They are adored like favorite offspring among Florida's bed-and-breakfast keepers because of their devotion to the B&B trade and because of their two Shih Tzu dogs without whom they can't bear to travel.

Celeste is a painter, Sandy a retired Washington lawyer who is a director of the Greater Miami Convention & Visitors Bureau.

Just south and across Indian Creek from their Bal Harbour home, they operate the Bay Harbor Inn.

One part of the inn is the oldest building in Bay Harbor Islands, dating from the late 1940s when the town was formed. The other was once the Albert Pick Hotella (later the Bay Crest), where guests of the wintering chic were lodged. Times change. The little neighborhood at one point degenerated into an enclave of drug users and prostitutes. Sandy cleaned it up for the powers that be.

Now his and Celeste's corner compound, just north of the drawbridge that connects Bal Harbour and Bay Harbor Islands, is where the towering Norfolk pine in front becomes the community Christmas tree for three towns each year.

Sandy says the compound is modeled on the old Cortland Inn he knew in New York in the Forties and Fifties. It was a place where Rotary met and politicians held court.

The inn is friendly, with a staff treated as if they were family. Everybody calls Sandy Sandy. Lee Machette, who runs the place, used to run Sandy's Washington law office. Joann Howard, who's executive housekeeper, was a licensed practical nurse from Georgia looking for a change when she discovered the Bay Crest and was kept when Sandy acquired it. Jo Nolan, at the front desk, a Bay Harbor Islands resident, read that Sandy was taking over the properties, wrote, and was hired. Sandy and Celeste acquire friends who get involved with them. Guests get befriended.

For all the friendliness, the inn is professionally run, though not without its curious feature. This becomes apparent on entering the townside building where guests register. Though the building is a half-century old, it's full of antiques that go back twice as long and longer. Here are oak and pine desks, handmills, scales, and grandfather clocks. In the mid-century modern space, the antiques feel free-floating, marching to a different drummer.

Rooms are the same, a mix of antiques, like oval oak mirrors, cherrywood and walnut pieces, against more modern backgrounds of louvered closets and good commercial carpet. Some rooms have stunning petitpoint chairs and Eastlake beds. All have modern baths, with tub-shower stalls.

There's also a little air-conditioned upstairs alcove where, without windows, you can imagine yourself happy, reading on a rainy day. Select from Romain Gary, Stephen King, and shelves about Washington personalities. There's also a first-floor oak meeting room full of rare Florida maps you can buy at prices from $400 to $4,000. Some of the maps are amusingly inaccurate, showing Lake Okeechobee draining north through the St. Johns River.

Across the street—"creekside," as Celeste says—the rooms are modern, with sliding screen doors over sliding glass doors, every room facing onto a loggia under palms. Upstairs is carpeted; downstairs has Spanish tiles. Rooms on this side come with refrigerators. The downstairs area creekside is a replica of a London bar with an old English mail chute. The mahogany bar, the brass plate valet stand, and trimming came from the Vanderbilt mansion in London. Off to the side is the Seafood Gardens Restaurant, a veritable palm grove, woody and casual at poolside. Inside it's pink and cream, beribboned and breezy, with rigged-down canvas for when the wind blows.

Across East Bay Harbor Drive is the Palm Restaurant, a branch of its namesake, which has been operating in New York since the Twenties. Waiters in white aprons carry oversized platters of hearty American food, and serve amidst walls covered in celebrity caricatures.

The Bay Harbor Inn is a hospitable respite in a notoriously touristy city. You're a five-minute walk from the beach, three minutes from the best shopping in the metropolis, the same from many of the best galleries. Choice little digs. And you can bring the dogs.

Bay Harbor Inn, 9660 E. Bay Harbor Dr., Bay Harbor Islands, FL 33154. (305) 868-4141. Sandy and Celeste Lankler, owners. 36 rooms with private bathrooms, AC, heat. Color cable TV, direct dial phone. Children under 16 in same room with parents, no charge. 3rd person in room $15. Selected rooms okay for pets, $12 nightly. AmEx, CB, DC, MC, Visa. 20 creekside rooms with refrigerator. Rates: townside, Dec.-Apr., $75-$110; May-Nov. $60-$80; creekside, $95-$115, $70-$85, includes continental breakfast and high tea, daily newspaper on the yacht "Celeste." Swimming pool (heated), 2 restaurants and bars plus London Bar with $5 menu. Seafood Garden $5-$13 per entree lunch, $15.95 fixed-price dinner, a la carte $15 up. The Palm, $20-$50, dinner only. Smoking permitted. Free off-street parking.

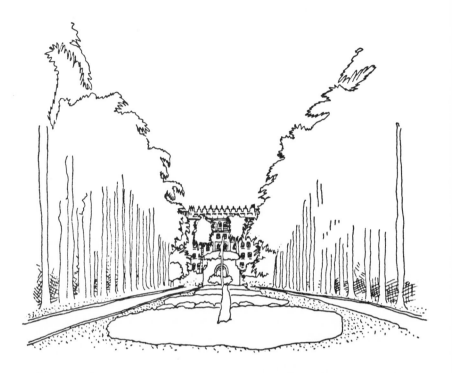

Boca Raton – BOCA RATON HOTEL & CLUB

East Coast lyrical grandeur from the ocean to the Intracoastal Waterway.

No Florida hotel has been more closely linked with its place than the Boca Raton with its namesake town. For more than 60 years hotel history has been town destiny, from development by legendary rogues to management by three-piece-suiters.

Architect Addison Mizner, society's darling who created the heyday look of Palm Beach but felt confined by mere million-dollar commissions, shifted his flamboyant talents 40 coastal miles south to Boca Raton, where in the mid-20s he sought to equal his celebrity in riches. With his scheming brother Wilson and a hardly more savory press agent, whose advice was "Get the big snobs and the little snobs will follow," within a year Mizner was raking $2 million a week into his land development office. Checks came so fast, legend has it they were dumped into baskets and filed by amount!

The heart of the scheme was a 1.25-million-dollar hotel Mizner named the

Cloister Inn. It opened with all the pomp that duPonts, Vanderbilts and Whitneys could assure for the development they had all invested in.

The hotel was unmistakably palatial and opened the same year as the rebuilt Breakers in Palm Beach. Mizner was miffed because the Palm Beach commission was denied him. The two hotels immediately set a standard never since equaled in Florida. Of the two, the Cloister (now called the Boca Raton or simply "the Boca") is the more sensuous, and to this time, lit on a rainy evening, it glows in lyrical warmth.

That Mizner's dream of a winter colony to rival Palm Beach failed within a year belied no vision. His failure was merely personal—unless you lump his failure with the wipe-out of thousands who lacked his notoriety but nevertheless went down with the collapse of the land boom. But he left one of America's great hotels and a tradition of larger-than-life entrepreneurs to run it.

Why the hotel survived is hard to say. It hardly ever earned a return for its investors during its long middle years to the present. The owners who followed Mizner must have been intrigued by his legacy and the property's beauty.

After ownership by Charles Dawes, a U.S. vice president, and then by utilities millionaire Clarence Geist, who expanded the property fourfold during the Depression years, the Army made the hotel into a barracks during World War II. In 1944, J. Myer Schine was able to buy it for only $3 million. Schine got the little town going with a shopping center and developments along the ocean.

The hotel's greatest change, however, was to come from the man Schine sold to in 1965 for $22.5 million. Arthur Vining Davis, who had made his fortune in aluminum, was 88 when he bought the Boca. He set up a land development company he named Arvida (for himself) and linked the hotel with beachfront land and vast acreage he owned west of town. His managers and successor built a 22-story tower, added convention facilities, golf villas, a beachfront hotel, and then developed one after another of Florida's finest residential communities west toward the Everglades.

The hotel began operating year-round in the early 1970s during its time of greatest expansion. Mizner's sense of proportion and beauty has generally been vouchsafed; even today the dimensions of the hotel are so out of the ordinary that they appear natural—man as nature, man's handcraft as natural. Great inner spaces seem natural carvings of the outdoors.

Everything is textured, ornamented, graced by decorative arts. The guest rooms resemble sets from films featuring memorable European resorts. The ambient legacy of great craftsmen textures our imagination, and so balances what we see with what we feel inside. The air of subtlety keeps the grandeur human and elevates us.

Even in summer the sometimes empty grounds and lobbies are filled with the presence of our own disoveries. The mood is not unlike Monday in a museum, or a performance hall where recitalists are rehearsing. As it is is right for the moment.

Grand hotels must know their markets and satisfy them. They have to be consistent. They must be willing to spend the dollars to stay in front. They are expected to be there. In recent years, a multi-million-dollar improvement to the Cloister has included the new Palm Court, refurbishment of all Club rooms with marble baths, porcelain sinks, and brass fixtures, and a lavish floor of 48 rooms and five parlors, complete with concierge, in-room champagne and private lounge. Value of this sort does not derive from inexpensiveness. certainly not from indecisiveness. In the first instance it derives from attraction. Although guests grouse about nickle-and-diming, they return because the Boca delivers value.

Boca Raton Hotel & Club, 501 E. Camino Real, Boca Raton, FL 33432. (305) 395-3000. Michael Glennie, president. 1,000 rooms and suites with TV, AC, heat, room phone, bathrooms with tubs, his-and-her terry robes, hair dryers. Restaurants, bars, pool, complete outdoor recreational activities including water sports, lighted tennis courts, 18-hole golf course, croquet green. Elevators. Children of any age accepted, free in parents' room to 12. No pets. All major credit cards. Rates based on location. For winter (Dec. 21-April): $200 to $390 single or double; spring/fall (May, Oct-Dec. 20): $185 to $365 single or double; summer (June-Sept.): $110 to $240 single or double. Dine around plan, $45 per person MAP (excludes Nick's). Fish market. Off-street parking.

Cocoa – BREVARD HOTEL
Renewed popularity likely for Twenties Moorish hotel on the Indian River.

Walk into the Brevard Hotel today and you'd have to say it's on the up side of flux. Flux being what it is, you can't be absolutely sure what's next, but a betting person could wager the corner's been turned and the Brevard won't get torn down for condos, as was bruited.

At the beginning of 1991, a corporation had taken over from Georgia and Tony Ninos, who'd been here for years. New owners are totally renovating under general manager David Guilderson. David has in mind the fine-dining equivalent of white-glove service for the lower-level restaurant, while upgrading room furnishings and keeping the Twenties-Thirties look.

Consider the hotel and its location.

The Brevard is on a beautiful stretch of Riverside Drive in the old part of Cocoa where the action hasn't been for some time.

Consider the kind of people Georgia and Tony are, and the quality of the place next door to their retirement home.

"I'm the only guy who's ever said this," admits Tony, "but hoteliers like to be waited on as much as they like being hospitable. They like getting up in the morning knowing there are people around to hop to it. It's like having a home with private servants. You can have anything you want. We always invited someone to breakfast. Your friends can come, and you can have them stay. It really adds to your own good living."

The Brevard is one of the remaining stucco, oasis-like Moorish hotels that once prevailed around Florida. The 57 rooms spread out behind spacious lawns and cabbage palms on the scenic Indian River.

An earlier owner, Ralph Laycock, lately recalled the site as one of the most beautiful in Florida.

"Cocoa was a beautiful, quiet, typical Florida citrus town with a beautiful beach," recalls Laycock, now retired in Orlando. "We were located at a natural point in the Indian River. There was a wooden causeway across and then you went south on Merritt Island about two miles and then across another mile-long rickety bridge to Cocoa Beach. Getting there was a day's excursion, no question about that.

"We used to take the entire guest list once a week for a beach buffet, and the chef and the waiters would go in uniform. But if you forgot something for that meal there was not much chance of going back for it.

"Of course it was a time too when guests could sit on the seawall, catch fish, and bring them to the kitchen door for dinner that evening. And mind you, those 'fishermen' would have been the envy of any hotel in Florida. We had presidents of universities, W.T. Grant Company, Montgomery Ward, famous surgeons, business people from practically every walk of life."

The hotel had been built in the mid-Twenties, but closed after the bust until the Laycocks reopened it in 1934. When Tony and Georgia bought it in 1961 they were only the second owners.

Tony found the place 15 years after relocating in Florida from Lockport, New York. He was out of the Army after the Battle of the Bulge. He'd taken some vows. He'd never get up early again. He'd never go without a car. He never wanted to see snow again. He settled on the east coast, Boca Raton, met Georgia in Clearwater, and after they married, moved to Cocoa when they read about $40 million to be spent there for space exploration.

Tony has seen the old order pass before the onslaught of chain-age modernism. For 15 years he was prominent in state affairs, first as councilman and Mayor of Cocoa, then as president of the Florida Hotel & Motel Association, later Hotel Commissioner and director of the state's Division of Hotels and Restaurants.

Today even as the Brevard changes, guests can still enjoy the revived historic district just down the block and the beauties of the Riverside Drive for miles south and north. The staff can arrange horse-drawn carriage rides.

The lobby has working fireplaces at either end. Guest rooms are spacious, easy to plop in. Rooms are being updated.

Arriving at sunset, you'll see the few houses that show through the trees across the river reflectively lit, as if glowing from inside, warming the settling darkness. Halyards pong so evenly on masts in the marina that you think it's the warning ring for opening of the Hubert H. Humphrey Bridge. The former Vice President stayed with Tony and Georgia when Tony was mayor of Cocoa, so you know how the bridge got its name.

The simple give-and-take style of the Brevard Hotel has seemed strangely dated for years, making us wistful about the world of privilege Tony and Georgia enjoyed. They enjoyed it because they shared it. We can only hope new management does the same.

Brevard Hotel, 112 Riverside Drive, Cocoa, FL 32922. (407) 636-1411. David Guilderson, manager. All data subject to change. 56 rooms with baths and tubs, color cable TV, AC, heat, room phone. Restaurant, bar. Children of any age accepted, $5 extra in room with parents, cribs free. No pets. MC, Visa. Year-round rates: single $30; double $40. Breakfast $2 to $5; lunch $3-$5; dinner $5-$10. Off-street parking. Smoking OK.

Coconut Grove — GROVE ISLE HOTEL
Small luxury hotel on condominium island,
priority to club members.

January each year in Miami they stage an event called "A Taste of the Grove" where restaurants from the city's oldest settlement set up stalls in the historic park and sell samples of their specialties at a festive occasion for charity.

The annual taste is a bare trace of the mouthful Miami tore off when in the summer of 1925 its revenue-starved commisioners swallowed prosperous Coconut Grove whole.

The seizure of the Grove is now repeated without annexation formalities when every Friday and Saturday night otherwise sober-sided citizens exploit its historic tolerance of nonconformity by pouring into its small downtown and celebrating their own need to let loose. Streets are packed with cars full of gawkers whose inclination to go slow is reinforced by daredevil rickshaw haulers and madcap rollerskaters who swerve in and out of traffic and make even normally unpredictable bicyclists wish for a little respect.

From its beginnings more than 100 years ago, Coconut Grove has attracted eccentrics and provided their lodgings as well as in every generation increasingly more genteel accommodations for those more inclined to spectate than get fully involved.

Temple Pent and Joseph Frow came in the second quarter of the 19th century as lighthouse keepers. Later came Ralph Munroe, a sailor and boat designer known as the Commodore, who attracted a colony of artists and writers at a time still before the turn of the century, when the only way here was by steamer to Key West and packet boat back up the coast to the Grove—then known as Jack's Bight.

Once the railroad joined Miami to the rest of America, throngs poured in. Many wealthy visitors who had heard of Coconut Grove especially from writings of world-traveled Kirk Munroe (no relation to the Commodore) chose to settle in the Grove or carve out a piece of wilderness between the Grove and downtown Miami.

Much of Miami's age-graced charm is now displayed along this route, called South Miami Avenue and Bayshore Drive. A trip from downtown is scenically enjoyed along a road arched over by royal poincianas, past the virgin hammock preserved in rock-walled Simpson Park, past the entrance to Rickenbacker Causeway and the city's best beaches, on by Vizcaya, which was James Deering's early 20th century Renaissance palazzo, now a county art museum, and into the Grove.

A little more than halfway on the five-mile road from downtown Miami to the Grove is a 20-acre island where, among towering apartments, a small hotel shares acres of gardens bejeweled with one of America's finest collections of contemporary sculpture, including works by Calder, de Kooning, Liberman, Nevelson, and Noguchi.

Here the bay is wide and open. Across are Key Biscayne and Cape Florida. North, the new high bridge to the key. South, open water to the Bahamas.

Though 500 apartments loom in three huge buildings behind, during weekdays people pass along the parklike perimeter of the island by the ones. To one edge of the island a little beach faces toward where the sun sets behind the skyline rising in the Grove. A hot orange streak blazes blindingly across the water. A sand crab sidles over, a tiny fly probably born in the morning settles on a leaf.

The hotel is used by members but is also open to others, with priority to guests of the Grove Isle Club and those interested in membership ($1,755 a year), for it has only 49 rooms, of which 10 are suites. All are furnished in tropical island style with Spanish tile floors set off by area rugs, lilac and gray colorations, with ceiling fans. Very spacious, maybe 450 square feet to a room, these accommodations include individual balconies all with bay view, ice delivery to rooms and stocked bar. Bathrooms are equipped with hair dryers and extension telephones.

Guests enjoy a complete health spa, restaurant, cocktail lounge, two tennis courts lit for night play, swimming pool, marina store, and tight security. An outdoor Ship's Deck dining area looks directly onto the bay and is topped by a peaked canvas roof which has ceiling fans for summer comfort, and heaters for winter. Greenery is pervasive. The sculptures are inside as well as out. In open passageways, decorative fragments of historic New York buildings provide an ornamental motif.

The living space is like a luxurious ocean liner, for everywhere you look is the bay. You savor the vast resource. Miami reveals itself the city on the bay. By its shore, Grove Isle is a retreat from the pulsing metropolis, and in its own way, a taste of the Grove.

Grove Isle Hotel, Grove Isle, Coconut Grove, FL 33133. (305) 858-8300. Joel Gray, managing director. 49 rooms and suites with AC, heat, color cable TV, direct-dial phone, bathrooms with tub and velour robes and hair dryer, and servi-bar. Restaurants, bars, pool, health spa, lighted tennis courts, marina, store, elevators, valet parking only. Children of any age accepted, free in parents' room to 18. No pets. AmEx, Diners, MC, Visa. Rates for winter: single from $175, double from $195. Balance of year: approximately 30 percent less. Turndown service, continental breakfast, morning newspaper (Wall Street Journal optional), nightly chocolate included. Meals: lunch $6 to $15; dinner $9.50 to $27.50.

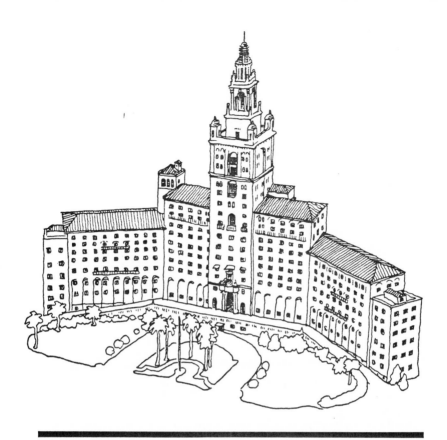

Coral Gables — THE BILTMORE HOTEL
Magnificently restored grand hotel of the Twenties set in
the beautiful residential district of Coral Gables.

The Biltmore Hotel was closed in 1990, but as this book goes to press news is
that it has been bought by a European investment group and is scheduled to
reopen in the summer of 1991. We are hoping that there is now a new, more
secure long-term plan for the hotel.

However extended the recent closure proves, it's not likely to compare with
the one that, until the winter of 1986-87, had left the hotel unavailable to guests
for 45 years. Coral Gables was never imagined without it. The 350-foot tower of
opulence was George Merrick's ultimate grace for the Mediterranean city he
dreamed out of a tomato patch. Its revival restored faith in the American Dream.

George Merrick was a preacher's son and a poet with a messianic faith in
the happiness money could buy. He was loyal to a vision few could have imagined.

He dreamed of a city that would be "the most magnificent gateway [to] the only American tropics."

At the hotel opening in January, 1926, surrounded by the wealthy who had come on special trains from the North to glory in the realization of his dream, he stated his belief that "every man will dig up more dollars for or work harder to retain the piece of ground that has in its neighborhood the inspiration of such beauty . . . like this Biltmore tower can yield."

Testifying to his vision and tenacity, the *Miami Riviera* described the opening as "a scene of splendor, rivaling a pageant from the Arabian Nights."

The Biltmore chain of hotels projected a way of life that appealed to the moneyed elite Merrick wooed. He backed his appeal with an array of promotions that set a standard hardly equaled in Florida during the ensuing half century.

The great orator William Jennings Bryan was hired for $100,000 a year to help sell Coral Gables land. Bandleader Paul Whiteman serenaded buying throngs at the Venetian Pool. Land advertisements for the first time began telling readers of *Forbes*, *The Saturday Evening Post*, and *Vogue* about Florida, about Coral Gables. Offices were opened on New York's Fifth Avenue and elsewhere up North, extolling "America's finest suburb."

The hotel's wedding-cake look, patterned on the Giralda Tower in Seville, Spain, immediately became an inland landmark, visible from across Biscayne Bay. Its baroque ornaments rose 18 stories above a level of splendid shops that were arched over by a sweeping elevated driveway. Architect Leonard Schultz incorporated high interior spaces and grand exterior courtyards with elaborate fountains, colonnades, and staircases, all of classical stone forms that recalled Renaissance origins. Light and cross ventilation were balanced by the brooding opulence of millions spent for heavy Mediterranean antiques, and for the skills of artisans who painted open-beamed ceilings and prepared reproductions of chandeliers and tapestries.

Nine months later a killer hurricane struck, driving thousands to the Biltmore for refuge. The sturdy hotel withstood the storm, but the real estate boom was over for south Florida, and with it went the flow of dollars from America's moneyed set. Merrick's bankrupt Coral Gables Corporation was succeeded by other moneyed interests, but in 1943, a year after Merrick died almost a pauper, the hotel became a military hospital.

Many schemes were proposed for the property after the government closed it in the mid-Sixties. In 1973 a federal agency presented the property free to the city. Ten years later the Coral Gables Biltmore Corporation was formed and won a city contract to restore the hotel.

The $40 million restoration included the colors, materials, windows, and details of the outside of the building, the original and oversized swimming pool, the approach ramp, the loggias, courtyard and terraces. Inside, the magnificent lobby, dining room, lounge, mezzanine, 13th and 15th floor suites were brought back to their original grandeur.

The lobby is starry dazzling under mottled sky-blue groin vaults, and in another section, a coffered Spanish Renaissance painted ceiling. Tiffany glazes on walls give an added sense of age as do the travertine and rough stucco finishes to the plaster. Although most of the furniture is superbly reproduced from period pieces, there are 13th-century case pieces, including a vestment chest acquired from Whitehall, the Flagler estate in Palm Beach.

A huge fireplace is the focal point at one end of the lobby, while massive carved oak doors lead off the center of the area to two banquet halls. Both open onto the terrace overlooking the 18-hole Biltmore Golf Course, and both also have arched passageways to a columned loggia surrounding a ground-level courtyard.

Stone stairs lead to the second floor, which has nine guest rooms, and down to the ground level, where restaurants, bars, and a spa are located. In the center of the area is a lushly landscaped courtyard, framed by the rooms available for outdoor dining and entertaining in good weather. In 1989, the original hotel casino, which later became an art museum, was reintegrated with the hotel as a grand room for special events.

Guest rooms and suites are located on 10 floors in the main body of the hotel and in the tower. All of the headboards are hand-painted and hand-carved by artisans from Europe and Latin America. Antique double-doored armoires hide cable TV sets. All of the overscale casement windows open onto spectacular views—of the golf course, Gables treetops, and the distant Miami skyline.

A former project director, Joseph Herndon, has said that although the Biltmore is very much one of a kind, it broadens the public dimension of life here. "We are," he says of the metropolis, "the glamor capital south of Manhattan, an international glamor city. The history is exotic. The hotel is part of that exoticism.

"It was my pleasure to hear a guest say, 'To think that this hotel has been here all these year.' Then I knew the project was a success. I didn't want the hotel to look too new. I wanted people who hadn't been here before to think it was a grand hotel continuously in operation. I'm very satisfied how it has been restored. It's going to remain open for at least another 100 years." One trusts with no more closings, however brief.

The Biltmore Hotel, 1200 Anastasia Ave., Coral Gables, FL 33134. Note: the following data should all be verified as the hotel was closed (presumably briefly) at the time of this writing. (305) 445-1926; (800) 223-6620. Heinz Schutz, general manager. 275 rooms and suites with AC, heat, bathrooms with tub, direct-dial phone, color cable TV, bathrobes, restaurants, bars, elevators, pool, spa, lighted tennis courts, 18-hole golf course, 24-hour room service, nightly entertainment, boutiques. Children of any age accepted, free in parents' room to 12. No pets. All major credit cards accepted. Rates: winter from $115 to $400, off-season (Apr. 15-Dec. 31) from $90 to $400. 3rd person in room $10. Meal prices: breakfast from $5.50; lunch from $6.50; dinner from $17. Off-street parking.

Coral Gables – HOTEL PLACE ST. MICHEL

A superior small hotel in a downtown of high-rise offices.

Sunday morning while corporate Coral Gables sleeps, a musician parks his car in the shadow of a glass tower and totes his bass viol toward a squat Italianate building. A factotum waters the flowerboxes. A bicyclist locks his 10-speed to the municipal No Parking stanchion. Lovers kiss under the awning. Sunday brunch at Hotel Place St. Michel awakens the possibilities of the country in the city.

They call Coral Gables the City Beautiful, mindful of its dreamy Mediterranean buildings, canopied roads, and storybook street ornaments. Its graceful features contrast sharply with the ordinary look of suburban Miami blocks adjacent to the north and east. New sleek high-rise offices are bunched in the Gables' downtown, where their sudden modernity strains at the way things used to be. The small hotel among them mediates. Its time is yesterday; its place, today.

"It's funny how that's happened," says Stuart Bornstein, the owner of Hotel Place St. Michel. "Jet-set businessmen stay with us from all over the world to make money in the high-rises, and at the end of the day change into shorts to play tennis at Salvadore Park or swim in the Venetian Pool—local places equal to the best anywhere."

You will have seen nothing like the ivy-clad Place St. Michel in the 10-minute drive along the gasoline alley from the airport. If you have stayed elsewhere before in Miami, odds are it was bigger. This place is so small and anomalous in its setting that even if you have walked in from a stroll along the Gables' tree-lined, boutique-filled sidewalks, you have to slow down. The bass fiddler, the bicyclist, the caretaker of the flowers, and the lovers have all added to the glow of caring, and they, like Jimmy Buffet, Rudolf Nureyev, Susan Sontag, Derek Walcott, and

240

Tom Wolfe, have only recently discovered the place.

For the charm of the hotel is new again after decades, Stuart Bornstein's gift of a re-creation as much for himself and a partner during the last few years as for guests.

The entry is vaulted above and tiled, while below the floor of checkerboard terrazzo is flanked on one side by French doors that lead into a garden-like restaurant, and opposite by a wall accented by palms and corn-plants and bordered by eye-popping purple mums.

Upstairs, the two stories with 28 guest rooms have more the aspect of a Coral Gables mansion than hotel. The staircase and old-fashioned elevator split the two floors into wings, carpeted, with ceiling fans. Curtained windows, a rarity in hotel corridors, soften the look, as do bookcases, antique breakfronts, chairs and tables, and vases of flowers.

The rooms are all different, individually laid out and furnished. They share in common the look of care. All are done in antiques. Instead of closets there are armoires. Area rugs accent teak parquet floors. TVs rest on old Singer treadle sewing machine tables. All rooms have firm new beds, period headboards, and a variety of furniture for a random aesthetic rather than for matched lineage. Bathrooms are modern.

Room ceilings are high, and decorative stenciling outlines chair-height moldings. All rooms also have air conditioners, ceiling fans and telephones.

The look was never previously thus. When put up in 1926, the building was intended for offices. But there was more demand for hotel rooms. The building was renamed Hotel Sevilla and remained popular until modern hotels first appeared in Coral Gables during the 1950s and '60s.

The hotel suffered twice more on its way down, and at first interested Stuart only as protection for an investment he had made in a creperie successfully opened where the full-service restaurant now operates. When the hotel went on the market in 1978, he and his partner took it over. Improvements, including the Restaurant St. Michel and adjacent take-out deli, have continued steadily. The newest addition is Stuart's, a pub-like piano bar you enter either through the lobby or from the street. It has become instantly popular with the high-rise set for down-to-basics socializing.

The place could hardly be better as it settles into its second 60 years among the superior small hotels of America.

Hotel Place St. Michel, 162 Alcazar Ave., Coral Gables, FL 33134. (305) 444-1666. Stuart Bornstein, proprietor. 28 rooms with AC, ceiling fan, heat, color TV, bathrooms with tub in most, direct-dial phone. Restaurant, Stuart's Bar & Lounge, deli, elevator. Children of any age accepted, free under 12. No pets. All major credit cards accepted. Year-round rates: $75 to $105, suites $125, includes basket of fresh fruits and cheese on arrival. Italian chocolates with turndown service, morning newspaper, continental breakfast. Restaurant prices: breakfast $3 - $6; lunch $4 - $7 in deli, $10-$15 in restaurant; dinner $30-$50. Free garage parking across street.

Delray Beach – THE COLONY HOTEL
In-town and unchanging Mediterranean memory.

"Nobody's made an offer we can't refuse," says manager John Banta, so the Colony goes on oblivious to change, survivor of the Twenties, still profitable operating only three months a year, and in its way stylish more than 60 years later.

Too striking to be forgotten, but no longer busy with locals, the old sculpted Mediterranean-style compound balances the fun-in-the-sun revival of downtown Delray and helps keep the small city midway between Palm Beach and Fort Lauderdale prideful about its past.

Its fascination is that guests keep returning as if it were still the only place to be. It is not as if the hotel surroundings were magical for vacationing.

The Colony is a theatrical landmark from when it was more important to build resort hotels closer to the train station than to the ocean. Atlantic Avenue, which it once dominated with its romantic twin cupolas and rounded white stucco facade, has prospered east toward the beach, while the shops nearest the hotel, though of interest to vacationers, have come to depend on year-round clientele, so that winter colonists seem year by year more cast in a stubborn plot to resist by cordial interaction among themselves the proof of their own transiency.

Life goes on without dramatic change because some of the same people keep managing, many of the same guests keep returning. John Banta first worked the kitchen in 1939, and has had charge of the property since 1949. Bud Nicklaw, the cabana manager, has been here since 1935, though his wife Christine, who managed the hotel liquor store most of that time, has retired, as have George Whitin, Bud's assistant since 1951, and social hostess Elizabeth Ohmer who came in 1960.

From winter to winter guests come back to the same pillared lobby and molded ceiling and old-fashioned front desk (postcards still 5 cents, six for a quarter). Recent touch-ups include new chintz on the repainted white wicker, and a new "pink sand" carpet John doesn't think looks either pink or sandy.

He'll tell you there are still "the same tired 1926 rooms," all now with original Banta water colors (except he forgets sometimes that he may have sold one), all with baths and phones, all heated, but only a third air-conditioned, the rest with ceiling fans, and none with TV.

The dining room, where almost everyone continues to take breakfast and dinner on the Modified American Plan, still is reminiscent of the Twenties, though it has been air-conditioned and has new coral and aqua carpet, still floral like the remaining patch of the original from '26 that's been stored away for old time's sake.

"Hyatt will try something like this and call it a Gatsby Room," says John, with a sweep around his public rooms, taking in old lobby writing desks, drawing and cartoons of bygone events, Moroccan urns, ashtrays on tall stands with weighted bottoms that rock, a clock with sweep second hand behind the front desk. A bar with TV is adjacent.

"But here it's all still as it was. When we change, it's an adjustment to our guests. Take the fireplace. We don't light it as often as we used to. Get the heat up too much and the liquor goes right to the old people's heads."

Un-air-conditioned, this is Florida of thrown-open windows, billowing curtains, sunlight streaming through skylights. Guests daily are shuttled between hotel and the beach, where the Colony maintains its cabana club with pool and chaises and offers a midday buffet and grill lunch.

"It's an old way of life," says John. "Guests get used to it. They don't want to stay in hotels where people could care less about you.

"Younger people come here all the time to join their parents and grandparents. They like the style, too. Nobody's confined. We arrange golf, tennis. We're interested in people. The town is mystified by the hotel, that it keeps going. But the family who owns the property doesn't need to make a lot of money from it. We get offers every week. We'd rather keep operating than sell."

There is no make-believe about the place, no pretense that it's European or restyled modern. Its Twenties genre long ago became its own authentic style. It's an old Florida hotel still operating. Delray is kept special by it.

The Colony, 525 East Atlantic Ave., Delray Beach, FL 33444. (407) 276-4123. John Banta, manager. 103 rooms with heat, about a third with AC, almost all with baths, tubs, a few connecting bathrooms, phone (50¢ for each use). Children of any age accepted. Pets $10 per day (no meals). Elevator, gift shop, dining room and cocktail lounge, liquor store on premises, TV in downstairs parlor, beach club with heated salt-water pool, free shuttle bus. No credit cards. As we go to press we learn that John Banta has retired. Dick Foss, internal auditor at The Colony since 1981, has become manager. Postcards are still 5¢, six for a quarter, "nor will anything else change," he says, "but touch-ups."

243

Florida City — GRANDMA NEWTON'S BED AND BREAKFAST
Nothin' more friendly.

Down in Florida City where urban rush gives way to rural drawl, Mildred Newton runs—you might say pokes along with—an in-town bed-and-breakfast full of country notions.

If it started slow catching on, that's right up to speed in Florida City. a town that mainly lives off laboring in America's growingest winter vegetable patch, and looking after tourists bound for Everglades National Park and the Florida Keys.

Mildred's place might as well be Uncle Newton's as Grandma's because the same kids of Richard's brother Philip who make grandma Grandma make Richard Uncle, and 47-year-old Richard is just as much the prize of this four-room B&B as his mom. He's kind of the resident PR man, as well as handyman-builder.

Ask if they take kids and he'll chide, "What's a grandma's place without kids?" He'll make you believe the place is right-down-the-middle stylish just the way he's fixed it up, "not all formica and fiberglass like a lot of those fancy places we hear about," but "if you want TV in your room and double deadbolt locks, we'll be happy to send you down to the Days Inn."

At first you'll focus on Richard's mismatched plaid shirt and shorts, the bulky sneakers and patterned athletic socks—and the stub of cigar stuck in the corner of his mouth that gives him a boss look and befits his sayings like "Mom's down-home, and I'm redneck."

Richard, who turns out to be easygoing as a hound in a fruit pile, gets the job done. Erica Jong has stayed, and a lot of Sierra Club people come by. Folks recommend Grandma's down at the vegetable stand, at the airboat rides, and at Coral Castle, and she was featured on local TV during Heritage Week.

Just in case you missed that, Richard is happy for you to see the tape on the living room VCR, especially the part where one of the TV fellows says:

"If it's old-fashioned, country-style hospitality you want, Grandma Newton's is the place for you. She sure knows how to put on the breakfast. The part Grandma likes best is sitting around the breakfast table visiting with guests from all over the country. Umm, umm, it's the part I like best too."

"Well, yes, it is a big part," says Mildred, looking sweetly seventy-ish, plump and gray-haired, and slow-talking from living 40 years in the sticks after growing up in a coastal Carolina backwater. "I serve lots of fruit and meat and biscuits and grits—the whole bit. After they ran that TV show I had people wanting to come just for breakfast. But that would infringe on the pleasure of the guests. We don't want people tromping through the door all the time disturbing them."

Not much else is likely to either. The two-story vinyl-clad Dade County pine house, oldest in the area, started in 1914, sits on a quiet corner a block from Palm Drive. A grassy yard surrounds the house with coconut palms, shrubs, and borders of artillery fern behind a cyclone fence. Chairs and tables are set around, and there's a porch swing under the wood canopy.

It's a place of screen doors and open windows with breezy curtains. You walk into a narrow hall that has stairs going up one side. To the right is Grandma's breakfast room and kitchen. Left is the living room, and you notice the boxcar siding walls and ceilings that mark the house from early in the century.

Furniture is a mix of antiques and just plain old. Some of the paneling, the candy-bright colors, and shag carpets make you think of mobile home decor.

Guest rooms are less dowdy. Upstairs to the front is a room full of windows and white curtains that's bright and airy with twin beds. Spacious. Next to it is a darker room that sports fishermen's artifacts. Sound passes freely between these rooms.

Quieter to the other side is Grandma's Room (Mildred actually uses the Cowboy Room downstairs) with a king-sized bed, country-white curtains with patchwork trim, white-painted and contrasting dark furniture.

There are two hall bathrooms, one walled in cedar with only a shower, the other in pine with tub large enough for two.

Downstairs in the addition back of the house is the Blue Room, where Richard admits he went a little crazy with different kinds of wood: barnboard, roughed-out cedar, composition board of wood chips. The hall bathroom (private for this bedroom) is all paneled in cedar. Ceiling too.

Two houses across the street built between 1927 and 1932 have been acquired by Grandma and are being readied slowly (of course). Efficiencies as well as guest rooms will be available in time. You might ask.

How the house came to be a bed-and-breakfast is because when Mildred and Richard were looking for property it was too good to pass up but too big for a single family.

"I like people," says Mildred, "and I'd heard about bed-and-breakfast. So I got some books from the library and we plunged in." That was 1986, and since then folks have been coming from all over, including Europe.

"The foreign folks don't always understand English too well. I've actually been asked by some of them to slow down. Can you imagine! Asking me to slow down! I couldn't help but laugh. I had to explain that if I slowed down any I'd stop."

Grandma Newton's Bed-and-Breakfast, 40 NW 5th Ave., Florida City, FL 33034. (305) 247-4413. Mildred and Richard Newton, proprietors. 4 rooms, 3 baths (2 with tubs). AC, heat, ceiling fan. No credit cards. House phone for taking messages, local calls, credit-card and collect LD calls. Children of any age accepted, no charge for infants. Extra person in room $5. Fenced-in area for pets. Dec. 15-Easter: $40 single, $60 double; off-season: $30, $45. Longer stays discounted. Inquire about rates for efficiencies.

Fort Lauderdale — RIVERSIDE HOTEL
Downtown surrounded by fashionable shopping and the river.

Among Florida's few intimate downtown hotels, none relates better to its urban surroundings than the Riverside in Fort Lauderdale. For more than 50 years it has set the style on fashionable Las Olas Boulevard. Its front-door access to shopping plus its pool and garden setting on the New River—some call it "the loveliest stream in the world"—make it a good choice for vacationers as well as business travelers.

Its aspect is smaller than its actual size. In the absence of overstatement, nothing overwhelms simple courtesy. An example: A guest rests a moment in the outer lobby. Someone from the kitchen walks by. "Are you being looked after?" he asks. "Yes," the guest replies, but thinks to ask for a cup of decaffeinated coffee. The solicitous employee returns with it. The guest later learns he is the head chef.

Absence of pretense marks the place. You can imagine that whatever brings you to Fort Lauderdale will go better because you are lodged here. Why not, if setting has anything to do with anything?

The hotel has 116 rooms in a three-story wing built in 1936 and a six-story addition raised one year later. The hotel was immediately impressive on the street whose only distinction was as the first road to the beach. The name Las Olas means "the waves," and the hotel stood near the center of town, $2\frac{1}{2}$ miles from the ocean.

It was first the Hotel Champ Carr, named for the mate of a small charter fleet docked on the river. The hotel's developers made him their first manager. He was a great storyteller who wove woolly takes of seafaring adventure, cloaking his hotel with the allure of what he termed, grievously today, "The white man's tropics."

The grounds are still tree-shaded and planted with flowering gardens that recall the ambiance of the Thirties when beach hotels were not yet the rage because tanning was still the mark of people who labored in the sun. Guests carried parasols and wore broad-brimmed silk hats.

In time the boulevard developed and Las Olas became synonymous with high fashion. Two traffic lanes were built in each direction, mitigated by a lane of plantings between, and on either side wide, tree-shaded sidewalks with places to rest that flow into well proportioned, imaginatively designed shops. The town side of the hotel facing the boulevard is decidedly Southern with a wrought-iron balcony, hooked-back shutters, porch furniture, curtained French doors, and newly added tropical mural. Brick, glass, and matte-finish mullions make the street level elegant yet subdued.

More than ever, the mood contrasts on the other side, where the New River flows with that independence that gently mocks city grids and refreshes our admiration for natural nonconformity. Across the stream—no wider than a coconut toss—are private homes and garden apartments.

Interiors of the hotel are varied and well set off from each other. Contrast these discrete spaces with trendy cavernous lobbies that often look like shopping malls. The boutique style of Las Olas prevails inside the hotel as out.

There is an entry foyer, inner lobby, main lobby with reception desk, and two restaurants, one with a piano bar. The building's original design has left old-style lobby posts that have been half-mirrored and allow for conversation areas backed up to them.

Materials are crafted, earthy, and warm. Here are coral fireplaces, tile walls, cushioned braided wicker, potted palms, philodendron, cornplants, poinsettias in season. Paddle fans stir the air. There are ornamental carved and sculptured pieces, and tinted wall art of exotic birds that lends an Art Deco look.

Guest rooms are spacious and comfortable, with ample lighting. Typically, there is a Queen Anne armchair with desk and chair. The furniture is original oak, restored, solid, and handsome. The bed is firm. A dresser hides the TV, and there is a small refrigerator in a large closet.

Views are variously of the boulevard, the river, and the city. From some rooms you can see the ocean. Wherever you look you have the feeling of being centered.

One of the pleasures of the Riverside is its walking proximity to downtown business and attractions. Among these latter is the turn-of-the-century home—and once the business place—of Frank and Ivy Stranahan. The house is a two-story, broad-porched mansion completely restored and booked today for business and social affairs. It has a fine gift shop. Regular tours are offered. The Fort Lauderdale Historical Museum is a little farther west along the riverwalk, the new and highly rated Fort Lauderdale Museum of Art just a six-block walk.

Together with the museums, the Riverside Hotel remains a unique asset of Fort Lauderdale's downtown.

Riverside Hotel, 620 E. Las Olas Blvd., Fort Lauderdale, FL 33301. (305) 467-0671; (800) 325-3280; (800) 421-7666 (FL). Mary Mathurin, acting manager. 117 rooms with AC, AM/FM radio, heat, cable TV, bathrooms with tub, room phone, restaurants, bars, elevator, pool, boat dock, morning newspapers in restaurant. Children of any age accepted, free in parents' room to 16. No pets. All major credit cards accepted. Winter rates: $110-$150 single or double; rest of year $65-$90. 3rd person in room $10. Meals: breakfast about $6.50; lunch $12; dinner $15 and up. Off-street parking. Non-smoking rooms available.

Hollywood – DI VITO BY THE SEA
Irresistible kitsch on the ocean.

There's a small motel in Hollywood Beach on what they call the broadwalk—what you might think is a deliberate mispronunciation by some burlesque comic who wants to make sure you know what he likes best about the parade of acned skateboarders, bikers with ghetto blasters strapped to their racks, and buxom teenagers exposed like the engineering of unfinished condos barely clad when their developers go bust.

Di Vito By The Sea pops up at the north end of the strip where all the forgettable motels and cut-and-paste towers lose their punch after the long visual assault.

Up on the beach, divinely garish, Di Vito's appears like a gaudy riverboat stuck in a dried-up riverbed with its tower a misplaced Gothic smokestack, painted beachfront arches like the tops of sidewheels stuck in the sand, lower decks subsiding in farewell to a flagrant era.

To enjoy the place best you want to get in the ocean. Seen from there, Di Vito's fits, the Palace of Kitsch built by a master.

Tony Di Vito built it in 1958 when he was in his 50s. "We used to have a very good time in my younger age," he says. "I made living room, dining room and novelty furniture—like tables, most in French, Italian, Spanish style. My own creations.

"I moved to Florida to retire. I looked from North Miami up to Deerfield. I liked it here. I built this instead of a house. I wanted to spend a little something to keep myself occupied.

"I'm Italian. I got to where I needed an elevator to get to the third floor. I'm almost 90 years old. I'd been in Pisa. So I added the tower of Pisa. It leans a little. Nobody's straight in the world. I came to Chicago from Italy in 1920.

"I got the boat idea after my wife passed away. The whole thing looks like a ship. So I added the boat on the top. I wrote on it, 'Dry Dock Maria.' I mean it's not in the ocean. We're at the edge. There's actually the wheel of a boat up there.

"The back building? That represents the Castello di Sora, the city I come from, near Rome, and the castle is the castle we got over there up in the mountains. That's to me the kind of duplicate, you know."

Tony has given the furniture business to his son, one of six children, and more than 30 grandchildren and great-grandchildren. Tony lives in northwest Chicago with one of his daughters, but spends most of his time in Hollywood Beach.

"It's not like other places," says summer manager Austin Christman. "It's a family place. People get to know you. If they like you, they come back, If not, that's tough. We don't cut prices, like some."

Tony found Chris just after the place opened. Like Tony, Chris was vacationing back in the '50s. Miami Beach was getting congested. Motel Row was going up. So Chris went riding up the road. Happened to look over, saw this place. He and his wife checked in.

One day Tony was getting ready to go to Italy. He needed somebody to look after the place.

"Chris was going to build a house," Tony remembers. "I said, 'What do you want a house for?' I gave him the keys and told him to stay in the place. I knew he was an honest guy even if he didn't know anything about running a hotel. I told him. 'Do what you want to do.' We been friends since, and he comes nearly every year for two or three months."

There are only 10 apartments, each with its own bath and kitchen. Furnishings are nondescript tropical modern. Terrazzo floors. It's open all year, but people come mostly for a week or more. Chris will take you for a night if he has space, and it won't cost much, summer or winter.

"The place is equipped with friendship," says Chris. You get a lot of that.

Di Vito By The Sea, 3500 N. Broadwalk, Hollywood, FL 33019. (305) 929-7227. Austin Christman, summer manager; Ida and Dominick Corona, winter. 10 apartments and efficiencies with color TV, AC, heat, bathrooms with tubs, pay telephone. Children under 16 not accepted from Jan. 15 to March 25 (more or less), otherwise free "if not too many — we don't follow the plan religiously." Crib about $10 a week. Rates vary by time of year from $160 for up to 2 persons in a bedroom from May 1 to December 15, $180 for up to 2 in an efficiency, to $310 for up to 2 in a bedroom between Jan. 15 and April 1, $350 for up to 2 in an efficiency — all rates for week at a time. Overnight rates subject to negotiation when space available. Off-street parking.

Indiantown — SEMINOLE COUNTRY INN

Railroad-era lodge renewed as town center.

Give Charlie Miner high marks for hanging in. He thought it was going to be easy running a country inn. Anything looked good after a career as stockbroker in St. Louis. He came home one afternoon, told his wife he couldn't do it another day. The next morning he saw the ad for the Seminole Inn in the *Wall Street Journal*.

South Florida. Less than an hour from West Palm Beach. The best place in Indiantown.

The only thing was that competent help was hard to find. And then people would come out, lured by the history of the Duke and Duchess, look at the pictures in the lobby, then drive off again.

The part about the Duke and Duchess of Windsor still draws folks here. People have heard that Wallis Simpson, before she became a duchess, once ran the dining room for her uncle, and that's true. She did.

Her uncle, S. Davies Warfield, built the inn in 1925 when he was president of the Seaboard Air Line Railroad. A hunting and fishing lodge for his cronies is what he had in mind. Close to Lake Okeechobee; he didn't have to worry whether anybody else came. He would bring everybody he wanted on the train. For a while the track ended here. What else was there but the Seminole Inn?

A few years ago an old-timer described the place then as "a nice hotel, sitting right out in the swamp. Nice, but that was about it." People came only for a night on their way to Palm Beach or Jupiter. After the railroad extended to West Palm Beach, the train quit stopping and people didn't stay at all. The hotel closed and opened several times.

Holman Wall, who had become rich in lumber and ranching, fixed up the hotel and reopened it. Holman's daughter, Jonnie, ran the hotel for a while but lost interest. That's when Charlie saw the ad in the Journal.

He didn't have to change much. Anybody who sees the old Spanish-style place with the front porch rockers falls in love with it. The tile floors, wicker, and ceiling fans in the lobby make people feel right at home.

The rooms have never been much to write home about, but they're comfortable, with firm beds and chairs. The only drawback is the veneer paneling. It seems an inadequate way to style the place when the real thing is all around.

Out back there's a swimming pool in a yard of native trees. Side trips can include a tour through Owens Groves to see the peacocks, and a tour of the Barley Barber Swamp by arrangement with Florida Power & Light.

Charlie found that there were many retired people at the Indianwood Country Club, and some of them liked coming to help and meeting people who pass through. Now that some of the kitchen staff's been better trained, Charlie can provide the country cooking that suits the guys who stomp in in their boots and dusty jeans. They pack the place, putting away barbecued chicken and beef sandwiches and fries. And the gussied-up weekenders love the pork and beef tenderloin medallions in sauce, and the more elegant side of country cooking.

"It's a lot more work than I anticipated," admits Charlie. "People who come may find this a sleepy old inn, but I can't believe how busy I stay."

Part of his time is spent researching the history of town. So far, the only book about Indiantown in the local library is about Mayan Indians. That's because of the large influx of Guatemalans who have come to work the fields. Going to and from work in their colorful clothes, they follow a trail across the street from the hotel's front porch.

Just beyond the open field are the Seaboard Railroad tracks. These days they link Miami with the rest of America. You'd never know it from the porch of the Seminole. Okeechobee to West Palm is all anybody much thinks about. And these days not many fail to stop when they're along this route. Charlie's operation and his stick-to-it-iveness have won over a lot of people.

Seminole Country Inn, 15885 SW Warfield Blvd. (Highway 710), Indiantown, FL 34956. (407) 597-3777. Charles Miner, innkeeper. 26 rooms with AC, heat, color cable TV, bathrooms with tub, direct-dial phone, pool. Restaurant. Children of any age accepted, free in parents' room to 14 when accompanied by both parents. Pets $10. AmEx, MC, Visa. Year-round rates: $45 single, $50-$65 double. 3rd person in room $5. Meal prices: breakfast $1.95 to $3.25; lunch $2.95 to $4.95; dinner $4.95 to $11.95. Off-street parking.

Miami — MIAMI RIVER INN
Hidden dimension of downtown hospitality.

Like kids who whirl around, dizzying themselves into some hidden dimension, you can spin about downtown on a Saturday, a hub turned flea market for a hemisphere of immigrants and a world of tourists, then cross the First Street Bridge over the river and stun yourself into 1910 at the Miami River Inn.

Downtown Saturday the business suits are all in suburban closets. The office buildings and junior college are closed. Flagler Street teems with yellow-shirted kids on Globo Tours from Brazil, electronics bargain-hunters prowling mini-malls, pawn shop denizens, homeless panhandlers. Crew members from Jamaican-staffed cruise ships carry out ox-tail and curried goat from the Jamaican Eating Place, where North Miami Avenue pulses to reggae and Radio El Sol. Whatever you want is "no problem, Mon," from *precios bajos*—low prices—to stashing a Panamanian generalissimo under the courthouse for a couple weeks.

You cross the low bridge. Pelicans swoop through the draw, scavenging the trash of island freighters. Down the steep iron stairs from the bridge, the inn astounds with its antiquity.

This is no museum of remnant buildings relocated in huddled abstraction. The little compound nestles where it was developed between 1904 and 1910 after the land was sold by pioneers William Brickell, Julia Tuttle, and Henry Flagler. Winter guests were still boarding here in the 1980s, many in past seasons having come by train, their parents before them conveyed by horse and carriage from the Florida East Coast Railway depot once next to the county courthouse.

Gentility haunts the look. In a curious juxtaposition, women outside the inn's gates still carry parasols, and men wear Panama hats. Evoking yesteryear gentry, these modern passersby have fled Nicaragua. They populate a refugee neighborhood where kids play ball in the street, moms without cars tote groceries, and dads come home in the evening with lunchpails.

The inn compound combines five freshly painted, softly colored old guest-houses, and four mid-century masonry buildings of a modified Deco and Mediterranean look. The two sets fit together better today in the single courtyard than before because tall palms strategically buffer their eras.

The five older buildings are clapboard with dormers on four, high-pitched overhanging roofs, picket porch rails, and monumental green fire escapes. They are more elaborate versions of nearby bungalows that typified urban dwellings in much of America early in the century.

Former Dade County Historic Preservation Officer Ivan Rodriguez says the Miami River Inn "is important because these are the only remaining houses of the time built right close to the river. They are a good characterization of what the entire area once was like." Their historical integrity is matched by frosted street lamps that surround an oval lawn, and by cast-iron furniture on keystone walks.

Interiors have been restored to the straightforward craftsman-era style that favored hand detailing without showy Victorian ornamentation. Rooms and suites feature hardwood floors and high ceilings with paddle fans. Alcoves harbor mirrored armoires. Mantels and claw-foot tubs are gaily painted, and porches are inviting with their wicker and chintz.

The houses are two and two-and-a-half stories, the masonry apartments two and three. Masonry exteriors are beige with white trim. Here and there, Deco details speak to their own era, with little portholes under ziggurat trim.

The compound sits behind its high, black wrought-iron fence across South River Drive just north of Jose Marti Park. It has its own pool and jacuzzi, and off-street parking. The park, one of Miami's prettiest, has another pool, as well as playgrounds for children, raquetball courts, and recreational pavilions. Many guests will recognize the spectacular views of downtown from episodes of the TV show "Miami Vice."

Although there is no restaurant on the premises (there are plans), East Coast Fisheries is an easy walk. Big Fish for lunch, and Joe's for lunch and dinner are only a little farther.

The most dizzying aspect of the inn is that it took nearly five years to open. For months it remained ready but empty except for caretakers. Partners feuded until 1990, when Dr. Jim and Sallye Jude bought out the others. The Judes were original restorers of the Island City House in Key West.

Now—finally—phones ring busy at the inn. Preservationists who had watched and worried are booking out-of-town friends and groups.

Although some people question safety in the neighborhood, Sallye says the neighborhood couldn't be more hospitable. "People around all the time are what the property has needed," she says. "Our neighbors are friendly. We all look out for each other."

Guests fall in love with the little compound and are quick to recommend it.

Neighborliness, you reflect, is just further into that hidden dimension where the Miami River Inn spins you.

Miami River Inn, 118 SW S. River Drive, Miami, FL 33130. (305) 325-0045. Sallye Jude, proprietor. 40 rooms with 38 baths (2 rooms use bath across hall) (32 with showers, some with tubs, 5 with tubs only), AC, heat, most with ceiling fans, direct-dial phones (50¢ local calls, 40% mark-up on LD calls). Children of any age accepted ($10 for cot, rollaway, or crib). No pets. AmEx, MC, Visa. Year-round rates: $60-$70, includes continental breakfast. Daily paper available. Pool, jacuzzi, croquet lawn. Small meeting facility. Off-street parking.

Miami Beach – ESSEX HOUSE, PARK CENTRAL, WALDORF TOWERS HOTEL, HOTELS CAVALIER, CARDOZO, LESLIE, CLEVELANDER, EDISON, BREAKWATER, AVALON, BEACON

The look and the beach and the ocean are everything,
though rooms are small and managements are unpredictable.
Essex House stands out.

Introduction

Barbara Capitman was the true believer of the Miami Beach preservation movement. She lived to relish how renewal of that shabby little Art Deco District began the revival of all of Miami Beach. Just like she said it would.

But now, even though some 500 of 800 buildings in the Deco District have new facades, and the city enjoys world recognition, the situation, according to Barbara in one of her last interviews (she died early in 1990), "has never been more precarious." Nor did she think that the tourists or the fashion models and their camera crews for the hip magazines were doing enough to preserve the city they all value as stage set.

"They need to throw themselves down in front of the bulldozers," she cried, recalling how she had done that in two notable losing causes that late in the Eighties saw destruction of the Flamingo Hotel and then the Senator, the latter for 37 parking spaces.

Barbara's concern was that developers would keep getting exceptions to knock down buildings here and there in the district until the area would lose its integrity. She saw the wolf past the door and already in the hen house when the city in 1990 won more compliant preservationists over to a plan to destroy several hotels for a new megahotel across from the convention center. The plan called for gutting interiors for conversion to boutiques and restaurants. In return, an expanded preservation district was enacted with guarantees—how good have they ever been?—against further demolition.

For Barbara, the to-the-barricades fury that saved the district has been neutered by quiche-eaters. Gone are the aroused architects, intellectuals, and museum directors who got it all going (too many gone to AIDS, Barbara lamented), replaced by middle-class, real estate people interested only in money. The 1990 Art Deco Weekend summed it all up for Barbara.

"They don't care about scheduling lectures and old films and design displays any more so that people get to learn what it all means," she said. "It's just money now. You see the same battered food carts from all the other festivals.

"Loving care is what's lacking here."

Nevertheless, Barbara would acknowledge that it's wonderful to see the thousands of people again along the streets of South Beach.

"People are coming from all over the country to live here," she said. "Musicians, writers, designers with a whole life of their own are here—though we didn't envision moving out the elderly so unmercifully, or people willing to come but unwilling to fight."

Newcomers, now that Barbara is gone, may wonder how the transformation happened.

Denis Russ, who heads a Miami Beach redevelopment agency, recalls that "Barbara waved her wand over us, and everything changed. She said, 'You have Art Deco buildings,' and all of a sudden all of us who thought we were living in a problem area were living in the Art Deco District. Naturally, we all wanted to find out what that was."

Thus began the revival of Miami Beach in the 1970s, a slow process for its enthusiasts, too slow to interest banks, but inevitable for risk-takers. And finally for politicians, including early naysayers, so that in the Nineties a coalition is cautiously forming that will link the vision with the practical steps for realizing at last the renascence of this great American resort in the tropics.

Revival of the Miami Beach Art Deco District gives vacationers potentially dozens of restored historic hotels to stay at along a scenic drive beside a mile of broad Atlantic Beach. More than a dozen hotels have reopened, though of widely different standards. Many more have been readied: the Avalon, the Beacon, the Majestic. With them are coming bagel shops to bodegas, health clubs to nightclubs. Everything is Deco-styled, so that even souvenirs from the Deco District are special.

But these properties are still in their early stages of resurrection from rundown housing for the elderly to nostalgically trend-setting hotels. They have been plagued by high management turnover, financial disputes, and the hyper-salesmanship of unabashed real estate promoters. Moreover, the national press has been more concerned with promoting the Deco District than with careful reporting about what it's like to be lodged in these properties. Charming they are, but not without problems.

Let's put the scene in perspective.

Except for Key West and St. Augustine, nowhere in Florida is historic preservation more valued for tourism than in the Deco District. Developers and municipal agencies are working together because preservationists led the way with a series of conferences and Deco celebrations that revealed property in the district to be greatly undervalued. Still cautious lenders will join in as soon as there are sustained operating results. Their alliance bids well to keep the district unique, and vacationing a mix of sunshine pleasures and one-of-a-kind shopping and entertainment.

Withal, the Beach is a place of contradictions. At the same time revived Deco hotels were already gratifying fashion-minded yuppies, data of the community-based development agency led by Denis Russ depicted South Beach as more depressed economically than even riot-scarred Liberty City. Banks continue to evaluate hotel projects by their residual appeal to seniors of limited means, who are the district's only established clientele, in case proposed new markets of the affluent young fail. (Banks clearly are not the heroes of this scenario.)

South Beach is a place where the nationally acclaimed Miami City Ballet rehearses behind see-through windows on Lincoln Road, a reviving arts street, even while impatient politicians talk of tearing out the pedestrian mall to bring cars back. Even aesthetic expansion of beachfront Lummus Park and broadening of the beach get mixed reviews. The grassy expanse wilts in winter's droughts and looks awful. Young parents of tots complain about the long walk over hot sand to the water, while seniors complain that their energy gives out before they get to the water at all.

Miami Beach will stay in the news. A review of the Deco District's dynamics can help visitors better evaluate what it is like vacationing in the district's hotels.

Recent Miami Beach History

By the mid-Eighties, Miami Beach had turned around so many times looking to recapture its lost tourist trade that it had screwed itself near permanently stuck. From queen of resorts 30 years before, the city had run down and acted indecisively. At different times in recent years Miami Beach glimpsed salvation among boozing college kids, nesting yuppies, empty-nest seniors, on-the-cheap U.K. charter tourists, rich South American escapists, gambling addicts, and nudists. It elected and rejected mayors and hired and fired directors of tourism almost as loosely as George Steinbrenner changed Yankee managers, but with no superstars to show for its spending.

Tinsel towns "in" become tinsel towns "out." Tourists, retirees, and refugees don't make for stable communities. The lack of permanent families to make a real city leaves fashion the passing tourist allure. Hotels can't pick up and leave when the tourists do.

There was a time during the Forties and Fifties when Miami Beach was a middle-class community with two- and many three-generation families. Schools and churches were well attended. Tourists and residents mixed among crowds in fine Lincoln Road shops. Many hotels, filled with vacationers in winter, were busy with cabana club residents in summer.

But a series of changes—mostly the fault of hoteliers themselves—caused demise of the beach.

Some say the end was in sight in the mid-Forties when crime-buster Estes Kefauver closed illicit gambling. That led new hotels to install star entertainers in their own palatial showrooms. Coupled with inclusive meal plans, the hotels drained the action from big-name night clubs and restaurants that had given the Beach its glamor and made the mainland a playland, too.

Hotel guests became further captive when the huge resorts next began adding shops and services in competition with established town retailers. Many hoteliers were seen to be greedy and uninterested in anything else happening on the Beach—or on the mainland, where full-scale cities of permanent populations were developing.

While new jet airplanes let warm-weather seekers overfly Miami for the Caribbean (where cold fronts don't threaten spells of low temperatures), tourism managers were adopting a throwaway attitude toward their trade. Instead of updating, old hotels were supplanted by new ones built in a flashy parade as tourism marched its way north along the oceanfront. Developers built bigger all the time, encroaching further onto the sand, building seawalls that quickened erosion.

After 1968 there were no grand new hotels. A subsequent generation of vacationers was turned off by the kibbitzing style of their parents who loved Miami Beach so well they started buying apartments in the new residential high-rises and quit patronizing the hotels altogether. Like the hotels, the condos eroded the beach. In time there was little sand between the megastructures and the sea. The beach was gone. Town life was going. There was the Strip. And before long that became an embarrassment, the symbol of failure. Property values fell so low that once famed Miami Beach became a convenient dumping ground for thousands of impoverished Cubans who fled their island in the late Seventies and in their new ghetto of feeble oldsters fed on crime.

Tourism, after a flamboyant heyday, had become a neglected seat-of-the-pants operation, costly to investors, shunned by people of competence, mindlessly competitive, and contributing the relatively benign pre-crime, pre-riot image of Miami as a place for fun in the sun where you might retire but certainly didn't want your brightest kids to pursue careers.

Now the stigma of crime and riot has subsided as Miami visionaries erect a shiny celebrity city of skyscrapers, chain hotels, rapid transit, parks, major league sports, and entertainments they hope will attract people to live downtown and enjoy the good life that jobs in international commerce and fueled by the drug trade make possible.

The spectre of casino gambling has faded. As recently as the mid-Eighties, the prospect was real enough to have threatened a new cycle of tear-down and replace—this time the entire beachfront with megastructures as in Las Vegas and Atlantic City—instead of heritage-based revival.

Probably "Miami Vice" killed the future for casinos. That and presidential leadership against drugs. Responsible people no longer want to be linked with fast money.

Besides, families are moving back to the Beach. A huge new vertical suburb is likely to rise in a few years on the vast nondescript acreage below the Deco District rimmed on one side by the Atlantic, on the other by Biscayne Bay. Says Denis Russ, "The Art Deco phenomenon has demonstrated the vitality of Miami Beach to renew itself."

The Art Deco Inheritance

The Art Deco District came together during the 1930s and '40s. The style seemed to spread spontaneously along the Beach. It was popular because its playfulness fit with a town that had no business but pleasure. Everyone, it seemed, walked daily with a towel around his shoulders to the beach, carried a canvas beach chair, drank piña coladas. The rest of America struggled with Depression, but Miami and Miami Beach had been only temporarily slowed by the hurricanes and land boom collapse of the late Twenties. The Beach was described as "a world of moneyed industrialists, boulevardiers, and stars of stage and screen, its atmosphere gay, carefree, and expensive."

The Deco style was derived from more sources than practicing architects might have acknowledged. Cubism, deStijl, the Bauhaus, Art Nouveau, and German Expressionism all contributed. Some movements were in opposition to each other: deStijl's rectangular abstractions repudiated the sculptural plasticity of Expressionism. Never mind in Miami Beach!

The elements merged at the 1925 Paris International Exposition of Decorative and Industrial Arts, where the immanent style became known as Art Moderne, and later in America as Art Deco. It was marked by streamlining, strong vertical movement, horizontal banding, and decorative friezes. The style complemented the futurism that was finding expression in new swept-back railroad, ship, and automotive designs. Playfulness merged with a wind-blown mythic look that seemed to signal the strength America would need for the war ahead.

All elements were employed unrestrained in the new hotels, apartment buildings, and houses that began to line Ocean Drive and filled blocks of the lower end of the Beach. It was low-rise and relatively democratic. Farther up, the Beach was "restricted" and grand, as was much of the rest of lower east coast resortdom. In South Beach, townfolk and tourists mixed easily. Residential and tourist architecture looked alike. To this day, stores and houses along South Beach are among the finest examples of Art Deco style included in tours of the Miami Design Preservation League.

The League was founded in 1976 and became the vehicle for art historian Barbara Capitman to mount the preservation campaign for South Beach. She succeeded in attracting national support before local leaders were convinced. After all, they were being asked to invest their prestige in a collection of shabby buildings in a part of town that everybody but the pensioners had been avoiding for years. More, conservative preservationists resisted Barbara's urgings because Miami Beach and its elderly Jewish population, long the butt of jokes, weren't dignified enough for still elitist tinged preservation. For them, Barbara's transgression was the democratizing of preservation. She talked of Art Deco as folk art and equated the style's whimsy with its sophistication.

Any first-time visitor immediately recognizes that, aesthetics aside, what appeals most about the Deco District is how it's part of the real world. There are no admission gates to Ocean Drive. Young and old mix easily. Couples hold hands. Older men walk and talk with each other while their wives walk and talk a few steps behind. Some gesture animatedly, arguing old causes. They speak many languages. They are black and white and shades of brown.

You come around 16th Street off Collins Avenue onto Ocean Drive and the restored colorful Deco facades pop out. They are frozen lemonade popsicles, sugary wedding cakes. Full of brows and neon, they put you in mind of old movie theaters, when admission was a nickel and you tried to get in free by walking backwards when the show broke.

Some are pink on pink, others multi-colored. One— yellow, coral, white, and blue—has perfect proportions. Another has streams of neon that pour into channels and flow dazzling around the sides.

On the grass, Cuban patriots sing songs of home and clap, annoying Pepsi-popping Anglos on lunch break from a restoration job. Retirees carry their aluminum beach-chairs, some in the undershirts, shorts, and socks they used to wear to work with black shoes.

At the Cardozo Hotel, Stuart Bornstein, who runs Stuart's Lounge, calls Ocean Drive "consummate people-watching. It's glamorous and funky, not sterile. Marriott didn't do it."

A jogger does stretch exercises against the prop of a yellowing tall palm. Models and those down on their luck share the widened pink sidewalks. Galaxy Tours cruise the street, offering fast looks at the hotels. A bus so big that only a star could own it goes by. A dog named Cosmo runs beside his mealticket on a bike.

At 9th and Ocean Drive, Waldorf Towers rates a prize for the art posters under glass at its veranda cafe. At the Revere, the old folks still keep to their chairs on the shaded porch, as they have ever since the magic first ran out of the Beach 40 years ago. The News Cafe is very Ipanema, very Tel Aviv. If it were a performance, the SRO sign would be up. You can get a big bowl of fresh fruit and baskets of crusty rye and pumpernickel while reading *Rolling Stone* or *Mirabella*. Waitresses make good tips because the place is owned by beach-experienced guys, not clothiers who jumped ship for a fast buck.

A man in black sportswear in an open black Mercedes convertible nestles into black leather with a black cellular phone. Everything stops when a boyish-looking woman in a ribbed undershirt walks by. If somebody sounded a long, low whistle, the street would break into applause.

ESSEX HOUSE

The beauty of Patricia Murphy's Essex House, an original of architect Henry Hohauser, is that you don't have to worry about anything jolting you. After you're fully lulled into confidence by the serenity of Patricia's Deco spaces—with the Earl LaPan Everglades mural, the etched flamingos, the pink mirrored glass, and the fiber-optic Yamaha disclavier player piano—nothing's going to grab you and shout, "Gotcha!" Patricia's a self-styled spoiled brat from Newport who spent $3 million and 18 months to get her 51 rooms and suites opened. That was in 1989. She knew what she wanted.

Consider bedroom essentials.

All doors are card-locked. They're solid. You don't hear sounds from next door or from the hallways. Towels and linens are designer matched. Pillows and sofa rolls are feather and down. Lights are on dimmers. Bed lamps have three-way bulbs. Room furniture has ziggurat arch bottoms and includes firm beds, desk with chair, night table, and more in the suites.

Bathrooms, though new, are all ceramic. They have pull-out clotheslines above tubs, wall-hung sinks, make-up lights, and paintwork done between the lines. Fresh flowers, at least sometimes, are in rooms. There's Evian water.

Speakers carry music of the Thirties everywhere, crisply and without distortion. When you return from dinner, you can listen to "The Man I Love," "Love for Sale," or maybe "How Long Has This Been Going On" in the elevator, then find your room completely remade, the drapes pulled, the bed turned down, and the lights turned low.

Essex House is a block away from Ocean Drive, but some suites overlook the beach. You're in such elegance and among such competence that you can be happy and thankful. Patricia Murphy has done it right.

PARK CENTRAL HOTEL

The stylish, six-story Park Central reopened in 1987, 50 years after the first time around. It's under control: the look from outside, the smart bars and restaurant, the art, the rooms, the rooftop gardens.

The good news is that the assured hand of owner Tony Goldman is also at work reviving a half dozen other properties, including 800 Ocean Drive, where the popular News Cafe is.

The Park Central is palm-fringed, with lavender and blue Deco styling. It has portholes, brows, fluting, and neon-channeled letters.

The bi-level lobby has high ceilings and the feel of an atrium garden. Rose's Cafe is down, Lucky's Cafe up.

Rose's is for mornings among potted palms behind glass that holds in the aroma of breakfast coffee. People pass in and out in beachwear, in every imaginable sandal, sunglass, and shades of sunburn. A dozen languages mix, a dozen tour company bags, a hundred points of origin.

Lucky's is one of the stellar Beach dining spots. It's mauve and sea green with mirrors and hanging Deco lamps, long-stemmed glassware, and cushioned banquettes. Dinners have featured pastas, mesquite grill items, and goodies like a garlic custard surrounded by portobello and shiitake mushrooms in a buttery white wine sauce topped with slivers of fresh basil.

On the mezzanine a couple of imaginative montages catch the eye. One of entertainment stars features Fred Astaire, Betty Boop, Bette Midler, and Baby Snooks. The other is a scene of Havana Harbor with owner Tony Goldman among tourists and their cameras along the Malecon. The photo blow-ups of hurricanes withering the beach rivet attention.

Rooms have been redone with their original maple furniture restored. There are twin night tables and lamps, white carpets, small tile baths, and awning windows covered with wide-slatted venetian blinds behind white curtains. Oceanfront rooms also have new wicker pieces.

The rooftop gardens are set up with a bar, tables, and chairs. Remarkable how the turquoise and lavender walls are exactly the colors of the sea beyond the palm-fringed beach.

Admire. Enjoy.

WALDORF TOWERS HOTEL

The new owner here is a Swedish contractor who bought out Jerry Sanchez in 1989. Or have things changed again?

There is flair in the public look. The facade is rose, yellow, and white, with channeled neon letters. There are the typical vertical fluting, horizontal brows, curved corners, and abrupt color juxtapositions, here with a cupola atop the third floor. The front terrace has become the Italian-styled Waldorf Cafe, with its exceptional art posters under glass.

The lobby is typically light-hearted, now with a little bar also used for breakfasting. Terrazzo tiles are uncarpeted. There are Deco posters. Ceiling fixtures feature the segmented details of a grand chandelier as might be seen in the Radio City Music Hall. The ceiling is edged in molded bands painted green, rose, and white, surrounding the broad center space that is yellow, with three lighting fixtures. Above the elevator door is a keystone arch in a burst design. There are various potted plants and glass-brick partitions.

Downstairs, the club has been totally remodeled and now is "Sempers," redolent in antiques of Czarist Russia, a seductive mishmash of classical paintings, statuary, gilt, cushions, and upholstered banquettes. It's plushly Victorian/Edwardian, Thirties, vaguely Egyptian, with its drapery over fringe, its dimness perfect for espionage or escapades. It's the work of Barbara Hulanicki, creator of the once successful Biba's in London. They say it's private, but non-members get in.

Hallways are bright with recessed fluorescence from artfully dropped ceilings, and decorative wall mountings that imitate sconces. Doorways are in a beige rose with louvered insets of dusty green, and door moldings of dark green. A rose hall carpet extends into guest rooms.

A typical room is Deco in its pastels, in its streamlining, its fantasy motifs. Rooms are sparse, uncluttered. Nothing gets in the way of the Deco mood but the TV. Drapes are fantasy designs, puffy pastel clouds all coral, sky-blue, green tinged, colors picked up in the moldings, trim, and doors. Bedcover, ruffle, carpet, bed lamps, and cornices are more rose. Lamps are scalloped, and overhead fixtures are variations of those in the lobby. Headboards, sidetables, dressers and desks are all in a streamlined marbleized mica.

Bathrooms are small (as they always have been) but with tubs and showers. Beds are firm. There is a room phone. Wall art consists of Deco-themed posters.

Oceanfront suites have foyers, sitting rooms, and a bedroom facing the beach. Furniture consists of upholstered easy chairs in shades of gray. The round sitting room mirror is etched with a woman and two hounds in Twenties fashion. The bedroom corner is curved, a delicious touch.

THE CAVALIER

Someone is always walking around here with vases of fresh flowers: bursting blossoms of allamanda, bird of paradise, lustrous red gingers, great white hibiscus. Beautiful young people as fresh and real as the flowers pop in and out of the staircases.

The hotel stays very busy. The standard is high. The flowers tell it all.

The Cavalier is first rate because of long-time former manager Don Meginley. Don set the standard for the district. When the bank took over from the exploitative Royale group something went wrong, and Don, who had begun competently upgrading the other Royale properties, too, was let go. Everybody loses from this move.

If Don's competence can be equaled, guests will continue to enjoy a European cold breakfast: fresh croissants, muffins, cheeses, cold meats, yogurts, cereal, dark breads. The orange juice will still be freshly squeezed, the coffee beans freshly ground each morning. In the lobby each Thursday evening maybe the flutist and pianist will still perform as guests enjoy wine and cheese before dining out.

As for rooms, there have been fluffy towels changed every evening, real water glasses, and bottled Evian water. Miami water may not give you *la turista*, but nobody locally concerned with long term health drinks it unfiltered. There's a morning newspaper in front of every room.

No rock and roll, no jazz, no late-night restaurants in the lobby. This is a hotel you can sleep in.

Service may not make the rooms larger but they look better because caring has gone in rather than just the obligatory "look." The paint trim is all within the lines. Desks are of the era. Inside the front center drawer are pen racks and a well for an ink bottle. Beds are firm, and most headboards are original.

Color tones are softer than the typically affected Deco themes. Wheat-colored drapes, white sheer curtains, blonde furniture, russet carpet, walls of palest yellow, bedcovers a pale gold-on-gold boxy check, Deco-fluted yellow ceramic ashtrays, more colorful Deco framed prints—the look is reposeful as would befit those tuxedoed gents and their bobbed and gowned women who show up in all the brochures, evoking an era when nobody thought of pleasure without service and style, both.

In the lobby, Deco's Egyptian heritage surfaces in bordered geometrics of silver, gold, bronze tones embellishing terrazzo, tile, glass, and metal tubing, with the usual fluting, beveling, and recessing. On the best days, you turn away for a moment and someone has replaced the floral arrangement of an hour ago with sterling roses and Princess Gracias purple lilies, yellow lilies, heliconia and white fresias. Around the walls are exotic potted false bananas, areca, and pygmy date palms.

On lesser days the lobby looks neglected, sisal undermatting masquerading as carpet, the flowers few and tired, the wicker furniture unimaginatively arranged. One suspects the place sparkles more when a fashion shoot is going on, less at other times.

Risk inquiring. At its best the Cavalier rates tops.

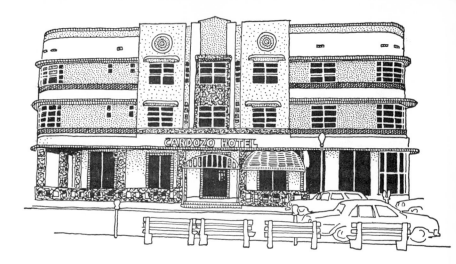

HOTEL CARDOZO

Though the Cardozo was one of the first hotels in the district to be revived, its restorers ran out of money, the hotel lapsed, new owners left it to languish for three years while they turned elsewhere. Now its banded curves in dark winey colors sweeping around the corner of Ocean Drive and 13th Street make it again one of the most attractive, inside as well as out.

The hotel was designed in 1939 by Henry Hohauser, the most prolific of the district's architects. It is named for Benjamin N. Cardozo, a U.S. Supreme Court Justice during the Roosevelt administration. Some remember the hotel more because in 1958 it was featured in the movie "A Hole In The Head" that starred Frank Sinatra, Edward G. Robinson, Keenan Wynn, and Thelma Ritter. The song "High Hopes" was taken seriously by Don Meginley of the Cavalier, when he was also in charge here.

The lobby and terrace-level Cafe Cardozo has been reestablished as Stuart's Cafe, with Tuesday-through-Saturday music that is again popular among the trend-setters. The lobby is striking in its marble veneer in swirl pattern, its dramatic duotoned ceiling mirror radiating from an incised Neptune, its banded terrazzo floors, and the cherrywood, mauve, and pewter tones of furniture. The brass elevator door features portholes and a peacock motif. Even the stairs open as a decorative recess.

Guest rooms feature hardwood floors, dramatic headboards in flared crown geometric patterns. All the furniture is original from the Deco era. New lamps are in keeping.

Though the Cardozo has been beautifully restored in its public spaces, and at least modestly so in its guest rooms, it is not without problems for guests. Noise travels easily from room to room, and the swinging entertainment so appealing to young guests and the oldsters who like to be around them makes sleep impossible upstairs until bands quit for the night—well past midnight.

Some might argue that vacationers have no business going to sleep early. Enough will disagree, and somehow successor restorers to those now at work will have to deal with the problem here and at the other hotels of the district.

The problem may also be that too many would-be restorers see only dollars to be made in these properties. They are not necessarily successful hotel operators with a developed sense of hospitality. Certainly that seems to have been part of the problem for owners of the Art Deco hotels, whose litigation with lenders slowed their plans for development of additional properties before ousting them from control altogether. Managers have not stayed long enough to have an impact. One suspects publicists have been valued more highly.

Without doubt, if you are careful to try for rooms not above and preferably with nobody checked in on either side of you, the Cardozo is an excellent choice.

HOTEL LESLIE

Just south of the inexplicably closed Carlyle, lately a Deco favorite, the Leslie is equally dazzling, three stories symmetrical in pink, white, and apricot, with its own sitting porch. The manic subdues here. The incompleteness of the street stays outside. The place is calm, befitting its small size.

Every lobby table has a vase of astromerias, and chairs to one side where hotel guests can enjoy breakfast. The sign in one window given over to a salon reads, "Hannah and Her Scissors."

Guest rooms are newly redone with platform beds. The furniture is wood, clean and neatly painted. Deco lamps are in white and mauve. Quilt and drapes are candy-banded in the room's soft adobe tones. A pair of Deco prints are on the walls. There are metal wire wall sculptures and wire magazine racks. There is a beach feeling that especially suits the oceanfront and oceanview rooms. These feel like cottage rooms. Non-oceanview rooms are less interesting—but where aren't they!

THE CLEVELANDER

Here the sound lately has been British, down the street Italian, and—when the SAS charters are coming in—Swedish all over. Virginia Kay and her sons stir in Jamaican reggae poolside on Sundays. It's a winning mix and likely to prevail in the ever-changing Deco District, where the Kays have stuck it out since the mid-Eighties.

"It's not just us and the other hoteliers who are making it go now," says Virginia. "It's almost as if the city were finally in favor of reviving the district. I can complain about a trash pile one day and the city removes it the next."

Mirabile dictu!

Certainly everybody likes the Clevelander style. Miami Heat players stay here, owners of reviving restaurants. Vegetarians come for the natural food service in the outside restaurant. Models tend bar, run the shop. There are old-timers, local residents and international guests.

Softly colored in green, yellow, beige, and lavender, the hotel is a temple of horizontal brows and vertical banding, topped off by a triumphal Deco pediment.

The lobby features a neon-ringed pink and blue clock above the pigeonholes. Further recessed sits a glass-brick, marble-topped bar with vinyl swivel chairs. There's a shop where the Kays design their own T-shirts and shorts. At night, the Inside Outside patio restaurant by the sculptural pool and gardens has become an "in" watering hole.

Still there's the improv look. Maybe it's the guests in and out in swimsuits. The Clevelander seems to have a leftover look of permanent flux from when it was taking guests before everything was ready. Many of the youthful trippers from the United Kingdom who helped get the property together have stayed on.

"I still seem to live out of a suitcase, but I don't mind," says Virginia, a Chicagoan. "I came to Miami Beach because it's the playground of Florida. We didn't know Art Deco from anything. This was a slum property. Where else could you find this kind of a buy on the beach? Now everybody comes here for the fun."

There is in fact always entertainment for seniors across Ocean Drive at the 10th Street Auditorium. There's Penrod's just back of that for the college spring-break crowd. Now and then among the bikini crowd a Jesus preacher pauses.

"For nightlife," says Virginia's son, Kent, "you can stand an hour just to get into someplace. Next morning you get up to start work, and some people are still dressed in holiday costumes from the night before."

The Clevelander, finished now, is one of the better properties in the district. Rooms feature restored original heavy mahogany furniture, and soft peach-toned walls with plum, white, and magenta trim. All bathrooms have their original tubs. Rooms have ceiling fans and central air-conditioning and heat. And if the Deco rooms are small, they help remind you you're here for Ocean Drive and the authentic Deco gulp.

THE EDISON and THE BREAKWATER HOTELS

The Edison is a Middle-Eastern pastiche. The Breakwater is a ship thinking about becoming a rocket. Episodes in fantasy: rounds and squares, history and future, tents and nomads, space cadets, two soldiers on a road to fortune.

Who knows who this year's manager is, but last year's was Al Sainz, who came from the Cavalier. Al threw the switch 180 degrees from the no-frills operation the Edison was to the fluffy towels and Evian water standards he learned training with Don Meginley.

"I found the guys like tractor-trailer operators," Al said about when he took over. He began catering to the fashion industry. No local walk-ins. Valet parking.

The Breakwater was to reopen in 1991 with 46 rooms, mostly small, only a few with views of the ocean. Even the penthouse suite, though it has two rooftop terraces, has no windows directly on the ocean. Who can explain? Furniture on reopening was standard contract, something Al thought filled an order left years ago by Jerry Sanchez, the first grandly self-promoting reviver of the Deco District after Barbara Capitman, and still a mortgage holder at the Edison. Al wanted to replace what he was given with a more Deco styling.

In the lobby is I Paparazzi, an established trendy restaurant, all green and coral with scrolled upholstered armchairs, gorgeous black flatware with green napkins, and white cloths over pink.

The Edison, with 56 rooms, lies north of the shared courtyard that features fountains, canvas gondola umbrellas, palms, and flowering bananas. It attracts by its image of exotic revival, more Mediterranean than Deco, a playful style to suit playful moments. The building has no wish to appear ordinary. It flaunts its facade of natural shades—from cream to coffee brown—with ornament etched, braided, molded, and appliqué. False balconies top a ground-level colonnade, and the elevation is crowned by pale blue epaulet-like trim.

Downstairs front is given over to Tropics International, a leased cafe open from breakfast to early-next-morning-jazz. Bold and gaily painted storybook shapes decorate cafe columns. Zigzag cut-outs hang from the high blue ceiling like fantasy clouds in a Beatles-dreamed sky.

The lobby is coolly tropical in expanses of wicker-set paneled terrazzo, two-story-high open beam ceilings, and a phalanx of fanlight windows.

Standard rooms are small, basic, supplied with clean contract furniture that covers the essentials. Minimal styling is supplied by floral quilts, a piece of wall art, pale carpets, and creamy peach plaster walls. Oceanfront rooms are more spacious. Neither of the two penthouse suites (Romeo and Juliet, and Papa Hemingway) is oceanfront, though they do have kitchens.

AVALON HOTEL

Here the *de rigeur* sidewalk terrace is perfect for cocktails. A small bar by the lobby has an old radio converted to a diamond-shaped fish tank. The elevator squeals and whines, then opens with a sigh onto off-white corridors cooled by paddle fans.

Rooms are clean with a faint smell of a grandmother's room. They might remind older beachgoers of sleep-over cabanas beneath a bit of peeling paint, but rooms are otherwise tidy, with crisp peach and ecru sheets, leaf print spreads, and dusty rose carpet. Each comes with a closet safe, compact refrigerator, TV, small table and chairs; bathrooms have fluffy towels, designer toiletries, and laundry soap for hand washables.

Low pretense at the Avalon, and—thanks to Helen Moller's competence—a sense of being in a right place.

THE BEACON HOTEL

You'd love to find this one in a big-city downtown. Its colorful banding and verticals with piqué fabric-like cutouts, its Aztec friezes outside and floor mural within elsewhere would make it the pick of the pack. On Ocean Drive we're thankful for another good piece of work.

Enter teak doors shaped to surround flamingo-etched semicircles. There's an intimate bar, plus a Texas-style steak restaurant that extends seating onto the patio. Sit here especially when the moon is full.

Of 84 rooms, 30 are upgraded with aqua and dust-rose-speckled carpeting, pink and green-scalloped Deco lamps, pastel easy chairs, and new wood furniture. Older rooms are comfortable and less plush. All bathrooms have an attractive black tile trim.

Louvered room doors open onto a hallway under paddle fans. Very Bogart-like. Assistant manager Greg Gilbride is an ace with guests.

Hotels Leslie and Cardozo, 1300 and 1244 Ocean Drive, Miami Beach, FL 33139. (305) 534-2135; (800) 423-1981 (national). Leslie 49 rooms, Cardozo 56, with AC, heat, bathrooms (most with tubs), color TV, direct-dial phone, elevators, restaurant and lounge (Cardozo). Children of any age accepted, free in parents' room to 16. No pets. AmEx, MC, Visa. Winter rates: Cardozo: $105-$185 single or double; Leslie: $10 less. Rate includes expanded continental breakfast; off-season: $95-$165. Average breakfast $6, lunch $9, dinner $16.

The Cavalier, 1320 Ocean Drive, Miami Beach, FL 33139. (305) 531-6424. (800) 338-9076 (national and Canadian). 46 rooms including 2 suites with AC, heat, bathrooms (most with tubs), color TV, direct-dial phone, elevator. Children of any age accepted, free in parents' room through 16 years. No pets. AmEx, MC, Visa. Winter rates: $105-$175, summer $90-$150, includes expanded continental breakfast, fresh flowers, newspaper, Evian water. Free indoor parking.

Waldorf Towers Hotel and Edison Hotel, 860 Ocean Drive and 960 Ocean Drive, Miami Beach, FL 33139. (305) 531-7684 (Waldorf Towers); 531-0461 (Edison); (800) 237-3522 (national); (800) 237-5926 (Canada). Waldorf Towers 45 rooms, Edison 65, with AC, heat, color TV, direct-dial phone, bathroom (most with tubs). Sempers nightclub; Tropics International restaurant and club at the Edison. Children of any age accepted, free in parents' room to 12. 3rd person in room $10. No pets. AmEx, DC, MC, Visa. Elevators. Winter rates: $75 to $95, suites to $150; off-season, $55 to $75, suites to $110. Average meal rates in Tropics International: breakfast $1.75; lunch $2.95 to $9.95; dinner $8.95 to $19.

The Breakwater Hotel (inquire at Edison).

The Clevelander Hotel, 1020 Ocean Drive, Miami Beach, FL 33139. (305)

531-3485. Kent Kay, manager. 65 rooms with AC, heat, ceiling fan, bathrooms *(all with tub), color cable TV, direct-dial phone, elevator, pool, bar, outdoor grill. Children of any age accepted, free to 12 in parents' room. Inquire about pets. All major credit cards. Rates: summer $50-$70; winter $60-$90. Also weekly and monthly rates. Off-street parking. 3rd person in room $10. Average lunch: $5-$10. Informal dinner: $5-$10.*

Park Central Hotel, 640 Ocean Drive, Miami Beach, FL 33139. (800) 533-3397 (USA), (800) 433-9642 (Canada), (305) 538-1611. *Tony Goldman, proprietor. 76 rooms and baths with AC, heat, ceiling fan, color cable TV, direct-dial phone (50-cents for local calls; LD surcharge), elevator, rooftop sun terrace, restaurant and lounge, swimming pool. Children of any age accepted ($10 for crib or rollaway). No pets. AmEx, MC, Visa. Winter rates: $75-$125 per room; summer: $60-$100, includes continental breakfast, turndown service, bottled water, fruit in rooms on arrival. A charge for off-street parking. Smoking allowed.*

Essex House, 1001 Collins Ave., Miami Beach, 33139. (800) 44-ESSEX, (305) 534-2700. *Patricia Murphy, hostess. 50 rooms and baths (tubs in all but 2), with AC, heat, ceiling fan, color cable TV, direct-dial phone (local calls 50-cents), elevator. No 3rd person in rooms. No pets. AmEx, MC, Visa. Winter rates: $98-$218; summer: $78-$198. Includes deluxe continental breakfast, turndown, bottled water. On-street parking. No smoking 2nd floor.*

Avalon Hotel, 700 Ocean Drive, Miami Beach, FL 33139. (305) 538-0133. *Helen Moller, resident manager. (Also operates Majestic Hotel next door.) 55 rooms with bath (shower and tub), AC, heat, ceiling fan, color cable TV and radio, direct-dial phone (50-cents local calls, surcharge on LD calls), room refrigerator, safe, elevator, bar and restaurant. Children of any age accepted, free in parents' room to 10. Each additional person in room $10. No pets. AmEx, MC, Visa. Rates through May 14, 1991: $85-$150; after, inquire (were $55-$125 off-season 1990). Includes continental breakfast, beach chairs, beach toys, exercise room, recreation/game room. Smoking allowed. On-street parking. Inquire about meal rates.*

Beacon Hotel, 720 Ocean Drive, Miami Beach, FL 33139. (800) 541-4477 (U.S. and Florida), (305) 531-5891. *Peter A. Pearson, general manager. 84 rooms and baths (tubs and shower), AC, heat, 34 with ceiling fan, color cable TV, direct-dial phone (50-cents local calls, LD calls surcharged), elevator, restaurant and bar. Children free in parents' room to 18. No pets. No rollaways, no charge for crib. All major credit cards. Rates (from 1 to 4 persons in room): winter: $70-$90, summer $40-$60. Non-smoking rooms available. Small off-street parking lot for cars, no charge, space available. Average meal prices: breakfast buffet $6; lunch (high season only) $5.50; dinner $15.*

Palm Beach – BRAZILIAN COURT HOTEL

Long-time favorite garden hotel for the guests of Palm Beachites, off the beach in a residential neighborhood.

If you lived well in subtropical Florida, you would hear the same birds, see the same flowers, be happy in the same way about the absence of traffic as you would on a morning awakening at the Brazilian Court. Palm Beachites think so, which is why they regularly book rooms here when for one reason or another they or their guests can't be at home.

The Brazilian Court is a mix of the hotel and the house-guest experience. Not surprising in this time when bed-and-breakfasts and inns have become popular in America, and chain hotels have begun personalizing their services and de-institutionalizing their look.

The BC, as it's called, has had over 60 years of making its influence felt, from when shortly after its opening in 1925 as an apartment house it lodged the girlfriends of well-to-do Palm Beach men, girlfriends who for obvious reasons were not placed at the Breakers nor, it goes without saying, invited as houseguests.

The reputation soon improved when the property was converted to a hotel and Elliott F. Bishop, the first of several legendary managers, introduced himself to the town mayor by declaring that his first guest would be cereal heiress Marjorie Merriwether Post, arriving early with her servants to prepare Mar-a-Lago for the season.

So almost to our own time it has served as a romper room for Kennedy heirs when the family of Joe and Rose wanted to keep the children from underfoot at the family quarters and sent them to the BC for fun and games. It was here in 1984 that David Kennedy, one of Robert and Ethel's sons, died of a drug overdose.

But the hotel has undergone such change since then that what was old shoe has become stylish new pump. Comfortable all the same. Color and verve have returned to the two-and-three-story yellow stucco compound that occupies three tropical acres in a residential district two blocks from Worth Avenue and only a few more from the beach.

What most makes it special are the twin courtyards girdled by rooms. Guests feel themselves inheritors of a lifestyle where gardens are indispensable to good living. Nothing grandiose, but an accessible setting for delighting in burbling fountains, orange, banana, and African tulip trees, for savoring the scent of evening jasmine, and in good weather, which is most of the time, for relishing meals from breakfast through dinner under yellow and white-banded beach umbrellas on the keystone patio.

The setting is equally special in stormy weather, when guests tend to draw closer to each other in the manner of allies threatened by common deprivation: loss of tanning time or a golf game. While they chat in the charming loggia before cable knit-sweatered carhops escort them under cheery umbrellas to limousines, potted palms inside the wooden entry doors dance with abandon to the improvised jazz of the blowing wind.

After a $7.5 million renovation for the 134-room property, guests awaken to morning sun that embarrasses mere electrical light. Yellow sheets glow rich like butter on corn. Brass glistens, and white curtains become white on white. You imagine yourself in the country and someone softly calling, "Jean! Breakfast is ready when you are!"

That breakfast can be enjoyed in bed (part of 24-hour room service) with a *Wall Street Journal, USA Today,* and local paper in spacious rooms and suites in themes of yellow, green, and blue, each with patterned white carpets on floors of bone-gray washed wood. There are comfortable upholstered chairs, dressers, desks, lamps, mirrors, wall prints, curtains and drapes. Bathrooms are large, marble-tiled, supplied with gourmet toiletries. The bright look is almost collegiate—as at a privileged campus, to be sure.

New management plans few changes. Small but important changes nonetheless: since 1989 the BC has been open all year. And a guided bicycle tour now departs every Saturday with all riders receiving a free copy of *Brazilian Court's View of the Island,* a little tongue-in-cheek review of some of the folklore of what Palm Beachites call "The Island."

The dining room, the Rio Bar with its Bistro for informal dining, the pool area, and various meeting rooms, complete the facility. Really quite splendid. Welcome.

Brazilian Court Hotel, 301 Australian Ave., Palm Beach, FL 33480. (407) 655-7740. George Terpilowski, general manager. 134 rooms including 6 suites with AC, heat, bathrooms with tub, cable TV, turndown service, overnight shoeshine, newspapers, restaurant, bar, pool, dining patio, room phones. Non-smoking rooms available. Children of any age accepted, free in parents' room to 12. No pets. All major credit cards. Rates: winter: $180 to $270 single or double, $70-$140 rest of year. Inquire about suites. Extra person $25. Meal prices: breakfast $8, lunch $10 and up, dinner $10 and up. Complimentary continental breakfast left at door at designated hour.

Palm Beach — THE BREAKERS
One of America's distinguished hotels.

Henry Flagler made Palm Beach, Addison Mizner made it fun to live here, and the Breakers made ordinary visitors acceptable. Or as Flagler heirs explained in 1969 when for the first time the hotel stayed open all year instead of closing after winter, "The people who will come here will come up to our standards rather than pull them down."

The legacies of Flagler and Mizner have fused the sacred and profane into an attitude as much Palm Beach as its standards of money and influence, which have always been important in this barely four-square-mile bastion of privilege.

The standards accord equal respect to fortunes from bootlegging as those more conventionally acquired. Eccentricity and celebrity are courted so long as their subjects, like the Palm Beach author of *The Sensuous Woman*, remain self assured. All that is asked is the forbearance of spectators, that commentary be not judgmental, and that all the while we please be smartly dressed and do good works for those less fortunate than ourselves.

Flagler, after all, paid the price for a divorce law that succored no one but himself, and Mizner behaved so mischievously that one writer declared his and his brother Wilson's regard for money "as simply something to keep score with."

The town was first named Palm City after a shipwreck of coconuts washed ashore and were planted along the beach. The name was changed because another Palm City existed. Flagler called his hotel the Palm Beach Inn and later changed its name after it burned the first time, was rebuilt, and people who stayed at his larger, earlier hotel on the lakeside would say, "Let's go down to the other hotel by the breakers."

Flagler was already established in the north Florida hotel trade, and had decreed that well-to-do Americans would winter in Florida rather than on the Riviera. "Europe is a place people come *from*," he was reported to have said when his sickly first wife proposed a winter abroad.

Flagler began building hotels in St. Augustine because he could find nothing there to suit him. He developed his railroad to ensure that vacationers could reach the hotels he kept adding southward along the coast. His agricultural investments on the mainland opposite Palm Beach led him to the island which he fell in love with. By 1894 he had extended his railroad here and opened the Royal Poinciana Hotel. It became so successful that he doubled its size in 1899 and again added rooms in 1901 to make it the largest wooden structure in the world and the largest resort ever built. Antiquated, the Royal Poinciana was torn down in 1935.

The Palm Beach Inn at first was for those who objected to the strict formality of the Royal Poinciana. It was the first oceanfront hotel in southeast Florida. Flagler quickly enlarged it. After the fire in 1903, he rebuilt, renamed it the Breakers, and promptly lost interest, instead extending his railroad and hotel chain farther south to Miami, finally to Key West just before he died at 83 in 1913.

After the hotel burned a second time, Flagler's heirs opted for grandeur and permanence. They might well have had Mizner design it. He had shown up in Palm Beach in 1918 promoting himself as an architect, which seemed reasonable enough because as an artist he was a superb draftsman, and as a diplomat's son he was world traveled and able to get away with whatever outrage he dared, thanks to the fortune of a newly acquired friend, Paris Singer, the sewing machine heir, who backed him.

But Flagler's principal heir was an engineer. No mere artist, however lionized—no matter that he had built the Everglades Club, fabulous mansions, and all of Worth Avenue which became the shopping playground for royalty, millionaires, and star entertainers—was going to design what he intended to be the greatest hotel in the world. The assignment instead was given to the architects of the Waldorf-Astoria.

Within 12 months after the 1925 fire, and on a record 11-month construction schedule, the new Breakers was complete. But for the addition of two wings mostly for meeting rooms, the hotel today, with 528 rooms, is much as it was.

Its facade and twin towers, seen at an exalting distance from South County Road, were inspired by the Villa Medici in Florence. The lobby, with its beautifully decorated, vaulted ceiling, was modeled after a palace in Genoa. The majestic ballrooms are also modeled after the great halls of Italian palaces. Its great fountain in the center of the entry drive is modeled after one in the Boboli Gardens in Florence.

Today, says historian Jim Ponce, the hotel is almost like a civic center to Palm Beach. "From the monthly chamber of commerce breakfast to the big charity balls, everything takes place at the Breakers. The hotel's invitation list is the largest single source of charity funds in the country," he says.

Inevitably, the hotel's guest rooms seem plain compared to its gilded public rooms, though they are complete in comfort and detail. As part of a $50 million, five-year renovation, more than 400 guest rooms and suites have so far been upgraded—all will be by 1992—and feature historic photographs of The Breakers, armoires, and consolidated TV/mini-bar/refrigerator/ice bucket/extra clothes storage units. Two new guest elevators embody the spirit of the renovation by blending high technology with opulent cabins suggestive of the lobby's frescoed ceilings. New landscaping includes towering clusters of Canary Island palms at the porte cochere and beautiful flowerbeds of annuals.

Conventioners and incentive groups dominate the scene much of the year. There is a constant surge of check-ins, check-outs, guests on historical tours, the feeling of a great museum obliged to house guests in order to defray its upkeep. The hubbub makes democracy seem a handicap. Preservation and recycling seem less than perfect endeavors. Latter-day use seems fictional. No one can again be to-the-manner-born. The Breakers makes us nostalgic for the days when most of us would never have entered its premises. Where once we would only have imagined it, today we imagine how it used to be. It remains one of America's most distinguished hotels.

The Breakers, South County Road, Palm Beach, FL 33480. (305) 655-6611. Thomas Wicky, president and general manager. 528 rooms, including 40 suites with AC, heat, cable TV, phone, bathrooms with tub, special toiletries kit. Suites and deluxe rooms provide velour robes. Evening turndown service. Outdoor heated pool, elevators, various restaurants and bars, boutiques, service desk, newsstand. Two 18-hole golf courses, tennis courts, croquet lawns, bicycles and bicycle paths, health club, jogging path, complete water sports. Children of any age accepted, free in parents' room to age 17 in summer. In season, $75 for additional person in double room (MAP). No pets. All major credit cards. Rates: winter: from $260 to $400, suites from $350 to $795 EP; summer: $95-$220; suites, $195-$575. Various intermediate season rates. All rates single or double. Daily service charge $10 per room, $15 per suite per day. Additional person in room or suite $12 and $5 service per day. Breakfast plan $10 per person plus $7 service; MAP $40 and $7; AP $55 and $9. Various summer packages. No-smoking rooms, and no-smoking areas in dining rooms. Handicapped accessible guest rooms.

Palm Beach – CHESTERFIELD HOTEL DELUXE
Intimate, elegant, and good value.

Mayor Yveline "Deedy" Marix christened Maurice Shawzin's baby by sprinkling peach champagne over a glorious arrangement of pink carnations. Bagpipers played. Utterly English Maurice (actually South African born) declared, "I may talk funny, but I am an American citizen and proud to bring my English and European roots to this proud island."

The island is Palm Beach. The occasion was a preview of the new Chesterfield Hotel Deluxe. In a matter of months, the Chesterfield became a Palm Beach favorite.

Where else can you get four newspapers at your door: *The New York Times, Wall Street Journal, Palm Beach Post,* and *Palm Beach News?* Or English high tea daily, with traditional cucumber and smoked salmon sandwiches, scones that critics rate superior to the English, fruit tarts, and tea leaves for those who disdain tea bags?

Worth Avenue may be only three blocks away, but the Chesterfield will usher you there in a chauffeured English taxi with bar and TV.

"If you loved the hotel previously, you will adore it now," says Maurice, a genial boniface ever with pink carnation in lapel. He chaperones the 55-room, eight-suite property where the traditional English chintz is unsparing as the traditional English floral arrangements which fill lustrous porcelain bowls in the lobby.

Today's Chesterfield in 1926 was the Royal Palm, later the Vineta and Royal Park. What looks like a Mizner original, though it was merely a copy, enjoyed its first brief revival as the resplendent Palm Court in the mid-1980s. Dreadful squabbles among partners ended that, and the hotel closed. This revival, since late 1989, flies the banner of Toddman-Hundley Hotels, an experienced private operator around the world, notably including the paragon Chesterfield hotels in London's Mayfair and in Los Angeles's Century City.

The Palm Beach version is in a residential neighborhood. Guests enter a piazza-like courtyard beneath green and white awning. Geraniums and azaleas bloom seasonally in window boxes.

The lobby may look familiar to previous visitors, but as Maurice Shawzin points out, "We did a number of things to freshen it up and make it aesthetically pleasing. The interior was completely redone. Lights and chandeliers were strategically placed for a lovely nocturnal effect, and we softened the walls with fabrics, and used lots of flowers. It's not a pretentious look."

There's a pair of unobtrusive Chippendale desks where receptionist and concierge quickly service guest needs.

Guests will find diversion in two rooms off the lobby. Across from each other are the carpeted library with its leather sofa, English chairs, rich paneling, and fireplace; and the passionately red game room with TV and upholstered chairs.

Locals were the first to herald Butler's, the dining room, and the Leopard Lounge and bar. Butler's cossets diners in green velvet banquettes. Wallpapers are floral, and fresh buds ornament tables set in peach napery. Executive chef Kevin Kenny creates classical cuisine that features a roast wagon of the day and exclusively free-range poultry. All breads, pastries, and preserves are prepared here daily. Chef Kenny, who earned a Michelin star abroad, sets out an excellent cheese board, notably with a creamy stilton, served with port wine.

Leopard's Lounge is jungle-like in its spotted fabrics, and pukka in its tartans, brass and cane chairs. Behind the bar a Rousseauean painting splashes jungle color which spills over in fresh roses and orchids on the tables.

Guests make good use of the new swimming pool, whirlpool spa, and sun deck behind high walls of tropical plants.

Wallpapers, fabrics, and bedcovers in guest rooms are an imaginative salad of greens, radish reds, pinks, and whites. Blues mute the mix. Unpatterned yellow walls are crowned by classical white moldings and topped by stucco white ceilings. That white is pulled down into lamps and into the backgrounds of framed botanical prints. An upholstered armchair is comfortably supplied with hassock. Desks have their own firm, cushioned armchair.

Bathrooms include a hair dryer, a caddy of soaps and conditioner, wraparound mirrors, bottled water. Towels are thick and plentiful. The Chesterfield's deluxe aspirations are sumptuously realized.

Chesterfield Hotel Deluxe, 363 Cocoanut Row, Palm Beach, FL 33480. (407) 659-5800. Maurice Shawzin, managing director. 55 rooms, 8 suites, 70 baths, all with shower and tub, hair dryer, robes; AC, heat, direct-dial phone, color cable TV. Pool, whirpool spa. Restaurant, bar, library, game room. Children of any age accepted, free in parents' room. Pets accepted. Rates: mid-Dec.-end Apr. $155-$235 and up, suites $275 and up; May-mid-Dec. $65-$125 and up, suites $150 and up. Includes continental breakfast, daily high tea, newspapers, fresh flowers, fruits on check-in and in lobby, ice in rooms. All major credit cards; checks accepted with credit card. On-street parking.

Stuart — HARBORFRONT
Beautifully sited architect's house.

Stuart is becoming one of Florida's most talked-about cities—not because of its size or because of scandal, but because Stuart has cannily decided to renew its historic look and keep its downtown alive and well. Stuart people believe that much of recent America has been interruptive and is no model for the future. They prefer to reaffirm what's been continuous and go on from there.

Bed-and-breakfast is already a part of this sane scenario. There is an affinity between towns where people are at home living and working, and where visitors are welcomed in home settings. The message is that people are weaning themselves from lives split between work and play. They don't want workplace immorality spilling into their personal lives.

Stuart has hired city planners who understand how this change in American morality is changing the way people choose where to live, how to work, and where to vacation. They see that towns derive marketing advantage for attracting the kind of people they want—earnest newcomers with compatible values—when they deliberately reaffirm their traditions by investing in historic renewal.

This municipality is leading the way in making the downtown viable again by burying utility lines underground. Landscaping, sensitive lighting, and wider sidewalks are going in. A new urban code addresses setbacks and parking requirements. A design code prescribes materials prevalent in the 1940s—wood, brick, stone, stucco (no glitter)—and color palettes, window and porch treatments, and roof slopes. Living upstairs from the store has been zoned back in.

A major breakthrough occurred when planners Andres Duany and Elizabeth Plater-Zyberk convinced the Florida Department of Transportation to leave two lanes of the old bridge in place even after completing the new viaduct that vaults U.S. 1 over the old town on the south side of the river. The commercial part of the old town will flow beneath the overpass to the residential west and regain its local traffic patterns.

Local businesses are refurbishing and new ones are opening. Mahoney's Pub is renowned for its fresh seafood and varieties of hot sauce and quality beers. Downtown Products Fruits & Vegetables is new. The Thirsty Whale has extended a sidewalk service patio under shady oaks. The old Plaza Cafe storefront is becoming shops.

Architect Peter Jefferson, who has championed the revival of downtown with his wife Joan, three-time mayor until her retirement in 1990, is shepherding through a grant application for restoring Stuart Feed Supply. The store, which dates back to 1905, will sell merchandise from the early part of the century and will house a 30-seat presentation area. Peter also designed a 1910-style bandstand by the river.

This reviving area east of the new bridge will tie west with a riverwalk that, when finished in about 1995, will link the entire waterfront of more than two miles. Shuttle trams will also connect the two sides of town.

It is in the west section where JoAyne and John Elbert have turned Peter and Joan Jefferson's old house into the bed-and-breakfast they call Harborfront.

The house is all cedar shake shingles with trim ranging from brown to blue-gray and patches of sailboat canvas. It has tin-tile eaves and many gables. The grassy yard slopes to the river under maleleucas and moss-draped oaks. From stone benches you can see the harbor full of moored sailboats.

Inside, most of the features that made this a fine architect's house after Peter and Joan remodeled it in 1980 remain after the Elberts' adapted it for guests. The church pew rails remain on the porch. A large common area with fireplace is next to an atrium. Sliding glass doors lead to a porch with small tables for breakfast. The ceiling is copper-coated steel and reed. Much of the cabinetry is built in, including a cypress buffet. Floors are oak. The hall gallery is lighted for display of art. The house is otherwise indirectly lit, and features transom doors and pine ceilings. The breeze reaches even the overstuffed sofas. Though the house was built in 1908, it's not Victorian but a comfortable old southern cottage.

The master bedroom has high wainscoting and tongue-in-groove walls and ceilings. The look is traditional in navy, burgundy, paisley, with full carpet. The bathroom has a $2/3$ tub with handrails for the elderly, as well as a view onto landscaping of hibiscus and night-blooming jasmine.

The smaller Grey Room has a queen-sized bed, wingback chair, table, a built-in desk, and its own bath. A separate guest house is being set up with two suites and a shared common area with kitchen. The cottage where Peter Jefferson had his office has been set up with its own kitchen.

A full breakfast is included with all rooms except the cottage. A champagne breakfast in bed can be arranged. So can breakfast baskets-to-go for sunrise at the beach. Both of these arrangements have an additional charge, as do Friday evening fish barbecues in season, and candlelight dinners on request. Weather cooperating, sunset is celebrated with complimentary snacks and wine. Guests find fruit snacks and beverages provided throughout the day.

Just down little Atlanta Avenue, an old fishertown lane quietly tucked off South Federal Highway, is Frazier Park. It has picnic tables, barbecue stands, and a playground. Coming as part of downtown renewal are rental paddleboats. These will be a delightful option for enjoying all of waterfront Stuart, west side to east and back, from Harborfront.

Harborfront Bed & Breakfast, 407 Atlanta Ave., Stuart, FL 34994. (407) 288-7289. John, JoAyne and Amy Elbert owner/hosts. 3 suites and 1 room, all with private baths, color cable remote-control TV, AC, heat, ceiling fan. Two suites share kitchen in cottage. Children accepted 12 years and up, $10 extra (same as for additional person in any accommodation). No pets. Phone in porch reception area for local and for 3rd party and credit-card calls. Checks accepted. Smoking allowed outside only. Fresh flowers, ice in rooms. Fruit snacks, beverages provided all day on sideboard. Daily newspaper available, board games, cards. Rates: Grey Room $60, master bedroom suite $70; in guest house (available in 1991) Whirlpool Suite $85, Family Suite $100. All rates double, and include tax. Singles subtract $10. May 1-Dec. 31, approximately 20% less. Cottage $85 daily, $450 week, $1,500 month. Kitchen included. All rates except cottage include full breakfast. Also available, champagne breakfast in bed, breakfast baskets, Friday night fish barbecue, dinner, candlelight dinners. Sunset (weather cooperating) complimentary snacks, wine. Off-street parking.

Stuart — THE HOMEPLACE
Perfectly scaled in a jewel-like setting.

Jean Bell, who likes to pull weeds and make baskets, saw the old abandoned house under a big tree. It was about to be demolished. She moved it, restored it, and made it Stuart's first bed-and-breakfast inn. It was a pioneer builder's house that now serves, at least in the back, as the office for an imaginative, small, tree-filled development—Creekside Commons—that is reviving old downtown Stuart. A portion of the new Stuart riverwalk will wind past.

Jean Bell gently rocks you in the bosom of now, between the past and future.

The house is short blocks from U.S. 1 on a cul-de-sac by Frazier's Creek, named after R. Russell Frazier. Frazier, his wife and children were the first settlers, in 1887, of the town that became Stuart.

The house Jean rescued was built in 1913 by Sam Matthews. He had come in 1902 to help Henry Flagler complete development of West Palm Beach. The house remained in his family until the 1960s.

It was Sam Matthews' daughter Edith Sadler, now living in North Carolina, who told Jean the stories about "the old homeplace" that gave rise to the inn's name.

The house charms behind a picket fence. It has Victorian rose and white trim, and is part shingle, part clapboard. The exterior is of several woods, suggesting that Matthews used leftovers from other jobs. He built the house up on blocks to ensure a dry foundation and a breeze circulating beneath. The house has many windows, and a screened front porch is still used for comfortable evenings.

On the first floor are an elegant living room, dining room, and kitchen filled with old-time household tins and colored bottles that the sun shines through. A lovely sun porch overlooks a patio and pool that in time will be shared by the development behind.

The living room is in two distinct sections, one in Eastlake Literary style, with a brass oil lamp with cherubs. Separating the parlor to the other side is a rosewood grand piano under a silk-embroidered fringed piano shawl. In the parlor is a mid-to-late 1800s empire sideboard of mahogany, incised with pineapples, and fitted with tassled cabinet keys. An oak secretary with brass hardware serves as a bar.

A charm of breakfast is to look from the dining room through the wicker and ferns of the sun room while listening to an antique coffeemaker rumble.

Among treasures in the sun porch is a concertina that came with the house.

The foyer has a pressed tin ceiling. A bucolic Italian tapestry hangs at the back of the stairs. The staircase is of red oak with long slender spindles Jean added as replacements for damaged ones. Stairs, risers, and wainscoting are also new, though you wouldn't know it.

Of three guest rooms, Opal's has the loveliest story. Opal Taylor was the great-aunt of one of the first visitors to the house after Jean restored it. Jean's guest shortly thereafter donated to the house a copy of *The Girl Graduate*, her great-aunt's diary. It has the class will of 1909 from the village of Marysville, Ohio, and entries of her later life as an operatic performer abroad.

The room has floral carpet, floral night table covers, a floral tissue box, and a rose-colored little book of poems called *Brilliants* by Whittier, inscribed 1915. There is an oil-finished walnut cheval dresser with tilt mirror and hatbox drawer, carpentered with triangular dovetails. The oak bed has oakleaf and acorn ornamentation and brass fittings. A wood lamp is made to look like hammered brass. The bathroom has a white tub with brass fixtures.

Captain's Quarters feels solid. It has a deep red carpet, cypress wainscoting, a walnut dresser, upholstered rocker, steamer trunk, armchair and night tables. Shipshape accessories include an ancient globe, a bosomy figurehead, a long-stemmed pipe, and a hanging bedlamp meant to sway at sea. The double bed is brass.

Prissy's Porch is frilly Victorian but lighthearted, with wainscoting, floral bedcover and sheets, sidechair, ferns, plants, and wall hangings. A white brick chimney passes through the room. Twin night tables, each with its own lamp, surround a frilly iron double bed with lacy pillows. The bathroom has a shower built into a rose-colored, deep clawfoot tub.

The Homeplace is richly satisfying.

The Homeplace, 501 Akron Ave., Stuart, FL 34994. (407) 220-9148. Jean Bell, innkeeper. 3 rooms and baths with AC, heat, ceiling fan. Pool, heated spa. Bicycles and tandem bike for free use. No TV. Phone in kitchen hallway for free local calls and credit-card LD calls. Children accepted 12 and older. No pets. MC, Visa. Checks accepted. Rates: May-Nov., $60-$80; Dec-Apr., $80-$100, single or double. Includes full breakfast, fruits in room, and ice. Newspaper available. No smoking. Free off-street parking.

West Palm Beach — HIBISCUS HOUSE
Superb hospitality in a veritable antique gallery.

Soulfully handsome, youthfully assured, Raleigh Hill in his early 50s restores houses, moves in, sells, and moves on. His houses are the proof of a career he has imagined, and that now for the first time calls for taking in B&B guests.

It's incidental that now he happens to be in a pleasant middle-class neighborhood near downtown West Palm Beach. At other times he has been in a Manhattan walk-up, Toronto Queen Annes, and West Palm Spanish revivals. Hibiscus House is shingle colonial, built in 1921 by then West Palm Beach Mayor John Dunkle. Raleigh noticed it as he went for a stroll while waiting for the lawyer to close on another a few blocks away. He strolled back, cancelled the other, and bought this. It needed more work. He looks after guests with the same avuncular indulgence.

Certainly he might long ago have begun taking in B&B guests. He has always enjoyed entertaining house guests with dinners and poolside parties. But it only occurred to him lately when he stayed for the first time in a north Canada B&B. And then, he says, "I saw a copy of *Country Inns*. I knew this was for me."

The only way his mother would let him travel from Miami to New York after high school was to accompany the family preacher.

"He drove 30 miles an hour and preached all the way," recalls Raleigh. "We couldn't agree on anything before we reached Washington. There we agreed we couldn't stand each other any longer. And then we agreed never to tell anyone that I got out and took the train the rest of the way. I didn't move back to Florida for 12 years."

His career found him when evenings and weekends, after Wall Street studies and office work, he would hunt affordable antiques for improving his $26-a-month five-story walk-up where he began taking out walls, built archways and bookshelves, and unsealed fireplaces. "I never wanted to be stifled or ordinary," he says.

He has since, for more than 30 years, invested in real estate, collected antiques, designed other people's spaces. But Raleigh's essential spirit has been at work restoring his own places, moving from one to the next with his favorite pieces, celebrating the moving-on man who knows how to make the most of his stops.

This took him back to Florida, where in the early Seventies he chose less busy West Palm Beach. He began buying properties, and set up as interior designer. That was a time when condominiums were going up all along south Palm Beach and he was much in demand.

His sure sense about serial moves seems to have settled Hibiscus House into an ambiance mixed of sentiment and impermanence that assures B&B guests that mere transiency is knowingly accommodated.

How that happens is that—surrounded by a room full of Louis XV and XVI tables and chairs, an early 19th-century American oak dining room, cathedral arches, stained glass panels, and split wall-mounted columns saved from a Manhattan demolition site (need one point out that this is the merest recitation of what's to be discovered here?)—guests feel in no way disrespectful to putter around shoes off, as if in fact house guests and not precisely paying guests.

The living room intimates Egyptian. It's the mix of period French and English, of tall potted palms in porcelain bowls, of Mediterranean arches parallel-trimmed in green and beige lacquer. It's the sweet eclecticism of a crossroads bazaar. Only a wood-carved candelabrum is authentically Egyptian, though on a little table is an Egyptian-like obelisk surrounded by quaquaversal turtles.

Guest spaces are many and change all the time with Raleigh's newest installations. "Little pockets where guests can come sit," is how he describes these, "And I bring coffee to them."

Newly set up is a casually furnished sun room inside from the deck at one end of the pool. He has lately converted utility space to a poolside breakfast and game room. The pool itself is set in a pine deck surrounded by almost fully mature plantings. His varied hibiscus bushes, a loquat, and avocado tree are long established and bearing, as is an orange tree on the far side of the house where guests can pick fresh fruit from a bedroom window.

Most use is made of the library and TV room that picks up midday and afternoon sun. There's a mix of pickle-finish Louis XV chairs, others with cane backs and sides. The cushiony sofa is where you might spend hours with the Sunday papers. There's a bay window seat for discarding perused sections. The room is full of blue and white original and faux Oriental canisters, and collections of books about world history, the Civil War, antiques and art, and contemporary fiction.

Bedrooms are all different, variously whimsical with Raleigh's headboard creations of castoff wood ornaments trumped up as antique. There are Persian rugs on polished pine floors, matched English chairs, and pine four-posters. The largest room is salmon-colored with headboard and canopy in dramatic wood parquet. Most bedrooms have private decks and bathrooms, all have potted green plants, all look thought about.

Just as Raleigh has always invited house guests to his new places, it's likely too that B&B clients will also follow as he, with his ever-changing effects, keeps on the move.

Hibiscus House, 501 30th Street, West Palm Beach, FL 33407. (407) 863-5633. Raleigh Hill, owner. 7 bedrooms, 6-1/2 baths (2 with tubs). Kitchen available for use. AC, some with heat, ceiling fan, telephones, digital clock radio. Children accepted, but no rollaways or cribs. Messages taken, free local calls, credit-card and collect LD calls okay. Well-behaved pets. No credit cards. Rates: Dec.1-Apr.30: rooms with private terrace $75, without $65; May 1-Nov. 30: $65, $55. Includes full breakfast. Swimming pool. Washer-dryer available to guests.

KEY WEST LOCATIONS

Artist House	Lamppost House
The Banyan Resort	La Te Da
Colours	Marquesa Hotel
Curry Mansion Inn	Marriott's Casa Marina Resort
Duval House	Merlinn Guest House
Eaton Lodge	The Mermaid & The Aligator
Eden House	The Palms
Heron House	The Poplar House
Hollinsed House	Seascape
Island City House	Simonton Court
La Concha	Tropical Inn
La Mer	Watson House
	Whispers at the Gideon Lowe House

KEY LARGO

ISLAMORADA

ATLANTIC OCEAN

GULF OF MEXICO

MARATHON·

KEY WEST

BIG PINE KEY
The Barnacle
LITTLE TORCH KEY   Casa Grande
Little Palm Island

FLORIDA KEYS AND KEY WEST

Key West is in every way its own place—removed, quirky, front porch on the tropics. But so are the rest of the Keys unique to the mainland. For the first time in this edition we can recommend three properties with the character that innkeeping vacationers look for.

Two are side by side, the **Barnacle** and **Casa Grande** on Big Pine Key. Longtime friends operate these, so that guests find an extra dimension of hospitality, more like-minded vacationers to meet—or to stay apart from if you wish.

Exceptional for its chic, management, and remoteness is **Little Palm Island**, the hideaway that well might have slid off the edge if the the world hadn't proved to be round.

There is a fourth to consider about which I have heard good things. This is the **Hopp Inn** in Marathon [5 Man-O-War Drive, Marathon, 33050, (305) 743-4118].

There's always turnover in Key West guest houses. **Artist House** has a new manager who has brought stability to management of this exceptional Victorian. **Banyan Resort** has more professional management. new owners at **Duval House**

285

seem committed to maintaining its high standards. Mark Anderson if he had all the money he needs would have a restaurant added by now to **Eaton Lodge**. As is, the historic gardens are restored and the house is newly lightened in decor. **Eden House** is no longer hippie. Now yuppie. **Island City House** and **The Palms** are now owned by Bruce Corneal, who's ambitious to acquire additional properties. **Lamppost House** has new owners who have given up the rest cure house next door. New owners at the Gideon Lowe House have changed its name to **Whispers at the Gideon Lowe House**. They're conscious of marketing subtleties.

New to the book—TaDa!—is **Curry Mansion Inn** with marvelously idiosyncratic owner-operators. Al and Edith Amsterdam make every morning and evening a social hour. Relaxing and friendly.

The **Marquesa Hotel** is as fine a small hotel as there is in Florida. It's become the standard, and with its restaurant seems to have anticipated a trend toward more full-service inns in the state.

The **Mermaid & The Alligator** is new, also stylish and with sophisticated owners with backgrounds in TV news. **The Popular House** is as friendly an establishment as you're going to find thanks to Jody Carlson, who can't help doing things to make guest happy.

Exceptional for its color, its style, and for its singular location in the Bahama Village section of Key West is **Caribbean House**. Rooms are tiny but stylish, the clientele younger and from around the world—one of these places that word of mouth quickly makes popular. Bahamian descendants once were the exclusive residents of this part of town that's now being re-invested in. Gentrification may or may not move the old-timers out. Inquire at 226 Petronia St., Key West 33040, (800) 543-3418, (305) 296-1600.

Though not detailed in the book, you might also want to consider the **Chelsea House** [707 Truman Ave., Key West, 33040, (305) 296-2211], **The Cottages** [1512 Dennis St., Key West, 33040, (305) 294-6003], and **Pilot House** [414 Simonton St., Key West, 33040, (800) 648-3780, (800) GUEST-O, (305) 294-8719], **Blue Parrot Inn** [916 Elizabeth St., Key West, 33040, (305) 296-0033], and newly opened in 1991, **La Pensione** [809 Truman Ave., Key West, 33040, (305) 292-9923].

Much of the guest house charm in Key West stems from the highly personal style of operators. Hardly any two are alike. How they differ one from each other is described in the entries that follow.

But in one respect all are alike: all accept guests of every lifestyle. Gay guests frequent all of the guest houses, some more than others. Many are run by gay couples. But be assured there isn't the slightest suggestion from operators that their guests indulge in their gay preferences. While some innkeepers are more professional than others, all respect the privacy of their guests.

For those readers interested in exclusively gay guest houses, there are some 15 in Key West, including some of the most hospitably run and finest appointed lodgings in Florida. A list can be obtained from the Key West Business Guild, P.O. Box 1208, Key West 33041, (305) 294-4603.

Note that at all Key West lodgings, the higher (winter) rates are charged for all national holiday weekends and for special festive weekends, and there is probably also a two- or three-night minimum requirement. Ask in advance of booking whether your requested date includes one of the special weekends.

Keep in mind that because Key West guest houses change hands fairly often, new operators often mean changes in facilities, style of hospitality, and often of rates. Remodeling may be going on. Ask if there has been a change to anything noted in the guidebook. Don't be hesitant to ask about everything on your mind. A good innkeeper will be enthusiastic about the changes and will answer your questions openly.

Between the mainland and Key West there are resorts galore but few that fit the format of the guidebook. There is an attractive motel-like little resort on the Gulf side of the Overseas Highway in Layton, about Mile Marker 68. This is **Lime Tree Bay Resort** [Box 839, Long Key 33001, (305) 664-4740]. Its location is just north of the once famous Long Key Fishing Club where Zane Grey was among notable members.

Big Pine Key — THE BARNACLE and CASA GRANDE

Value and innovation in bed-and-breakfasts next door to each other.

Many vacationers, after finding this pair of outstanding bed-and-breakfasts on the way to Key West, won't continue all the way. What's the point, they'll say. This is as good as it gets.

There's something compulsive about driving to the end of the road, about reaching Key West, and though most people love that town, Key West *is* commercial (though still brash). You can always complete the drive another time or fly there.

So that if what you want is an affordable island getaway, and especially if you want bed-and-breakfast comfort without a lot of other people around, this neighboring pair of B&Bs fronting the Straits of Florida fully satisfies.

The lure of the Middle Keys is nature. Some 7,000 acres of Big Pine Key make up the National Key Deer Refuge where, in addition to this two-foot-short endangered subspecies of the whitetail deer family, visitors can spot the Florida Keys marsh rabbit, and with snorkeling gear, loggerhead and green turtles and West Indian manatees.

Snorkelers and divers find the most diversified of the 160 miles of Florida Keys reef formations at Looe Key National Marine Sanctuary, within five miles of the Big Pine Key bed-and-breakfasts. Strike Zone Charters, operated by Captain Larry Threlkeld (a son of Jon and Kathleen, who run Casa Grande), can arrange for dive and snorkel trips, as well as offshore and backcountry fishing, and for trips to the offshore Great White Heron National Wildlife Refuge.

Marathon, the largest town between the mainland and Key West, is the site of Crane Point Hammock, a rare 63.5-acre tract of historic and ecological importance in the Keys. It has nature walks, a museum of natural history, and the Florida Keys Children's Museum (though it should be noted that both the Barnacle and Casa Grande accept only adults).

What makes this pair of bed-and-breakfasts so good is their sophisticated lodgings in a remote area. Guests enjoy the physical pleasures of good looking-after while looking after themselves, striving for inner renewal.

Part of the reward stems from the Cornells and the Threlkelds being side by side, each offering B&B lodgings. This didn't happen by accident.

Wood and Joan Cornell and the Threlkelds have known each other for about 40 years, ever since Jon worked for the Cornell family lumber business in Carmel, New York. They both bought property on Big Pine Key, they both built, but while

Jon and Kathleen chose to live here much of the year, Wood and Joan spent most of their time in Vermont.

In Manchester, the Cornells operated the Reluctant Panther, a nine-room B&B with a 60-seat restaurant, while they raised their family. When the children of both families were grown, the idea occurred to make the children's rooms at the Big Pine Key house available to guests: four rooms in the Cornells' Barnacle, three in the Threlkelds' Casa Grande.

Though the Barnacle and Casa Grande operate independently, they share a common pond between their heavily landscaped lots and the waterfront. Parties sometimes bring visitors together, and off-shore excursions typically are more economical when guests from the two B&Bs go off together.

The Barnacle is full of architectural surprises. Although one of its units, the Cottage, is off slightly on its own, all guests share an edenic garden in a second-story atrium of the main house. Screened atop, it shows the Star of David six-sided shape that Jon figured would bring in maximum breeze. At times that breeze is enough to nearly lift you off the ground.

The atrium has wildly eclectic furnishings: an oak chest carved with fruits and scrolled with a horned god; a vertical sea chest with ancient hinges full of games, deer head and mounted horns. When it rains up here, it rains through, so breakfast on those mornings is served in the kitchen just inside. That indoor space is almost as large and almost as open.

All rooms have easy-care comfortable furniture with plenty of built-ins. Wood Cornell's stained glass windows show up especially well over the bed in the Cottage, where brilliant blue tropical scenes imprint matching sheets, pillow cases, and coverlet. Here and elsewhere floors are paver tiled.

The Ocean Room is very pink and lollipop green. Fucshia folding shades drop across a decorative block wall full of openings (but thoughtfully screened). The Bobcat and Bear rooms both have Oriental pieces—an old Chinese chest, a Mt. Fuji tapestry. Bear has a bear head on a slice of redwood.

Casa Grande is more traditional—if you call massive Spanish doors in the Keys traditional. The house is more country, with bough wreaths, baths not as exotically colorful as next door, a lot of open beams, and carpet. Colors are softer. There are Mexican touches. One room is rose and palest blue, beautifully set off by Mexican fabric art. Here, too, is a second-story screened patio with a garden that would do most people proud. Breakfast is served here.

Both houses are built like forts because of their waterfront vulnerability to storms, yet both are remarkably open. The waterfront is not good for swimming because the sea here is shallow and rocky. About 50 yards out, the bottom turns sandy. Sneakers are provided in various sizes for walking in the water, and both houses share sandy beach. Each B&B provides small boats that guests can use to get to where the swimming's better, and there are sandy swimming beaches at many state recreation areas just a few miles north or south.

Both houses also are full of books and informative pamphlets about the Keys, as well as novels for leisurely passing time. However spent at these two places, time is gentled and rewarded by uncommonly thoughtful hosts.

The Barnacle, Rte. 1, Box 780A, Big Pine Key, FL 33043. (1-1/2 miles east off U.S. 1 on Long Beach Rd., including 1/2 mile beyond private gateposts). (305) 872-3298. Wood and Joan Cornell, hosts. 4 rooms (1 with complete kitchen except for oven, others with refrigerator) with private bath, AC, fan, color TV, phone (all on 1 line, free local calls, no LD surcharge, messages taken). No children, no pets, no credit cards. Rates: May 15-Dec. 14: $70-$80 cottage, $90-$100 main house, includes full breakfast, outdoor tiki hut and barbecue, private ocean beach, floating rafts, rubber boat, kayak, hot tub, bicycles, canal fishing, swimming, boat ramp, dock, snorkels, masks, coolers. No 3rd person in rooms. Off-street parking.

Casa Grande, Long Beach Drive, P.O. Box 378, Big Pine Key, FL 33043 (same local routing directions as The Barnacle). (305) 872-2878. Jon and Kathleen Threlkeld, hosts. 3 rooms with private bath, AC, fan, refrigerator. Color TVs, phones for guest use (free local calls, no surcharge on credit-card or collect LD calls). No children, no pets, no credit cards. Year-round rates: $75 with full breakfast. 3rd person in room $15. Rate also includes hot tub, paddleboats, and much the same as The Barnacle. Off-street parking.

Little Torch Key – LITTLE PALM ISLAND

Chic island hideaway for stopping the world and getting off.

Show up at Little Palm Island at low tide. Later watch your perimeter shrink. The water's rising and you're miles from nowhere. No bridge, no phone in your room, no TV, no radio. Around you a comely group of tanned, sandaled people with wet hair in floral shifts and loose print dresses. At the edge of the Atlantic you joke about the tide. The shared seclusion brings you together easily, intimately. Location is eveything, and not just in business.

Of course, Little Palm Island is business for Ben Woodson and his mostly Memphis partners. Good business. Couples pay $573 a night in season, tips and meals included. Meals are gourmet. Chef Michel Reymond works with a kitchen staff of 20. The 80 who make up the full staff always outnumber guests.

Ben and his colleagues dreamed of an American island easy to get to but unimaginably remote. They found it off Little Torch Key, 120 miles south of Miami. Once they'd found it, the problems weren't the ordinary ones about convincing bankers.

Land-use authorities were just saying no to new businesses on unbridged islands. Beekeeping was the only exception.

Little Palm had been a celebrity fish camp. They say that Roosevelt, Truman, Kennedy, and Nixon all came.

The Memphians have given it their own magical style. They have kept it to 30 well-appointed suites, 28 of these in thatched-roof bungalows. They converted the old great house to a restaurant-bar with two suites, and improved the utilities. The authorities liked it, no small matter, even though the partners had been assured of exactly one attempt at the project by a grandfather clause. Partner Jack Rice will tell you that Holiday Inns would have wanted 500 rooms, not 30, on any five acres they had.

Holiday Inns was his line of work, as it was for Joseph Roth, Jr., the only non-Memphis partner. Restaurants were Ben Woodson's trade. Worthington Brown, Jr., is a lawyer, Richard Raines an M.D. All are successful. At Little Palm Island they dreamed up a way of vacationing for people like themselves.

It took three years of paperwork, building, and detailing before the place opened in late 1988. The look remains tropical: palms, villas, beaches, blue water, and wading birds.

Villas are up off the ground and thatched to withstand up to 150-mile-an-hour winds. The palm fronds form 12 to 14 inches of natural gutters. Only the first inch or two gets wet in a rain. Villas stay naturally cool. Wind flutters the thatch softly. Under millions of stars that long ago vanished from cities, you imagine you're at sea—which of course you are.

Each of the 14 villas divides into two suites. These are pine with pecky cypress paneling and cedar trim. Each extends from a furnished porch to a living room, large bathroom-dressing area, and bedroom. Furniture is comfortably cushioned wicker and rattan. Beds are firm as an old-fashioned handsake, with twin night tables and lamps with three-way bulbs. There are inside and outside showers and deep whirlpool tubs. Each suite has a coffee maker and tea. There are mini-bars and closet safes. The look is luxurious yet simple in pale pink and green, shades of sunset, water, and sky.

You get around barefoot along a fringe of beach. Palms and salt-resistant flowering shrubs enclose the pool. Dining room and bar are stepped up and down to covered and open cypress decks. Though nature is all around, service and settings are artful, not rustic.

Most guests come together at dinner, joined by yachtsmen and a few others who come by launch from the mainland. Charter boats tie up at the island's wharf. Scuba and snorkeling gear, canoes, kayaks, and sailboats are freely available. Pontoon boats rent by the two hours or the day. The island is surrounded by Coupon Bight Aquatic Preserve. It's four miles south to the reef at Looe Key National Marine Sanctuary. The setting is privileged.

Offshore activities leave the island quiet by day. When the wind is calm a crescent of flats breaks at low tide. The little beach lies unruffled but for soft jazz and an occasional outboard. Pelicans and anhingas scout and dive.

Guests welcome a passing shower. They share the shudder of a storm. They lie in hammocks, curl up in the leather and lattice chairs on the porch, sink into sofas, stretch out on firm beds, maybe turning on the overhead fan or untying the mosquito netting. Laid-on diversion is limited to a shop with Bloomingdale-style selections, and a few small TVs with VCRs you can rent. Classic films are free.

At first when guests arrive, they're full of ideas about completing the last 25 miles to Key West. By the second day they're not so sure. A morning newscast from a kitchen radio crashes in the dining room more rudely than a pile of dishes falling off a tray. Earliest sun turns clouds to gilded pewter. Pelicans dive for their breakfast. Spoonbills vacuum theirs, while egrets stand stock still waiting for breakfast to pass beneath their mangrove-like legs before snapping their traps shut. A smiling waiter will be happy to bring yours to your cottage, or you can walk the beach and fully savor the quiet style of the island before your first coffee, smiling yourself.

Little Palm Island, Mile Marker (MM) 28.5, Little Torch Key, FL; Rt. 4, Box 1036, Little Torch Key, FL 33042. (800) 343-8567, (305) 872-2524. Ben H. Woodson, managing general partner. 30 suites with bath (tub, inside and outside shower) with whirlpool, AC, heat, ceiling fans. Pool, color cable TV with

VCR for rent (limited numbers). Telephone in great house. Gift shop, exercise room, restaurant, bar. Children accepted 9 and over. No pets. AmEx, MC, Visa. Ice, newspaper provided daily. Free use of sailboats, windsurfers, canoes, kayaks, snorkel and fishing gear. Dive shop. Small rental boats, fishing charters on request. Free launch service for guests to and from mainland office. Rates per suite (AP) July 16-Oct. 15, $410; Oct. 16-Dec. 20, $460; Dec. 21-Apr. 30, $573; (EP) $288, $340, $489; (rate including food, beverage, special activities: $600, $650, $700). Rates include 15% gratuity. 3rd or 4th person in suite, add $100 on AP rate. Suite for single occupancy deduct $55 from AP rate.

Key West – ARTIST HOUSE
One of Key West's most photographed houses; large guest
spaces, tiny yard, bygone style.

Artist House is the living space everyone wants to get into. It is high Victorian artistry, of a time when wealth was displayed as obligation, not merely flaunted.

The Conch Train and the tour trolleys stop so tourists can take pictures. Key West features the house on brochures. Posh stores as far away as San Francisco pose catalog photos in front of its Charles Addams facade.

An artist, Thomas Otto, who was world traveled and famous, built the house. His father Joseph, a medical doctor, had been a Union prisoner of war at Fort Jefferson in the Dry Tortugas who later settled in Key West as an apothecary.

Thomas, one of six children, bought the lot on lower Eaton Street and built the house between 1898 and 1900. He lived here for 40 years.

Thomas's son Eugene was the last of the family to live here—and the most famous. He was born in the house in 1900 and returned in the 1940s with his bride. He, too, was an artist. His scenes of Key West, full of sun and pastel-colored in white tropical light, were exhibited at the Boston Museum of Fine Arts, the Corcoran Gallery, and the High Museum of Art in Atlanta. Flower shows he put on were acclaimed by the *National Geographic*. He was an authentic Key West legend, similar to Hemingway and Tennessee Williams, but different from them in that he was a third generation Conch.

It was only in 1979, after the passing of Gene Otto and his wife, that the house for the first time was opened to guests. Its four owners since then have each lavished funds and attention on the property, three only to lose interest after a while and leave.

The house looks today much as always, and it is one of the pleasures of staying here that one feels ensconced in a home more than a commercial establishment. It is a harmonious composition of those elements that most evoke Queen Anne style: bays, porches, balconies, turrets, gables, gingerbread, jigsaw-cut balustrade, sculpted wooden columns, etched glass transoms, broad picture windows. The whole of it is painted lavender and gray with white trim, as if not merely to arrest by its style but seduce by its finery.

You move through the place as if in a museum. The rooms and suites are treasures of bygone style. Ceilings are 12 feet with crown moldings. Antique armoires, chinoiserie, fireplaces with marble mantels, French doors with chain-pull closures are all original with the house.

Consider the Oriental and dhurry rugs, the William Morris reproduction wallpapers. One room is done with rosewood and cherry pieces that match wallpapers and rugs in their sumptuousness. There are Queen Anne upholstered pieces in exquisite fabrics, decorative lamp shades, swag curtains, and four-poster beds.

The entry door is an Everglades scene in etched glass. The foyer holds a large mirror in an elaborate gilt frame above a marble-topped table. There is an enamel umbrella stand. Oriental runners extend on heart pine floors. A heavy, carved newel post anchors the carved banister leading up.

Some compromises have seen elimination of pocket doors, now kept permanently closed, forming walls against which headboards have been set for queen-sized beds. So you can't walk from one room to another as you once could, nor can you walk the entire wraparound porch because it has been enclosed by a series of private bathrooms. But these have their charm, with high ceilings that are the undersides of an upstairs balcony, antique fixtures, and thanks to fencing, a feeling of being outdoors in these intimate chambers. You shower under classical pediments and transom in sight of gingerbread.

The turret suite upstairs may be the most intriguing guest accommodation in Key West. Interior space eddies about to fill the bay with mostly Queen Anne pieces, plush sofa, brass queen bed on a dhurry rug atop pine plank floors, and Chinese and antique rosewood cabinetry. Rich texturing includes floral wallpaper in a diamond pattern, a white bed coverlet, and elaborate crown moldings. Long white curtains hang at long casement windows. Two sets of French doors lead to a little porch. A Cinderella closet under the stairwell has room for not more than a single frock or two. There is also a larger closet, the only one in the house.

Along the inside of the bay is an eye-popping staircase that grandly hugs the angled walls, curved like the fantasy of a childhood memory that goes on and on about something that could never be.

You mount the 17 steps to the turret into an octagonal space with seven six-on-six sash windows. You are high among tin roofs, at the top of a tamarind tree. To the southwest is a forest of church steeples that seem in communion with this secular tower.

Artist House gardens are small, with jacuzzi and goldfish pond, and filled with double hibiscus, thunburgia, kalanchoe, gardenias, orchids, bromeliads, and palms. This house enjoys more lovers than any other object of desire in Key West.

Artist House, 534 Eaton St., Key West, FL 33040. (305) 296-3977. Ed Cox, innkeeper. Two rooms and three 1-room suites with AC, ceiling fan, 3 bathrooms with tub, color TV. Make-yourself-at-home kitchen. No children. No pets. MC, Visa. Telephones downstairs and up. Continental breakfast included, expanded on weekends. Rates: winter $99-$175 double; summer $69-$99. No smoking inside.

Key West — THE BANYAN RESORT
Spacious, historic, worth a trip to Key West.

After time away from Key West you want to sneak up, catch it unawares, rediscover the shadow and breeze, color and reflection, slack pacing that issues from a source prescient about what America needs.

Here again are tin roofs awash in morning sun, broad lacy verandas, white clapboard eaves, boxy glassed French doors. On cool evenings the breeze slides along slanty tin roofs, tickling trees in full foliage. Key West is the ordered tropics, temperate order and tropical fullness.

The old town's heady mix of order and ease is well rooted at the Banyan Resort on lower Whitehead Street, a block from the Audubon House, four from the Hemingway, and across from the new multi-use development at Truman Annex that may make the vicinity one of the most popular in Old Town. Don't rent a car if you fly in. You don't need it and there's hardly any place to park.

The Banyan is an adult place of middle-class style. Garden apartments in historic homes away from the kids. A wood canopied garden bar and little sandwich kiosk. Two pools. Yards of pebble walks, palms, crotons, frangipani, hibiscus, ixora, schefflera. They have catalogued 65 different species of flora.

Morning, people in a compound this size, almost two acres in straitened Key West, cluster in private conversations like counselors coaxing new openings into lives constrained by elsewhere. Too bad about this one who was doing drugs. Good news about that one who got married. The jibber-jabber of relaxed swimsuit living. The free fall of our prejudices and joys. A week away.

It's Saturday-to-Saturday for many guests because the Banyan is a time-share. Key West softens the negative inference. People buy here for investment as much as use. So there are always apartments available overnight or longer, and visitors to take them. The Banyan feels like any first-class property in Key West. Only more spacious. Who wants to complain?

The two oldest buildings are the Cosgrove House and the Delaney-Holtsberg House, both in the classic revival style, in Key West marked by square posts, jig-cut balustrades, and scroll-cut corner brackets. Giant banyan trees shadow the pair and combine to make this block a favorite for photographers and painters who year-round work at their easels.

The houses are rich in history. Cosgrove is on property owned early in the 19th century by a Bahamian native who fought in the War of 1812 and died in 1891 at the age of 108. The Cosgrove family acquired the land in 1871, immediately built the house, and continued to live here until 1947. In their very first years the back of the house was Key West's first bottling works. D.T. Sweeny had two carriages on the trot serving the entire island with his famous rum, gin, whiskey, liquors and bitters, as well as pure bottled water from the well on the property.

Two generations of Cosgrove men were Coast Guard ship captains. The elder, Philip L., commanded the first rescue vessel to reach the stricken battleship Maine in 1898 in Havana harbor.

The Delaney house at the turn of the century replaced a two-story masonry structure that had been on the site since the early 1840s. The Holtsbergs acquired the house from an interim owning family of cigar-makers. Frank and Theo Holtsberg, brothers from Rumania, were among the first Jewish emigres to come to Key West. The family is still active in dry goods on Duval Street.

As operated today, the property has 38 apartments. The spaces are decorator burnished with brushed carpets, perfect-home upholstery fabrics, haute wicker furniture, thin venetian blinds.

They are done in subdued coordinated tones that heighten architecturally interesting interior angles formed by exterior eaves. There are French doors and windows for textured appeal that leave an otherwise clean, spacious look unaffected by wall art or by wallpapering except in bathrooms. Apart from the architectural geometry, only a ceiling fan protrudes in living rooms. These are tidy, organized spaces.

Each apartment has a full kitchen complete with microwave oven and quality cookware and coordinated tableware.

Bedrooms are wickerful and textured. Two ovoid mirrors, a lesser and a greater, gracefully plain ceramic lamps, a humorously languid artificial banana plant potted in a corner—these are the only decorative accessorizing. Beds are queens. There are ceiling fans and TV, with venetian blinds.

Bathrooms are spacious, modern, and supplied with bath towels thick enough to sop up an island squall.

All suites have either upstairs private porches and/or balconies or downstairs patios furnished with strapped lawn furniture.

Resort manager Gilbert Russell is a former Alaskan who came in 1984 looking for a warm climate. He'd read that Key West was the only frost-free city in the continental United States. Sounded good. The satisfactions are more subtle now. One is finding a tropical garden as spacious as the one at the Banyan, only a block from the busy end of the city's main street.

"Where else?" he asks.

No place. Good reason to visit while in Key West.

The Banyan Resort, 323 Whitehead St., Key West, FL 33040. (800) 225-0639 (No. America), (305) 296-7786. Gilbert Russell, resort manager. 38 apartments completely equipped (2 with tubs), AC, heat, ceiling fan, direct-dial phone (50¢ local calls, surcharge for LD calls), color cable TV. No pets. AmEx, MC, Visa. 2 pools (1 heated), jacuzzi. Balconies, porches or patio. Pool bar and snack bar. Rates: Dec. 16-end-April $185-$265, May through Dec. 15 $115-$165 (double), $20 for 3rd or 4th person. Limited off-street parking.

Key West – COLOURS
Fun and games hospitality in Queen Anne house with large
private yard, spacious guest rooms.

James Remes is playful. Like Nixon opening China, or Reagan buddying up to
the Evil Empire, only a CPA could get away with running a business playfully.
Here he is telling guests about how he was envoy of the Conch Republic to the
French Bicentennial.

"Of course Mitterand didn't receive me, but I was in Greece in October, and
just lately in Costa Rica. Every place I tell them I'm the Ambassador of the Conch
Republic, and they go around introducing me that way. People remember when
you play, and there's nothing more you have to do about it."

James's plenipotentiary status was conferred by a recent Key West mayor playing
out the Conch Republic game. The Conch Republic was created in 1982 when the
Keys declared their "independence" from the United States in a dispute over the
federal government's stopping and searching cars leaving the island chain. The object
was to exploit every opportunity for publicity to attract tourists to Key West.

A lot of people wind up at Colours, what with James traipsing the globe
and making himself unforgettable. Guests get looked after well. They play, too.

They come back.

James will tell you there is "extreme difference between guests and tourists in Key West. Size of the place has a lot to do with it. Tourists get filed away. Guests are entertained by hosts in more family-type accommodations. Not 'families' with kids, you understand, but among kindred adults. Long-term guests will leave like family."

Getting his place to that point has taken seven years. Few people run guests houses that long. James may be playing, but he plays smart.

Usually there are 10 in staff to look after the 12 rooms. The staff are called hosts. They do the work, but they interact with guests without any barriers between "them" and "us." Often the comment is, "Who's the owner?" Guests do mistake staff for other guests.

Most guests use Colours as what James calls a "base for expeditions" to all the scenes of nightlife, for skiing, parasailing, snorkeling, and movies. Others never have to leave the property.

James makes it more home-like by serving food. There's never a menu. He creates what guests want. This goes on in season almost every night. People come back because they like the people they meet here. There is no little partying at this "inn for the avant garde."

James, you might imagine, sorted himself out for Key West. He'd been raised in back-roads Iowa, graduated from Drake University, joined a Big Eight accounting firm in Des Moines, got transferred to Denver, and came to Key West on a vacation.

"I stayed from March through Easter. My mind, body, and soul were already hunting for real estate. It was difficult getting back on the plane. In July I left Denver for Key West again. I knew instantly I wanted a guest house. I hunted up this situation, which was in foreclosure, changed the name to Colours, and started from scratch."

The house was the final residence of Francisco Marrero, a Cuban who fought early for his island's independence, was sent to a Spanish prison in Africa, escaped to Liverpool, then to New York where he learned the cigar trade. After establishing his business he moved it to Key West and here became one of the city's most prominent manufacturers at a time when Key West's 165 factories were producing 100 million cigars a year, contributing 19/20ths of the internal revenue collected at that time in the state of Florida.

The house changed hands many times, but fortunately has suffered little exterior change. It sits back from lower Fleming Street behind a little masonry wall, its ornate Queen Anne architecture is separated from the sidewalk by plantings that set off its stark white frame and ornamentation like some still tall slender dowager dressed in a white shirtwaist, not so much out of touch with her times as demanding respect for the times she herself keeps current.

Sharply angled eaves slant their way atop a flat second story roof below which a series of five porch openings between columns are set off by gingerbread brackets that resemble the spread of eagles' wings. Framed behind these are numerous doorways with framed transoms, inset glass panels, and shutters latched back. A spindle balustrade protects the walk.

Below, the columns mark off higher arched spans than above, more lacily ornamented asymmetrically, to one side framing the double entry doors.

The back-facing part of the house has been stabilized, upgraded, and painted creamy yellow. There are new plantings. The old kitchen has been fixed up.

Rooms are more grandly antique than ever. Here is a huge mahogany and burl sideboard with mirrors and rattan inlay. There, a room all in greens and blues, Queen Anne tables, a six-panel bamboo screen, Oriental tables, Aubusson rug, wicker armoire. The rooms today are well-ordered, the hippie look gone, their high ceilings and distinctive shapes highlighted by strategic placements of furniture and wall art.

Among intriguing features are a six-globe, spider-foot chandelier. Several chandeliers have been converted from gas to electricity. Set off by sculpted balusters and carved newel post, there is Lincresta wainscoting up the sharply rising staircase. Lincresta is a texturing process from turn-of-the-century England that presses insects and flowers into design work.

To the rear on the first floor is a living room-lounge with stereo, Cinemax, and complete entertainment center, as well as a full bath for use by guests who want to enjoy the premises after check-out but before flight departures—playing to the last.

Colours, 410 Fleming St., Key West, FL 33040. (305) 294-6977. James Remes, hotelier; James Seally, manager. 12 rooms with AC, ceiling fan, some space heaters, all private baths except one connect, some tubs, some with TV. Direct-dial phones. Heated pool. Stereo and video entertainment center. All but 2 rooms with refrigerators, 2 with kitchenettes. No children. No pets. AmEx, Discover, EnRoute, MC, Visa. Sunset cocktails, evening turndown and mint service. Rates: winter $100-$140 double, summer $80-$120. 3rd or 4th person in room $15. Continental breakfast and airport pick-up included.

Key West – CURRY MANSION INN
Richly mom-and-pop, a couple you'd like to be adopted by.

Persist, and you can bed down in the museum. Why would you want to? It's the most elegant part of the house. It *is* the house. It's the house of Milton Curry, Florida's first home-grown millionaire. You'll ensconce in bedrooms with bay windows of ormolu on mahogany, and Chippendale chairs. Hallways have Tiffany beveled-glass windows and glass sliding doors, bird's-eye maple paneling, and marble-topped console tables.

Where others come on the $5 tour, you're at home. Just like Al and Edith Amsterdam, who bought the Curry Mansion in 1975 and spent 10 years restoring it.

Curry's father, William, made his fortune in lumbering, wrecking, and ship equipment. The Amsterdams had taken early retirement from growing apples on 1,000 acres in upstate New York. They moved to Fort Lauderdale, visited Key West, and realized what a mistake they'd made. They saw the mansion all lit up, with a big "For Sale" sign. The realtor saw Al and said, " A man like you needs a house like this." Al bought it.

It didn't look then the way it does now.

Though only one couple had lived in the mansion after the Currys sold it in 1918, they became reclusive and let the house run down. For seven years nobody lived in it. Of the original furniture, only the dining room and the piano remained.

"It wasn't too hard to refurnish, strange as that might seem," says Edith, given the dozen or so rooms. "Al and I had sisters and brothers with really terrible taste, so between the two of us we inherited a lot of good stuff from both our families. Most was from the period of the original mansion."

The house is a version of a townhouse that Milton Curry and his wife, Elaine, had seen in Paris on their honeymoon. The style is modified French Empire, three symmetrical stories with two full front balconies and a partial balcony on the third story. It is all grandly flowing in a rising series of porticos, with fanlight windows and pedimented dormers. To one side is a rotunda; atop is a widow's walk you can ascend for a grand view.

The house is an eclectic mix of antiques in an intuitive museum. Many ornate figured pieces are Dresden: ginger jars and oil lamps from the Meissen factory. A silver epergne made in France in 1795 is identical to another displayed in L'Hermitage in Leningrad. An inlaid table of brass and tortoise shell is attributed to Andre Boule in 1798. Amsterdam family Limoges and acquired pieces of Coalport, Minton, Royal Crown Derby, Wedgwood, and Worcester sit in glass cases in the carriage hall.

The gold-colored tableware in the dining room suggests the grandeur of the original Curry solid gold Tiffany service for 24, remnants of which are on display at the Audubon House.

The 1853 Chickering grand piano belonged to Henry James. Early Edison cylinder players still work. Listen to a very low fidelity version of Paderewski playing Chopin's "Valse Brilliante." Audubon prints are original, as are the prints by Mario Sanchez, Key West's legendary keeper of the cultural memory.

They say that Key lime pie was first created in the Curry kitchen by Aunt Sally, a cook, but they don't say when. It might have been around the time of a kitchen photograph from 1912 that marked completion of the railroad to Key West. The photo shows the rear of the mansion from the Fogarty House next door where railroader Henry Flagler reviewed the commemorative parade. Fogarty was mayor of Key West. His house was built by the same architect as the Curry mansion, built by father William for Milton's older sister when she married in 1888. In 1912, Mayor Fogarty lived there.

One of the pleasures of the mansion is that even though it's museum quality, you can sit on the furniture. Apart from the elevator, there may not be another piece in the house with a Do Not Touch sign. In the kitchen a notice reads, "Curry Mansion Inn Rules." It starts with a "1" and that's all there is.

Al and Edith live in the master bedroom of the house, but so much in the other rooms is antique and probably not meant to be used (even if there aren't signs to that effect) that they prefer to house their guests in the addition around the pool.

The addition has 15 rooms on two stories. These are airy and bright, full of wicker and chintz, with modern bathrooms. Best of these are those numbered 1, 2, 3, 8, and especially the very large 16.

What holds the modern addition and the antique mansion together is Al and Edith's presence. They're here, and they're enjoying the place and themselves in it. They love guests. Early evenings they entertain guests by the pool with drinks and hors d'oeuvres. People tell their stories of all the ways they've arrived in Key West. The sun sets, spirits rise. It's not unusual for guests and the Amsterdams to head out for dinner together. You return feeling you belong. Good people, you'll say to yourself; good people, good place, good living—good night.

Curry Mansion Inn, 511 Caroline St., Key West, FL 33040. (800) 253-3466, (305) 294-5349. Al and Edith Amsterdam, innkeepers. 15 rooms with bath (1 with tub), AC, heat, ceiling fan, color cable TV, digital alarm clock-radio, wet bar, refrigerator in most rooms, direct-dial phone (no local call charge or LD surcharge), pool. Well-mannered children welcomed, free in parents' room. Crib free. 3rd person in room $25. All major credit cards. Rates (double): high season (Dec.22-Apr. 29), $160-$225; rest of year, $125-$200, includes continental breakfast, afternoon cocktails, use of Pier House beach facility and health club. Handicap rooms (with wheelchair elevator). Free off-street parking.

Key West – DUVAL HOUSE
In the midst of town yet quiet in its spacious gardens.

"We were going to put in telephones. 'No!' said the guests. We were going to put in TVs. 'No!' they said again. Terry robes, Neutrogena soaps, Evian water? We nixed those ourselves. Nothing wrong with any of them, but when you have 85 percent repeat guests, you want to be real careful before you change anything."

That's Richard Kamradt talking. With partner Walter Goldstein of Los Angeles, he recently bought the Duval House that under former owners Bob Zurbrigen and the late Ben Conners was one of Old Town's favorites in the Eighties.

Duval House is in the heart of town, where a lot of visitors think they want to be. They may think twice, though, once they arrive. But Duval House, though it fronts on its namesake main street, which is where the action is, extends back into a private compound that's instant jungle and leaves you feeling far away from the bustle. So you get the best of both worlds.

Lodgings are in a pair of 100-year-old buildings lately with a smaller third with three kitchen apartments on Petronia Street. Interiors are tropically textured and toned with a bright clean look. Whereas pool areas elsewhere may dominate the setting and you're either into the scene or left out, here in addition are a fully furnished poolhouse with kitchen for communal use and the one TV, spacious gardens that are composed and meditative, and broad balconies for enjoying the outdoors pretty much by yourself.

The place is immediately appealing from the street. Original sand-colored lodgings and the third on an adjacent lot are trimmed in green, porches downstairs, balconies up. Between the first two houses an outdoor corridor extends into the densely landscaped yard. An additional structure houses a book and card store.

Bob excelled with his guest rooms. These Richard and Walter have left alone. The feeling is equally Southern and tropical. It shows in bed covers, custom wall colors, dramatic cane and wicker headboards, quality ceiling fans and venetian blinds, and a light touch of stenciling beneath crown moldings.

Even the smallest rooms—which are about 14x14—feel spacious and airy because of multiple windows and doors. French doors make you feel in elegant digs if you choose to stay and read indoors on a rainy afternoon.

Beds are firm. Baths are modern with quality vinyl tiles that complement room decor (and instead of the pricey amenities still feature welcome Key West aloe and frangipani soaps—the first of Key West guest houses to do so). Doors have weight and feel solid. Paintwork is done without wavy lines. Reading lamps have three-way bulbs.

Some of the rooms are exceptionally proportioned and well furnished. A rear second floor room has 11-foot ceilings and French doors to a broad deck. There are scalloped-back armchairs, shelves stylishly filled with carefully selected decorative accessories: a collection of Oriental canisters, a stone-carved *art nouveau* bird, antique clock, flowing bougainvillea.

Almost all the rooms feature exquisite armoires. Among the more memorable is one of inlaid burl with antique mirrors inside. You exult to be in rooms decorated with this care.

The original houses were built as cigarmaker tenements in the 1880s. They were unused when Ben and Bob found them in the early 1980s and moved them forward on the lot toward the street so the land behind could be developed as their recreational compound.

Richard had first come to Key West in the mid-Sixties. "You could buy turtle steak and soup cheap. Everything was primitive, dangerous, rough," he recalls. Now he finds it upscale, colorful.

He and Walter were investing in rental apartments in Los Angeles, but "getting pretty sick of eviction court," as Richard recalls. "Apartment people just complain. But B&B guests arrive frazzled, are real happy to be with you, and thank you when they leave. You're the beneficiary of the change you've helped them find."

When Bob decided to retire and put the property up for sale, Richard and Walter quickly made their move to Key West.

So what changes have they made? Small but good ones. China replaces styrofoam cups at breakfast, where baked goods are bakery fresh, not commercial. More shade plants have been added in the yard.

No room phones, no room TVs. Escape as good as it was before.

Duval House, 815 Duval St., Key West, FL 33040. (305) 294-1666. Richard Kamradt and Walter Goldstein, owners. 28 rooms, including 3 suites with kitchens, with AC, ceiling fan, private bath, some with tubs, fresh flowers, tropical garden. Pool, poolhouse, central TV in poolhouse. Phone booth, and messages taken. Children accepted 17 and older. No pets. AmEx, MC, Visa. Rates: winter $92-$150, single or double; summer $54-$96. Additional person(s) in rooms $15. Continental breakfast included. Limited off-street parking.

Key West — EATON LODGE
New artistic owner restores gardens, renews hospitality.

Here was one of the best guest houses in Key West, and when it was sold you wondered what would happen. People can do radical things with otherwise good ideas in a place where fantasy rules. Sellers, when they're burned out, often don't care who gets the place next.

In the case of Eaton Lodge, we can relax. What was good is better.

Sam Maxwell and Denison Tempel had made this well-proportioned Victorian behind the white clapboard and muted red shutters very English, uniquely among Key West guest houses. They were English. Their living room was dark mahogany, and English interiors fit as well as any others in Key West.

Denison was an architect, and the house had a smart, arts look to it inside and out.

Mark Anderson has come and made the house still more arts appealing. He's a potter, and the partner who first came with him was a porcelain designer with other art skills as well. Some of his works remain. So that today the house is art-filled. It's lighter, more tropical than it was. And inside is only part of the story. Outside Mark is restoring the palm gardens that made this house a favorite of touring garden clubbers for more than a half century.

Downstairs in the living room, where the dark pieces used to be, Mark has introduced an eclectic mix of Scandinavian modern, Edwardian, and Deco, with paintings varied as a 19th-century Russian wolf-attack-in-the-snow to contemporary American watercolors.

The Scandinavian pieces are upholstered with white bamboo-patterned cushions. The Edwardian is a pine washstand that Mark uses as an unobtrusive foyer registration desk. A screen is French Deco with veneers of walnut, cherry, and mahogany; there are Deco area rugs on the red plank Dade County pine floors, and twin 1930s mahogany loveseats with early rayon brocade. A Victorian settee has lion head, arms and feet.

It's a mishmash, Mark admits, but so skillfully put together that it works.

Art that Mark has installed includes a salt-glazed tea jar by his master, Byron Temple, that comes with bamboo handle. Some of Mark's own pieces are here, too. Mark's former partner, Val Roy Gerischer, who returned North because Key West didn't suit his need for a vigorous work environment, has contributed a superb piece called "Ratatouille," three stained glass garden panels, one behind the other on a mahogany drop-leaf table.

After years of studying with Temple in England and New Jersey, Mark was attracted by the warmth of Key West, and quickly fell in love with the Eaton Lodge gardens.

These had been planted early in the century during the time that a Dr. Warren and his wife were in residence. Though Dr. Warren died in the 1930s, his widow continued in the house to the Seventies. Her rose garden extended almost to Duval Street. It was said that Mrs. Warren was one of the few who could afford a gardener during Key West's dismal Depression years.

Paul Keener, an authority on palms hired by Mark to help create vignette gardens out of bush, found the challenge irresistible. He can point to a pair of huge Washingtonians that flank the front, each maybe a hundred years old. Many mature specimens date from the 1920s. Ponytail palms rise to nearly 20 feet. A thatch palm supports an enormous orchid cultivation that Paul estimates was placed on the palm at least 40 years ago. There are caladiums, bromeliads, arecas, and traveler palms around the jacuzzi, exotic heliconia and other tropical shrubs surrounded by brick.

Guest rooms are in the upper two stories of the main house and in back on the two floors of the carriage house.

Guests climb stairs with flared bottom and paneled stairwell wainscoting. The Dade County pine floors have been uncovered. Rooms are smartly decorated with Oriental prints and mirrors, with sheer drapes against casement windows. Fabric draperies in large floral prints stretch across beautiful French doors in rooms that open onto the upstairs front porch.

Wicker is being put in all the main house rooms to add lightness. New mattresses have improved some beds, but some softer mattresses remain. Ask for a firm bed if that's your choice. The garden rooms in the carriage house are a pleasant mix of antique and contemporary. One bedchamber is Edwardian, and has a king bed made of two twins with white-painted iron bedposts and a white chenille bedcover. By contrast, the sitting area—again it works—is almost Bauhaus, with blue upholstered steel chairs and a glass-topped starkly square table. Full kitchens downstairs have tacky cabinets that Mark plans to replace in 1991. At the same time he will replace vinyl floors that show from under tightly woven carpet by the sink.

If other plans go his way, Mark will open a restaurant in the house, using part of the quarters that previous owners used behind the sliding wall, and opening the house to the south from the living room.

Whether more or less change happens, Eaton House remains one of the choice places for overnighting in Key West.

Eaton Lodge, 511 Eaton St., Key West, FL 33040. (305) 294-3800. Mark Anderson, innkeeper. 13 rooms and suites with AC, heat, ceiling fan, bathrooms, refrigerator, some with tub. TV available on request, no charge. Telephone room for free local calls, no surcharge for LD calls. Jacuzzi. Some rooms with kitchens. Not suitable for children. No pets. MC, Visa. Rates: winter $105-$150, off-season $75-$105. Rates for suites $220; $150. Special long-term rates. Extra person in room $15, in season. Inquire for off season. Full breakfast included (home-baked). Airport courtesy car in season. Street parking.

Key West – EDEN HOUSE
The hippie pad now a yuppie pick.

If you want a look at what Eden House used to look like, catch the Goldie Hawn movie "Criss Cross." It's about a single mother who struggles with drugs, sex, and hippies in Key West in the late 1960s. Scott Sommer stayed at Eden House and used it as a backdrop when he wrote the novella from which the movie is adapted.

When the production crew showed up in 1990, Mike Eden had just finished the renovations that changed the place forever. Every room had been fitted with air-conditioning, classy wicker, and new carpet. New upscaled suites had just been installed in the back. Everything was newly painted a crisp white. Ceiling fans and awnings were installed on the rear porch by Rich's Cafe. Next door to the west, renovations had just begun on the newly acquired 100-year-old house. When finished, it would add six more luxury suites to Eden House for 1991.

So comes the movie crowd. They want the place as it was in the old days. "They took everything out," says Ulf Zimpel, Mike's manager, himself a Key West personality from his days at distinctly off-beat Big Ruby's. "Asphalt tile floor put back in, and they aged the outside extremely as if it hadn't seen a renovation for 20 years. A very, very tacky neon sign went up outside."

That's how it looked, changing slowly like life itself. Since it was built in 1924, before air-conditioning, all the rooms off central corridors opened at both ends for better ventilation.

The building was first a general store and a residence. Earlier visitors had come by horse and buggy from the Havana Ferry docks, and later, railroad workers

311

called it home. By 1935 it was the Gibson Hotel. Jack Gibson, who owned it, was born in one of the rooms.

Mike and his brother, Stan, bought it in 1974. Mike figured out how to operate a budget hotel for the times. As he and Stan used to say, "We own, manage, and clean the Eden House." Guests paid hostel rates—$7 a night. "We were probably the first guest house in Key West," Mike recalls. "We took exactly what we had to work with. The dressers were here, not much more."

In the late Eighties, Mike was looking for investors to bankroll the upgrade. All Key West was going upscale. Change came slowly as Mike, largely working on his own, was able to phase it in. No sooner did he have most of the work done, than the movie crew shows up and wants the place the way it used to be.

At least in the movie, Eden House will always have its historic look as one of Florida's old blue-collar hotels. Its plaster-in-the-sun plainness will speak again for all the people who've ever come to Key West by bus and explored the town by walking or pedaling a clunker bike. The look will forever be nearly gimmick-free, and leave you in mind of a time before folks bit the apple, exited paradise, and fell into organized tourism, self-conscious preservation and gay lifestyles.

Then, as now, still a saving grace, Eden House remained among the last places in Key West where Floridians built sensibly for the climate, extending canopies over sidewalks to keep walkers shaded from intense sun and sudden downpours, and providing rooms upstairs where people could catch the breeze on tropical nights.

More than just the sensible canopies remain. Upstairs in the original building, Mike has kept some of the European-style rooms with the bath and shower down the hall. There are still semi-private rooms where guests share baths with adjoining rooms. But with everything air-conditioned, the hostel rate is gone: rooms with bath down the hall now *start* at $55 in the off-season.

The new spaces all have kitchenettes (no ovens), smooth walls, track lighting and dimmers in bathrooms—all very up-to-date. Imagine: in Eden House, where hippies used to sit on the floor when the free keg of beer was tapped in the afternoon, guests now get chairs with levered footrests. There are eave windows covered with narrow decorator blinds. Guests find twin lavatories in the baths. Sofas open to queen beds. Rattan tables have two chairs for tete-a-tete dining in alcoves. The look is all beige and tan, floors covered in indoor-out cocoa-mat carpet. Suites have ample closets.

Newcomers will probably love it. The rest of us will have to go to the movies for Eden House the way we love and remember it.

Eden House, 1015 Fleming St., Key West, FL 33040. (305) 296-6868. Mike Eden, proprietor; Ulf Zimpel, manager. 38 rooms, suites, 16 with private baths, 10 with semi-private, 12 that use hall baths. Some suites with kitchens. AC, fans, phone. Lobby color TV. "Well-behaved" children accepted, free in parents room to 16. No pets. AmEx, MC, Visa. Restaurant. Pool. Rates: summer $45-$145; winter $75-$195. Off-street parking. Inquire about house next door.

Key West — HERON HOUSE
Good value in a spacious compound that a restless owner keeps improving.

"Thank God I have so many credit cards!" says Fred Geibelt, papering walls, putting up glass-brick partitions, and sawing porch rails. "This business is often a cliffhanger.

"People sometimes wonder why it's expensive to stay in Key West," says Fred. "Guest houses are expensive to operate anywhere. You can't spread the costs over hundreds of units. Especially in Key West, where there's so much regulation. You have to have faith in yourself and the town.

"In Key West you're at the end of the earth. There are no relatives around. You can't easily run home."

In seven years, Fred has never stopped spending on his place. He gave up a successful ginseng distributing business in New Jersey to finance conversion of a weed-filled Key West yard into a stylish compound.

First he underwrote renewal of the row of rooms along the pool he built. Then he bought a pre-Civil War frame house to the other side. Now he's digging deep to complete renovations on two stories of deluxe rooms on the far side of the pool, and getting cost estimates for the waterfall he's always dreamed of.

Despite Fred's penchant for doing things right, he is always hoping—never taking for granted—that guests will love the result. He can relax. The value is there.

When you open the redwood and cedar gates leading from Simonton Street, you enter a large sunny and shady compound filled with the kinds of uses Fred thinks people will like: a pool with lots of deck, gardens, a shady patio, a breezeway reading room.

But for the large shade trees—avocado, gumbo limbo, mango—Fred has added almost everything. He has planted sugar apple, sapodilla, traveler palms, anthuriums, orchids, bromeliads, staghorn ferns, bird of paradise, flowering vines.

Rooms that used to be as dark as tenements are now deluxe, with private decks, stained glass panels, and gardens. They have wicker and cane furniture with glass table tops, tile floors, Hunter fans, and lights on dimmers. You get five-foot by six-foot crank-out windows, recessed lighting, and exposed beam ceilings. Fine touches include stained glass transoms with three-dimensional bougainvilleas worked into them, cut-glass lamps, and original watercolors by longtime Key West artist Diana Quigley. Rooms have cedar closets, walls of mirrors, and twin swing-out wall lamps to either side of firm new beds.

Signature features are the crafted wood walls and the splendid bathrooms.

Carpenter Dan Peloquin, one-time Econo Lodge maintenance man redeemed by Fred, has done an entire wall of cedar worked in a diamond pattern, of oak and cedar lattice, of beveled wood bricks. You don't see the work anywhere else, nor for that matter, the wood-worked bed frames, custom moldings, and cedar door frames, all hand made.

New baths are sumptuous in redwood with granite-like river gravel tubs fitted with deep jacuzzis. There are blue granite sinks and counter tops, with lights on dimmers. Shower enclosures are granite and glass.

Always pushing himself to improve things, Fred has returned to the first rooms he built, upgrading them with marbleized vanities and chrome fixtures, smart rattan furniture, thin decorator blinds, and new French doors.

Guests enjoy easygoing sociability. There are no room phones, no TV. Guests mingle. They share the good feelings of a place free of aggressive chasing, with no put-on whatsoever. Others who want a beach scene, a non-stop party, or a place where they can stay in touch with business, next time stay elsewhere.

When guests are stretched out by the pool dozing, sunning, reading, or when they're talking about Key West days under a starry sky at a poolside cookout, the place looks right, it feels right. Used. Fred is happy.

Heron House, 512 Simonton Street, Key West, FL 33040. (305) 294-9227. Fred Geibelt, owner. 19 rooms with AC, ceiling fans, all with private baths; pool, color cable TV in deluxe rooms. Children accepted 15 and older. No pets. AmEx, MC, Visa. Pay phone. Rates: winter $95-$175; summer $55-$95, includes continental breakfast. Seventh night free except February and March.

Key West – HOLLINSED HOUSE
Six fully-equiped Caribbean-styled apartments with a lot of privacy.

Key West was as close to Jamaica as Judy and Mickie Hollinsed could relocate. She was from New York in insurance. He was from Bath, Jamaica, in real estate. Life in Montego Bay had become unpredictable. They'd begun to look over their shoulders.

It was a major dislocation starting life again in their 60s. They had lived and worked around tourism in Jamaica. They got the idea to make hospitality their new career.

A friend in Key West had done over a building for himself and recommended the same. So in 1977 they bought their own place, a Conch house abandoned for years. They restored its old Key West look themselves. Today the Hollinsed House that Mickie continues to run since Judy's recent passing remains one of Key West's most satisfying places to vacation.

It's off the beach like almost all the guest houses, in the heart of Old Town near Duval Street. Whereas most such places stand shoulder to shoulder, Hollinsed House is in a tidy compound, a little apart, uncluttered by any studied look other than its nurturing of an informal Caribbean style. There is something normal about the ambiance. No posing, no strutting, no lovers trying to get lined up for the night.

Part of it is that, different from most guest houses, this place is fully set up as apartments, six of them in two old houses. You can quickly feel at home in these ample spaces. These aren't just rooms where you come at night to sleep after a day and night on the town. They're for spending time in. You might almost wish for rain.

And there **is** a look, though not fussy. The look on Southard Street is gingerbread and jigsaw-cut railings, white clapboard behind porches set off by two-story-high wood columns. You might detect the hint of a lived-in tilt. The place exudes fairytale charm, and all around are colorful hibiscus and bougainvillea, tall royal palms, and fruiting papaya, sapodilla, and hogplum in season.

The tropical look, after all, is what you expect. People come all the way to Key West to be as near to the tropics as they can without leaving the continent. When an occasional cold front moves through Florida and winter temperatures in Miami sometimes dip into the 30s, it's usually 20 degrees warmer in Key West.

Many come here as a Caribbean substitute, to avoid customs and immigrations hassles, dealing with another language and a foreign currency—and, of course, because of the cost.

Inside as well as out, Hollinsed House satisfies. The place looks Caribbean but is conveniently American.

Most of the decor is from Judy and Mickie's Mo Bay home. Wicker, rattan, and slatback chairs combine well with tropical colors. Like a lemon wedge on the lip of a tall cooler, compatibility counts.

There is nothing earnest or forced about the look, no sense of anyone fearful of making a mistake or having copied. What is here is what worked best in the tropics. The way some places tug at Northern remembrances, this one easily refers to life in another island of honeyed accents.

Though the look of the place is well lived in, there is nothing tatty. Louvers and open-beam ceilings keep the indoor space open, fresh, and textured, different from the outside but sensual in its own way.

Walls and ceilings are white, set off by foam green carpet and colorful fabrics on chairs, beds, in wall hangings. The feeling is clean, breezy, bright. You want to greet morning with a fling of improvisation. You come back after a day of fishing or swimming feeling soft and loving on a cushiony sofa or at ease with a magazine or book on a shady porch. After a night out, you return to quarters that feel like home with a separate access, no sense of hordes fumbling with room keys along factory-like corridors. You are aware that an individual hand is at work, not a corporate one.

Part of the charm is how the compound has been laid out. Like most guest houses, this one ensures enclave satisfaction. There are the two houses and the little blue pool and deck positioned at the center like three squares on a checkerboard: the house up front with three stories, the low deck and pool to the side connected by a yard of river rock, and the two-story house behind.

All the apartments have kitchens, they are air-conditioned, there are lots of blankets and space heaters just in case, fresh towels daily, maid service weekly, use of Mickie's living room phone, and TV in each of the apartments. Very sensible, very comfortable.

Hollinsed House, 609-11 Southard St., Key West, FL 33040. (305) 296-8031. Mickie Hollinsed, innkeeper. 6 apartments with AC, heaters available, bathrooms, full kitchens, TV, porches, pool, jacuzzi. Living room phone downstairs for free local calls, credit-card LD calls. No children. No pets. No credit cards. Rates: winter $85 to $150 double; summer $65 to $105. $10 extra person per night. Limited off-street parking.

Key West – ISLAND CITY HOUSE
New owner further renews grandly architectural small hotel.

Bruce Corneal, the latest improver of the Island City House, brings to mind a long-overlooked Florida connection with empire-builder Henry Flagler.

In 1897, already well into his development of Florida hotels and railroads, Flagler acquired the 1804 Bedford Springs Hotel in western Pennsylvania. Florida turned out to be one of the biggest markets for Flagler's Bedford bottled water, which arrived here on Flagler trains.

Bruce recalls the connection because in the 1980s he came into possession of the Bedford Springs property, and then later, like Flagler, albeit more modestly, made his move to Key West. The Island City Hotel that Bruce now owns had been a private home but was converted to a hotel when its owner learned that

Flagler was bringing his railroad to Key West.

Island City House today is the oldest (albeit discontinuously) operating guest lodging in Key West. With its neighboring Arch House and Cigar House, it makes one of the most attractive guest compounds in Old Town.

The Island City House was almost lost. By 1972 the structure had been condemned as unsafe. Its last owner had been forcefully removed, and when she died the property passed to the Catholic Archdiocese of Miami. The property out back joined L-shape to the Arch House. Preservationists Jim and Sallye Jude learned that the Church had no real use for it. They equaled the highest offer, so that in 1976 Jim and Sallye—who already owned the Arch House—began work on the second phase of their compound.

Like the Island City House, the Arch House had been built in the 1880s. Today it is the only remaining carriage house in Key West.

When the Judes saw it in 1973 it was a derelicts' den still distinguished by the 16-foot arch off Eaton Street that linked its twin quarters around the wide passageway. Sallye and Jim bought it just after they first got involved with the Old Island Restoration Foundation, and Sallye restored it working with a carpenter and helper.

It took three years and almost a million dollars to restore the two properties. Island City House had been collapsing and had to be carefully stabilized before almost total reconstruction could begin. The front porches, stairs, and long side veranda on each floor were rebuilt, the original parapet reconstructed. Rear porches were added, and broad staircases parallel to but offset from the rear facade.

Today, all white and pale yellow outside behind white picket fence, with thousands of spindle balusters, airy post and beam porch framing, its zig-zagging exterior staircases, brown shutters, glass transoms over glass-paneled double doors, and inside with rooms outfitted in antiques and period-recalling fabrics and wallpapers, the house is a triumph of preservationist vision.

Last addition to the property was the Cigar House. This two-and-a-half-story all red cypress addition re-creates the Alfonso Cigar Factory that once occupied its site. It sits at the angle of the compound's L, its front porch a step above the wooden deck around the bougainvillea-draped pool and jacuzzi. Largest suites in the compound, also in period style, are here.

The three house are linked by wood and brick walkways embowered by a tamed jungle of tall trees and flowering shrubs, including a hill of bromeliads. There are 25 units in all, all different, all with private bathrooms and kitchens.

Bruce bought the property as part of a plan not yet fully realized that would complement the Bedford Springs Hotel's strong summer season with Key West's strong winter one. He had become active in restoring historic properties in Washington, D.C., and in Philadelphia, and by the 1980s had become attracted to restoration and tourism.

Alas, Bedford Springs wound up in litigation and isn't operating, and that in turn has held back Bruce's acquisition of additional Key West properties.

However, it hasn't slowed improvements at the Island City House compound.

The Arch House, which had been furnished with odds and ends, is somewhat improved with wicker and rattan. Hanging lights have been installed underneath the arch. The high fence that had blocked the interior garden view from Eaton Street has been removed and the arch left open. Second-floor units are getting little porches overlooking either gardens or Eaton Street. The feeling is altogether lighter and more airy than before.

An unfortunate lean-to kind of serving area next to the Cigar House has been replaced by a bright little canopied red and yellow wagon with big wooden wheels where guests now can enjoy an improved continental breakfast of fresh orange juice, croissants, and breads fresh from a neighborhood bakery. Plastic soap dispensers have been replaced with little lined wicker baskets. New specimen plants have been added to the gardens, and new deck furniture and white canvas umbrellas to the pool area.

Guests who remember the property from the Judes' time will feel well-rewarded in these sumptuous digs. Bruce Corneal may not be Henry Flagler, but he shares the vision and the gift of hospitality.

Island City House, 810 Eaton St. or 411 William St., Key West, FL 33040. (800) 634-8230 (U.S. and Florida) (305) 294-5702. Bruce Corneal, innkeeper. 24 units with AC, heat, ceiling fan, color cable TV, complete kitchen, pool, jacuzzi, direct-dial phone. Children of any age accepted. No pets. AmEx, MC, Visa. Rates: winter from $105 to $295 per one- or two-bedroom suite; summer from $75 to $135. 3rd person in 1-bedroom unit or 5th person in 2-bedroom unit $10. Rates include continental breakfast.

Key West – LA CONCHA
Savvy street scene loosens up Holiday Inn stodginess.

The new place for getting high in Key West is the same place for looking down on natives and tourists. No disdain meant. We're talking high-rise. Key West's first in 1926, and still tallest building. The magic of millions has transformed the long-time drab shell of La Concha into the green-awninged pink life of the party.

The view from atop seven floors was always spectacular, but for a long time the hotel beneath was shuttered. When La Concha opened in the boom years, the *Key West Citizen* said it was just in time. The city had a "reputation none too good due to its lack of sufficient hotel accommodation." In those days guests stayed only a night or two before riding the ferry to Havana.

Even if Key West hasn't lacked rooms lately, La Concha, larger than life but wasting away, was about as appealing as a port-a-potty at a banquet. Duval Street deserved better.

Today the revived hotel, as anyone driving the Overseas Highway knows from its billboards, promotes the old town's spirit of artful living, of leisure and history tied together like the convergence of the Atlantic and the Gulf of Mexico that's part of the visual lagniappe from the hotel's rooftop.

The best of this town is still daily and plebeian. The most imaginative store windows can't compare with the self-styled fashion that parades buxom young bicycling women in halter tops pedaling a tot or a pup in a handlebar basket, gold-chained yuppies toting shopping bags from Fast Buck Freddies, and map-in-hand camera-groomed tourists more intent on the passing scene than precisely locating themselves.

Most people on Duval Street rediscover the pleasures of walking. People, when they're walking, like that nothing passes faster than a bike—even if it's a car.

La Concha adds to the scene a streetfront that's already slightly dissolute by 11 in the morning. There's a more subdued off-street motor entrance for guests checking into its refurbished accommodations. This set-apartness lets guests in need feel protected by an enclave on the island, a retreat for visitors who more want to tease than go all the way—or at least feel better about a little debauchery in a setting that leaves them feeling in control.

The hotel lobby is soft and dreamy, lush in taped jazz and potted palms. The bright subtropical light slants through geometric glass walls. The crowded style of life on a small island reflects subtly inside in the steps and dividers that make of the lobby a tight cluster of uniformed service stations, conversation areas, lounge for bar service, and dining room. It's a close-together urban space that concedes to the faster pace guests are getting away from, while by pastel colors and reliance on natural lighting instead of artificial, the space helps assert a tropical claim on urban gusto that guests can use as a bridge for crossing more into the local style.

Though operating today under a Holiday Inn franchise, the hotel is no cookie-cut replica of standard design. Four years were spent restoring it to its grand dame status. As writer Jane Sutton describes, "The architect, owners, builders and designers—working without original plans—dug through yellowed photographs, interviewed old-timers, and stripped away layers of wallpaper and paneling for clues to the original structure." The restoration won a 1987 award from the Historic Florida Keys Preservation Board.

Original guest rooms have been beautifully redone in coral, green, and blue versions, many enlarged or expanded, and matched in style by a new wing. Poster beds, armoires, and wallpapers are period reproductions. Chenille spreads, lace curtains, and white sturdy wicker bring back the Twenties look. Night tables, desks, and dressers are antiques as are bathroom accessory tables and wicker corner shelves. Louvered doors and transoms are dark-stained in the tropical plantation style. Hallways are unusually well treated with the same quality well-lit lamps, wallpaper, and carpeting. Decorative wall tiles designate room numbers.

Only second-floor rooms of the original section have balconies. These overlook Duval Street and are furnished with white Adirondack chairs. Planters separate one from the next. A swimming pool is on the mezzanine level.

Open-air bars for many years have been popular in Key West, and some were synonymous with Ernest Hemingway and Tennessee Williams. (Hemingway placed bootlegger Harry Morgan in *To Have and Have Not* at La Concha, and Williams lived at the hotel while completing *A Streetcar Named Desire*.) Crazy Daizy'z at La Concha (athough it is air-conditioned) reflects the colorful saloons of yesteryear decorated in the rum-runner tradition.

Good weather, which is most of the time, brings guests out onto the Play Doh-colored wood furniture of the roof among pots and trellises of colorful bougainvillea. A favorite perch is along the well-rubbed rail of aromatic cedar looking over the tightly packed townscape. Trees and tin roofs make up a tight plaid. Stipped between are communications antennas, flagpoles, church steeples, power plant stacks striped white and red.

Especially for first-time visitors, La Concha is a good choice for a Key West overview that is likely to bring them back for more intimate engagement on return visits.

La Concha (Holiday Inn), 430 Duval St., Key West, FL 33040. (305) 296-2991. 800-HOLIDAY. In FL: 800-227-6151. Terry Horton, general manager. 160 rooms including 2 suites with AC, heat, color cable TV, direct-dial phones, baths with tubs. Pool, gift shop, sundries shop, restaurants, bars. Balconies: 2nd floor rooms on Duval St. Children under 19 free in parents' room. Rollaway bed: $10. Non-smoking rooms available. All major credit cards. Rates from $70 to $275 depending on time of year and category. Average breakfast: $7; lunch: $12; dinner: $25. Parking free to guests. Handicap rooms.

Key West — LA MER

Queen Anne on the beach where the Mallory Square
sundown crowd likes to gather by day.

Around the corner from the ocean end of what the tour guides hype as the longest main street in the world (because it runs from the Gulf of Mexico to the Atlantic), La Mer has the minor distinction of being the only intimate lodging for Key West guests on the beach.

The beach is as small as the distinction, with coarse sand washed by grayish brown-blue water that deposits a seaweed fringe.

Still, the beach attracts a savvy Key West crowd who leave the broader strand north of the new condos to more obvious tourists. Here instead by day come many of the sundown buskers who entertain at Mallory Square near the Gulf end of Duval Street.

Others, men wearing bandanas, earrings, and hibiscus flowers in their hair, entertain by their appearance. Still others create their own entertainment, like sanitation workers on a goof snickering about how to surprise a sunbather who has loosened her bra string while lying on her stomach.

The easygoing style, the all-you-can-eat Eatery, and the stand-out Southernmost House on the other side of Duval Street make this beachfront quarter especially attractive to guests at La Mer. Guests also can use a pair of swimming pools at nearby motels under the same ownership.

The house was built between 1900 and 1903 and for more than 75 years was lived in by kindred families. Louis Harris bought it in 1903. He was an attorney and brother of Judge Vining Harris, who built the Southernmost House. Both houses were in the Queen Anne style, the Judge's more resplendent to this day.

"They were very wealthy people," recalls Ingurtha Pinder, who in her 80s is last remaining of those with early memories of the Louis Harris house. She was the second Mrs. Luther Pinder, whose first wife was the sister of Louis Harris. Although Luther Pinder bought the house in 1920, Ingurtha Pinder never lived there.

"I had married Luther's brother, Greyburn. When he died, and after Luther's wife died, Luther gave the house to his daughter, and he and I lived together in my house on Flagler Avenue.

"But I was very intimate with the house. It was two stories, and much bigger than the Harrises needed because they never had any children. But people of wealth built big houses in those days whether they needed them or not.

"One evening when we were all playing cards, the top story caught fire and burned. That left the house with just one story. Later, when it was sold, those weren't the booming times, and it only brought $75,000."

The buyer in the early 1980s was a Frenchman named Didier Moritz. He changed none of the outside except for rebuilding the second story according to the original plans, and letting a slender palm that already poked through the first floor poke through the floor above, where it now towers over the lodging between two gabled second-story bays.

The outside of La Mer looks wonderful as it always has. Its gabled tin roof shines in the sun. Repainted white with dark gray trim, its balconies, bays, dormers, porches, spindles, turret and latticework fencing play hide-and-seek through swaying palm fronds for passersby along Front Street.

Those who enter find La Mer pleasantly modern and clean. Rooms are mostly furnished the same, attractive if nondescript, but varied in sizes and shapes. Colors are mauve, browns and beige, some orange tones, a little blue contrast in bed quilts, bud vases, and wall art. Upholstery is textured over cane and rattan furniture. Lamps, mirror frames, and headboards are of natural materials. A night table and desk are included in each room. Some rooms have sofa sleepers.

Beds are firm, floors are carpeted, ceilings are high–to 12 feet in some of the rooms. Downstairs rooms have porches; those upstairs, balconies. An attractive feature of No. 8 upstairs is a private porch with an awning that can be cranked down to ward off too much midday or early afternoon sun.

A few rooms come with their own kitchens that are nicely angled away from the bedchambers and separated by a small breakfast bar. There is an extra charge of $50 to set up the kitchen for any length of use, though it is waived for repeat guests who have left kitchens immaculate after prior visits.

Current owner Sigmund Blum, a Michigan architect who came to Key West on vacation in 1985 and decided to invest and stay, refers to La Mer as a small hotel. "We don't like the terminology guest house or inn," he says. "We are moving in the direction of being a bed-and-breakfast."

So far only a continental breakfast is served, but the Eatery more than suffices for nearby meals. You can order less than all you can eat and pay accordingly–though waitresses have also been known to pour all-you-can-drink coffee, genially shushing confessors, who admit to having already had refills, with a homey, "So who's counting?"

The restaurant is reached by a wooden walk across the sand that runs on the far side of a barrier of Spanish bayonet and cactus from the lodging. La Mer is close to the scene as well as secure from it.

La Mer, 506 South St., Key West, FL 33040. (800) 354-4455, (305) 296-5611. Sigmund Blum, owner. 11 rooms with private baths, tub, AC, heat, color TV, direct-dial phone (66¢ for each call), fan, pools (one heated), jacuzzis. All rooms but one with either balcony or porch, some with kitchen. Children 16 and older accepted. 3rd person in room $10. No pets. AmEx, MC, Visa accepted. Rates: winter $155-$230 single or double; rest of year $104-$144. Off-street parking.

Key West — LAMPPOST HOUSE

Restorative as a hammock. Just a few large rooms in a rich tropical setting, and owners who know to leave you alone.

With Debbie Rosenblum's enthusiasm for Key West, the 100-plus-year-old Lamppost House operates with the air of a place likely to keep on keeping on. Good to know in Key West, where four or five guest houses are for sale at any time. Or operators may be nearing burn-out or running low on personal commitment.

Lamppost House was one of those for sale just a couple years ago after Ed Carr and Casey Rafferty had made it, even if not well known, one of the places guests returned to year after year.

The house has its four units and a cottage that Casey used to run as a therapeutic hideaway for the over-stressed, and that Debbie has now made available to the rest of us only routinely stressed. The plant-plentiful site is at the end of a quiet street that backs to a city park and is across from married officers' quarters at the navy base. The site itself is restorative.

No surprise to hear Debbie say that Lamppost House guests aren't frantic tourists. That may be the last thing you hear before you nod off in a hammock. (Why don't all guest houses have them?)

New projects don't daunt Debbie. She and her husband Howard were urban pioneers in Chicago. He's a contractor. Together they brought back a huge house with four enormous four-bedroom, two-bath apartments in an iffy neighborhood.

"You had to be kind of gutsy to live there," Debbie recalls. "There were gangs and gunshot at night. You have to feel if an area is declining or on the upswing." Debbie helped determine that by becoming volunteer president for two years of the Humboldt Boulevard Association, and helping ensure that their tenants made the right choice by moving there.

Debbie and Howard had come to Key West on vacation because Howard had been here in the Navy. Debbie fell in love with the architecture. "The place was something you'd read about or see in the movies, so tropical. We thought we'd look at property."

Lamppost House was the first place they looked at and quickly the one they chose. "Key West is expensive," says Debbie, "but we're used to big price tags in Chicago."

Now Debbie and Howard are completing work on their own new home at 1200 Whitehead Street. That restored eyebrow house just around the corner and two houses down will be the check-in for Lamppost House.

Fortunately, not much had to be changed at their guest property. Lamppost

House fits amiably into the yard where it once was a carriage house, and long since has accommodated the lush plantings that cover and surround it. You would hardly think of it as a boxy four-unit house. It has more the feeling of a tree house with two spacious kitchen-equipped studios upstairs, two down, wide covered balconies up, open patios down.

Deep cleaning has done wonders for the studios with their large bedrooms that flow back from living areas entered by triple panes of sliding doors. All have queen or twin beds plus double or queen day beds—all firm and all with bright new floral bedspreads. Lighting is good. There is plenty storage space. Expect small modern bathrooms, varied wall art, accent rugs on carpet, wood, canvas, and upholstered furniture, with comfortable pieces on the porches and patios, ceiling fans, peaked open-beam ceilings upstairs. No particular look, just comfortable, casual, less thought out than thought about.

The cottage has a wraparound deck with spindles on two sides and another deck, all letting the breeze flow through the house. There are two bedrooms and a bath, living and dining rooms. Debbie has added a floral couch, comfortable upholstered chairs, and floral pictures. The dining room is a bright mint green. Guests have the use of an electric kitchen.

Between the cottage and the wood house is the pool with gardens all around. Orchid trees, gumbo limbo, mulberry, shefflera, frangipani, and palms shade the yard and the street, ignoring the lattice fence which nevertheless keeps the compound private. Hibiscus, bougainvillea, thunburgia, pencil cactus, and ferns out of the sun keep the space colorful.

Debbie serves a continental breakfast poolside from 8:30 to 10:00. The jacuzzi is available until midnight.

The grown-in look of the place seems to reject notions of modern-day marketing, as if to say this place is for young people or old or gays or straights. It's for anyone who likes the feeling that nothing is about to change—certainly not while you're here, and not from year to year.

The place is as close to country as you get in Key West. Sounds come at you by the ones. A dog yelp. Palms riffled by the wind. The wafted Conch Train spiel, something about yellow fever once upon a time in Key West. Long ago has a liking for this place. Long ago is in for a long run here.

Lamppost House, 309 Louisa St., Key West 33040, (305) 294-7709. Debbie and Howard Rosenblum, owners. 4 studios and 1 2-bedroom, 1 bath cottage with AC, ceiling fan, color cable TV, bathroom, porch or patio, complete kitchen, clock and radio, heated pool, jacuzzi, floor heaters when needed, public phone by the pool. Children under 12 free. No pets. Rates: for studios Dec. 16-May14 $125; rest of year $80. MC, Visa. Rates for cottage on request. Rate includes continental breakfast. Each additional person $15. Dead-end street parking.

Key West — LA TE DA

Modest to deluxe lodgings in the action center of Old Town, a "must" while in Key West.

At the end of the road where everything stops but anything goes, only the sun rivals Lawrence Formica, the owner of La Terraza de Marti—now officially La Te Da, as everyone has called it all along. Only sunset at Mallory Square attracts the loyalty of Key Westers as much as his tea dances and charity balls do. Every day at his small European hotel is an affair of the town's heart.

By his innovations in style and hospitality at La Te Da, he suggests the limits of public behavior. That the limits stretch sometimes to include topless sunning at his poolside restaurant offends maybe a few gays, who otherwise celebrate with him their fullest emancipation anywhere in America in this fantasy-rich town where he has become chief fantast.

For those who let nothing escape them, La Te Da is the place to be.

Its 18 rooms are only part of the scene, and no offense meant, they're strictly for tourists. They range from small and comfortable, to suites set up like a Manhattan penthouse—or what else do you call vacationing with a private jacuzzi, Oriental rugs, stereo cassette system, microwave oven, wet bar, make-up mirror, bottled water, pink carnations, Godiva chocolates?

Good as they are, the suites are almost afterthoughts because Lawrence's mind trips more engagedly over the here and now of Key West for which he has, for many years now, been the standard for what the place is about.

He was already successful as retailer, impresario, builder, when in 1977 he came to Key West to build a few apartments for income and a place to stay until spring warmed Philadelphia. He chose a house once the exile home of Cuban patriot Jose Marti that had become dilapidated beyond the glamorous end of Duval Street. Four apartments led to a few more, to a cook, a waiter, a manager, computerized reservations.

Over time his place has become a pink wooden compound packed to its balconies and bougainvillea with people who can't resist his stagy version of what otherwise in Old Town has taken decades to evolve naturally. It's his flamboyant energy that charges the place up and makes it popular with banker types and politicos as well as the gays for whom it was a rendezvous back when the idea was shocking. Everyone now comes to eat and drink, to see and be seen, to be a part of the excitement when languor is aroused and only shuts down in exhaustion.

Today La Te Da is impressive not only for the daily goings on, but for its arty influence on the ways things get done around town.

Until the end of 1985 Key West remained largely controlled by the "bubbas," old-timers with ties to the Spaniards and the wreckers who gave the town its easy-to-get-along early 19th-century style. A fortuitous federal project of the 1930s to revitalize the town combined the arts and tourism and sparked a new economy. In time, after the navy pulled out, and later when drug-trafficking got notoriously risky, control passed to a mix of preservationists, developers, gays, and those like Lawrence who could work their quality-of-life concerns into a year-round series of celebrations the rest of America could believe as real and buy into.

Lawrence calls Key West "a tropical island with something to do. All the advantages of the U.S. and none of the hang-ups."

Some of the events are aimed at tourists, some more for home folks, but even these, as word gets out, bring the visitors down. Any excuse will do.

Fantasy Fest is the Halloween orgy. There's the January Key West Literary Seminar. Old Island Days in late winter celebrates history and preservation. Conch Republic Day, April 23rd, commemorates the mock secession provoked by massive traffic jams when the Border Patrol in 1982 began searching cars for illegal drugs. Hemingway Days are in late July.

Among Lawrence's special credits have been the Alice in Wonderland, Derby Day, Dreamland, and Stardust & Memories fund-raisers—that last one for the Monroe County Fine Arts Council that included everything in black and white—except for 1,000 roses—cigaret girls, pages, limousines, and the Guy Lombardo Orchestra.

Regular but not ordinary are the Sunday tea dances that locals say give them the only occasion worth dressing up for, and that have become a must for everybody new on the island, these days including the sometimes thousands who fill condos, hotels and motels looming on the edge of Old Town. In summertime, weekenders from Miami and Fort Lauderdale stay an extra day for the Sunday event, driving home Mondays.

La Te Da stays attuned to where the mainstream would like to be tomorrow. Everybody is on roller skates. Everything has a place like in a dream where order needn't be comprehensible. So much is pink that you think the place might suddenly flap off like a flamingo, leaving a trail of stardust blown into shape and use.

You cannot believe that across the street is a working car garage. La Te Da is a movie. Some people have trouble readjusting to daylight.

La Te Da, 1125 Duval St., Key West, FL 33040. (305) 294-8435. Lawrence J. Formica, proprietor. 18 rooms and suites with AC, heat, ceiling fan, all but two with private bathrooms, some with tub, color TV, pool, direct-dial phone. Children not accepted. Pets if small and well-behaved may be accepted. Major credit cards. Restaurants and bars. Rates vary by location, time of year, time of week. Dec. 16-April 15 $178-$183 double; rest of year $48-$108 double during the week, and $58-$128 Friday, Saturday, Sunday nights. Breakfast and lunch from $5.95 to $16; dinner from approximately $20 up with 4-course prix fixe dinner at $29.95.

Key West – MARQUESA HOTEL
Refined and unexcelled.

You can only believe that a genie was rubbed from the lamp to transform the southeast corner of Simonton and Fleming Streets from a food market, a car dealership, and a bike shop over the last 100 years into the exquisite small hotel and restaurant called the Marquesa.

Talk about kissing a frog!

The Marquesa is all about color, texture, and shape, not to overlook service, style, and comfort. But its sea-blue-green sides trimmed in white, with its green shutters, its tin roof over dormers, and its great flights of exterior stairs that trail up to bedrooms, define the Marquesa as inspiration as much as lodgings, and remind you there's more to life than just finding a roof over your head.

Where elsewhere there are lobbies, the Marquesa provides a common room of upholstered comfort, antiques, and reproductions. Botanical prints are framed under glass, the music is classical, jazz, and New Age, and the floral arrangements are colorful yellow fuji mums, pastel astromerias, and laqueur-red anthuriums. Atop a glass table are neat rows of the pictoral magazines.

Rooms of the Marquesa are not Victorian or gingerbread. They establish themselves more formally with mahogany dressers and fine millwork. But they relax in your gaze. You stand admiring any room before you enter.

In one, the sloping ceilings are highlighted by a bathroom door cut at a slant. In another, apple potpourri scents the air. The fans are timed only to waft rather than to cool. The air-conditioner takes care of that.

A junior suite in beige twinkles lavender: lavender accents on throw pillows, on chair cushion, below glass on magazine covers, on fabric-topped tables in far corners, on a tufted utility bench at the foot of the queen-sized bed, on the quilted cover.

The mood of another traipses through a Deco arrangement of flowers and greens, by a high-tech Hong Kong telephone, a Victorian armoire, a pair of rattan chairs, and lamp-base Chinoiserie, all pulled together by the print of the drapes, bedcover, and sofa pillows. No energy escapes outward to be lost.

Shower stalls close with assurance. Bath table and floors are marble. The twin pedestal lavatories have fluted bases and twin gilded octagonal mirrors. There are more and different lights (including double heating lamps) than on some city streets. White towels are thick as parkas. A cane caddy holds Caswell-Massey toiletries, including a bar of glycerine soap. Heating lamps are on timers. Their soft click may be the only sound you hear in these sound-proofed rooms.

Poolside is pleasingly green-blue, trimmed in white. It isn't large. A traveler palm is perfectly flanked by bird of paradise palms. Under an umbrella here, you can enjoy a superb continental breakfast of freshly-squeezed orange juice, pecan toast, homemade granola with Michigan dried cherries, and freshly brewed coffee.

The house that became the Marquesa was built in 1884 as a private residence of James Haskins, but became a boarding house by about 1900. It had 21 rooms. For the Marquesa, these were remodeled to nine, each with private bath. Two small buildings were added and attached, bringing the total number of rooms to 15.

When it first opened, the restaurant was the acclaimed Mira's. Lately it has been the more successful, and locally popular, Marquesa Cafe, with 15 tables and banquettes, mahogany bar, and open kitchen with a trompe l'oeil pantry mural.

The Marquesa is the work of Richard Manley and Erik deBoer, well regarded general contractors in Key West. Architect Tom Pope designed the restoration and new buildings. The project earned the only Master Craftsmanship Award for 1988 issued by the Historic Florida Keys Preservation Board. The property is on the National Register of Historic Places. Erik's wife, Carol Wightman, is manager. It is wonderful that they didn't run out of money before finishing, and that they didn't lose faith that their care would justify the rate. Find out why for yourself.

Marquesa Hotel, 600 Fleming St., Key West, FL 33040. (800) 869-4631 (North America), (305) 292-1919. Carol Wightman, manager. 15 rooms, suites with bath, AC, heat, 12 with ceiling fan, color cable TV, direct-dial phone, heated pool. Children of all ages accepted, free in parents' room to 16. No pets. AmEx, MC, Visa. Rates: Dec. 17-Apr. 8: $165-$260; Apr. 9-Apr. 29: $140-$215; Apr. 30-Dec. 16: $105-$175, includes fresh flowers, ice, turndown service with fresh towels, Godiva chocolates, cotton bathrobes, floor-mounted safe, choice of 5 newspapers. $15 additional person in suites, junior suites. Restaurant, bar. Average prices: $5 expanded continental breakfast poolside or in room; $20-$30 dinner. Free off-street parking.

Key West – MARRIOTT'S CASA MARINA RESORT

Flagler's legacy; corporate-style luxury on the beach in Margaritaville.

Spectacle extends out the Overseas Highway like a sentence of run-on superlatives that Key West pokes stop to with an exclamation point.

Language goes limp in the shimmer of sunset, the way subsequent history pales in the afterglow of that spectacular achievement when, in 1912, at a cost of $20 million and the seven-year labors of 3,000 men, Henry M. Flagler completed his railroad that connected what once had been Florida's wealthiest city–soon to be poorest–to the mainland.The Key West extension emphatically linked Flagler in the public mind with railroads, though trains for him at first were secondary investments for reaching his hotels.

The hotel he promised at the end of the line opened eight years after his death in 1921. Maybe because of its posthumous completion, the Casa Marina has lived and died the lives of a cat. It lives today as Florida's finest chain hotel of historical distinction.

The Casa Marina linked the temperate and tropical worlds. Equidistant from the North American mainland and Cuba, the hotel early on mixed calypso and corporate style. Today palms rustle, computers whirr.

Key West slips in and out of vogue. Fire, hurricane, depression have all battered its popular hold. The Casa Marina enjoyed only 10 good years through the Twenties before losses closed it. Its reopening for Christmas, 1934, was part of an ambitious federal scheme to revive bankrupt Key West–once wealthy from salvage, then from cigarmaking, later from sponges–as a mecca for tourists.

Frustration struck with the 1935 Labor Day hurricane that destroyed the railroad. Would-be visitors were left with the multiple but dubious travel choices of on-and-off ferries, the novelty of air, or the old way by steamer.

Business continued in fits and starts for 30 more years by operators who included the navy during World War II, the army during the Cuban Missile Crisis, the Peace Corps in the mid-Sixties. After that the place was shut altogether.

The savior came from Baltimore, a man named Stephan Alex who had rehabbed the old Stafford Hotel there. That was 1972 when hotels were dark in downtowns everywhere. Trade journals played up the revival. Key West native John Spottswood, who had come to own the Casa where he had worked as a child, flew Steve Alex in.

"Key West was down," Steve recalls. "The navy base was closed. Duval Street was just about empty. It was hard to attract financing. We eventually got two and a half million from a Chase banker. A brave guy. He really liked the old hotel.

"The plumbing was antiquated and the electrical system had to be replaced. But the structure was sound except for the wooden beams underneath. These were rotting out because the hotel had a massive water supply system that served the entire city. There was no navy pipeline, no desalinization plant in the early days. Just that tank under the hotel."

The first group of investors brought in a second with $13 million more and Marriott management. In 1978 the hotel reopened as the Marriott Casa Marina Resort.

Today marketing dictates that business meetings are as important as tourists. Guest rooms, now up to 314, including two new wings, the first void of historic character, the newer wing better in keeping, are comfortably conservative. They support the style of executive life more than they induce play. Bathrooms are awash in napery. Bedrooms—and living rooms of suites—are complete with gadgetry, neutral in color. Nothing is missing that a corporate hand deems worth giving.

Grand dimension and tropical exuberance survive in the lobby, the loggias, everywhere outdoors from grassy gardens, poolside, and onto the beach. Texture and color abound where guests inevitably play in swimwear and sporty plaids. Dining in Henry's is presidential.

Chain management doesn't get ahead of its market. It manages it. At the Casa Marina hundreds of guests and employees move through a luxurious setting as expected. It is not laid-back Key West. Henry Flagler was no laid-back guy. The Casa Marina has revived true to its corporate origins. Guests who come for what it offers receive value for money—and a grand helping of history.

Marriott's Casa Marina Resort, 1500 Reynolds St., Key West, FL 33040. (305) 296-3535. Michael Tierney, general manager. 314 rooms and suites with AC, heat, bathrooms with tub, color cable TV, direct-dial phone (local calls 80-cents; LD surcharge), elevators, restaurants, bars, pool, health club, lighted tennis courts, whirlpool, beauty salon, game room, gift shops, courtesy airport service, beach, turndown service on request, newspaper, night-time mints in high season. Children of any age accepted, free in parents' room to 18. Extra person in room $25-$35 (depending on season). No pets. All major credit cards. Rates: Dec. 21-May 17: $210-$695; May 18-July 12: $155-$415; July 13-Oct. 4: $135-$415; Oct. 5-Dec. 22: $155-$415. Inquire about special packages. Buffet breakfast $9.50 ($4.75 for children under 12); Sunday brunch $24.95 ($12.50); lunch $6.95 up; dinner $17 up. Complete water sports center. Off-street parking. No-smoking rooms.

Key West — MERLINN GUEST HOUSE
Wide range of rooms, but all guests share in good public spaces and homelike socializing

Key West guest houses do more for the continuity of Old Town than the people who run them. Not to disparage anyone's contribution, but people come and go. Once restored, the houses attract newcomers to look after them.

When the right restorer comes up with the right concept, and guests return year after year, next owners usually stick with it.

No question about it: what makes Key West special is that elsewhere so much of heritage has been lost. Here let eccentricity flourish if that's what it takes to keep the spirit alive.

Hence when Pat Hoffman came to Merlinn it wasn't so much to change what Stuart Gold and Jay Richards had done, but to preserve and adapt.

Merlinn remains the same oasis of Orientalia hidden behind its little stone wall and fence on Simonton Street. Here as before are the same Japanese gates, the pools and plantings, wood carvings, fabric kites, bestiary, arched wooden bridges, all overhung by frangipani, poinciana, and hibiscus among the ficus trees.

Same as before, the placid gardens provide entry to the animated spaces where guests mostly gather, the open deck by the pool for leisurely breakfast, and the spacious bi-level living room where evenings guests mingle for cocktails before nights on the town.

Innkeeper Pat Hoffman and assistant Kathy Klingerman serve breakfast between 8:30 and 11 from the airy high-ceilinged kitchen where Stuart the impresario used to dominate.

But of course the quiche is no less flavorful, the muffins and biscuits equally fresh each morning, and even if the jams are no longer blended with Grand Marnier, the service continues accompanied by soft music. The level of care is undiminished.

"The space remains an island within an island," says Kathy. "Guests feel like they're staying in a friend's house. Our fence calls so little attention to itself that people, unless they're coming to Merlinn, don't even know it's here.

"I like to believe that how we do things reflects the same spirit. We all do everything. I can play in the garden, cook, do the quiche for breakfast, help fix up rooms. In a place like this you want to do everything. You want to feel yourself part of the spirit of the place."

Pat came from Ohio, where she had been a professional social worker, divorced, and looking for change. After the idea of running a guest house, she returned home and apprenticed herself for a year at the Honey Run Inn in Millersburg.

"Though Merlinn is much smaller, I liked it as soon as I saw it among maybe eight guest houses I'd been shown. People can be a little apart here or easily mix together.

"After I decided on it, so many of the staff at Honey Run gave up their vacations to come down and help me work here and see Key West. My friend Kathy was one, and she has stayed on."

Pat came to stay in December, 1986. She repainted, put on a new roof, improved the electrical, put in fire alarms. She brought the place up to code so that returning guests find a spruced-up look that reaffirms Merlinn as it was. New are two aviaries with finches and cockatiels.

There are five full apartments and 13 more varied guest rooms. The early rooms of the house, which was built as a tiny hotel for dubious purpose in the 1940s, are still windowless and small—almost monkish, minimally furnished, though by being kept scrupulously clean with improved lighting and colorful linens, they almost shine and so appear brighter.

Better are the new guest quarters, the Pool House, Patio House, Deck House, and best, the Tree House. These are lavish spaces for guest house vacationing. Some of the juxtapositions remain unfathomable: Greco-Roman faux columns among the rattan and paper flowers.

The Tree House has a private sundeck and broad view over pool and gardens, high-ceilinged, open-beamed. It's airy, wonderfully open to a three-way breeze, walls covered in straw, so you feel there's only the skin of a shelter that's otherwise open. A few throw rugs are on polished pine floors, with cross ventilation also in the bathroom.

The parlor is rich in Orientalia, set off by potted palms, cornplants, cut flowers, against walls filled with stero equipment, records, and books.

Now in place of Jay Richards' sophisticated baby grand piano stylings there's a player piano that makes evening cocktails a little less formal and more down-home.

Says Michael Bishop, a helper from when Jay and Stuart ran Merlinn and still here today, "The atmosphere is perfect for guests getting to know each other. Some people come to Key West a little afraid about guest houses. Once they try they never want anything else."

Past guests do return. Some remark that for a change, it's agreeable to find a woman's touch. Old Town guest houses continue to choose their innkeepers well.

Merlinn Guest House, 811 Simonton St., Key West, FL 33040. (305) 296-3336. Pat Hoffman, innkeeper. 18 rooms with AC (except 2), some with heat, all with fans, private baths (some with tubs), color or black and white TV. Central pay phone, pool, whirlpool. Well-behaved children and small dogs accepted. AmEx, MC, Visa. Rates: Apr. 16-Dec. 19: single $36 to $79, double $59 to $79; Dec. 20-Apr. 15: single $45 to $84, double $72 to $94. $15 extra per person over 2 in suites. Rates include full breakfast and evening cocktails.

Key West – THE MERMAID & THE ALLIGATOR

Stylish, contemporary, especially good for
vacationers who like looking after themselves.

Ursula and Michael Keating are sophisticated people who have slivered a subtle innkeeping slice from the loaf of life's possibilities. They attend to guests, but don't spoon feed. If you need them you can find them. Guests sense they are being looked after by looking after themselves. That's how Michael and Ursula like to be treated. It's how they discovered Key West.

They needed a getaway from fast-paced lives in TV. They drove to Key West.

They had booked two nights at a guest house. Nice place, but nobody bothered to serve breakfast. Both mornings, Ursula and Michael stepped in. The other guests loved it. So did the owner. He asked Ursula and Michael to stay another two days as his guest. Then he asked them to house sit for another 10. Ursula and Michael started looking at real estate.

The house they bought on Truman Avenue was built in 1904 by a city attorney. Later Mayor John Malone lived here. Malone was defeated in the early 1930s when he tried to shut down the bars on Duval Street. An owner during the 1950s and 1960s, when the town was pretty much broke, started taking guests.

Ceilings had to be replaced, and plumbing and electrical updated. Ursula and Michael added the pool and deck, and a breakfast area under a shed roof under lacy poinciana and gumbo limbo trees.

Rooms were completely redone.

"My taste," says Ursula, "is not inexpensive. You can't have fabric furniture and shared baths. You can't just have a daughter's room, that after she moves out you rent for the money. Rooms should be different, built on people's fantasy. All the people who have never slept in a four-poster bed should have the chance to do that on vacation. Every room has to be a little stage setting."

Most everyone enters through the kitchen from the shuttered, gabled, and latticed back of the house, because the car park's there. Busy Truman Avenue can be noisy.

The living room contrasts upholstered sculptural sofas with hardwood floors and walls of Dade County pine. Though the walls are unfinished, the floors are lightly polished and dressed with silk Bokhara rugs from Ursula's parents' house in Vienna. Ursula has added smart caneback and empire pieces, and a brilliant efflorescent painting of faces masked by a luminous burst of color.

Hallways are exceptional, downstairs with a free-standing armoire, a rack for umbrellas and canes, a full wall of books, and a pew bench. Up a veritable forest of spindle balusters, the second floor displays a gallery's worth of Haitian, scenic, and abstract paintings, a piece of Art Nouveau stained glass, and a lovely dusty blue armoire.

The Garden Room downstairs is modern, with tile floors and Oriental furnishings. The shower feels like it's outdoors, with its triangular window atop. There are double doors to the garden.

Upstairs, the Blue Room has the four-poster of Ursula's dream for guests, a big soaking tub, and balcony on two sides. Sets of double doors in cypress and Cuban mahogany have glass insets and European-style brass hardware, all exquisitely detailed. The Pink Room is airy and looks into the royal poinciana tree with its cereus cactus. A chrome glass side table imparts a Deco touch.

Smallest of the five rooms, the little Sun Room has five shuttered windows. The entire room is a bay. It's wickery bright and faces west.

The rooftop suite is up a private angular staircase. The eave of the house triangulates space. There are rough-finished rafters and an oatmeal-textured carpet. To one side is a sitting area, to the other the bedchamber with a very firm queen bed and desert-toned designer bedding. Color is subdued. Here, as throughout the house, the best goose-down pillows are used. There are books by John Hersey, Bill Cosby, Stewart Alsop, Anne Tyler, Calvin Trillin, John Erlichman.

Breakfast is convivial. Guests sit around the mother-in-law-tongue wood table, with Michael's fresh-squeezed orange juice, fresh fruits, rye bread, cold platter of eggs, avocados, cheeses, cold cuts, coffee and tea. Guests might be from England, Trinidad, or Ohio, typically swapping stories about glass-bottom boat rides and the joys of East Martello Towers.

The deck extends two levels around to an octagonal jacuzzi, with cushioned deck chairs, and gay beach towels in straw baskets. Budgees twitter in a cage. Chimes ring in the breeze atop baskets of yellow mums and orchids. By the pool stands a statue of a mermaid and an alligator. Guests can figure out most everything they need to know.

The Mermaid & The Alligator, 729 Truman Ave., Key West, FL 33040. (305) 294-1894. Michael and Ursula Keating, innkeepers. 5 rooms, suites, all with bath (all with showers, 2 with tubs), 2 with AC, 1 with heat, all with ceiling fan, fresh flowers, color cable TV in living room, house phone for free local calls, no surcharge for credit-card LD calls, large jacuzzi. Children 17 and up. No pets. 3rd person in room $20. All major credit cards. Rates: May 1-Fantasy Fest (Hallowe'en celebration), $60-$85; rest of year $85-$145, all rates single or double occupancy. Rate includes full European (cold) breakfast. Off-street parking.

Key West — THE PALMS
Commenably revived at the east end of Old Town.

Sleuthing and luck—plus bucks—are reviving this historic property at the eastern fringe of Old Town.

The Palms before had had the right look up top, where its picturesque turret and cupola showed, but all that was available to guests were two flanks of motel-like rooms. These are still here, but newly deep-cleaned and lightened in color, and what's up front at least is more than facade.

The property was developed by John Sherman Williams in the mid-1880s. It was one of a group of splendid houses along White Street that he built for his prospering family, which owned most of the block. They were early saloon keepers and dry goods retailers.

This house, finest of the group, stayed in the Williams family until the mid-1950s. Because it had a big lot behind, purchasers in 1978 saw guest house potential. The house featured hand-carpentered railings, bays, a three-sided porch, and a cupola tower full of gingerbread trim—perfect for fronting a motel-like addition they could put out back, figured Kees Vandegraff and Terry Clarkson, who were phtographers and merchandisers.

To their credit, Kees and Terry came on scene when the guest house trade was still new. Superficial charm was better than none at all. Kees and Terry installed themselves in the grand Victorian space atop their acquisition and put guests in the easy-care new spaces out back. Guests were happy because Kees and Terry were terrific hosts. They featured poolside cookouts.

It was Kees and Terry, their world adventure stories, and Kees's affability in talking religion, politics, and all about Key West's "latitudes and attitudes" that attracted a clan following here to the White Street edge of Old Town.

Kees was one of the first to talk about "burnout, the time it takes for you to lose your illusions and give up the dream of running a guest house. People think it's very romantic," he would say. "You start up, you give your life to it. You turn all the space over to your guests, you leave yourself a bedroom and a sitting room. But you need more than that and you have to get away. People quit because they can't stand it anymore. New people take over. Five years is about it."

Kees and Terry lasted 10. New owner Bruce Corneal is an investor more than merely a guest house operator. But he cares about preservation. Regardless of how long he stays, his aesthetic commitment has made a big difference to The Palms.

For years the beautiful palm gardens and porches of this property were hidden from the street behind high fencing. To enter, guests had to push a security buzzer that had all the charm of big-city paranoia. That fence is gone now. The whole front of the house has been opened to its palms and other plants, some new.

The opaque fence is to be replaced—maybe has been by now—by four-foot-high, recessed, see-through pickets. These reproduce the original fencing, thanks to a piece of the original found underneath one of the neighboring Williams' family houses.

Next door a little horror of a one-story concrete commercial building that was built in front of one of the old houses is to be torn down. This will allow expansion of the Palms to a second house, and afford off-street parking.

Also restored are the original doors of The Palms. Bruce assumed they had been lost long ago. Then he found out that Kees and Terry had just removed them one day. Williams' family members had rescued them, but couldn't remember, some seven years back, where they'd put them. Bruce found them, still with original pediments in place. These two sets of French doors are now back, top panels in glass, bottoms of raised moldings and mother-of-pearl knobs. To mark their re-installation, the entire house has been repainted a soft peach color, and the gingerbread trim a lacy white.

Inside, sheetrocking has been removed to re-expose wood walls. Wicker has replaced an old, cheap lobby desk. Ceiling fans have been installed. The tacky little kitchen by the entry is being converted to another guest room. Dade County pine floors have been refinished.

Upstairs, a half dozen rooms are being completed and will be filled with antiques. A duplex turret suite with red Dade County pine floors is likely to be a standout. It is reached by a wrought-iron spiral staircase.

Though removed from the heart of Old Town, The Palms is also away from the hustle of Duval Street. It's a 10-minute bike ride to the island's best public beaches, a 10-minute drive to the airport. No doubt Bruce's improvements will spur further restoration efforts in the neighborhood, where many historic properties await the sleuthing and luck of others.

The Palms, 820 White St., Key West, FL 33040. (800) 558-9374, (305) 294-3146. Bruce Corneal, innkeeper. 23 rooms with baths, AC, ceiling fan, color cable TV, push-button phone (60¢ for local calls, surcharge for LD calls), refrigerator for guest use, pool. Children accepted. No pets. AmEx, MC, Visa. 3rd person in room $10. Rates: Dec. 22-May 15, $129-$149; rest of year, $59-$89. Limited off-street parking.

Key West — THE POPULAR HOUSE
Easygoing, happy guest mix in a ship's carpenter's house.

Jody keeps the door open. She understands Key West. She loves Key West. She has the long view. She's been here since the 1970s, long enough for it.

Before she opened The Popular House, Jody was tending bar at the Pier House. She managed their gourmet food shop. She ran the Bagatelle Restaurant. She owned a tiny bar on Appelrouth Lane. All the time there was this innkeeper trying to get out.

When it happened, December of '87, Jody was so up for it that she streaked through the mess and neglect of the house in four days and opened with all seven rooms filled. Today, when other places are half empty, Jody is still at the max.

Why? It has to do with keeping the door open.

So who's afraid? Jody has Sam and Dave, two of the friendliest golden retrievers around. It helps, too, that she's single and likes to meet people. Ask guests how they feel about the house and they'll tell you to give it five stars.

The house is comfortable, and Jody knows her town. She's brought much of the best of it inside, and tells guests how to find the best outside.

The house is a two-story ship's carpenter's house, all pink clapboard with white jigsaw bracketing, turned baluster porch rails, and picket fence. The yard has areca palms and ficus trees, with a huge saguaro cactus that follows the rows of thin white double columns up the two stories.

It was built in 1898 for a wife who threatened to leave her husband. She did anyway. But at least he had the house. For much of the century it stayed in the William Russell family, for a time a guest house, then for much of the Eighties a fat farm, since moved elsewhere in town.

The seven rooms have board walls with big bright copies of Gauguins or Key West paintings. A pair of signature features are the top sheet of beds bunched and folded in a rosette centered decoratively between double sets of pillows, and colorful large serapes sashed across beds and rockers. Beds are firm enough, likely with one lamp between twin doubles. Straw rugs cover wood floors. Barefoot feels good in this house.

The two downstairs rooms have private baths. The five upstairs share two in the hall. One room upstairs is a little single. The downstairs front room has two high windows that open onto the porch, where there are four Adirondack chairs. These and the sofa, loveseat, and hammock upstairs are front row for the passing theater of William Street. To the accompaniment of Jody's morning Vivaldi, a woman passes in a baseball cap pedaling her big-basket bike. Palms and greenery wave in the breeze, shadow-dappling white-posted, balustered house fronts and sloping tin overhangs. The order of good taste reigns prominent as a

Victorian bosom, though a less prim humor hangs in the air.

Breakfast bursts from the kitchen on a huge wood tray of freshly cut tropical fruits. Jody squeezes her own orange juice. She makes her own sticky buns. Freshly brewed Cuban coffee accents the living room and turns the breeze out open windows pungent through the neighborhood. Comfortably cushioned guests adopt a decorum that bespeaks one big family all unusually happy, with intense tete-a-tetes, typically intellectual, chewing over last evening's production at the Tennessee Williams Theater, or the virtues of Caribbean style.

Wood and straw, cane and wicker, and ceiling fans set the tropical mood. Books include *Different Drummers, Florida Landscape Plants, I'm With the Band: Confessions Of A Groupie.* All the doors and windows are open.

The wall art is eclectic, modern splash-and-dash to Aztec primitive, Audubon prints, and the bold, pink, and balmy Keys watercolors of David Harrison Wright. Wood floors here and there are covered with floor cloths, copies of 18th-century floor coverings that were forerunners of linoleum. Plants brighten every corner and shelf.

Jody helps guests to offbeat and inexpensive pleasures. When it rains she shoos them out to the above-ground cemetery. She can get guests a half-day on the water for $25. She sends them to Fort Zachary Taylor for $1.50. She'll send them to the bike rental to spend a day just getting lost. She recommends the Key West Museum at East Martello Towers, one of the red brick forts from the 19th century.

"I'll always live in Key West," says Jody. "Something gets in your bones. Life is just too free. You don't have to pass muster with anyone. Everywhere people are creative here, writers, painters, cooks, and you never have to dress up."

What's good for Jody is good for her guests. No wonder she calls her place The Popular House.

The Popular House, 415 William St., Key West, FL 33040. (305) 294-3630, 296-7274. Jody Carlson, innkeeper. 7 rooms, 2 with private bath, 5 share 2 hall baths (shower and tub), with AC, 2 with heat, ceiling fan. House phone available (no charge for local calls, no LD surcharge). Not a good house for children. No pets. AmEx, MC, Visa. Rates: in-season (Dec. 15-end-Apr.) $75 (for the 1 single room) to $115; rest of year $45-$85, includes full breakfast. On-street parking.

Key West — SEASCAPE
Sailor-suit trim and legitimately theatrical.

It's unpretentious but nonetheless show biz at the little white and blue-trimmed clapboard house on Key West's Olivia Street just off Duval.

The lawyer Alan Melnick and performer Danny Weathers were only looking for a business to take them out of New York, a place to invest savings and start new lives.

They made the move that pharmacists, accountants, bankers, window trimmers, and all you can name have made before them, heady about Key West. They opened a guest house.

Theirs, called Seascape (not on the water), is one of the oldest and smallest. Though they can't date it exactly, when they started tearing out walls in the insulation they found sheets from an 1886 newspaper. They've been told the house dates from '89. It's in the National Register of Historic Places.

Not long ago the building had been the annex for a Duval Street guest house, though Alan and Danny said it looked more like a flophouse when they bought it in mid-1986, just months after they'd first vacationed in Key West.

"The weather was so gorgeous in winter we fell in love with it," says Alan, 12 years a Manhattan lawyer and fed up.

"Right away I started comparing Key West with all those years I'd spent in New York. I was practicing maritime law, traveling all over the world. Sometimes you flew halfway around the globe for an overnight meeting. In New York it was subways.

"Here, you come downstairs and you're at work."

For Danny, most recently Gregory Gardener in "Chorus Line," the next move had to be for himself. No more auditioning, no more mouthing other people's lines.

"After 12 years on the New York stage, you need more than a creative line pause to make things different. I'd really had it with agents and casting directors. This is easier. Just the fact that the hours change whenever you want to is something different.

"New York is tough. Show business is tough. The two are meant for each other. But what an impossible way to live!

"Still Key West is a very theatrical town, too. I don't mean just show-offy. There are three theaters here and all do well. This is a town made for actors. I don't know anyplace else in America—outside of New York, of course—where tourists support theater the way they do here.

"After we had the house finished and were in the slow time of year, I sent my pictures and resume around. Amazing. I heard from all.

"That's a little different from the cold shoulder of New York."

So Seascape is the guest house where show biz people are made to feel welcome, a fillip to fill days differently for guests on this narrow street of modern houses and tall cactus.

It's three doors down from the Hemingway House, and a five-minute walk to the beach.

Blue shutters and blue-and-white awnings set Seascape apart in a town that prefers greens and yellows. It's the boutique look Bloomie's might install for a total Key West look. White picket fencing, white wicker and floral cushions, umbrella-topped tables with blue- and white-strapped lawn furniture, newly heated spa-pool, old transatlantic shipline prints: a classic winter fashion look.

There are five rooms to start, with two more possible in an upstairs apartment. All have pedestal-based queen-sized beds, firm and new; air conditioning, color TV, Bahama fans. Small bathrooms in each of the rooms have the basics.

While Danny works some theater into his schedule, Alan has been admitted to the Florida bar.

"I always liked the idea of a neighborhood practice," he says. "It's another way of helping us get known in town—though if one of us is going to bring home the business, let it be Danny with rave reviews."

Whoever comes will enjoy continental breakfast, the attentions of a friendly cat or two, bike racks, and the earnest hospitality of a couple of fellows eager to please.

Seascape, 420 Olivia St., Key West, FL 33040. (305) 296-7776. Alan Melnick and Danny Weathers, innkeepers. 5 rooms with baths, AC, ceiling fans, with color cable TV, house phone for incoming messages, pay phone for outgoing calls. Adults only. No pets. AmEx, MC, Visa. Rates: winter (December through April): $79-$94 single or double; summer (May through November): $59-$69. Includes continental breakfast, in-season sunset wine hour, spa-pool.

Key West – SIMONTON COURT
Three pools on two acres, rustic, one of a kind.

Ask Toby Nichols of Simonton Court and he'll tell you that what sets Key West apart is that "It has no moral standards whatsoever. It's live and let live. We don't consider it part of Florida at all. Somebody wrote that it's as if by mistake someone gave Key West a Florida zip code and area code."

His place combines what Key West is with what it was in a way that bespeaks easy liaisons.

You sense a creative high reaching to the sidewalk along Simonton Street where the pebble-laid, wood-fenced alley veers off. No security apparatus blocks curiosity about entering. Who doesn't like to discover pleasures tucked out of sight that reward our venturing to step out of line?

There's that camp feeling that must have been felt by artists who revived Monterey's Cannery Row or Manhattan's Soho. You can imagine that the first people who saw a future for Old Town guest houses had places like this in mind. It unfolds as a retreat of turns and textures that might approximate the arboreal possibilities of squirrelhood lived in the branches of great trees.

More so than any compound in Key West, Simonton Court has the out-island feeling of the Bahamas where so many of the settlers came from. The houses are spread over these almost two acres like in a small settlement, peak-roofed with canopied porches, simple like down any conch lane in the Abacos. Bright pastels color the clapboard behind porches set two or three stairs up from flowering shrubs. Hard as the sun beats, high arching boughs break the light into shady patches. A kind of "no-problem" languor hangs around.

The absence of directional signs is its own simple pleasure. You learn the lay of this spread the way you learn language. From use. No pointy signs to the nouns and the verbs. You might not find the office at first. You might discover one of the pools, then another, maybe the third. For that you will have walked past the Hurricane Alley cottages, and if they're open, explored their imaginative lofts, and if they're not, peered through their windows.

There's a kind of "Who was that masked rider?" feeling of admiration and wonder about this place. There's enough to be found from looking around that, coupled with the discovery of Key West itself, by the end of a stay you feel urged to come back. Places like this nest vagabond notions in your own tree.

In 1880, when the place was built, it was a Cuban cigar factory. The five cottages out back were housing for workers.

When the place was redone for guests, the idea was for minimum maintenance as a boon for owners and guests alike. So most of the furniture was built in. The look is modular, all wood. The idea of sparseness is as apparent as the uncluttered look that contrasts sharply with the century-old building, more spread out than most on the street, its appearance a little more plantation-style because of that.

The nine efficiencies make use of the original hardwood floors and walls, now with private baths and kitchens. It's not luxurious, but no longer spartan as it was a few years ago. The lustrous wood is set off by many windows with great fanfares of fan palms poking through—the thoroughly island aspect of the place. Straw rugs, straw chairseats, sectional mattresses that make up into sofas on pedestal bedframes all help make inside and outside informal and easy together.

The cottages are now all privately owned and so have widely varied looks. All but #6 remain rustic. That has a Miami Vice look with white plaster walls, green rattan, blue kitchen, and the only king-sized bed. Also #3 is dressed up with Deco prints and paintings. Some have upstairs beds tightly tucked under eaves, so watch your head. Only #2 still has a stretch of taut undisguised cable eye-hooked into opposite walls, designed to keep the cottage from blowing apart in a hurricane. Most cottages are now showing their hardwood floors and have floral cushions on rattan furniture. French doors have replaced sliding glass. There are skylights, and unfinished wood walls. Open kitchens have a rough-finish appearance. Exposed sleeping lofts are reached by ladder stairs. Almost all have private outdoor showers.

There are porch swings, private patios, and the three pools. Prettiest is set in a wood deck where black paint was worked into the gunite so the water reflects a black-cast blue. It seems jewel-like set apart in wood coping, surrounded by greenery, and off to one side a canvas-draped cabana that lends the whole space an oasis mood.

Toby came from stints with Hyatt and Westin hotels. Too corporate. He'd been managing a restaurant closed for the summer on Worth Avenue when he checked in for a three-day weekend. He never left. Bought the place in mid-'83 (has since sold the cottages but manages the rentals), and has been improving it since.

Despite the added dress-ups, Toby says he'll keep the rustic outdoor look. "That's the whole thing." The place remains so distinctive that not only is it not like the rest of Florida, even trendy Key West has hardly anything to do with this compound. Off-beat, but no longer off-the-wall.

Simonton Court, 320 Simonton St., Key West, FL 33040. (305) 294-6386. Toby Nichols, owner. Nine rooms with AC, some with heat, cable TV, clock radio, all with baths, ceiling fan, kitchens (only one with oven), telephones (60-cents for local calls, LD surcharge). Six cottages with first floor and loft sleeping spaces, AC, fan, all amenities (as in the rooms) plus full kitchens, bathrooms with tubs. Children under 18 not accepted. No pets. AmEx, MC, Visa. Rates: winter $90 to $145 main house; from $185 to $235 for cottage (up to 4); off-season, $70 to $105 main house; $145 cottage. 3rd person in room $10 winter, $5 off-season. Off-street parking 1 block away.

Key West — TROPICAL INN
Beautifully furnished little guest house on Duval Street.

Eunice Liebert, an Oklahoman from Midwest City, each winter returns to work at the downtown Tropical Inn. She arrives every October for Fantasy Fest. "I wouldn't miss it," she says. "They just act out everything!"

She is, according to the Tropical Inn's brochure, the "resident grandmother."

"We're the only guest house with a grandmother at work," says proprietor (and grandson) Dennis Beaver. "The visitors love her. Let the people make the messes. We'll clean up after them."

What makes Eunice a favorite, as she makes the beds and helps clean rooms, is her steady patter about Key West—which she loves—and the rest of the world, which she knows she has to live with. "Everybody in Key West calls me Grandma," says Eunice. "Dennis always called me Grandma. Then his friends started. Then it spread like wildfire.

"I'd never been on an island before. No, I take that back. I lived in California awhile. I'd been out around Alcatraz, but come to think of it, I never stopped.

"I'd love to live here, but I don't think I ever will. If I could find something I could afford I would. But what I could sell my house for in Midwest City would pay for just about half of one here."

"Midwest City is pretty lively, too. Dennis's brother is a policeman. He's been knocked down, but he's not afraid of anything. But we have good policemen—and women—here, too. This li'l ole girl here, she'll tackle anything. She'll catch 'em and make 'em put their hands right up on top of the car."

Dennis and Eunice offer a quiet style of hospitality. Talk about rarity! They don't intrude. They don't gush. Many guest house operators need their guests' approval more than they need their money. Their places are cloying like mangoes, perfumed like guavas. Dennis's is subtle as a pear.

There are five rooms and an apartment, most on the second floor of a house that's been around since at least 1840. Dennis is the first to take guests here.

It took him two vacations before he moved. He'd heard about Key West and stayed with friends. First he leased another place, lost the lease, then bought the place he calls Tropical Inn in 1983.

"You can earn a living if things work right," he says. "You have to have personality, a nice place. All the threads have to twine together. You meet people from all over, but you don't have to get attached to them.

"This place is very homey, yet completely cosmopolitan. You can be friendly or not. You don't have to talk with everybody here, as at a boarding house. You can be completely alone or mingle.

"We want to make everything the way we'd expect it to be if we went to a guest house. It's clean because we work at it. We'll answer any questions. But once people are in their rooms we want them to feel they're on their own."

The guest rooms are homelike, surprisingly clean on Duval Street (which didn't have the tidiest reputation when Key West was a navy town).

There is an aspect of connoisseurship about the rooms because of the quality of the wicker and furnishings. Things fit. You are aware of caring and intelligence at work. What you find are one-of-a-kind wicker and rattan furnishings, beiges, soft greens and yellows, lacy bedcovers, lots of Key West prints and posters, tightly woven nubby neutral carpets, green plants, louvered window shutters, ceiling fans, all rooms with private baths, air-conditioning, and clock radios.

Largest of the four is a wicker suite with an exquisite rattan chair that has a stowaway leg rest that pulls out to maybe 30 inches. The anteroom features an intricate cane, wood, and wicker free-standing storage unit. There is a private back porch with chairs overlooking the garden patio.

Even the smallest room doesn't feel tight. It, too, has a private porch.

Out front upstairs a balcony overlooks Duval Street with Kennedy rockers behind turned balusters.

No breakfast is served. There is no central lobby. So the rooms are meant for sleeping and times of day when you'd rather be quiet, out of the Key West hustle for awhile. From inside, in comfort and style, you might wonder whether what's outside is real. After a few days the inner and outer are less disjointed. Tropical Inn is a good place for entering into the mood of Key West.

Tropical Inn, 812 Duval Street, Key West, FL 33040. (305) 294-9977. Dennis Beaver, proprietor. Five rooms and apartment with AC, ceiling fans, private bathrooms, clock radios, balconies. Children of any age accepted, $10 for each additional person in room. $10 per day for pet. Discover, MC, Visa. Rates: single or double June 1-Oct. 31: $50-$110; Nov. 1-May 31: $55-$110.

Key West – WATSON HOUSE
Well appointed and wonderfully private.

Watson House may be the most get-away-from-it-all of all Key West guest houses. The "all" of Duval Street is only a block away, but it might as well be a protective mile.

The lodgings are removed even from their own street, opening only at the back of the house, beautifully landscaped on a narrow lot slivered like the shape of a secret.

If it is a secret, Ed Czaplicki wants it out, but operating his Key West Real Estate offices on the street side, his commercial sign above the little Watson House medallion gives the impression of an historic structure converted to business where inquiring vacationers at best will politely be smiled at by a receptionist who agrees that, Yes, the house is beautiful, isn't it, but No, sorry, it's no longer for overnighting.

Of course it is, though it is more often enjoyed in private than with a random mix of guests. With only three accommodations—a cabana, a second floor apartment, and an adjacent bedroom—Watson House is frequently taken over by friends traveling together, and otherwise, often as not, engaged by no more than a couple at a time or just a single who lucks out—lucks out good if wanting to be alone, bad if looking for company, though Key West has plenty of that and nobody looking ever goes wanting.

From Simonton Street the house looks pampered and inaccessible like a Southern beauty queen, set behind a black wrought-iron fence, white pilastered and picketed, balconied upstairs and down, demure in cream-colored clapboard, beige-shuttered, white-trimmed, shiny bright in its west-facing afternoon sun.

Its aspect around back is more yielding and affectionate. Balconies set with lawn tables and chairs are meant for use. And like an imaginative carpet there extends a patio that rises in textured tiers planted in red ginger and palms, and hung with wedeelia and bougainvillea that spread across terra cotta tiles.

At one level under a billowing sapodilla tree a swimming pool of bluest water issues a waterfall, while behind is a throne-like deck with strapped furniture between rectangular little housings covered by an eight-sided tin roof Ed calls a gazebo.

All accommodations look onto this setting, and guests are equally pleasured by looking from here to the main house. It is tall, narrow, and symmetrical. Double pairs of French doors match up each of the three floors, the second and third with white picket fencing, and doors on the third floor, to Ed's apartment, under etched glass transoms.

Just a step up from the patio are outside and inside parlors for guest use, outside set with cast-metal, and inside with chintz-cushioned wicker. The south side of the house has one off-street parking space in an attractive slate-like drive. Close to the north side hangs an elaborate white picket fire escape that serves regularly as a covered exterior staircase.

To the south of the patio is the cabana apartment. When its three sets of French doors are open, it shows its cool black and white floor tiles, partially covered by a rug of pink flamingos on black, walls of flamingo paintings, and comfortable Deco-styled furniture throughout. A kitchen is included.

The house was apparently already built in 1860. Four years before, the property had sold for $200. The resale price in 1860 was $2,000. Over the years the house escaped a devastating fire in 1886 but underwent remodelings. The balconies were added late in the last century but removed in 1940.

Ed, who came to Key West in 1978 from Chicago, admired the building, and after selling a guest house he had earlier set up, acquired the Watson House when it came on the market. His first move was to restore the front balconies and add the back ones. In 1986 he opened the house to guests.

The second-story apartment is deep and divided into a rich variety of tropical spaces. In from its balcony it first offers a parlor of coarse-braided wicker furniture with glass tops and contrasting striped and solid upholstery. Smooth plaster walls display Haitian art. On shiny pine floors is a Grecian key rug. There are recessed spotlights and floor lamps.

Three steps up is a bright white kitchen fully equipped with dishwasher and disposal in one of double shiny white—almost see-your-face—porcelain sinks.

The pastel pink bedroom has a firm four-poster double antique pine bed under pink quilt, sheets, and dust ruffle. A single recessed ceiling light operates on dimmer to illuminate a pine armoire, four-paneled Chinese wall tapestry, and two side tables, though with only a single reading lamp. There is an overhead fan.

To the rear is the 1940s bath with its mixed little geometric floor tiles and modern deep lavatory. A notice on the wall explains that hot and cold shower and tub faucets are reversed because when indoor plumbing was first installed in Key West homes, most of the plumbers were Spanish-speaking Cubans for whom Spanish "C" stands for *caliente* or hot.

The adjoining bedroom is in white wicker, including the queen-sized head- and footboards. An easy chair and ottoman are covered in lacy paisley. Pink to mauve colorations complement the wicker and white bedcover. There is a single wicker end table with lamp. The room includes a little cedar-lined closet. There are framed heirloom photos, stage-curtain shades, polished pine floor with throw rugs, Hunter fans, and an attractive fan-topped pine-framed mirror above the dresser.

The little bath has only a shower, but is decorated with a striking red, white, and blue boat print.

Guests at Watson House are mostly on their own. For vacationers who want comfort and beauty without mandated socializing, Watson House mercifully offers everything—but not "all."

Watson House, 525 Simonton St., Key West, FL 33040. (305) 294-6712. Ed Czaplicki and Joe Beres, proprietors. 2 apartments with kitchens, AC, heat, ceiling fans, color cable TV, telephone. Room with bath also available. Adults only. No pets. AmEx, MC, Visa. Pool, heated jacuzzi. Rates: Dec. 20 through Easter: bedroom $105, apartment $185, both combined $295, cabana $210 (single or double); Easter through July 31: $95, $150, $245, $165; Aug. 1- Dec. 20: $85, $115, $195, $130. Limited off-street parking.

Key West – WHISPERS AT THE GIDEON LOWE HOUSE
Earnest innkeeping in a classical Key West inn.

Guest houses are lifesavers for the people who acquire them before they're ever respites for guests. Their buyers need them most. They come from all over, fleeing every which career. These houses shelter their transition. They're where they want to be, doing something they figure to enjoy. Bed-and-breakfast is expensive adult therapy.

This one house alone in a half-dozen years has succored decorators, a bureaucrat, an insurance salesman, and a graphic artist. All bed-and-breakfast hosts. All here today, gone tomorrow. They must have worked something out doing it.

The current owners, Les and Marilyn Tipton, are house renovators. Jiggled themselves all up and around Florida before they grabbed their Key West chance.

Les first came from Toronto around 1980, stayed three days, two nights, hated it and left. On his way to California he met Marilyn in Tampa. So much for California. For 18 monthe, he and Marilyn played around in a camper, came down to Big Pine Key, couldn't resist another look at Key West. It was heaven as a couple. They had honeymooned in Key West at the Island City House, never knowing they'd one day own the house next door.

Back in Tampa, Marilyn each fall would raise a beautiful garden. Each winter it would freeze. She had the idea for bed-and-breakfast in Sarasota—or any place south. Les was getting the Key West paper weekly. He saw the ad for the Gideon Lowe. They came on a Wednesday. They bought it.

For anybody who's ever been to the Gideon Lowe before, it's okay to come back. Les and Marilyn and the old house work together.

All the house asks is to be looked after. It would be a crime against history to let this one go neglected.

The Gideon Lowe House was started in 1845 by the youngest son of one of Key West's earliest Bahamian settlers and is typical of the architecture of the island. It sits on a sleepy tree-shaded street within upstairs view of the gulf.

The oldest part is the kitchen, which was used for living quarters when the main house was being built. Today it rests on large coquina rocks in the bricked garden with its goldfish pond, swing chaise, fan palm, avocado, and sour orange trees. The diminutive yard is set off by soaring palms, where on a soft cool morning the fresh air curls around bare legs like a cat nestling up for a bowl of milk.

The main house was completed around 1866 and reflects a typical Greek revival floor plan, but with Victorian embellishments. The scuttles, porches, shuttered windows, and numerous doors show the Bahamian influence and are features well suited to the tropics.

Behind its picket fence and tiny front yard, the two-and-a-half-story wood structure is supported by squared columns that mark off front porches, topped by a shuttered attic window under the eaves. The inside is narrow, each floor front divided between hallway and stairs. Each floor, including the attic, has two rooms and one bath. All the rooms are different.

People who are wary of shared bathrooms might accept the arrangement here. Though two rooms each share a bath, the bathrooms are all in the hall, so there's no squeamishness about clicking a lock that's going to be heard in the next room, or otherwise feeling intruding or intruded on.

The room they call the Doll House has a half canopy bed, plant walls, and a Dade County Pine floor. Old green shutters latch behind casement windows. The rooms feel antique, done in a mix of period furnishings. There are old grass and porcelain doorknobs, lace curtains, and an impressive English constable's hat and a pitcher.

The Verandah Room has a four-poster king bed, gilded antique mirrors, and a ship's bench. It's homey and bright with the door to the veranda open.

The Bridal Suite has the mood of passionate collecting: a king bed under mosquito netting, lace curtains, and a huge sofa full of floral cushions.

Periwinkle is full of blues and mauves, with a steamer trunk, hatbox bureau, and twin double beds under chintz covers. It leads onto the second floor porch, which is full of cane and slat rockers, palms and cactus.

In the attic, Grandma's Attic is L-shaped with bright reds, and pink trim windows against gray-green plank walls. The beams are open under the gables, all white.

In Captain's Hideaway there's a coral-encrusted anchor, antique wooden anchor, coal oil lamp, and high single and double beds in an open-beamed room with a hatch door cover. Air-conditioning, a fan, and color TV, too. Very cozy, hidden away.

Les's petitpoints and needlepoint are featured throughout. The breakfasts are Marilyn's: French toast l'orange, homemade orange sauce and almond slivers, snow pea and shaved carrot omelets with sesame seeds, sausages—always a meat, always an omelet, always a pancake, and freshly-squeezed orange juice, teas, coffees, sour cream waffles with raspberry-mango sauce, and fresh cream whipped by hand.

The house lends itself well to couples here alone. Nude sunbathing is permitted on the deck. Or equally well to when a crowd's on hand. Says Marilyn, "Twelve people in the house makes us feel like celebrating. We'll do wine and cheese, or sometimes guests will just go out and bring food for all."

And why "Whispers"? Les says he likes the adult imagery.

Whispers at the Gideon Lowe House, 409 William St., Key West, FL 33040. (305) 294-5969. Les and Marilyn Tipton, innkeepers. 6 rooms with color TV, AC, ceiling fan, three hall baths, one with tub. Pay phone on 2nd floor. House refrigerator for storing beer, wine. No children. No pets. AmEx, MC, Visa. Rates: winter $95-$105, summer $69-$75, with full breakfast. $10 additional person in room. Tropical patio. No smoking inside.

APPENDIX:
IMPORTANT ADDRESSES

Florida's Association of Innkeepers

Inn Route, Inc.
377 E. Fairbanks Avenue
Suite 200
Winter Park, FL 32789
(407) 629-5442
Free brochure available

Bed-and-Breakfast Referral Agencies
in Florida

A & A Bed & Breakfast of Florida, Inc.
P.O. Box 1316
Winter Park, FL 32790
(407) 628-3233

Bed & Breakfast Company, Tropical
    Florida
P.O. Box 262
Miami, FL 33243
(305) 661-3270

Bed & Breakfast of the Florida Keys
P.O. Box 1373
Marathon, FL 33050
(305) 743-4118

Bed & Breakfast of Greater Daytona Beach
P.O. Box 1081
Ormond Beach, FL 32074
(904) 673-2232

Bed & Breakfast of Volusia County
P.O. Box 573
De Leon Springs, FL 32130
(904) 985-5068

Open House Bed & Breakfast
P.O. Box 3025
Palm Beach, FL 33480
(407) 842-5190

Suncoast Accommodations of Florida
8690 Gulf Blvd.
St. Petersburg Beach, FL 333706
(813) 360-1753

General Tourist Information

Florida Division of Tourism
Visitor Inquiry
126 W. Van Buren St.
Tallahassee, FL 32399-2000
(904) 487-1462

Information About Florida Parks &
Camping

Florida Department of Natural Resources
Florida Parks Service
Mail Station 525
3900 Commonwealth Blvd.
Tallahassee, FL 32399-3000
(904) 487-2319

Florida County Road Maps

Florida Department of Transportation
Maps and Publications
Mail Station 12
605 Suwannee St.
Tallahassee, FL 32399-0450
(904) 488-9220

Florida Bicycle Maps

State Bicycle Coordinator
Florida Department of Transportation
605 Suwannee St.
Tallahassee, FL 32399-0450
(904) 488-8006

Florida Council, American Youth
Hostels, Inc.

Florida Council
American Youth Hostels, Inc.
P.O. Box 533097
Orlando, FL 32853-3097
(407) 649-8761

NOTES

NOTES

NOTES

NOTES

NOTES

NOTES

NOTES

NOTES